INTERNATIONAL TRADE

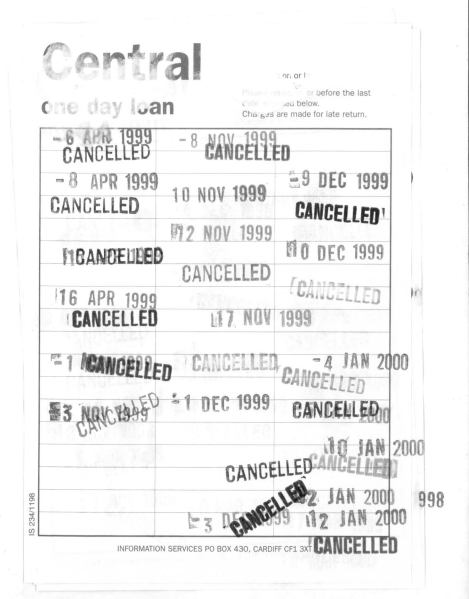

Central

one day loan

on, or before the last
date ...... below.
Charges are made for late return.

-6 APR 1999 CANCELLED	-8 NOV 1999 CANCELLED	
-8 APR 1999 CANCELLED	10 NOV 1999	-9 DEC 1999 CANCELLED
CANCELLED	12 NOV 1999 CANCELLED	10 DEC 1999
16 APR 1999 CANCELLED	17 NOV 1999	CANCELLED
-1 CANCELLED	CANCELLED	-4 JAN 2000 CANCELLED
3 NOV 1999 CANCELLED	-1 DEC 1999	CANCELLED
	CANCELLED	10 JAN 2000 CANCELLED
		2 JAN 2000 998
	3 DEC 1999 CANCELLED	12 JAN 2000 CANCELLED

IS 234/1198

INFORMATION SERVICES PO BOX 430, CARDIFF CF1 3XT

International Trade

A EUROPEAN TEXT

PAUL BRENTON
HENRY SCOTT
PETER SINCLAIR

Oxford University Press
1997

Oxford University Press, Great Clarendon Street, Oxford OX2 6DP

Oxford New York

Athens Auckland Bangkok Bogota Bombay
Buenos Aires Calcutta Cape Town Dar es Salaam
Delhi Florence Hong Kong Istanbul Karachi
Kuala Lumpur Madras Madrid Melbourne
Mexico City Nairobi Paris Singapore
Taipei Tokyo Toronto Warsaw

and associated companies in
Berlin Ibadan

Oxford is a trade mark of Oxford University Press

Published in the United States
by Oxford University Press Inc., New York

British Library Cataloguing in Publication Data
Data available

Library of Congress Cataloging in Publication Data
Brenton, Paul
International trade : a European text / Paul Brenton,
Henry Scott, Peter Sinclair.
Includes bibliographical references.
1. International trade. 2. Europe—Commerce. I. Scott, Henry G.
II. Sinclair, P. J. N. III. Title
HF1379.S58 1997 382'.094—dc21 97–6264
ISBN 0–19–877443–5
ISBN 0–19–877444–3 (Pbk)

1 3 5 7 9 10 8 6 4 2

Typeset by Hope Services (Abingdon) Ltd.
Printed in Great Britain
on acid-free paper by
Bookcraft Ltd.
Midsomer Norton, Somerset

For Rachel, Jean, and Shelagh

ACKNOWLEDGEMENTS

Writing this book has incurred many debts of gratitude, debts it is a pleasure to acknowledge here. Susan Redding and Joanne Quarry did an excellent job collating and typing the manuscript. We thank them very much. Barry Thomas read the whole draft, San Bilal, Rosemary Clarke, Greg Farrell, and Daniel Gros particular chapters; all provided valuable suggestions, while San helped us with bibliographical material and Barry with some tables. We are most grateful to all of them. We should like to thank our collegues at the Department of Economics Birmingham for intellectual comradeship, and record special thanks to many economists elsewhere, particularly Christopher Bliss, Max Corden, Peter Neary, Ashok Parikh, Joseph Stiglitz, and Alan Winters. We are also very grateful to Jessica Clayton, Thomas Donnelly, Nicola Gardiner, Neil Gostelow, Matthew Hazell, Richard Martin, Stuart Richards, and Laura Wilson who helped with proofreading and indexing, and Angela Griffin and Tracy Mawson and their colleagues at Oxford University Press.

Henry Scott would like to thank the members of the International Economics Study Group, of which he was secretary for many years, for stimulating discussions. Paul Brenton has benefited from working with Paul Luyton and John Whalley on EU Commission funded TACIS projects in Russia and the Ukraine, and from his many discussions with Cillian Ryan.

Paul Brenton and Peter Sinclair thank H. M. Treasury for the opportunity to prepare a report on the British export performance, recently completed, and Greg Farrell and Inma Martinez Zarzoso for econometric assistance. Peter Sinclair is most grateful to David Vines, with whom he has been researching on trade blocs; the European University Institute at Florence, and particularly Mike Artis, for excellent hospitality and research discussions; participants at IESG conferences for feedback on the papers he has presented there; and the Oxford Institute of Economics and Statistics and the European Commision, for invaluable opportunities to discuss ideas and work.

Our greatest debt is to our wives, without whose unstinting support this book could not have been written. We dedicate it to them.

CONTENTS

LIST OF FIGURES

LIST OF TABLES

ABBREVIATIONS

ACP	African, Caribbean, and Pacific
CEC	Commission for the European Communities
CES	Constant Elasticity of Substitution
CMEA	Council for Mutual Economic Assistance
CU	Customs Union
EU	European Union
FTA	Free Trade Area
GATT	General Agreement on Tariffs and Trade
GDP	Gross Domestic Product
GSP	Generalized System of Preferences
MFN	Most Favoured Nation
MPC	Marginal Private Costs
MSC	Marginal Social Costs
NAFTA	North Atlantic Free Trade Area
NBER	National Bureau of Economic Research
NICS	Newly Industrializing Countries
OECD	Organization for Economic Cooperation and Development
QR	Quantitative Restriction
SEM	Single European Market
TRIP	Trade Related Intellectual Property
UNCTAD	United Nations Conference for Trade and Development
VER	Voluntary Export Restraint
WTO	World Trade Organization

1

INTRODUCTION AND OVERVIEW

1.1 European union trade

Exports account for a large share of national income in European countries. In 1995, Europe's largest economy, Germany, displayed an exports-to-GDP ratio of two-ninths. For West Germany alone, the figure was 33.8 per cent, close to the EU average.

The EU's next four most populous economies, France, the UK, Italy, and Spain, all registered figures between these two German statistics: Italy and the UK, both benefiting from exchange-rate depreciations, came top of this group with about 28 per cent, with France and Spain some 4 per cent behind.

Most of the smaller EU economies exhibited greater openness. All else being equal, larger economies tend to have more diversified patterns of production, leaving less room for exports and imports. The most open EU economy was Luxembourg, where 86 per cent of GDP was exported. Ireland and Belgium, both on 71 per cent, came close behind. After them comes the Netherlands (52 per cent), and the Union's three new members, Austria, Finland, and Sweden (all close to 40 per cent), and Denmark (35 per cent).

The normal relationship between size and openness breaks down, however, in the case of Greece. Greece exported a mere 18 per cent of its GDP. This testifies to its lack of proximity to the main EU markets, and also perhaps to the fact that the process of trade integration with the EU is still recent. Greece only joined the EU in 1981. Distance and the recency of accession (1986) also help to explain another small economy outlier, Portugal, where the 1995 export–GDP ratio was 27.5 per cent.

Although EU countries are large exporters, they trade more with each other than the rest of the world. Intra-EU exports accounted for 58 per cent of total EU exports in 1994. The ratio of extra-EU exports to EU GDP was less than 14 per cent in 1995, close to that of the USA (11.3 per cent).

All the fifteen countries export more of their output now than they did two or three decades ago. This trend towards greater openness was strongest in the 1960s and early 1970s, slackening off somewhat in the later 1970s and 1980s. Four EU economies (Belgium, Luxembourg, the Netherlands, and Portugal) were actually less open in 1995 than they had been, on average, in the 1980s. Japan was also in this position. These are instances of a general slowdown in the expansion of world trade from its meteoric growth in earlier postwar decades, which appears to have occurred between the mid-1970s and mid-1980s and is examined by Sinclair (1993).

The EU countries differ widely in the percentages of their exports sent outside the EU. In 1994 this was highest for Germany (52 per cent), and above average for Denmark, Italy, the UK, and Greece. It was lowest for Portugal (24 per cent) and Belgium and Luxembourg (28 per cent combined).

The EU's largest outside export market is the United States. Almost one fifth of extra-EU exports were sent there in 1995. Behind the US came Switzerland (8 per cent), and two countries to join the EU that year (Austria, 6 per cent and Sweden, 4.4 per cent). The other countries each accounting for at least 2 per cent of extra-EU exports that year were Japan, Hong Kong, and Russia.

Turning to trade within the European Union (or rather the twelve countries comprising it in 1992), we can see from Table 1.1 that Germany is the leading trade partner for most members. The only exceptions are Ireland and (in its imports) Portugal. The UK dominates Ireland's exports and imports, and Spain is Portugal's leading source of imports. Both these exceptions testify to the importance of geographical proximity: international transport costs tilt trade in favour of near neighbours. Distant Greece trades relatively highly with Italy, and negligibly with far-off Denmark, Ireland, and Portugal. Germany trades much more with the Netherlands, a close neighbour, than with the UK. The three countries with which the Belgium–Luxembourg economic union shares a common border (France, Germany, and the Netherlands) account for some 80 per cent of its EU exports and imports. Yet distance is clearly not the only consideration: all else being equal, the countries tend to trade more with larger economies than with smaller ones.

These two principles are observable in the trade statistics for non-EU countries, or previously non-EU countries , too, as seen in Table 1.2. Switzerland, almost at the geographical centre of the EU but outside it, sends nearly 60 per cent of its exports to the EU. The EU accounts for 72 per cent of its imports. The statistics for Austria, Finland, Norway, and Sweden also display large EU shares in exports and imports. EU trade with the world's giant economies, the US and Japan, is larger in absolute terms; but the EU is a small player in their trade. Canada, with a GDP of barely one-twelfth of the US, registers large ratios of exports and imports to GDP; but the EU shares in this trade, dominated as it is by the United States, are in fact the lowest in the table. Turkey's GDP is barely one-eighth of Canada's, which explains why its total exports and imports are so much smaller than hers; but Turkey's proximity makes it almost as large a trading partner in absolute terms for the EU as Canada.

The former Czechoslovakia in 1992, in its last year before dissolving into the Czech Republic and Slovakia, conducted almost half its foreign trade with the EU. The EU's share in its trade had almost trebled there since 1988, as it had for many other formerly communist countries in Eastern and Central Europe. This bears witness to the effects of geography eventually establishing themselves, once the Cold War biases in trading patterns disappeared.

TABLE 1.1. Trade within the EU-12, 1992: in milliard (billion) ECUs

Imports from:	Belgium-Luxembourg	Denmark	Germany	Greece	Spain	France	Ireland	Italy	Netherlands	Portugal	UK
Exports to:											
Belgium-Luxembourg		0.6	23.0	0.1	1.5	15.8	0.6	4.3	18.7	0.4	7.3
Denmark	0.9		6.5	0.1	0.3	1.5	0.2	1.0	1.8	0.3	2.2
Germany	24.5	7.5		1.8	8.1	37.9	3.0	28.7	37.5	2.8	20.9
Greece	0.6	0.2	3.6		0.4	1.4	0.1	2.6	1.2		1.0
Spain	2.4	0.6	12.1	0.2		12.1	0.5	7.1	2.8	2.0	5.3
France	20.7	2.0	42.1	0.6	10.3		2.3	21.7	13.1	2.1	15.7
Ireland	0.4	0.2	1.4		0.1	0.8		0.4	0.9		8.0
Italy	7.1	1.5	31.4	1.3	4.9	21.1	1.0		8.6	0.5	8.3
Netherlands	14.8	1.4	28.2	0.2	1.8	8.2	1.2	3.8		0.6	9.0
Portugal	0.9	0.2	3.4		3.8	2.9		2.3	1.6		1.6
UK	7.5	3.2	25.4	0.5	3.9	16.4	6.8	9.2	12.4	1.6	

Source: Eurostat. External Trade Statistics, various issues.

Table 1.2. Exports and Imports for Selected Countries, 1992: in milliard (billion) ECUs

	Total exports	Exports to EU-12	Total imports	Imports from EU-12
Austria	34.2	22.6	41.8	28.3
Brazil	27.9	8.3	18.6	4.0
Canada	103.9	7.3	94.8	9.3
China	66.0	5.9	63.1	7.6
Czechoslovakia	10.9	4.9	13.6	6.5
Finland	18.5	9.8	16.3	7.7
Hong Kong	92.1	14.6	95.1	9.1
Japan	261.8	48.4	179.3	24.2
Norway	27.1	18.0	20.0	9.8
South Korea	57.6	7.1	62.7	7.4
Sweden	43.2	24.1	38.5	21.4
Switzerland	50.5	29.7	50.6	36.5
Turkey	11.3	5.9	17.6	7.7
United States	344.7	79.2	409.3	72.5

Source: Eurostat; International Financial Statistics

1.2. Arbitrage

A central concept in trade is *arbitrage*. This is defined as the riskless exploitation of price discrepancies for profit. Traders buy cheap and sell dear; and the cheaper source exports to the dearer destination.

What triggers arbitrage trade is price disparities. Countries tend to export goods that would otherwise have been cheaper there than in the countries that import them. If the costs of trade are trivial—if there are no costs of transport or legal restrictions, for example, and entry into trading activities is free—trade tends to equalize the prices.

So what are the main effects of this? Take two countries, A and B. In the absence of trade, price should settle where the local market in each country is in equilibrium—that is, where excess demand is zero in both A and B. Figure 1.1 illustrates. A's demand and supply curves intersect at E, and B's at F. Pre-trade prices will be G and H.

Since G is less than H, there is scope for international arbitrage. The direction of trade follows profit. A should export this good to B; any trader buying in B and selling in A would make a loss! Unrestricted and costless trade between A and B should, eventually, establish a common price of J. Here, A's excess supply of our product just balances B's excess demand. A's excess supply is found by mapping the horizontal gap between its supply curve and its demand curve from the left-hand panel to the middle panel. Similarly with B's excess demand.

Before trade, when B's market was in equilibrium at E, its consumers enjoyed a surplus of area $a + x$. This is the area below the demand curve D_A, but above the price of G. Area y represents producers' surplus in A. This is the area below the price of G, but to the left of the supply curve S_A. With trade, consumers' surplus in A falls by a. But producers' surplus increases by $a + b$. If social welfare in A is

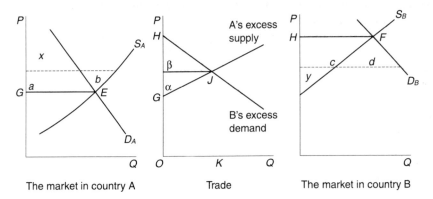

Fig. 1.1. Unrestricted arbitrage and the effects of trade

defined as the sum of consumers' and producers' surpluses (this is a simple but controversial assumption), A's social welfare rises by area *b*, or, equivalently, by area α in the middle panel. In B, trade squeezes producers' surplus by *c* but enlarges consumers' surplus by *c* + *d*, leaving a net gain of *d*, or β in the middle panel. The equilibrium level of trade is given by the distance *OK* in the middle panel.

Figure 1.1 illustrates some key effects of trade. There are large gains for some groups. Consumers in B are in this category. So, too, are those who benefit from an increased demand for the services of factors they own that rise in price in A in response to the higher level of production of our particular good there. But there are losers: consumers in A, certain factor owners in B. Yet the gainers' gains should exceed the losers' losses, at least in monetary terms, and this happens in both countries. Not everyone gains, but there are aggregate gains in both A and B.

Such are the major effects of free trade in a simple two-country, partial-equilibrium, perfectly competitive set-up. In later chapters we shall be exploring such effects in greater detail. We shall investigate knock-on effects on other sectors and industries ('general' equilibrium). We shall add in more industries, and more countries. We shall explore trade restrictions. And we shall extend the story to certain types of imperfect competition, for example, where many of the results will be found to change quite radically.

1.3. Duality and trade

One device we shall employ at several points comes under the general heading of duality. It is helpful to outline the main duality concepts at this point. One of these is the *income* function. This gives the value of a country's total output, of two goods, x and y, let us say. Let I denote income; make y numeraire, with a unit price of one, and let p stand for the price of x in terms of y. In units of y, I will equal $px + y$. What the income function gives us is the maximum value of $px + y$ that can be produced under perfect competition, with full use of existing resources. 'Resources' may denote the economy's endowment of two factors of production, capital and labour, for example, which we shall take to be given in total supply but perfectly mobile between the two industries.

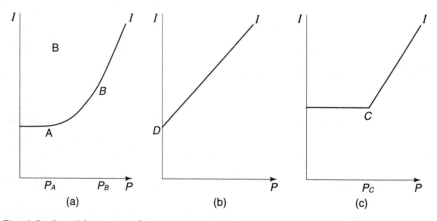

Fig. 1.2. Possible income functions

The gradient of the tangent to an income function gives the output of x. This could be zero, as evidenced by the horizontal sections of the income functions in panels (a) and (c). But if p is large enough, some y will be produced. A common type of income function is drawn in panel (a). Here, the output of x steadily increases as its price rises from P_A to P_B. Once point B is reached, the economy has withdrawn all its resources from the production of the other good y, so the output of x reaches a ceiling; beyond B, the income function is linear. In panel (b), the case of perfect complementarity in production (or fixed commodity endowments) is presented. Here there is no substitution between the sectors, and the output pattern is frozen, independently of prices. A third possibility is shown in (c). Here the economy produces all x and no y for any price above P_C, and all y and no x below P_C. Panel (c) corresponds to a linear production possibility frontier, which is explored in Chapter 2.

Another duality concept is the price indifference curve (Fig. 1.3). Take a typical consumer with normal, downward-sloping, convex-to-the-origin indifference curves drawn in the space of *quantities* of goods x and y. She will optimize by seeking a point of tangency with the highest indifference curve she can attain, given the constraint of her budget.

Now ask how she is affected by changes in the prices, P_x and P_y, of the two goods, with given money income, m. If both P_x and P_y fall, she is better off. Her

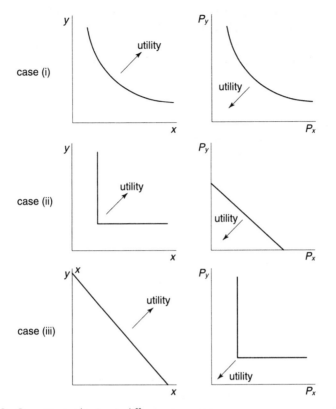

Fig. 1.3. Quantity and price indifference curves

utility will rise. The opposite happens if both P_x and P_y rise. But now confront her with a fall in P_x (which she will welcome) and a rise in P_y (which she will dislike). For any rise in P_y, there must be some fall in P_x that keeps her utility unchanged. The locus of all combinations of P_x and P_y where utility is the same is defined as a *price indifference curve.*

Figure 1.3 presents price indifference curves, in the right-hand column, corresponding to various types of quantity indifference curves to the left. Notice that utility rises as you move away from the origin with the latter, but towards it with the former. The gradient of the tangent to a quantity indifference curve gives the marginal rate of substitution, or (minus) the price ratio given that the consumer optimizes. The gradient of the tangent to a price indifference curve gives the ratio of *quantities* bought. That is why the 'perfect complements' quantity indifference curve—case (ii), on the left—with its L shape, corresponds to a linear price indifference curve on the right. No amount of juggling the prices for given utility and income can alter the ratio of y to x bought. The opposite case of perfect substitutes is shown in the bottom row. Here, it is the price indifference curve that is

L-shaped: if P_x is too high, the consumer will buy none of it anyway, so pushing up the price further leaves utility unchanged.

The price difference curve shows the combinations of P_x and P_y at which utility is unchanged for given money income. Let us now suppose that P_y is frozen at 1, and ask what must happen to money income, m, if utility is to be unaffected by a change in P_x (or simply p, since $p = P_x/P_y = P_x$). The answer is that m must rise if any x is to be bought.

This idea underlies the expenditure function. An expenditure function gives the minimum money income someone must have to enable him or her to reach a specified level of utility, when p is treated as a variable.

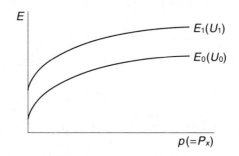

Fig. 1.4. The expenditure function

Figure 1.4 illustrates a typical expenditure function. It must slope up (unless no x is bought, in which case it will be horizontal). It must also be concave, tending to flatten off as p rises. This is because of the substitution effect, which must induce someone to buy less x, and not more, as it becomes more expensive (for a given level of utility). If utility were to rise, say from U_0 to U_1, we would draw a new expenditure function: this would certainly lie above the old one. If the substitution effect were zero (as in the limiting case shown in the middle row of Figure 1.3) the expenditure function would be linear.

We can now combine the income and expenditure function to illustrate how a simple, small, two-industry economy can gain from trade. Let us begin with equilibrium under autarky (a state without trade). This is illustrated by the point of tangency between two functions. The value of the price where this occurs, $\bar{p}$ in Figure 1.5, is the price ratio at which the demand and supply are in balance. The demand for x is the gradient of the expenditure function, while its output is the gradient of the income function. Equilibrium in autarky occurs at the tangency point between them. Since the expenditure function is concave and the income function convex, tangency can occur nowhere else—at least, and we must stress this, consumers have common preferences and factor-ownership patterns.

Now confront our economy with the opportunity to trade at a given world price, $\tilde{p}$. If $\tilde{p} = \bar{p}$, there will be no trade, and no gains from trade. But with $\tilde{p} \neq \bar{p}$, there are gains from trade to be had. If $P = P_1$, for example, the home country will export y and import x, reaching a utility level U_1 which is higher than under

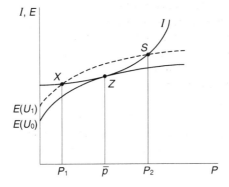

Fig. 1.5. Autarky and trading equilibrium

autarky (U_0). The new level of production of x slips to the gradient of the I function at X; home demand rises to the gradient of the E function at X.

Had the world price been P_2, we should have seen this opposite pattern of trade. Good x would be exported now. Its excess supply would equal the excess of the gradient of the I function at S over that of the E function at S. As it happens, utility is the same with P_1 and P_2. We may infer from this that the larger the gap between the home economy's autarkic price ratio and its value in world markets, the greater the gain from trade. The size of the gain from trade also depends on the degree of curvature of the E and I functions. If these are sharply concave and convex, the utility gain from trade will be much greater than if they are almost linear. The key idea here is the strength of substitution in demand and supply. This is also evident in our partial equilibrium diagram, Figure 1.1: the steeper the demand and supply curves, the smaller the gain in the sum of consumers' and producers' surpluses.

A final duality concept that we shall introduce here relates to factor prices. Just as isoquants depict the combinations of quantities of factors that yield a given output, with the isoquant gradient giving the ratio of the factors' prices when production is ideal, so an *isoprice* depicts the combination of the prices of a pair of factors at which average costs are given. The relationship between isoquants and isoprices is exactly the same as in Figure 1.3. When isoquants display perfect complementarity the associated isoprice is linear, and vice versa. Isoprices are very useful in showing how trade can affect the prices of factors of production, as we shall see in Chapter 3. Isoprices are also called *isocost* curves.

1.4 Controversial trade

Figure 1.5 has shown how trade can be welfare-enhancing for a simple small economy. This is indeed the general rule, which survives under a wide variety of cases (big economies, imperfect competition, many goods and factors, and so on). There are a few exceptions, which are studied in some detail in Chapter 10. But it is appropriate at this point to look briefly at the case of commodities or services where trade is often considered harmful.

Drugs, guns, slaves, animals threatened with extinction, pornography, acid rain, beef infected with BSE, spent nuclear fuels—what do these all have in common? All are goods which are liable to be traded with such potentially adverse welfare effects that international trade looks seriously damaging. Acid rain is an involuntary import for many countries, where noxious compounds of chemicals are borne by wind across international boundaries. The others are products that may be bought by residents in one country from residents in others, to the distress or repugnance of many observers. Should such trade be banned?

In some of these cases, social marginal benefit from consumption may be less than social marginal cost of production at any positive level of activity in any country. If this is so, it is clearly best that the activity in question should be prohibited. The optimal level of the activity is zero. Each country should make both production and consumption illegal, and devote some resources to ensure that the activity is brought as close as possible to vanishing point. A ban on international trade in the good may be helpful, but will not suffice on its own, because consumption and production could still flourish within economies even if international trade is blocked.

In other cases, the picture is less clear-cut. The availability of guns for farmers protects crops and livestock from vermin; their use by the police and armed forces may deter terrorism, serious crime, and war. Opium and heroin derivatives may be valuable for patients facing excruciating pain. In the wrong hands, or put to wrong uses, such products may be very damaging; yet the social marginal benefit may exceed social marginal cost at positive levels of consumption and production. If this is so, guns and narcotics may be deemed to join the list of 'moderate' bads (such as tobacco, ghetto-blasters, paint spray-cans and alcoholic spirits) which the authorities will seek to discourage by regulation and/or taxation rather than outright bans.

The best policy, if feasible, in an otherwise perfect world, would be to achieve the following:

1. a pattern of production with equal social marginal costs of production, wherever the good is produced;
2. a pattern of consumption with equal social marginal benefit from consumption, wherever it is consumed; and
3. equality between the equated social marginal costs of production on the one side, and the equated social marginal benefits of consumption on the other.

If the source of the problem is externalities, or agents not being deemed to act in their own interest, this optimum could be achieved by a set of taxes. If the gap between social and private marginal valuations was the same everywhere, each country should set the same rate of tax.

Compared with this ideal policy, a restriction or ban on international trade is less satisfactory. A trade ban might be better than nothing. But even this might not be true. A trade ban will mean less consumption of the good in a country that would otherwise have imported it. That is quite possibly, but not necessarily,[1] all to the good. But it will mean lower prices, and hence more consumption, in a country that would otherwise have exported it. When a trade ban is accompanied by national taxes designed to equate social marginal cost and benefit at a local level, that will typically be superior to a trade ban on its own; but both will be inferior to a set of optimum taxes in a setting of free trade.

We conclude from this that free trade will generally be a more efficient way of dealing with 'moderate bads' than trade restrictions, provided these are accompanied by appropriate national taxes. For really serious 'bads', for which social marginal cost outweighs social marginal benefit everywhere at any positive level of activity, prohibition—if feasible—is best. In those cases, a trade ban may be a valuable accompaniment to a set of domestic prohibitions on consumption and production. Which of our list of possible bads fall into the first category, and which into the second, is an important if controversial practical matter, but one which takes us too far from our main themes in this book.

1.5 Overview of the book

When you reflect on why a product costs what it does, it is natural to start by estimating the amount of labour time that goes into its production. Multiply this by the average wage rate, grossed up for tax and a plausible profit margin, and you can usually guess the price quite accurately.

This is the approach to predicting equilibrium prices which David Ricardo first applied to international trade nearly two centuries ago. It is the cornerstone of what is known as the Classical Theory of Value. Chapter 2 explores these ideas in detail. They still provide a very valuable foundation for the analysis of international trade. Allied to them is the efficient allocation of labour, which applies for individual workers at the micro level right up to the national level, and which also predicts how decentralized decisions should allocate labour.

Labour is an important factor of production, receiving about two-thirds of national income in most contemporary economies. Yet it is not the only factor. Capital matters, too. Some industries are labour-intensive, while for others capital per worker is very high. Just as industries differ in their capital–labour ratios, countries differ in their endowments of these two factors. The 'Heckscher-Ohlin' or 'neo-classical' theory of international trade based on these two observations forms the subject-matter of Chapter 3. The emphasis here is on competitive firms' choices of factors, and what this implies for relative prices and sectoral levels of output.

In Chapter 4 the theory of supply in separate economies built up in Chapters 2

---

[1] Not necessarily, because the trade ban might cut back consumption much too far.

and 3 is confronted with demand and trade. The key issue is what determines countries' patterns of exports and imports, and their relative price (the terms of trade). The roles of countries' factor endowments, and of technology, which provide critical foundations here, are examined further in Chapters 5 and 6. The emphasis in all these five chapters is on perfect competition.

Not all markets are perfectly competitive, however. Oligopoly and monopolistic competition are widespread, and not just at the level of an individual country. Imperfect competition and increasing returns have been dominant themes in research on trade in the past twenty years. Chapter 7 provides an analysis of the main types of imperfect competition in international trade.

Having run through the key elements of trade theory, the next issue is to examine evidence of trade patterns to determine what factors appear to govern trade in practice. This is the subject-matter of Chapter 8, where the main focus is on Europe. By this stage the book has covered the central *positive* questions of international trade, both theoretical and empirical. This leads naturally to normative questions about trade.

Should national governments espouse free trade? Or should they intervene, by restricting imports by tariffs or quotas? Should they leave exports to market forces, or should exports be subsidized—or taxed? What difference does imperfect competition make? These policy questions form the basis of Chapter 9 and Chapter 10.

International transfers between countries are not limited to goods. Factors of production—labour and capital—migrate between them. What effects do international capital movements or labour migration have? Who gains and who loses? Should governments try to restrict such movements? These are among the questions explored in Chapter 11.

While some of the foregoing analysis studies dynamic issues, the main focus is comparative static. It is the role of Chapter 12 to explore the linkages between international trade and economic growth. These run in both directions: growth effects trade, and trade effects growth.

A prominent feature of the postwar international trade environment has been the growing tendency for countries to enter trade blocs. This phenomenon is especially evident in Western Europe, with the gradual evolution of the fifteen-country European Union from its beginnings in the 1950s. Powerful trade blocs are also arising in North America, South America, and the Far East. Chapter 13 is devoted to the study of Free Trade Areas, Customs Unions, and Trade Bloc issues.

One of the driving forces behind the growth of trade blocs has been governments' concerns about trade competitiveness, employment, and wages. Trade policies are often seen as vital instruments for enhancing or protecting competitiveness and jobs. Chapter 14 explores these issues, with particular emphasis on Europe.

Sometimes trade restrictions can increase aggregate wages and output in a country; sometimes they can even enhance its national welfare, on certain definitions. Very often, however, trade restrictions are an inefficient and inappropriate instrument for securing such gains. At the world level, free trade is in general ideal. Yet we see trade restrictions of varying sorts in a vast variety of contexts: no longer, perhaps, on trade within the European Union, but certainly in many categories of trade between the EU and the outside world. Chapter 15 turns to the intriguing question of why we actually observe such restrictions despite the fact that they appear to be damaging.

In Chapter 16, the book turns to the issue of trade and the environment. Economists have been increasingly concerned with environmental issues, ranging from the problems of overfishing and deforestation to the varying fortunes of the energy and extractive industries; for some of these issues, such as the greenhouse effect, the externalities are literally global.

The substantial advances in prosperity in Western Europe in the postwar era, built partly on policies of trade liberalization, contrast markedly with both continuing poverty in much of Africa, Asia, and Latin America, and the much more rapid economic progress observed in recent decades in the Far East. Chapter 17 explores the economic links between Western Europe and less developed countries.

In Chapter 18, attention turns to Europe's trade policy *vis-à-vis* the world's more advanced countries. This substantial chapter starts by reviewing trade policy in manufactures, and then turns to the thorny question of the EU's Common Agricultural Policy and its internal and international effects.

2

LABOUR PRODUCTIVITY
AND COMPARATIVE ADVANTAGE

2.1 Introduction

Economists have always been interested in why nations trade. More specifically, they have been concerned with what determines the pattern of trade, that is, what goods are exported and imported; the terms of trade—at what prices does trade take place; and the gains from trade—who benefits, and are there any losers? Associated with these questions are policy issues: in particular what are the effects of various policy instruments such as tariffs, export taxes, quotas, and production and export subsidies? These questions are positive in the sense that in principle they are free of value judgements; but they have important normative implications for the desirability of using different policies to achieve social objectives.

In considering why countries trade, we should first note that this question is mis-specified. It is not countries that trade, but their residents: private individuals, merchants, and corporations. These, we shall assume, are motivated by the desire to acquire goods and services where they are cheapest, and to sell where they can obtain the highest price. Governments also engage directly in trade, but their motivation is often different. For example, the Commission of the European Union buys agricultural produce from Community farmers at high prices, and sells these outside the Union at lower prices. Governments often have procurement policies that involve purchasing domestic goods and services, although these may be obtainable from abroad at lower prices. We, however, shall be concentrating upon the trade motivated by the desire for profits. Such trade can be considered as arbitrage that exploits any differences in prices greater than transport and other trading costs that would exist in the absence of that trade. Such arbitrage trade is shown in Figure 2.1.

The left- and right-hand panels of this Figure show the partial equilibrium conditions of domestic demand and supply for a commodity in countries A and B respectively. The diagram has been drawn such that in the absence of trade, the market clearing price will be lower in A than in B ($P_A < P_B$). The central panel shows the excess supply of the commodity in A at prices above that country's no trade-price, and the excess demand in B at prices below its no-trade price; thus

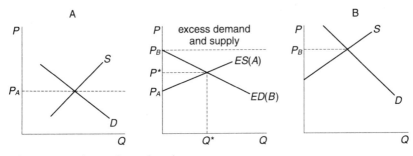

Fig. 2.1. Demand, supply, and trade

these are the supply of the product for export from country A and the demand for its import in country B respectively. In a world consisting of just these two countries, and in the absence of transport costs, equilibrium will occur at the common price P^*, with the price differential being eliminated by the export of Q^* of the product from A to B. At this price, world demand and supply are equalized.

Three points of interest arise from this simple diagram. First, there is no price differential observable when there is trade, but it would reappear if the volume of the trade fell below its equilibrium level. Secondly, the direction of trade is determined by the pre-trade prices, which in turn are determined by the conditions of demand and supply in the two countries. This suggests several possible explanations for the trade: the conditions of demand might differ because of differences in tastes or needs; for example, more income might be spent on fuel for heating in Finland than in Portugal because of the difference in climate; or trade might arise because of difference in supply conditions between countries. These, in turn, might arise because of differences in technology between countries, or because of differences in the availability of factors of production. The third point that may be noted is that if either the conditions of demand or of supply are perfectly elastic, then that will determine the price. There are two applications of this point. The first is that if a country is sufficiently small it will face a perfectly elastic demand for its exports and supply of its imports, even though the global demand for these products is inelastic. For example, the world supply of oil is clearly not perfectly elastic, but the supply to Luxembourg is so for the volume of imports that are relevant. Such a country is a price-taker. A second application, relevant to the discussion of the Ricardian model that follows, is that if a product can be produced at constant costs, then there is a perfectly elastic supply at that cost which determines the price.

Less obvious from the diagram is that international trade might also be influenced and explained by economies of scale and imperfect competition. In the real world trade is motivated by all of these considerations; but the methodology of economic theory is to focus on a particular determinant of trade, and to analyse the implications of that explanation. This is the procedure that we follow in this and the next several chapters.

Traditionally, international trade theory has concentrated upon supply-side considerations as the main determinants of trade. It was recognized that in some circumstances differences in demand between countries could determine the pattern of trade, but the main emphasis was on differences in costs of production.

In this chapter we consider trade based upon differences in the productivity of a single factor of production. Chapters 3 and 4 discuss the interaction of demand and supply when there are two factors of production. Chapter 5 is concerned with trade arising from differences in costs caused by differences in relative endowments of the factors of production between countries. Chapter 6 gives further consideration to trade arising from differences in technological capability of countries; and Chapter 7 discusses how international trade can be motivated by economies of scale and imperfect competition.

2.2 Ricardo's Theory of Comparative Advantage

We take as our starting point the Theory of Comparative Advantage, as formulated by David Ricardo in 1817. This famous theory is not only of historical interest. It demonstrates the fundamental insight that countries with different relative costs of production can benefit from trade. We shall see that Ricardo's theory of comparative advantage can be formulated in modern terminology as the recognition that it is Pareto-inefficient to have more than one country producing two or more goods at different relative marginal costs of production.[1] Ricardo demonstrated that mutually beneficial trade can be based upon the exploitation of this inefficiency. In addition to the insight about the gains from trade, Ricardo put forward a proposition about the pattern of trade. He postulated that trade is based upon differences between countries in the relative productivity of labour in the production of goods. This proposition, although very simple, has stood up surprisingly well to empirical examination.

We use the Ricardian model to introduce analytical concepts that are important in subsequent chapters. In particular we shall be combining assumptions about the endowments and productivity of the factors of production with assumptions about the working of the factor markets to develop the supply side of a trading economy. We shall also be examining the relationship between commodity and factor prices which is central to an understanding of the gains from trade.

The model is concerned with the following questions: what determines the pattern of trade and the terms of trade, and what are the gains from trade, and how are they distributed?

---

[1] Pareto efficiency is the condition where it is not possible to achieve a gain without sustaining some cost. It is closely linked with the concept of opportunity cost because a condition of Pareto inefficiency is one in which some economic desideratum is available at zero opportunity cost.

2.2.1 The assumptions

The Ricardian model, like any other economic model, is based on certain assumptions. Some of these are to maintain simplicity and to make the model amenable to analysis, others give the model its particular characteristics and distinguish it from other models.

The assumptions are:

1. There are two countries and two goods.
2. Production of each good in each country is subject to constant returns from the input of a single factor of production (labour).
3. The cost (price) of goods is determined by the cost of the constituent labour.
4. Labour is mobile between industries within a country but is immobile between countries, so wages are equalized within a country but can differ between countries.
5. There are no transport costs.

Before proceeding let us comment briefly on these assumptions.

1. These dimensions make the model simple, but will have to be extended if it is going to have empirical relevance.
2. This assumption is central to his proposition that the pattern of trade is based on differences in relative labour productivity.
3. This is the labour theory of value, and is also critical in determining the pattern of trade. It gives us the relationship between commodity prices and wages which is an important aspect of the model.
4. This is the assumption that distinguishes the conditions of trade within a country from that of trade between countries. Without this assumption we would need some explanation as to why labour does not migrate from low-productivity to high-productivity countries.
5. This assumption gives us clean results, with commodity prices being equalized by international trade. The main propositions can withstand the presence of moderate transport costs. But the case where there is a class of goods that are 'non-traded' because of prohibitive transport costs needs further consideration.

We shall see that although Ricardo's proposition that beneficial trade is based on different relative costs of production was formulated in the context of this model, it is not dependent upon any of these assumptions.

2.2.2 Labour productivity, comparative advantage, and opportunity cost

The simplicity of this model allows us to illustrate it with a simple numerical example, so we set it up in a general form and as a numerical example.

a_x is the labour required to produce one unit of X in country A   (2.1)
a_y is the labour required to produce one unit of Y in country A
b_x is the labour required to produce one unit of X in country B
b_y is the labour required to produce one unit of Y in country B

Table 2.1. Labour inputs

	X	Y	Opportunity Cost Y: X
A	a_x = 1	a_y = 2	$a_y/a_x = 2$
B	b_x = 4	b_y = 4	$b_y/b_x = 1$
Relative labour productivity A: B	$b_x/a_x = 4$	$b_y/a_y = 2$	

Since the coefficients a_x etc. represent the labour inputs required to produce a unit of output in a country, their inverses represent labour productivity in that good and country. Thus b_x/a_x is the productivity of labour in the production of good X in country A relative to country B. A country is described as having a comparative advantage in the production of a good when its relative labour productivity in that good is higher than that for the other good. Thus if $b_x/a_x > b_y/a_y$, then country A has a comparative advantage in the production of X, and necessarily, country B will have a comparative advantage in the production of good Y.

In the numerical example, labour is more productive in both industries in country A than in country B; but it is four times as productive in the X industry, and only twice as productive in the Y industry. Thus $b_x/a_x > b_y/a_y$ and country A has a comparative advantage in X, and B has a comparative advantage in Y.

Ricardo's insight that there can be gains from trade based on comparative advantage can most usefully be seen as a recognition that there can be gains from trade based on different opportunity costs. In the Ricardian model the opportunity cost of producing one good in terms of the other good depends only upon the labour inputs required for production. Thus the opportunity cost of good Y in terms of good X is a_y/a_x in country A, and is b_y/b_x in country B. If these opportunity costs differ, and both countries are producing both goods, there can be gains from reallocating production and engaging in trade. In particular, if $a_y/a_x > b_y/b_x$ as in the numerical example where the opportunity cost of Y in terms of X is 2 in country A and is 1 in country B, gains arise from shifting labour away from Y towards X in country A where two units of X can be obtained at the cost of one unit of Y, and doing the opposite in country B where each additional unit of Y obtained costs only one of X. Note that the condition $b_x/a_x > b_y/a_y$ so that country A has a comparative advantage in X, and B has a comparative advantage in Y is identically equivalent to $a_y/a_x > b_y/b_x$, i.e. that the opportunity cost of Y in terms of X is higher in country A than in country B. Ricardo's concept of a country having a comparative advantage in a product is equivalent to the concept that the opportunity cost of producing that product in that country is relatively low.[2]

It is important to appreciate that the potential for beneficial trade based on comparative advantage or differing opportunity costs is independent of Ricardo's labour theory of value, and is valid however these costs are determined. In more modern terminology it is Pareto inefficient if two producers are both producing the same goods at differing relative marginal costs of production. International trade based on comparative advantage generates gains from the removal or reduction of that inefficiency. The gains from trade based on comparative advantage can thus be seen as a gain in Pareto production efficiency yielding for the world as a whole more of at least one good.

2.2.3 Production possibility frontiers

A convenient way to illustrate the Ricardian model diagrammatically is to assume that there is a fixed supply of labour in each country: L_A and L_B. These fixed ·labour endowments in conjunction with the labour input requirements (production functions) yield constant cost-production possibility frontiers for each country:

$$L_A = Xa_x + Ya_y \quad \text{and} \quad L_B = Xb_x + Yb_y.$$

The slopes of these are the inverse of the opportunity cost of Y in terms of X in each country. Trade at intermediate opportunity costs makes available in each country consumption possibilities that are not available under autarky. The corollary of this is that production combinations in which both countries are producing both goods are Pareto-inefficient and lie inside the combined-production possibility frontier for the world as a whole. It should be noted that, although each country has a constant cost-production possibility frontier, there are increasing costs at the point of complete specialization for the world as a whole.

Figure 2.2 illustrates the production possibility frontiers for the given labour input coefficients for the case in which $L_A = 40$ and $L_B = 60$ units of labour. The inverse of the slopes of the production possibility curves are the opportunity costs of producing Y in terms of X in each country.

2.2.4 Prices, output, and consumption possibilities

In the absence of trade (autarky), and assuming that some of both goods will be demanded and will have to be produced domestically, the relative price of the goods will be the opportunity cost of production, and the consumption possibilities of the economy will be limited to the production possibilities of that country. If, however, a country is able to trade at any relative price different from the

---

[2] The theory of comparative advantage was reformulated in terms of opportunity costs by Haberler (1929).

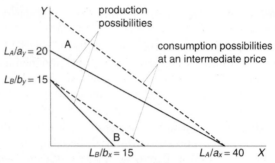

Fig. 2.2. Production and consumption possibilities

domestic opportunity costs, that country can specialize in the production of the good that is internationally relatively expensive, and import the good that is relatively cheap. In this model complete specialization occurs because of the assumption of constant costs of production.

In the two-country model there is the possibility of trade at any relative price intermediate between the two countries' opportunity costs. This is shown in Figure 2.2, with each country specializing in the product in which it has the comparative advantage, and importing the other product. The consumption possibilities for each country are determined by the value of production and the price, as shown in the Figure. The inverse of the slope of the consumption possibility lines is the price of Y in terms of X, which is assumed to be the same in both countries after trade. It can be seen that for both countries the consumption-possibility line lies outside the production-possibility frontier. This gives us an interpretation of the gains from trade. Trade has made available consumption possibilities that were not available in autarky. It is apparent that the distribution of the gains from trade between the countries will, in this model, depend only upon the relative price of the commodities. The greater the difference between the terms of trade and a country's domestic opportunity cost, the greater will be the benefit of the trade to that country. Trade at any intermediate price will result in complete specialization in both countries, and both will gain some benefit. It is possible, however, to have trade taking place at the opportunity costs of one of the countries. In which case, that country will be producing both goods, and will not be getting any of the gains from the trade.

What will be the terms of trade? This model only considers the production side of the economies, and can only provide a partial answer to this question: the terms of trade must lie within the range of the opportunity costs as determined by the labour productivities of the two countries, $a_y/a_x \geq P_y/P_x \geq b_y/b_x$. In order to determine where the terms of trade will be within this range it is necessary to have information about the demand conditions in the two countries. This model does not provide such information, but one might surmise that if a very small country were to engage in trade with a much larger one, then it is likely that the demand and supply conditions in the large country would dominate, and so the terms of trade would be close to that previously obtaining in that country and the small country would reap the gains from trade. Such a consideration might be relevant if a small country that was previously isolated from the world economy opened itself to world trade. It is unlikely, for example, that the liberalization of Albania will have much effect on world prices, so it is Albania that will benefit from the opportunity to engage in trade at international prices.

2.2.5 Wages and prices

Merchants engaged in the business of importing and exporting are concerned with money costs and prices, not the arcane concept of comparative advantage. The question to be considered next is how labour input requirements are converted into monetary costs and prices so as to enable trade to flow in accordance with comparative advantage. The link is, of course, wages. In this model costs and prices are determined only by the cost of the constituent labour.

Let the money wages in countries A and B be W_A and W_B respectively. Then the money costs of production (prices in autarky) can be shown as the matrix:

Table 2.2. Money costs of production

	X	Y	Relative price of Y to X
A	$W_A a_x$	$W_A a_y$	a_y/a_x
B	$W_B b_x$	$W_B b_y$	b_y/b_x

Notice that the wages are expressed in money terms and have a time dimension, such as, say, £4 per hour, and the input requirements also have a time dimension, say 2 hours of labour per unit of output; so the money costs of production are expressed in terms of money per unit. However, the money and wage terms drop out of the expression for the relative prices. In autarky the relative prices are the opportunity cost of producing the goods in each country, and these are independent of the wage rates provided that within each country the wage is the same in each industry, as is being assumed. The relative wage in the two countries is, however, very important in determining the terms of trade and in allowing two-way trade to flow in accordance with comparative advantage.

Since $b_x/a_x > b_y/a_y$ in the example given, A has a comparative advantage in X, and B in Y. In order for mutual trade to flow, it is necessary that the money costs of production reflect this comparative advantage: that is, that the money cost of producing X in A is less (not greater) than that of producing it in B. This condition is $W_A a_x \leq W_B b_x$. Similarly if country B is to export Y it is necessary that $W_A a_y \geq W_B b_y$. Therefore, to have two-way trade it is necessary that $b_x/a_x \geq W_A/W_B \geq b_y/a_y$.[3,4]

[3] In the absence of transport costs trade may take place if the cost of producing one of the two goods is the same in both countries. Under these circumstances one of the countries will produce both goods, whereas the other will be completely specialized.

[4] This relationship provides the basis of one of the best-known attempts to test the

Note that the feasible relative wage in the two countries must be bounded by their relative labour productivities in the two goods. Thus, in the numerical example given above, since the labour productivity in country A in the X industry is four times that of country B, whereas it is only twice as high in the Y industry, the wages in country A must be between four times and twice those in country B. The intuition of international trade based on relative labour productivities is quite simple. The low-wage, low-productivity country is able to export the product in which it has a comparative advantage, because for that good the low wage more than offsets the low productivity, so that the labour costs per unit of production are lower than that of its trading partner. On the other hand, the high-wage and high-labour-productivity country can export the good in which it has a comparative advantage, because for that good the high relative labour productivity fully offsets the high wages, so that labour costs of production are relatively low.

Let us consider what would happen if relative wages lay outside this range. Suppose the wage rate in country A was only one and a half times that of country B. For example, if the wage in country A was £6 and that in country B was £4, then the cost of producing good X would be £6 in A and £16 in B, and the cost of producing good Y would be £12 in A and £16 in B. At these relative wages, country B cannot compete in the production of either good. Both goods would be produced in A, and neither in B. This book is not concerned with issues of macroeconomic adjustment, but we might note that country B would face an unemployment problem and a balance-of-trade deficit, suggesting two possible adjustment mechanisms, both leading to a fall in the wage in country B relative to that of country A. Wages might fall directly in response to the unemployment, or the parity of the currency in country B with that of country A might be abandoned in response to the balance of trade deficit, so that at unchanged nominal wages real wages will have fallen.

Suppose that production and trade are in accordance with the pattern of comparative advantage. Then the free-trade price of X in both countries will be the cost of its production in country A: $P_x = W_A a_x$, and similarly the price of Y will be its cost of production in country B: $P_y = W_B b_y$. Thus $P_y/P_x = (b_y/a_x)/(W_A/W_B)$. The terms of trade and the relative wages are mutually determined by the demand conditions and the labour productivity conditions in the two countries. The relationship between the relative wages and the terms of trade is shown in Figure 2.3.

It can be seen that the range of feasible terms of trade is bounded by the opportunity costs of producing the goods in the two countries. The extreme point A is where the terms of trade are equal to country A's opportunity costs of production. At this point, country A may be producing both goods, and its wages relative to those in country B are as low as is feasible with two-way trade. In contrast, the point B is where the terms of trade are equal to country B's domestic relative costs of production, and are most favourable to country A. At these terms of trade,

labour-productivity version of the theory of comparative advantage: MacDougall (1951). This is described below.

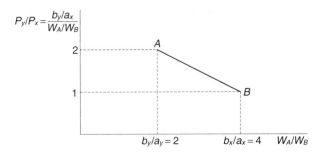

Fig. 2.3. Wages and the terms of trade

country B might be producing both goods, and country A's relative wages are at
their maximum.

2.2.6 Absolute advantage

Prior to Ricardo, economists such as Adam Smith had envisaged trade as being
based on absolute differences in labour productivity. This is a situation where in
one country labour is more productive in one good and less productive in the
other good than is labour in the other country. Absolute advantage and disadvantage of this sort implies a comparative advantage and disadvantage. The
analysis of trade based upon differing relative labour productivity and opportunity costs is therefore unchanged. The only point of note is that, in the absolute
advantage case, the range of feasible relative wages straddles unity, so we are
unable to know from the labour productivity conditions alone in which country
the wages will be highest.

2.2.7 Real wages

In autarky, the real wages in each country are determined by the productivity of
labour in the two industries. After trade based on comparative advantage, the real
wage in terms of the exported good remains unchanged, but the cost of the
imported good has fallen, so real wages in terms of the imported good in each
country have risen.

In country A the real wage in terms of Y has changed from $1/a_y$ to $W_A/W_B b_y$.
Since $W_A/W_B > b_y/a_y$, this is an increase. Similarly, in country B the real wage in
terms of X has changed from $1/b_x$ to $W_B/W_A a_x$. Since $b_x/a_x > W_A/W_B$, this is also
an increase.

The real wages in the two countries before trade and after trade at an arbitrarily chosen intermediate price are shown in Figure 2.4.

It will be noted that this diagram is similar, except in scale, to Figure 2.2 above.

Table 2.3.   Real wages

Before Trade			After Trade		
	X	Y		X	Y
A	$1/a_x$	$1/a_y$	A	$1/a_x$	$W_A/(W_Bb_y)$
B	$1/b_x$	$1/b_y$	B	$W_B/(W_Aa_x)$	$1/b_y$

The only economic agents in this model are workers, so the extended consumption possibilities made possible by trade can be seen as an increase in the real wage of workers. The extent to which a worker within a country can benefit from a fall in the price of the imported good depends upon his or her consumption pattern, and so is indeterminate within the model.

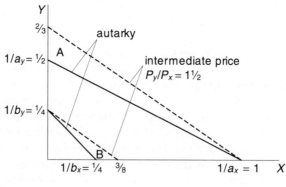

Fig. 2.4. Real wages

The numerical example illustrates the gains from trade given the postulated labour productivities for the *arbitrary*, but feasible case in which the money wage in country A is £4, whereas in country B it is £1.50. These wages will yield the prices P_x = £4 (cost of production in country A) and P_y = £6 (cost of production in country B). Thus the cost of the imported good has fallen in each country, and the real wage in terms of the imported good has risen. For the numerical example the real wage in terms of each good before and after trade are shown in Table 2.4.

2.2.8 Unequal exchange

In the above example it takes 8/3 hours of labour in country B to produce the Y which can be exchanged for the X which has been produced in one hour by a

Table 2.4. Real wages in terms of each good before and after trade

Autarky			Trade		
	X	Y		X	Y
A	1	1/2	A	1	2/3
B	1/4	1/4	B	3/8	1/4

worker in country A. This is described as exploitation in the Neo-Marxist dependency literature.[5] Such 'unequal exchange' is an intrinsic aspect of trade based on comparative advantage between a country with high absolute labour productivity and one in which labour productivity is generally low. The important point is that in the absence of trade the real wage in the poor country would be even lower in terms of the potentially imported good, as can be seen in this numerical example.

2.2.9 Productivity changes

Policy-makers and commentators are often concerned that their country is falling behind in competitiveness or failing to keep up in productivity. Issues of competitiveness and international trade are considered in Chapter 14 below. It is useful, however, to comment briefly at this stage upon what the simple Ricardian model has to suggest about the effects an increase in labour productivity in one country might be expected to have upon its trading partner. The basic point is that the gain from trade depends upon the terms of trade; thus the effect of increased labour productivity in country A upon welfare in country B depends only upon how the terms of trade have changed (assuming that there is no change in labour productivity in country B). Consider the case in which country A is producing both goods, but country B is completely specialized in the production of one good. In such a case the terms of trade are determined by the relative labour productivity in the industries of country A. Thus there is no general presumption that increased productivity in a trading partner will cause problems for a country, but it may do so if that productivity increase is biased in favour of the growing country's import competing industry. This is a scenario that may have some relevance to countries such as small tropical sugar producers trading with the European Union. Increased productivity in sugar production promoted by subsidies in Europe impact adversely upon the export prospects and the terms of trade of the tropical producers, causing them declining incomes and difficult adjustment problems.

[5] Emmanuel (1972).

On the other hand, increased productivity in Europe's export industries can be expected to have favourable terms of trade for trading partners that are importing those goods.

There is no general presumption that a country will be worse off as a result of productivity gains in its trading partners. The basic point, further developed in Chapter 14, is that it is productivity growth in Europe that is important for European living standards, rather than productivity growth relative to the United States, Japan, or anywhere else.

2.3 Extending the Ricardian model

We now consider how the Ricardian model can be extended so as to make it more relevant as a framework for discussing real-world issues, while maintaining its essential features.

2.3.1 Many products

The most natural extension, and one that is necessary for any empirical application, is to increase the number of products. We shall see that the model can withstand this extension without difficulty, although it is no longer possible to determine on the basis of labour productivity alone whether any particular good will be exported or imported by a country. First we note that the production set remains linear, in the sense that the production possibility frontier is linear in any pair of dimensions. Output is constrained by the total fixed labour supply and the fixed-labour requirement of each industry. Thus the production set is:

$$\bar{L} \geq \Sigma a_i Q_i$$

where a_i is the fixed labour requirement to produce one unit of good i, and Q_i is the quantity of good i that is produced.

The Ricardian model satisfies the requirements of the 'non-substitution theorem' which states that a production set will be linear if all of the following conditions are satisfied:

1. There are constant returns to scale in the production of each good.
2. There are no joint products.
3. There is only one primary factor of production which must be mobile between industries; or if there is more than one factor, they must be used in the same proportion in every industry, so that from a production perspective they constitute a single factor.

We shall see in Chapter 3 that the introduction of more than one factor of production causes the production-possibility frontier to be concave to the origin. Increasing returns to scale tend to make the production-possibility frontier convex, as will be discussed in Chapter 7. We do not discuss issues concerning joint products, and it is left to the readers' intuition to appreciate that joint production will tend to make the production-possibility frontier convex.

The Ricardian model, however, satisfies all of these requirements; and we have already seen that in the two-product case it yields a one-dimensional linear production-possibility frontier. The three-product case will yield a two-dimensional plane as a production-possibility frontier, as is shown in Figure 2.5. The opportunity cost of any product Y in terms of any other product X remains constant at a_Y/a_X.

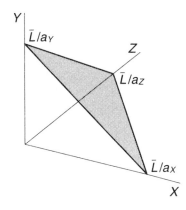

Fig. 2.5. Production possibilities: three goods

More generally, if there are N products there will be an $N-1$ hyperplane production-possibility frontier.

It is intuitively easy to appreciate that this multi-dimensional production possibility frontier will be linear in any pair of dimensions. Suppose that there are a hundred products; then if the output of ninety-eight of these is given, there will be a fixed amount of labour remaining to be allocated between the two remaining products, as in the two-product case. The opportunity cost of the products and their pre-trade prices are determined only by the technological requirement of their relative labour inputs. The cost of producing any good will be determined by its labour input: $P_i = Wa_i$. Under perfect competition the wage will be the same in all sectors, so the relative price of any pair of products will be equal to their opportunity cost: $P_i/P_j = a_i/a_j$. This, of course, is a constant in the absence of technological change.

We now must consider the conditions for trade. Let us suppose that we have two countries A and B, and N commodities. We can rank these commodities in order of A's labour productivity relative to that of B.

$$b_1/a_1 \geq b_2/a_2 \geq \ldots \geq b_i/a_i \geq \ldots \geq b_j/a_j \geq \ldots \geq b_n/a_n \qquad (2.2)$$

This gives us a chain in which country A's comparative advantage is greatest for good 1 and is least for good n. Apart from the goods at each end of the chain, we cannot tell, in the absence of information about demand, which products will be exported and imported by each country. It is possible, for example, if country A is small and is trading with the rest of the world, that it will be specialized in the production and export of good 1, and it will import everything else. More generally, we might expect each country to produce and export several of the products. Although the theory cannot determine which products will be exported from each country, it is able to tell us something about the pattern of trade and relative wages. If a good is to be exported from country A to country B it is necessary that its cost of production is not greater in A than in B, i.e. $W_A a_i \leq W_B b_i$. And conversely, if some other product is exported from country B to A, then $W_B b_j \leq W_A a_j$. Combining these conditions yields $b_i/a_i \geq W_A/W_B \geq b_j/a_j$, where good i is an export from country A, and good j is an export from country B. This is nothing more than the condition that the labour costs of production are lower in the exporting country than in the importing country. We shall call it the 'labour-cost condition'. Expressing it in this form draws attention to the role of relative wages in breaking the chain of comparative advantage to distinguish between exports and imports. This is shown for six commodities in Figure 2.6.

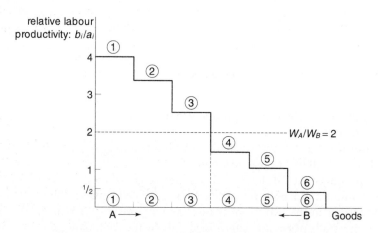

Fig. 2.6. Relative wages and the location of production

In this diagram, the commodities are numbered on the horizontal axis from 1 to 6 in order of country A's comparative advantage. The labour productivity in country A relative to country B for each of the products is shown on the vertical axis. These have been drawn for the values: 4, 3.5, 2.5, 1.5, 1, and 0.5. In this example, labour productivity in country A ranges from four times to half that in country B, so this defines the range of relative wages that is feasible with these productivities. As wages in country A relative to those in B rise, the range of goods that can be produced in A falls. For example, if wages in A were twice those in B, goods 1, 2, and 3 would be produced in A and the rest would be produced in B.

At relative wages of 2.5, good 3 could be produced in either country; but at relative wages greater than 2.5, good 3 could only be produced in country B.

It can be seen that the more a country is able to specialize in the product in which it has its greatest comparative advantage, the higher will be the relative wage in that country. Thus the result that we obtained in the two-commodity case—that the gains from trade are likely to be reaped mainly by a small country trading with a large one—continues to hold in the many-commodity case. The ability of the country to maximize its wages by specializing in just one product depends upon the world demand for that product being sufficient to employ all of the country's labour in its production. More generally, an increase in the demand for goods produced in a country will tend to raise wages in that country, and will tend to restrict the range of goods that it will produce.

The step-like relationship between relative labour productivities, relative wages, and location of production in Figure 2.6 arises because of the limited number of goods and the discrete labour productivities. If we have a very large number of products, we will tend to get a continuous relationship between relative wages, location of production, and the demand for labour in the two countries. This is discussed in Dornbusch, Fischer, and Samuelson (1977).

It can be seen that, in this model, the location of production is highly specialized in the sense that only one of the many products might be produced in both countries. This is in marked contrast to the real world, in which most countries produce and export a considerable number of products.

2.3.2 Many countries

We next consider what the model has to suggest about the pattern of trade and the gains from trade when we have many countries. We shall start with the case where there are several countries and just two products. The main difference between this case and that where there were only two countries is that each good is likely to be produced and exported by more than one country. Countries will tend to be specialized in production, and it is possible for only one country to be producing both goods. We can again establish a chain of comparative advantage by ranking the countries A to Z in order of their labour productivity in the production of good X relative to Y, thus: $a_Y/a_X > b_Y/b_X > \ldots$ and so on. Again, in the absence of information about demand, we can only be certain about the exports of the countries at each end of the chain. Furthermore, we cannot tell which exporting countries will supply which importing countries with a particular product. However, if country B is exporting good X and is importing good Y, whereas country C is exporting Y and importing X, then even though these countries may not be trading directly with each other we get the standard labour-cost condition showing the relationship between wages and the relative labour productivities in the two countries: $c_X/b_X > W_B/W_C > c_Y/b_Y$.

Figure 2.7 shows the production possibility frontier for a world consisting of four countries A to D, and two products X and Y. In this diagram the slope of the

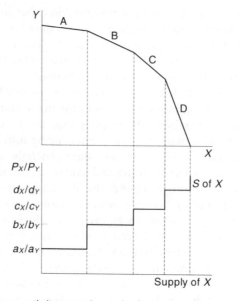

Fig. 2.7. Production possibilities and supply: four countries

production-possibility frontier indicates the opportunity cost of X in terms of Y in a particular country: $a_X/a_Y < b_X/b_Y < c_X/c_Y < d_X/d_Y$, where the coefficients are the labour requirement per unit of output for countries and industries, so country A has the strongest comparative advantage in X. Production on this frontier will depend upon world demand. It might be at a point where the frontier is kinked, in which case all of the countries will be completely specialized in one product or the other; or it might be at a point where world price equals the cost of production in one country, in which case that country could produce both goods. The lower panel shows the world supply curve for the good X with respect to its price in terms of good Y. If that price exceeds the opportunity cost in a country, then that country will specialize in the production of X. The world supply curve resembles a flight of steps with vertical sections where all countries are specialized, and flat sections where one of the countries is producing both goods. As the number of countries becomes large, the production-possibility frontier and the associated supply curves will become smooth.

2.3.3. Many products and countries

This discussion can be extended to cases where there are many products and countries. It is still possible to rank countries and products on the basis of relative labour productivity, and the labour-cost condition relating productivity to wages is maintained. The gains from trade are still in the form of an increase in real wages in terms of imported goods.

From a comparison of the case where there are two countries and many goods with that where there are many countries and two goods, it will be apparent that the number of countries relative to the number of products makes some difference to the pattern of specialization. When there are many products and few countries, each country will produce a range of products, but each product will be produced and exported from a very limited number of countries. On the other hand, if there are many countries and few products, countries will be highly specialized, while the products may each be produced in a number of countries. Countries will tend to be more concentrated in their exports than in their imports. This discussion leads to obvious empirical questions concerning the number of countries and products that there are in the international economy: questions which are not as straightforward as they might seem. A 'country', from a Ricardian perspective, is a region within which labour mobility is sufficiently high to equalize wages. On the other hand, labour mobility between 'countries' is low. Clearly the attempt to achieve a unified labour market with full mobility and uniform employment conditions within the European Union is an attempt to create a single 'country' in the Ricardian sense; but equally clearly, this has not yet been achieved. Furthermore, countries that are well-established politically may not have unified labour markets. Consider Italy, where high labour mobility has not yet been sufficient to eliminate the marked disparity in labour productivity between the north and the south of the country; or Canada, where language and cultural diversity reduce labour mobility. Clearly, these countries, like many others, fall short of the Ricardian ideal.

How do we define a good or product or industry in ways that are appropriate for relating to the Ricardian model? In principle this is not so difficult. If several goods are sufficiently similar in their labour requirements that the relative labour productivities between countries are the same for all of these goods, then they can be considered as a single good or industry from a Ricardian perspective. The problem, of course, is to find data which enable us to identify such industries.

2.3.4 Transport costs

We do not wish to discuss transport costs at any length, but there are some points that are relevant to reconciling the empirical evidence to the Ricardian model. First we should note a distinction between transport costs that are sufficiently high to prevent any trade in the product, and ones that are different between pairs of countries and which allow some trade. The former give rise to what are known as 'non-traded' goods. These tend to be products whose weight relative to value is high, such as aggregates used for construction, or products which are very perishable, such as ice-cream. Some coarse food-grains, such as millet, are usually consumed close to where they are produced, and are virtually non-traded. Services which have to be consumed where they are located may be non-traded; but care is needed here, because for some of these, such as postgraduate education and tourism, the value of the service is high relative to the travel costs of the consumer, and they have many of the characteristics of traded goods. Non-traded goods have an important role in open economy macroeconomics because exchange-rate changes will change the relative price of traded and non-traded goods, and so will affect the balance of trade and aggregate demand. The importance of the non-traded goods in the context of the Ricardian model is that they reduce the extreme specialization in production that the pure model predicts, since a country will produce a range of the non-traded goods as well as its export products.

Differential transport costs among countries also reduce specialization. Several countries might be able to export the same product even though they have different relative labour productivities, because in some markets the transport-cost advantage might offset a labour-cost disadvantage. For the same reason a country may be able to export several products, being effectively protected from competition in some markets by the transport costs.

Transport costs have generally been ignored in international trade theory. There is, however, a highly successful empirical model of trade, the 'gravity model', which emphasizes the significance of transport costs in determining the pattern of trade. This is discussed in Chapter 8.

2.4 Empirical relevance

The Ricardian version of comparative advantage, with its emphasis on a single factor of production, that of labour, is extremely simple. Can it explain the actual pattern of trade? Is the pattern of trade consistent with the view that trade is determined by differences in relative labour productivity?

An early attempt to 'test' the labour-productivity version of comparative advantage was published by the British economist Donald MacDougall in 1951. This has attracted considerable interest and controversy, and has been the prototype for several other studies. MacDougall had data on labour productivities in USA and British industry for 1937; and he observed that wages in the USA were about twice as high as those in Britain, i.e. $W_A/W_B = 2$. Thus in industries in which American labour productivity was more than twice the British, America should have the cost advantage and be expected to export; whereas in industries in which American productivity was less than twice the British, Britain would have the cost advantage. Using the notation previously developed, we can use the labour-cost condition to distinguish between products which the theory suggests America would export, and those that Britain would export: $b_i/a_i > W_A/W_B > b_j/a_j$, where b_i etc. is the labour requirement in industry i in Britain etc., so that b_i/a_i is American labour productivity relative to British in that industry. The two-country model would require a direct examination of bilateral trade between the countries. But in 1937, tariffs were very high and tended to offset the comparative advantage, and the amount of trade between the two countries was low; so MacDougall examined the level of each country's exports to the world as a whole.

In effect he was testing a three-country, many-product version of the model. The pure model suggests that in the industries in which American labour productivity was more than twice the British, Britain would not be able to compete with America in the world markets; and contrarily, America would not be able to compete with Britain in the industries in which American labour productivity was less than twice that of the British. But, as we have discussed earlier, transport costs and discriminatory tariffs may offset the labour-cost advantage or disadvantage, so that one country's dominance in an industry might be incomplete or even reversed. Furthermore, mis-specification and inappropriate aggregation of industries will cloud the results. Nevertheless, it is reasonable to expect that a country's comparative advantage and export share will be correlated to its labour-cost advantage. It is this that MacDougall tested, by fitting a regression line to the logarithms of output per worker US: UK and the quantity of exports US: UK, generating a diagram similar to that shown here.

Fig. 2.8. US and UK labour productivity and export share

MacDougall had twenty-five industries in his sample. The relative US: UK labour productivity ranged from 5.25 for tin cans to 1.1 for cement; and the quantity of US: UK exports ranged from 8 for wireless sets and valves to 1/250 for woollen and worsted (clothing). In general MacDougall found that 'where American output per worker was more than twice the British, the United States had in general the bulk of the export market, while for products where it was less than twice as high the bulk of the market was held by Britain'. The regression had a correlation coefficient of about 0.8 and an inverse slope of about 4, suggesting that a 1 per cent increase in labour productivity in one of the countries would give rise to about a 4 per cent increase in that country's export share. The regression line passed above the point where US wages were twice that of the UK and where the export shares were equal, suggesting that labour productivity in the US had to be somewhat more than twice that in the UK for the US exports to equal those of Britain. MacDougall suggested that this may have been the result of imperial preferences that discriminated in favour of Britain in the countries of the British

Commonwealth. He also postulated that the data may have over-estimated US labour productivity relative to the British.

MacDougall's methodology has been criticized, particularly by Bhagwati (1964), mainly on the grounds that it did not confirm the link between export price ratios and relative labour productivity; but the prevailing view now is that this and other similar studies have successfully demonstrated the importance of labour costs in determining the pattern of trade.[6] What is less satisfactory is that other models of the determination of trade—in particular the Heckscher-Ohlin model, which will be discussed in Chapter 5—generate the same relationship between labour costs and trade, and so the verification of the relationship cannot constitute a valid test of the Ricardian model in preference to others.

Satisfactory data on labour productivity are not easily obtained; but it seems that within Europe, and between industrial countries more generally, there is considerable variation in relative labour productivity among manufacturing sectors; so it is at least feasible that international trade in manufactured products could be based on such variation. The first table from Van Ark and Pilat (1993) shows relative labour productivity in manufacturing sectors in Germany and Japan compared with the United States.

Table 2.5. Value added per hour worked in manufacturing in Germany and Japan (United States = 100)

	1965	1990
Germany		
Food, beverages and tobacco	76.9	71.8
Textiles, apparel and leather	78.1	93.0
Chemicals and allied products	64.3	71.2
Basic and fabricated metal products	53.6	91.1
Machinery and equipment	77.1	83.2
Other manufacturing	56.6	78.2
Total manufacturing	66.7	82.1
Japan		
Food, beverages and tobacco	23.6	36.2
Textiles, apparel and leather	62.9	54.9
Chemicals and allied products	41.4	80.2
Basic and fabricated metal products	32.9	100.5
Machinery and equipment	25.7	116.3
Other manufacturing	21.3	63.2
Total manufacturing	29.3	82.1

Source: Van Ark and Pilat (1993).

These data—particularly the comparison between the United States and Japan—show great variation between industries in the relative labour-productivity of the two countries. This indicates that there is plenty of scope for trade between the countries based on differences in relative labour costs. It can also be

[6] In particular, Stern (1962) and Balassa (1963).

seen that comparative advantage has changed over time. For example, in 1965 Japan's labour productivity in machinery and equipment relative to the United States was low compared with that of manufacturing as a whole. But by 1990 this had become the industry of Japan's greatest comparative advantage. Comparing Germany with the United States, it can be seen that Germany's relative labour productivity in basic and fabricated metal products was low; but by 1990 this had become one of Germany's high-productivity industries relative to the United States.[7]

The second table compares labour productivity in British and German manufacturing industries. Labour productivity in 1987 was about 22 per cent higher in Germany than in Britain, but there was considerable variability between industries.

Table 2.6. British and German relative labour productivity

Labour productivity ratios: Germany/UK 1987	Per worker-hour
Metal manufacturing	110.8
Non-metallic mineral products	111.2
Chemicals	94.7
Metal products	131.4
Mechanical engineering	135.2
Electrical engineering	102.3
Vehicles	141.1
Instrument engineering	149.0
Food, drink, and tobacco	106.8
Textiles	95.8
Clothing, footwear, and leather	116.2
Timber and furniture	157.2
Paper and board	185.1
Rubber, plastics, and other manufactures	120.0
Total manufacturing	121.8

Source: O'Mahony (1992).

2.5 Revealed comparative advantage

Can the nature of a country's comparative advantage be deduced from or revealed by its trade performance? Care is needed in considering such a question. If comparative advantage is defined loosely as meaning that which the country is good at exporting, then the question is trivial. If, however, we have a clearly defined theory of the determination of comparative advantage, such as relative labour costs as in the Ricardian model, then it is reasonable to consider whether the trade performance indicates the presence of that source of comparative advantage. The validity of such a deduction depends upon the comprehensiveness of the

[7] Van Ark and Pilat's data are cited and the determinants of labour productivity are discussed in Englander and Gurney (1994a).

explanation of the trade performance. If there is only one determinant of trade, then that determinant is revealed by the trade; but if, as is the case in the real world, there are a number of explanations of trade, then we cannot deduce with any confidence that one particular explanation of the observed trade is the true one. The best that can be said is that the trade performance is consistent with a particular explanation. If we observe that Britain's trade performance relative to that of Germany is stronger in chemicals than in instrument-engineering products, could we deduce that Britain's labour productivity relative to that of Germany is relatively high in chemicals and relatively low in instrument engineering, as is the case in Table 2.2 above? Such a deduction is valid only to the extent that relative labour productivity is the dominant determinant of trade in these products.

The concept of revealed comparative advantage raises the issue of how trade performance should be measured. This is by no means straightforward. The main problems, apart from the availability of data, concern the appropriate level of aggregation of industries, the weighting of industries within the aggregates, and the distortions caused by trade and industrial policy.

A simple measure of trade performance in an industry is the net trade index $(X_i - M_i)/(X_i + M_i)$ where X_i and M_i are respectively exports and imports in industry i. This index ranges from plus to minus unity, and measures net trade relative to total trade in a product group. It is easily understood, and has the advantage of requiring only trade data for the product and country concerned. It is, however, subject to the limitations that it can be severely distorted by policy, and it gives little indication of the importance of the industry in trade or production. Its limitation can be seen by considering two countries in a multi-country world. The first might be the dominant world supplier of a product with high exports and virtually no imports. This country would have a net trade index close to plus one properly reflecting its strong trade performance. But the second country might prohibit all imports and might, as a result of subsidies, export a small amount of the product. This country would also have a net trade index of unity; but in this case the measure of strong trade performance is obviously inappropriate. More satisfactory are measures that normalize trade in a product with respect to a country's total trade or production. Thus Balassa (1965) developed an index that measures a country's share of world exports of the particular manufactured product relative to that country's share of world exports of all manufactured goods: $B = (X_{ij}/X_{wj})/(X_{im}/X_{wm})$ where i indicates the country, j is the commodity, m is total manufactures, and w is the world. This index only requires trade data, but it needs global in addition to domestic data, and it requires data for total manufactures. The OECD has developed an indicator of revealed comparative advantage in manufactured goods that is the ratio of an industry's share in a country's manufacturing exports to its share in that country's manufacturing output: $(X_{ij}/X_{im})/(Q_{ij}/Q_{im})$ where Q_{ij} and Q_{im} are country i's output of good j and of total manufactures respectively. This indicator requires data on production as well as trade, but it only requires domestic data. These normalized indicators are clearly more satisfactory than the simple net trade index, although they too can be distorted by trade policy.

The issue as to whether trade performance is being 'distorted' by policy is a difficult one. We would probably not want to consider European Union exports of butter at prices below the production costs as part of the Common Agricultural Policy disposal programme as reflecting comparative advantage. On the other hand exports by Germany of high-tech products made possible by state funding of education and research would normally be considered as reflecting comparative advantage. These are extreme cases, but where should the line be drawn between policies that distort comparative advantage and policies that determine it?[8]

2.6 Comparative advantage and policy reform

The location of a country's comparative advantage—however determined or revealed—has become an important issue in the integration of the former communist countries of Eastern Europe into the international economy. A difficulty faced by these countries is that their existing industrial and trade structures provide no indication of what might be appropriate for liberal and open economies. The problem is to ensure that the processes of liberalization and policy reform are consistent with the development of industries in which these countries have potential comparative advantage. An important issue, to be discussed further in Chapter 18, is whether the Eastern European countries should tend to specialize in standard labour-intensive products such as clothing, in which they may have a comparative advantage, when such industries are treated as 'sensitive' by the EU and receive high levels of protection.

2.7 Aspects of the Ricardian model

We conclude this chapter by briefly summarizing and evaluating the model. Ricardo successfully demonstrated that there can be gains from trade between countries when relative costs of production in autarky differ. We have seen that this proposition does not depend upon the labour theory of value used by Ricardo, but is an application of a general requirement for Pareto efficiency in production. There are gains from trade because the availability of goods for consumption has increased.

The model identifies a range of prices determined by the domestic opportunity costs of production at which bilateral trade can take place, but conditions of demand are required to determine the volume of trade and the terms of trade within this range, and thus to determine how the gains from trade are

---

[8] Concepts and the measurement of revealed comparative advantage are discussed in Balance (1988). Balassa (1989) discusses various aspects of comparative advantage.

distributed.[9] Since a country might be able to use trade policy to affect demand and thus improve its own terms of trade and increase its share of the gains from trade, the model demonstrates the case for some trade, not necessarily for free trade. This is discussed in Chapter 9 below.

The Ricardian model is formulated in terms of only one factor of production: labour. It therefore proposes that the pattern of trade, and the range of feasible prices and wages, are determined by relative labour productivities. The gains from trade take the form of an increase in real wages in terms of imported goods. Since Labour is the only economic agent in this model, we get the very strong result that there are no losers from trade, and that everyone who consumes any of an imported product gains. As we shall discuss in Chapter 3, this strong result cannot be maintained in models in which there is more than one factor of production.

The main deficiency of the model is the emphasis on one factor of production and the failure of the model to explain how the productivity of labour is determined. Most extensions of the theory of comparative advantage, and indeed most theories of the determinants of trade, provide explanations on how the productivity of labour and perhaps of other factors of production is determined. The most important of these are theories in which the productivity of labour depends upon the availability of complementary factors of production: land, natural resources, capital, and so on. These factor-endowment theories are the subject of subsequent Chapters. Also important are explanations based on differences in technology, differences in skills, and economies of scale. These are considered later.

The proposition that trade is based on relative labour productivities has been the subject of much empirical analysis, and has been surprisingly successful.[10] Van Ark (1990) provides both a justification for the emphasis on the single factor: labour, and of the robustness of the empirical results. He makes the point, which is reinforced in Chapter 14 below, that it is the productivity of labour that is the main determinant of a country's income and of the welfare of most of its population. Furthermore he points out that even in relatively capital-intensive manufacturing activities, labour constitutes about 70 per cent of the costs of production.

2.8 Summary

- If all goods are produced separately and competitively, from labour alone, at constant costs, a country's production possibility frontier will be linear.
- Gains from trade based on comparative advantage or differences in opportu-

---

[9] John Stuart Mill integrated demand considerations with the theory of comparative costs in 1848.

[10] See Deardorff (1984) for a discussion of issues in testing comparative advantage and for a survey of the empirical work.

nity costs of production between countries are gains arising from the reduction of a Pareto inefficiency in production.

- In the Ricardian model it is the difference in wages between countries that transforms comparative advantage into a money cost advantage thereby facilitating the flow of trade.
- In the Ricardian model there are no losers from trade. The gains are an increase in real wages in terms of the imported goods.

NEO-CLASSICAL PRODUCTION

3.1 Introduction

In this chapter we develop the elementary theory of the supply side of an economy in which there are two factors of production. This move from the one-factor Ricardian model to a two-factor one may not seem like much of an improvement in describing a world in which there are millions of factors. The two-factor model, however, is richer in the sense that it provides a framework for considering questions that the Ricardian model leaves unanswered: in particular, why factor productivity might differ between countries, and how international trade might affect income distribution within a country. This chapter concentrates on the basic theory, but subsequent chapters use this theory to consider these very important questions in the context of European trade and trade policy.

We shall limit our analysis to the case where there are two factors of production, thereby allowing a simple diagrammatic presentation of the topic. The discussion in this chapter is concerned with production and supply. This is in accordance with most of trade theory (including the Ricardian approach) that emphasizes differences in supply conditions between countries as being the basis of international trade. In Chapter 4 we shall be introducing considerations of demand. The supply side of the economy will then be integrated with the demand conditions to develop a model of a country's desire to trade.[1] This then enables us to consider a trading equilibrium between two countries that have differing desires to trade. Subsequent chapters explore various explanations of the causes of trade.

The supply-side model developed in this chapter is that of 'neo-classical' production. The neo-classical economists of the second half of the nineteenth and the early twentieth century, such as Edgeworth, Jevons, Marshall, and Walras, emphasized the importance of marginal values in determining conditions for economic equilibrium and optimization, thereby laying the foundations for modern microeconomics. In the context of neo-classical production, the emphasis is on the marginal productivity and marginal costs, in contrast to the classical

---

[1] We shall often refer rather loosely to 'a country' doing or desiring something. This is for ease of exposition. Actually the doing or desiring is by individual economic agents within a country: in particular, consumers, producers, workers, and owners of other factors of production.

approach that tended to formulate discussion in terms of average values. In the Ricardian trade model the assumption of constant costs and productivity ensures that the marginal and average values are the same, but the distinction is important when there is more than one factor.

3.2 Production functions and factor substitutability

The ability to substitute one factor for another in the production process is a fundamental characteristic of neo-classical production, so the production function must have at least two factors. We concentrate on the simplest case, in which there are two products, each produced by two factors of production. Outputs of the goods X and Y are assumed to be linear, homogenous functions of the inputs K (capital) and L (labour), for example $X = X(K_x,L_x)$ and $Y = Y(K_y,L_x)$.[2] (The subscripts which indicate in which products the factors are being used will be dropped when the product in question is unambiguous.) It is assumed that output will increase, but at a diminishing rate, when the input of one factor is increased while the other is held constant. This is to say that the marginal products of the factors are assumed to be positive but diminishing: i.e. X_K, X_L, Y_K, $Y_L > 0$ where X_K is the marginal product of capital in the production of X etc., and X_{KK}, X_{LL}, Y_{KK}, $Y_{LL} < 0$ are the second derivatives of the production function. This assumption of positive but diminishing marginal products is characteristic of neo-classical production functions. It is equivalent to assuming that the factors are imperfect substitutes.

In Figure 3.1 the isoquants indicate constant amounts of a good X, obtainable for various combinations of inputs as determined by the production function.

The neo-classical production isoquants have the following properties:[3]

1. They are convex to the origin (because of the diminishing substitutability between the factors).
2. Their absolute slopes equal the marginal rate of substitution between the factors: $dK/dL = X_L/X_K$.
3. Their slopes along a ray from the origin such as OZ are constant. This is a property of the homogeneity of the function, and means that the marginal rate of substitution between the factors depends only upon the proportion in which the factors are used.

---

[2] A widely used alternative notation that is analogous to that used in the previous chapter, is to represent the capital and labour used in the production of one unit of the good X as a_{KX} and a_{LX} respectively, and similarly a_{KY} and a_{LY} are the factor inputs in a unit of good Y. The two notations are linked by the identity $K_X = Xa_{KX}$, $L_X = Xa_{LX}$, and similarly for good Y. The fundamental difference between the Ricardian and the neo-classical coefficients is that the former are assumed to be technologically determined constants, whereas the latter vary subject to the production function.

[3] These properties are not proved here, but proofs and fuller discussions of production functions can be found in microeconomic textbooks.

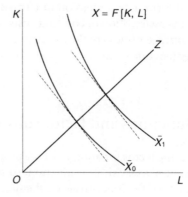

Fig. 3.1. Production isoquants

4.   Constant returns to scale imply that a given movement along a ray such as OZ (a proportional increase in the use of both factors) will yield an increase in output of the same proportion.

These last two properties ensure that the outputs per unit of factor input, and the marginal product of each factor depend only upon the proportion in which the factors are used. Thus a production function $X = F(K,L)$ can be written $X/L = f(K/L)$ and can be diagrammatically represented by Figure 3.2.

   In this formulation the slope at point T represents the marginal product of capital. It can be seen that as the capital–labour ratio (K/L) increases, output per labourer increases at a diminishing rate. This reflects the property of the production function that the marginal product of each factor is positive but diminishing.

   Returning to Figure 3.2, the convexity of the isoquant indicates that as we move up the curve using more capital and less labour to produce a given amount of the product, it becomes increasingly difficult to substitute capital for labour: the

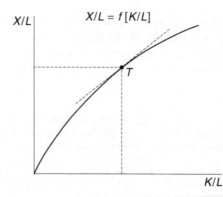

Fig. 3.2. Output per head

marginal rate of substitution of capital for labour increases. It is important to understand that this is symmetrical. As we move down the curve it becomes increasingly difficult to substitute labour for capital.

The convexity of the curve indicates the diminishing substitutability between the factors. Thus neo-classical production functions can range between the case where the factors are perfect substitutes, in which case the isoquant is a straight line; and the case where there is no substitutability, in which case the isoquants are rectangular.

3.3 Fixed factor endowments and efficient resource allocation

Now suppose that there are fixed amounts of the factors $\bar{K}$ and $\bar{L}$ to be fully utilized in the production of goods X and Y,

$$\bar{K} = K_X + K_Y, \qquad \bar{L} = L_X + L_Y \tag{3.1}$$

In Figure 3.3 these fixed endowments are represented by the sides of the box, and the factor inputs into X and Y respectively are measured from opposite corners.

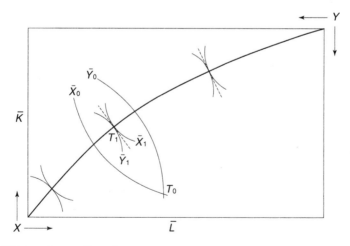

Fig. 3.3. Efficient factor allocation

Any point in the box such as T_0 represents a given allocation of the factors of production to the industries, and will be associated with a given level of output of each good as indicated by the isoquants $\bar{X}_0$ and $\bar{Y}_0$ each passing through T_0. But such points will only satisfy the Pareto condition for efficient resource allocation if the marginal rate of substitution between the factors is the same in both industries, that is, if the isoquants are tangential such as at T_1. The locus of all such tangency points is the locus of efficient factor allocation. It is analogous to the 'contract curve', as derived in the Edgeworth-Bowley box diagram (which represents the locus of efficient allocation of a fixed total endowment of two goods between two consumers). Indeed, the efficient factor (or resource) allocation locus is sometimes called a contract curve, although this is a misnomer, as it is derived purely from the technical conditions of production and the fixed factor endowments.

Since each point on the efficient factor allocation locus represents a specific level of output of each good, it can be converted into the production possibility curve showing the maximum combinations of output obtainable from the given factor endowments and technologies.

Thus point H' on the efficiency locus in Figure 3.4 shows the factor inputs into the two goods. The production functions tell us how much of each good is obtained from the inputs, so H' can also be shown as output of the goods as in Figure 3.5. H' is on the production possibility frontier of our economy because all of the resources are being efficiently used. At Point H'', which is also on the efficiency locus, more of the resources are going into the production of X.

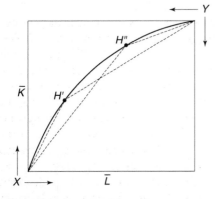

Fig. 3.4. Output and factor proportions

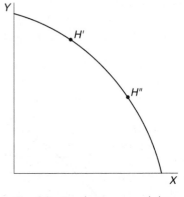

Fig. 3.5. Production possibilities

3.4 Factor intensities and increasing costs

In the box diagram shown in Figure 3.4 the efficiency locus has arbitrarily been drawn above the diagonal. Thus at any point on the curve such as H' the ray to the X origin is steeper than that to the Y origin, indicating that the ratio of K to L in the production of X is greater than in the production of Y. The X industry is described as being capital-intensive and the Y industry is labour-intensive. If it was the *Y* industry that was capital intensive, the efficiency locus would be below the diagonal. The relative factor intensities are determined by the production functions. Product *X* is capital-intensive and *Y* is labour-intensive, as in the diagram, if $K_X/L_X > K_Y/L_Y$, or using the alternative notation described in note 2 above, if $a_{KX}/a_{LX} > a_{KY}/a_{LY}$. It should be noted that the slope of the diagonal of the box represents our economy's overall factor endowment ratio. It is apparent that, if all of our resources are to be employed and both goods produced, then the capital-intensive industry (*X*) must use more capital relative to labour than the overall endowment, and conversely the labour-intensive industry (*Y*) must use less capital relative to labour than the overall endowment of the economy. It is sometimes useful to think of the overall factor endowment ratio as being a weighted average of the factor intensities of the industries, with the weights being determined by the relative size of the two industries.

The inverse of the slope of the production possibility frontier represents the opportunity cost of *Y* in terms of *X*. In Figure 3.5 the production possibility curve has been drawn concave to the origin, indicating that there are increasing costs in substituting one good for the other in production. Costs are increasing because of the diminishing marginal productivity of the factors in conjunction with an assumption that the goods use the factors of production in different proportions. There follows an informal explanation of this that the reader should fully understand, since it is basic to an understanding of many of the properties of the standard trade model.

We have chosen *X* to be the capital-intensive good. Now suppose that the production is originally at *H'* but it is desired to expand the production of *X*. Then as *X* is expanded and *Y* is contracted relatively more of capital and less of labour is required by the *X* industry than is released by the *Y* industry. If the industries attempted to maintain unaltered factor proportions there would be shortages of capital relative to labour. Thus at *H''*, where *X* has expanded and *Y* contracted, the *K/L* ratio in both industries has been reduced. Since it becomes increasingly difficult to substitute labour for capital in each industry as the *K/L* ratio falls, the further expansion of *X* is subject to increasing costs. The corresponding movement from *H'* to *H''* in Figure 3.5 is on an increasing cost (concave) production possibility curve. Note that it would make no difference to the conclusion of this argument if the *X* industry was labour-intensive so that the efficiency locus lay below the diagonal.

One of the most significant differences between the Ricardian and neo-classical production models is that the former generated a constant cost production possibility frontier, whereas the latter does not. It was noted in Chapter 2 that one of the conditions for the 'non-substitution theorem', which identifies the requirements for a linear production set, is that there is only one factor of production. The neo-classical production model does not satisfy this requirement.

An important implication of the increasing cost production possibility frontier is that there is a range of prices at which both goods can be produced. As a result the neo-classical production model generates a less specialized economy than does the constant-cost Ricardian model.

3.5 Factor prices and proportions

Nothing has been said so far about the economic forces that might result in efficient factor allocation. One might postulate that this could be achieved by an
omniscient planning authority. However, the approach taken in this book (and
indeed by most conventional trade theory) is to consider under what circumstances this will be achieved by market forces.[4] Assume that there is factor mobility between the industries so that the factor prices are the same in each industry,
and that there is perfect competition in the factor markets, and profit maximizing behaviour by the producers so that the factors are paid the value of their marginal products. Then, faced with given factor prices as indicated by the slope of *ab*
in Figure 3.6, i.e. $w/r = Oa/Ob$ where w (wage) is the price of L (labour) and r
(rent) is the price of K (capital), efficient production will be at a point such as Q
where a factor price line is tangential to an isoquant. That is, the marginal rate of
substitution between the factors in production is equal to the relative factor
prices.[5] A higher price of labour relative to capital (w/r) as shown by the slope of
$a'b'$ would be associated with a higher K/L ratio such as at Q'.

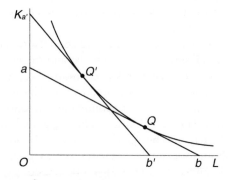

Fig. 3.6. Factor prices and proportions

On the assumption that the factors are mobile between and indifferent to
employment in the industries, then the price of each factor will be the same in
both industries, and production will take place at the same marginal rates of substitution between the factors, that is, at points of tangency on the efficiency locus.

In order to equate the value of the marginal products of the factors to their
prices we need commodity prices. In general let P_X be the price of X and P_Y be the
price of Y; but for the present, the exposition can be simplified by choosing one

---

[4] The important corollary is the analysis of constraints and distortions that may inhibit efficient
resource allocation. Some of these, e.g. factor market distortions, are discussed in Chapter 9 below.

[5] $w = P_X X_L = P_Y Y_L$, and $r = P_X K_X = P_Y Y_K$, so: $w/r = X_L/X_K = Y_L/Y_K$ where P_X and P_Y are respectively the price of X and Y.

good (X) as numeraire and letting its unit price be one. Then P can represent the price of Y in terms of X, and the factor prices w and r are also in terms of X. Thus the values of the marginal products of K and L in the X industry are respectively X_K and X_L, while in the Y industry they are PY_K and PY_L. Equating the factor prices to the value of their marginal products yields $w = X_L = PY_L$, and $r = X_K = PY_K$. Thus $w/r = X_L/X_K = Y_L/Y_K$ which is the condition for factor allocation to be on the efficiency locus.

3.6 General equilibrium

This system is the general equilibrium of the supply side of an economy with fixed factor endowments, given technologies (production functions) and the postulated factor market conditions. It can be expressed as eight equations:

$$X = X(K_X, L_X), \qquad Y = Y(K_Y, L_Y), 2 \qquad \text{production functions} \qquad (3.2)$$

$$\bar{K} = K_X + K_Y, \qquad \bar{L} = L_X + L_Y, \qquad \text{2 full employment conditions} \qquad (3.3)$$

$$w = X_L = PY_L, \qquad r = X_K = PY_K, \qquad \text{4 factor price conditions} \qquad (3.4)$$

There are nine variables, i.e. X, Y, K_X, K_Y, L_X, L_Y, P, w, and r, so the system is underdetermined. In Chapter 4 we shall be describing how in autarky this system is closed by demand conditions (preferences), and how in an open economy it is closed by price.[6] Fixing any of these variables would close the system and determine all the others; or any of these unknowns can be expressed as a function of any other. For example, the production possibility curve shows X and Y as an implicit function that satisfies all the other conditions of the system. Much of the standard model of international trade is concerned with the properties of this system, and in particular how trade (or trade-related policies) acts on commodity prices and hence affects output, factor inputs, and factor prices. The model can also be used to analyse the effects of growth in the form of changed factor endowments and/or changed technologies upon the variables of the system. As suggested by the formulation of the system in terms of the equations and variables, the analysis could be mathematical. In this book, however, the treatment is mainly diagrammatic and to some extent intuitive.

3.7 Factor and commodity prices

We now consider the relationship between commodity and factor prices in this neo-classical production model. This is extremely important because it suggests the effects that trade and trade-related policies might have upon the returns to the

---

[6] 'Closed' in this context means that the model is completed or fully determined.

factors of production, and thus upon the distribution of income within the trading economy.

In Figure 3.7 $\bar{X} = 1$ is the unit isoquant of X showing combinations of K and L that will produce one unit of X. At the relative factor prices shown by the slope of ab, cost-minimizing production will be at the tangency point Q. Since the price (cost) of $X = 1$, and the cost of the product is that of its constituent factors, at Q we have $rK + wL = 1$. Furthermore, this will obtain for any other factor combination on ab for the given factor prices, thus ab is the unit isocost line. This permits a diagrammatic representation of the factor prices, since at the extreme point a, $L = 0$ so $rK = 1$ or $K = 1/r$; and similarly at b, $L = 1/w$. For example, the numeraire, product X, might be a bottle of rum. So if point b represents two hours of labour, then the wage in terms of the numeraire is half a bottle of rum per hour. From the diagram it can easily be seen that an increase in the use of K and fall in the use of L in the production of X would not only be associated with a rise in wages relative to rents, but also in a rise in the real wage and a fall in real rent.

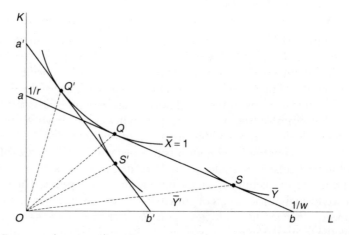

Fig. 3.7. Factor and commodity prices

Now introduce the other good Y facing the same factor prices as X. There will be some isoquant $\bar{Y}$ tangent to the unit isocost line ab. Suppose that this tangency is at S. In this case Y has arbitrarily been made labour-intensive and X is capital-intensive, since the K/L ratio for X at Q is greater than that for Y at S. The important point to note is that the price of Y relative to X is now determined. Since ab is the unit isocost line the amount of Y represented by the isoquant is equal in value (cost) to one unit of X, i.e. $P\bar{Y} = 1$ or

$$P = 1/\bar{Y} \qquad (3.5)$$

Now suppose that there is a rise in wages relative to rents shown by the slope of $a'b'$. Since this is now tangential to the X unit isoquant at Q', it has become the unit isocost line. A new Y isoquant $\bar{Y}'$ will now be tangent to the new isocost line at some point such as S' where the K/L ratio has risen. Note that the $\bar{Y}'$ isoquant represents less Y than did the original isoquant $\bar{Y}$, so the price of Y has risen in terms of X. The ordering of this argument makes no difference: an exogenous rise in the price of Y under the constraints of this model, given that Y is labour intensive, will have to be associated with a rise in the wage and a fall in rent. This is a fundamental result of this model that the reader should understand. It is in accordance with common sense and intuition that a rise in the price of one factor relative to the other is associated with a rise in the price of the commodity that uses that factor intensively. It may also be noted that the wage rate has risen not only in terms of X but also of Y; and similarly the price of capital has fallen in terms of both products. We have what is known as a 'magnification' effect in which a change in the commodity prices is associated with proportionally greater changes in factor prices (Jones 1965). Thus if the price of Y has risen more than the price of X, and Y is labour-intensive, we get the ranking $\hat{w} > \hat{P}_Y > \hat{P}_X > \hat{r}$ (where the circumflexes indicate proportional changes). This is easily comprehended when the commodity prices are considered as weighted averages of the factor prices, with the weights being the factor intensities.

An application of this analysis concerns the effect of a tariff on the distribution of income. The tariff will raise the internal price of the imported good, thereby encouraging its domestic production. Thus there will be an increase in the real rate of return to the factor of production used intensively in the import competing industry, and a fall to that of the other factor (Stolper and Samuelson 1941). More generally, we get the very important result that trade is beneficial to one factor of production, but makes the factor of production that is used intensively in the import competing industry worse off. This is discussed further in Chapter 4 in the context of factor endowments, and in Chapter 9 in the context of the gains from trade and trade policy.

3.8 Duality and commodity and factor prices

In our discussion of the two-sector model we have been focusing the analysis upon the production functions relating output of the goods to the inputs of the factors of production. Therefore we have been utilizing diagrams that are defined in factor space and that represent physical outputs by production isoquants. We have then used these physical relationships to deduce the relationship between commodity costs and factor prices. There is an alternative procedure that, in contrast, utilizes the cost-minimizing assumption that factors are paid the value of their marginal products to show directly the relationship between factor prices and commodity prices. This is useful because some of the central propositions of the standard trade model are concerned with the relationship between commodity and factor prices. This alternative procedure also facilitates the discussion of the effects of distortions in the factor markets. We therefore explain how the duality between the physical quantities and their monetary values can be applied in the context of neo-classical production.[7]

The relationship between factor inputs and commodity outputs can be described as the primary function. Its dual is the relation between commodity prices and factor prices. Thus the dual to the production function $X = [K, L]$ is the cost function $P_X = a_{KX}r + a_{LX}w$ where a_{KX} is the capital used to produce one unit of the commodity X and so on, and r and w are the prices of capital and labour respectively. Similarly $P_Y = a_{KY}r + a_{LY}w$. The price of each commodity is equal to the cost of its constituent factors because the production functions are linear and homogeneous, and the factors are being paid the value of their marginal products.

The basic diagram shows combinations of factor prices that are consistent with a given constant commodity price. The slope of the isocost curve is the capital–labour ratio consistent with the factor prices.[8] The isocost curve is convex to the origin because as w/r rises the technology becomes more capital-intensive, so larger changes in wages will be required to compensate for a given change in the price of capital if the cost of production is to remain constant. Note that, in contrast to the production isoquant diagram, a highly convex isocost curve indicates high substitutability between the factors, whereas a relatively straight curve indicates low substitutability.

Figure 3.8 compares the isocost with the corresponding production isoquants for products with varying degrees of factor substitutability. An increase in the price of the commodity will push out the isocost curve in proportion to that increase. An improvement in technology will also push out a given isocost curve, although not necessarily in proportion, since the technological change may be biased with respect to factor use.

Figure 3.9 shows isocost curves for two commodities X and Y at given prices. These have been drawn with similar degrees of curvature so that they intersect only once. The X isocost is steeper at any w/r ratio than that for Y, so X is the capital-intensive product and Y is labour-intensive.[9]

3.8.1 Feasible factor prices

It can be seen that there is only one point of intersection, A, and this determines the unique set of factor prices that enables the country to produce both the goods at the given commodity prices. However, there is a range of factor prices at which at least one of the goods could be produced. This is the shaded 'factor price frontier' shown in Figure 3.9. It is kinked at A, the point of incomplete specialization. It should be noted that a point such as B will be consistent with the factor prices

---

[7] A similar duality exists between consumer preferences and commodity consumption on the one hand, and consumer expenditure and commodity prices on the other.

[8] Differentiate the cost-function, letting $dP_X = 0$, and since with cost-minimizing use of inputs $rda_{KX} + wda_{LX} = 0$, thus $dw/dr = -a_{KX}/a_{LX}$.

[9] This discussion and diagrammatic representation has drawn upon Mussa (1979).

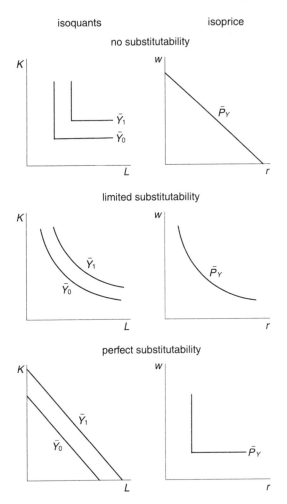

Fig. 3.8. Isoquants and isoprice

w^1 and r^1 if production is at the capital–labour ratio shown by the slope of the iso-cost curve at *B*. This will provide full employment for the country producing that one good only if the overall factor endowment ratio of the country is also equal to the slope at *B*. Production of both goods at the point *A* with factor prices w^0 and r^0 could be consistent with a range of overall factor endowments between the slopes of the two isocost curves at that point, since the combination of the two outputs can be varied to maintain full utilization of the factors. An application of this is that two countries with different overall factor endowments could produce both goods at the same commodity and factor prices using the same factor proportions, provided that each country produces relatively large amounts of the good which uses intensively the factor with which that country is relatively

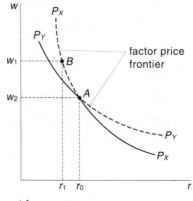

Fig. 3.9. Commodity and factor prices

well-endowed. This is the essence of the Heckscher-Ohlin proposition that is discussed in Chapter 5 below.

3.8.2 Change in commodity prices

In the preceding section we have discussed the relationship between commodity and factor prices. In particular, we have demonstrated that a rise in the price of one commodity relative to the other will be associated with a rise relative to both commodities in the return to the factor of production that is used intensively in the commodity that has risen in price, and a fall in the return to the other factor relative to the price of both commodities. This result is easily seen using the isocost diagram. In Figure 3.10 the price of the labour-intensive product Y rises, as is shown by the proportional expansion of its isocost curve from P_Y^0 to P_Y^1. The factor prices that are consistent with the commodity prices have moved from point A in the diagram to point B where the price of capital has fallen in terms of both goods, and where, as can be seen from the relative slopes of the curves, the wage has risen proportionally more than the price of Y. This is an illustration of what Jones (1965) describes as the magnification effect.

$$\hat{w} > \hat{P}_Y > \hat{P}_X > \hat{r} \tag{3.6}$$

where Y is labour-intensive, and the circumflexes indicate proportional change.

3.9 Factor market distortions

We now use this dual procedure to discuss factor market distortions.

   Factor market distortions are situations in which for one reason or another the

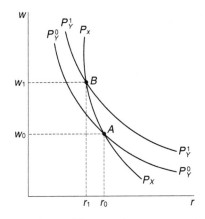

Fig. 3.10. Changing commodity and factor prices

value of the marginal product of one or more factors is not the same in the production of all goods. Two are considered here: subsidies and minimum wage constraints.

3.9.1 Subsidy

Consider the case where, in an otherwise undistorted economy, a subsidy is paid on the use of capital in the capital-intensive sector. Now, if the factor prices are still equalized between industries, the cost and marginal product of capital will be less in the capital-intensive sector than in the other. This is shown in Figure 3.11

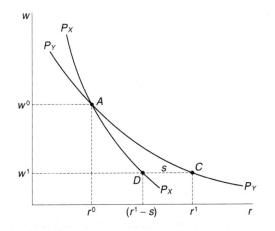

Fig. 3.11. Factor market distortions: capital subsidy

where, at unchanged commodity prices, cost equalization moves from point A to a pair of points C and D where the cost of labour is equal to the wage and is the same in both industries, but the cost of capital in the production of the capital intensive good X is below the price of capital r^1 by the amount of the subsidy S.

Note that the wage has fallen in both sectors and that the price of capital has risen more than the amount of the subsidy. Thus we get the paradoxical result that the subsidy on capital has increased its cost and made technologies more labour-intensive. The intuition for this result is that the subsidy in the capital-intensive sector tends to lower the cost of production in that sector. This can only be reconciled with the requirement that, at unchanged commodity prices, costs must remain the same if the cost of capital rises and wages fall. Note that if the subsidy on capital in the capital-intensive sector was replaced by a tax on the use of capital in the labour-intensive sector, the effects on wages and factor intensities would be the same, but the cost of capital in the labour-intensive sector would rise by more than the tax. Similarly it can be shown that a subsidy on the use of capital in the labour-intensive sector will, at unchanged commodity prices, induce a rise in wages and a fall in the returns to capital.

3.9.2 Minimum wage

Now suppose that a minimum wage w^* is introduced, as shown in Figure 3.12. First it can be seen that if this was effective in both sectors, then both goods could no longer be produced at the given commodity prices. The capital–intensive good X could be produced at point B with the price of capital falling to r_1. But it should be noted that if there was full employment at the original point A, then there must be unemployment at point B with only X being produced, since production has

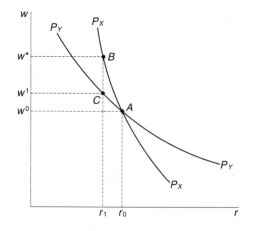

Fig. 3.12. Factor market distortions: minimum wage

become more capital-intensive and the capital-intensive industry has expanded. (The reader should remember from the box-diagram analysis earlier in this chapter that if the fixed endowment of factors is to be fully employed, an expansion of the capital-intensive sector requires a reduction in the capital intensity of production.)

Now suppose that the minimum wage was only effective in the capital-intensive sector. The labour-intensive good Y can be produced at point C in the diagram, where the price of capital has fallen to r_1 and the wage in the labour intensive sector has risen to w_1 which is less than the minimum wage. In this case a moderate minimum wage could be consistent with full employment, since the expansion of the labour-intensive sector would be compensated by the increased capital intensity of production.

It should be emphasized that all of these cases of factor market distortions would disturb Pareto-efficient allocation of the factors of production and move the economy away from its production possibility frontier. If, however, the factor market policies are introduced in situations that are initially non-optimal, then there is the possibility that the policies may be welfare enhancing. Such issues are discussed in Chapter 9.

3.10 Factor intensities again

To conclude this discussion of neo-classical production, we would like to emphasize that the most important results—increasing cost production possibilities, and the link between output, commodity, and factor prices—depend upon the assumption that the products differ in their requirements for the factors of production, that is, that they have different factor intensities. If the factor proportions at any factor prices were the same in the two industries, then the efficiency locus would lie along the diagonal of the endowment box. Therefore changes in output would not require any changes in the proportions in which the factors are used, and so could be accommodated at constant costs. It is the different factor intensities that drive the neo-classical model. The greater the differences in the factor intensities between the industries, the stronger will be the main results of the model.

3.11 Summary

- If a country produces two goods separately, competitively, under constant returns to scale, but using two factors of production in different proportions, its production possibility frontier is concave and there are increasing costs. An increase in the output of that good will therefore be associated with an increase in its relative price.

- An increase in the price of one good relative to that of the other will increase the returns to (price of) the factor of production that is used intensively in the production of that good, and will lower the returns to (price of) the other factor. An implication of this is that international trade will hurt and tariffs will benefit the owners of the factor of production used intensively in the import competing industry.
- These links between the pattern of output, commodity and factor prices are qualified in the presence of distortions.

4

RECIPROCAL DEMAND AND TRADE

....

4.1 Introduction

In this chapter we introduce the demand side of an economy and integrate it with the supply side. Under some assumptions, this completes the model for an economy in which there is no international trade, thereby determining the prices and all of the other variables of that economy. We then determine the conditions for equilibrium if such an economy were able to trade at prices differing from those obtaining in autarky, and we examine the conditions for a trading equilibrium of a world consisting of two such countries.

The discussion in this chapter is concerned with elementary theory; but, in conjunction with the previous chapter, it provides a framework for the consideration of many issues relating to European trade and trade policy which are the subjects of subsequent chapters.

4.2. Demand and the closed economy

We have developed the supply side of a neo-classical economy and represented it as a production possibility frontier. Where production will take place on that frontier will depend upon commodity prices. These, in turn, will be determined by the interaction of the supply with the demand conditions for the output of our economy. An equilibrium set of prices must satisfy the requirements that demand for each product is equal to its supply, and that producers and consumers have no incentive to change their production or consumption at those prices. For a closed economy which has no trade, such an equilibrium requires that domestic demand is equal to the output of each product, so consumption possibilities are limited to the production possibilities of the economy. But, for an open economy, consumption may differ from production subject to the budget constraint imposed upon that economy by the conditions of international trade.

Demand for each product is assumed to depend upon prices and income. In our two-commodity economy there is only one relative commodity price, P (the price of Y in terms of X); and income, I, is the value of national output: $I = X_S + PY_S$ where the subscripts S indicate the output of each product. Thus our demand system can be represented as:

$$X_D = [P, I] \qquad\qquad (4.1)$$
$$Y_D = [P, I] \qquad\qquad (4.2)$$
$$I = X_S + PY_S \qquad\qquad (4.3)$$

where the subscripts D indicate domestic demand for each product. Since in this model all income has to be spent, in the sense that output must be utilized, the two demand equations are not independent. Income that is not spent on X must be spent upon Y. Thus the demand system above can be considered as two independent equations. In addition, for the closed economy, we have the requirements that $X_D = X_S$, and $Y_D = Y_S$. We have therefore introduced four new equations into our equilibrium system, and there are three new unknowns: I, X_D, and Y_D. Since our supply analysis of Chapter 3 had left us underdetermined by one equation, we have now completed the system. The integration of the demand conditions with the supply side fully determines the levels of output, prices, consumption, and of the other variables of our economy which are the factor inputs into each commodity and the factor prices.

4.3 Community preferences and welfare

Before proceeding to consider the conditions of equilibrium of a trading economy, we must develop the diagrammatic interpretation of demand which, in conjunction with our supply-side diagrams, will be used as a framework for much of the discussion of policy issues in subsequent chapters.

We represent consumer preferences as a set of non-intersecting indifference curves as shown in Figure 4.1. These are analogous to the representation of an individual's preference system with which readers will be familiar. The curves show combinations of the two goods that yield constant levels of welfare, with movements to curves further out from the origin showing increases in welfare. The slope of a curve at any point shows the marginal rate of substitution between the goods at that point. In particular, the absolute slope of the indifference curve at point C shows how much of commodity Y would be needed to compensate for the loss of a small amount of X at that point. The curves are convex to the origin because of diminishing substitutability in consumption between the products. Thus at C_1, where consumers have more of Y and less of X than at C_0, the marginal rate of substitution of Y for X has risen because it now requires more Y to compensate consumers for further losses of X.

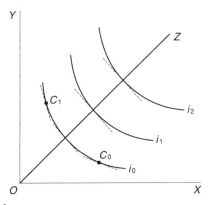

Fig. 4.1. Consumer preferences

There is, however, a serious problem in representing community preferences as a set of non-intersecting indifference curves. It is quite reasonable to consider that an individual has unambiguous and consistent ordering of preferences which is independent of income and prices, so that at any income and prices we can determine what the consumer will want to consume, and how his or her welfare ranks relative to that at other consumption combinations. For the community as a whole this is much more dubious. The problem is that for the community, preferences may not be independent of the way in which income is distributed. Thus, at a given level of aggregate income and prices, one combination of goods might be consumed at one income distribution, and another consumed at some different income distribution. For example, an uneven income distribution might give rise to a greater consumption of luxury goods at a given set of prices than would occur if the same aggregate income was more evenly distributed. Essentially we are questioning whether a set of non-intersecting indifference curves can be assumed when income distributions can change. We cannot comfortably ignore this problem by assuming that income distributions remain unchanged or are exogenous to our model, since a central theme of the neo-classical analysis developed in Chapter 3 is that commodity prices affect factor prices and thus affect income distribution. Indeed, one of the main purposes of the analysis of international trade and of trade policy concerns their impact upon income distribution. Nor can we adequately get around the problem by assuming that all consumers have the same tastes, since this is not sufficient to prevent demand for luxuries relative to necessities changing as income distribution changes. What we do assume, in order to justify the use of non-intersecting indifference curves, is that all consumers have the same tastes, and that those tastes are 'homothetic' in the sense that the ratio of goods consumed, or the proportion of expenditure upon each good, depends only upon relative prices, and not upon the level of income. It is therefore being assumed that the income elasticity of demand is unity for all of the products. Diagrammatically it is being assumed that all consumers have the same preference map, and that along any ray from the origin, such as OZ in Figure 4.1, the marginal rate of substitution between the goods (the slope of the indifference curves) is constant.

This assumption enables us to aggregate the individuals' preferences into a community set of indifference curves which have the same shape as each of the individual curves. Shifts of income from one individual to another will have no effect upon the community indifference curve.

Formally, individual preferences can be aggregated and used to represent welfare and aggregate demand under the following conditions.

1. Each individual has a clearly defined preference system. In the two-commodity case this can be represented by a set of non-intersecting indifference curves.
2. All consumers face the same commodity prices.

And at least two of:

3. All consumers have the same tastes.
4. All consumers have homothetic tastes.
5. The distribution of income between the consumers is unchanged.

We are unwilling to accept the last of these conditions, so to the extent that we use community indifference curves, we have to assume the other conditions.

We can now proceed to use the community indifference curves to represent the demand side of our economy. They are used in two ways. Firstly, they illustrate the conditions for consumer equilibrium and aggregate demand.[1] Generally this will be illustrated by the tangency of a budget constraint, determined by income and prices, to an indifference curve. Secondly, a movement from one indifference curve to a higher one is taken to indicate an improvement in community welfare. Here we must be aware of the important reservation that although the community as a whole is being assessed as better off, there may have been a change in the distribution of income that has worsened the welfare of some individuals.[2]

4.4 Closed economy equilibrium

In Figure 4.2 the supply side of our economy is represented by the production possibility frontier qq, and the demand side is illustrated by the set of community indifference curves i_0 and so on.

---

[1] The reader will appreciate that it would be inappropriate to use the community indifference curves to discuss such issues as the effect of trade policies on the demand for luxuries relative to necessities. This would be in breach of the assumption that tastes are homothetic.

[2] The issue as to whether the welfare of the community can be assessed as having increased when that of some individuals has worsened is considered in Chapter 9 below in the context of the gains from trade.

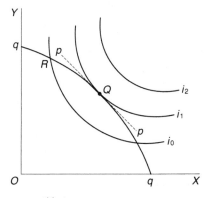

Fig. 4.2. Closed economy equilibrium

In the absence of taxes, subsidies and other distortions, full equilibrium for this economy is achieved at point Q where an indifference curve is tangent to the production possibility curve, and where the price (slope of pp) is the same for both producers and consumers. This price is equal to the marginal rate of substitution between the goods in consumption (the slope of the indifference curve at Q), and it is also equal to the relative marginal costs of production (the slope of the production possibility frontier at Q). These are requirements for consumer and producer equilibrium respectively. Furthermore, production is equal to consumption at Q for each good, satisfying the constraint that, in a closed economy, domestic demand must equal supply for each good.

It is the market mechanism that is presumed to move the economy to this equilibrium. Suppose production was at R on the production possibility frontier, with a price given by the slope of that curve at R. At this output and price producers would be in equilibrium, but consumers would not. At R the slope of the indifference curve is steeper than the price, so consumers would want more of good X and less of Y, and there would be upward pressure on the relative price of X encouraging production to shift away from Y towards X until equilibrium is achieved at Q.

Finally, it should be noted that in our non-distorted economy the market mechanism has generated the highest community welfare possible for the closed economy. A requirement for Pareto efficiency is that the marginal rate of substitution in consumption is equal to the marginal relative cost of production. This is being achieved at point Q.

4.5 Equilibrium for the open economy

We now consider the conditions for an economy which is able to trade. It is no longer necessary that the quantity consumed of each product must equal its output; however, the economy will, of course, be subject to some budget constraint related to its productive capacity and its ability to borrow. We shall limit discussion to the simplest case in which there is no borrowing or lending between countries, so that the current account of the balance of payments—exports minus imports, broadly defined—is in balance. Formally, we are replacing the two equations $X_S = X_D$, and $Y_S = Y_D$ by one budget constraint: $(X_S - X_D) + P(Y_S - Y_D) = 0$. Expressing the condition for balanced trade in this way leaves open the question as to which product is exported and which is imported. Since exports and imports are respectively the excess or the deficit of domestic supply relative to domestic demand, the budget constraint is that the value of exports is equal to the value of imports. It should be noted that this budget constraint can identically be expressed: $(X_S + PY_S) = (X_D + PY_D)$. This formulation states the budget constraint as a requirement that total income of the economy is equal to total expenditure.[3]

The replacement of the requirement that demand is equal to output for each of the two goods by a single budget constraint leaves our system underdetermined. We cannot know the level of trade or, indeed, of any other variable in the system unless we know or fix one of them. The natural way to proceed is to treat the commodity price P as a parameter, and then to determine the level of trade that is consistent with consumer and producer equilibrium and that satisfies the budget constraint at each particular price. In Figure 4.2 above, we identified the relative price that was consistent with no trade. This is shown again in Figure 4.3 as the slope p_0p_0 with production and consumption at point Q_0.[4]

Now suppose that the economy is able to trade at the price shown by the slope p_1p_1 which has arbitrarily been chosen so that the price of Y relative to X is higher than in the no-trade case. At this price producer equilibrium will be at Q_1, and the budget constraint will be along the price line p_1 passing through Q_1. Any consumption combination along this line will satisfy the budget constraint, and consumer equilibrium will be at point C_1 where the marginal rate of substitution between the goods is equal to the price. It might be noted that Figure 4.3 shows the budget constraint in both of its equivalent forms. Measuring from the consumption and production origin at O, consumption at C_1 is equal in value to output at Q_1. But by treating Q_1 and C_1 as the ends of a hypotenuse of a triangle with a right-angle at T_1, we can see that the value of the excess production over consumption

[3] The perception of the current account of the balance of payments as being identically equivalent to the balance of income and expenditure is extremely important in open economy macroeconomics, and is the basis of the absorption approach to the analysis of the balance of payments.

[4] To facilitate the exposition, we are rather casually referring to the price as being the slope. In fact, the absolute value of the slope is the price of X in terms of Y, and its inverse is the price of Y in terms of X.

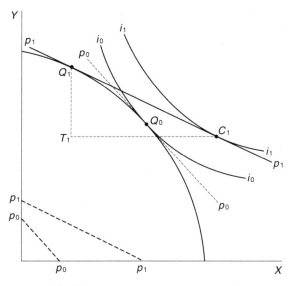

Fig. 4.3. Open economy equilibrium

(exports) of Y, $Q_1 T_1$, is equal in value to the excess consumption over production (imports) of X, $C_1 T_1$. Thus the trading triangle with an origin at T_1 represents an equilibrium at which the value of imports is equal to the value of exports at the given price.

4.6 The gains from trade

The trading equilibrium with production at Q_1 and consumption at C_1 maximizes community welfare at the price p_1 because the Pareto conditions for production and exchange are being met. More specifically, the relative marginal cost of producing the goods domestically (the slope of the production possibility curve) is equal to the marginal cost of obtaining the goods through trade, which is equal to the marginal rate of substitution between the goods in consumption.[5]

The gain from trade is reflected in the move from the autarky indifference curve i_0 to i_1. This gain can be decomposed into two parts. Suppose that production is completely rigid at Q_0, with the production possibility frontier being a rectangle at that point. Then the ability to trade at the price p_1 rather than at the autarky price p_0 would have no effect on production. The budget constraint (not shown) would

---

[5] We are assuming for the moment that the country can trade as much as it likes at the given price, so the marginal cost of the goods in trade is equal to the average cost. We relax this assumption later.

pass through Q_0 with the slope of p_1, allowing consumption at some point to the south-east of Q_0 on an indifference curve superior to i_0 although inferior to i_1. This source of gain has arisen because the ability to trade at some price different from that obtaining in autarky has extended consumer choice; and provided that consumers are not completely rigid in their consumption patterns they can benefit from the extended choice. This source of gain is an important consideration in any theoretical discussion of the gains from trade or of the effects of trade related policies. It may be of important practical consideration in assessing the gains from the implementation of the single European market, or more generally of economic liberalization or economic integration.

The rest of the gain from trade in this theoretical model arises from the shift in production. The value of production at world prices at Q_1 is greater than at Q_0. It should be noted that we can identify the increase in the value of production as a source of gain without having to make the restrictive assumptions that were needed to identify community preferences, so it is not necessary to assume that preferences are homothetic. The new income and price gives us a budget constraint that passes to the north-east of Q_0, so that consumption possibilities where there are more of both goods become available. The consumers may not choose to have more of all goods, but that is their decision.

It can be seen that welfare rises as the price of Y (the exported good) rises relative to that of X. We get the normal output response with production of Y rising and that of X falling. The consumption and import of X must rise; but whether the consumption and or the export of Y continues to rise will depend upon the elasticities of demand and supply as reflected in the shape of the curves. This is discussed further below.

The discussion has been formulated in the context of a relative price of commodity Y that is higher than it would be in the absence of trade. This is arbitrary. We could just as well have considered situations in which the relative price of Y was low compared with the no-trade situation, in which case Y would be the imported good, and welfare and the level of imports would rise as the price of Y fell.

4.7 Reciprocal demand and the offer curve

In the preceding discussion and diagram we determined the level of production and consumption that provided equilibrium at a particular price, and then identified the level of exports and imports that was consistent with that production and consumption. It is often convenient to be able to show the level of trade directly rather than as a residual, and for this purpose expositions of international trade theory and policy often make use of a diagrammatic version of a demand curve known as an offer curve or as a reciprocal demand curve. We have shown that our general equilibrium analysis enables us to derive the demand for an import or the supply of an export of each of the products as a function of its price. This could be shown diagrammatically as conventional demand and supply curves. Such curves are asymmetric in the sense that the *total* quantity demanded or supplied of one good is shown on one axis, whereas the *average* amount paid or received for that good is shown on the other axis. However, in international trade analysis it is sometimes useful to treat the products symmetrically, so that the total amount demanded of one product is shown on one axis, and the total amount of the product being offered in exchange for the first is shown on the other axis. This is the offer curve.

Before deriving the offer curve of our trading economy, it might be helpful to illustrate the relationship between a conventional (average-revenue) demand curve and the associated total-revenue offer curve. We shall also show how an individual's offer curve of money for a product can be derived from his or her preference system and income.

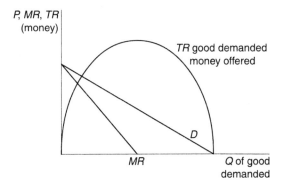

Fig. 4.4. A total-revenue demand curve

Figure 4.4 shows a conventional demand curve D showing the demand for the product Z as a function of its money price P. The diagram also shows the marginal-revenue curve, which becomes negative as the elasticity of demand falls below unity. We could show total revenue associated with each quantity and price as the area of a rectangle; but we could also plot it directly on the vertical axis as shown by the curve TR in the figure. Obviously total revenue will be zero if either price or quantity is zero, and it will be at a maximum where marginal revenue is zero and the elasticity of demand with respect to price is unity. Measuring from the origin, the total-revenue curve can be interpreted as an offer curve. On the horizontal axis it shows the total quantity of the good that is demanded, and on the vertical axis it shows the total amount of money being offered. It is a supply curve as well as a demand curve because it shows the quantity of money that is being supplied in exchange for the good. The price at any point on the total-revenue curve can be represented by the slope of a line from that point to the origin.

We now describe how the offer curve can be derived for a consumer who has an initial endowment of money and a preference system involving one commodity, and money available to spend on all other commodities.

In Figure 4.5, the horizontal axis measures the quantity of the one commodity, food, that is purchased and consumed. The initial endowment of money is shown as M^* on the vertical axis. The total amount of money spent on food is measured down from M^*. This leaves the rest of the money, measured up from the origin O, to be spent on all other goods in accordance with the preferences shown by the indifference curves.

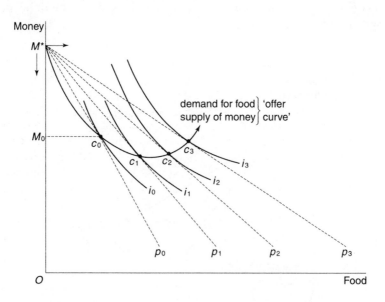

Fig. 4.5. A consumer's supply of money and demand for food

The budget constraint for this consumer is shown by a line passing through the initial money endowment, M^*, with a slope equal to the price of food in terms of money. Equilibrium expenditure on food occurs where the budget line with a slope equal to the price is tangential to an indifference curve, e.g. at c_0 and so on. Thus at a price equal to the slope p_0, the consumer would spend M^*M_0 on the purchase of M_0c_0 amount of food. This would leave OM_0 of money to be spent upon all other goods. As the price of food falls successively to p_1, then to p_2, and to p_3, equilibrium expenditure and consumption would move to c_1, c_2, and c_3, with more food being purchased as its price falls. Now if we put a curve through the endowment origin M^*, and through each of the equilibrium points c_0, c_1, and so on, we have an offer curve showing, from that origin, the demand for food and the supply of money for it.

4.8 Properties of an offer curve

An offer curve showing the demand for X and the supply of Y will characteristically take the shape shown in Figure 4.6, with the demand for a product continuously rising as its price falls. The quantity of Y supplied for X may be expected to rise at first, as the elasticity of demand for X will be high when its price is high (but not prohibitive); but it will fall eventually as demand becomes inelastic.

The price of X in terms of Y at any point, such as T in the figure, is the slope of a line from that point back to the origin; and the marginal revenue is the slope of the offer curve at that point. It may be intuitively obvious to the reader that the price elasticity of demand of an offer curve at a given point is reflected in the straightness of the curve between that point and the origin. We can, however, give a precise diagrammatic representation of the elasticity of demand, based on the definitional relationship between price, marginal revenue, and elasticity that holds for any demand curve. This relationship, which can be derived directly from the definition of the price elasticity of demand, is $e = p/(MR-p)$, where p and MR are respectively the price and marginal revenue of the product that is being demanded. In Figure 4.6 the price of X in terms of Y is OU/UT, and the marginal revenue is RU/UT, so $e = -OU/OR$. This confirms that the algebraic value of the elasticity of demand is negative; and we can see that the numerical value of the elasticity is unity when the quantity supplied (total revenue) is at its maximum. We can also see that an offer curve which is a straight line from the origin is perfectly elastic.

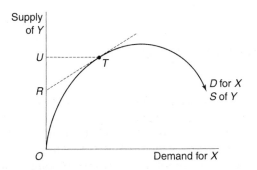

Fig. 4.6. The elasticity of an offer curve

We can also identify the elasticity of supply of Y with respect to the price of Y in terms of X at the point T in the diagram. Remembering that any demand function can be expressed as a supply function, and that the relationship between the elasticity of demand, e, and the associated elasticity of supply, n, is $e + n = -1$, we can see that at the point T, the elasticity of supply of Y with respect to its price in terms of X is RU/OR.

4.9   The trading economy's offer curve

We can now return to the diagrammatic representation of our trading economy. If the economy only produced a single good which it exchanged for an imported good, then we could use the same diagrammatic technique as Figure 4.5 above, which illustrated the demand of a consumer with a given income. If our country produced both goods, but in fixed amounts so that the economy can be represented as having a fixed endowment of goods at point Q in Figure 4.7, then we could still use the budget constraint at each price through Q to identify the desire to trade and to construct the offer curve.

In this case, however, the direction of trade would depend upon how the trade price compared with the no-trade price. At prices of X in terms of Y less than the slope of the indifference curve i_0 at Q, there will be a desire to import X and supply Y, so the offer curve will be in the quadrant to the South-East of Q. If, however, it is X that is expensive and Y that is cheap, the direction of trade will be reversed, and the economy will be demanding Y and supplying X as shown by the part of the offer curve that is to the North-West of Q. This figure has a consumption and production origin at O, and a trading origin at Q. It is possible to show consumption, production, and trade all on the same diagram because the assumption that production is fixed also fixes the origin of the offer curve to that point. In the more general case the endowment origin will shift as the pattern of production changes, so it will no longer be feasible to show the desire to trade at each price on the same diagram as shows production and consumption.

The reader will recall that the earlier diagram, Figure 4.3, and indeed our neoclassical production and supply analysis, enables us to determine the equilibrium volume of trade associated with particular prices. We now plot this information directly on to a diagram which measures the volume of trade from its origin. This is done in Figure 4.8.

At a price P_0 equal to the slope of the offer curve at the origin (T_0), production will equal consumption (not shown in the diagram), and there will be no desire to trade. At prices such as P_1, where the price of Y relative to X is above the no-trade price, there will be an excess of consumption over production of X, and so a demand for imports of X and supply of Y as shown at point T_1 on the offer curve. Conversely, if the relative price of X is high, as shown by the slope of P_2, there will

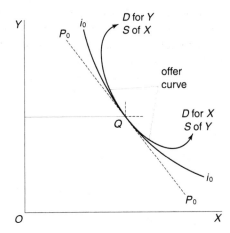

Fig. 4.7. Offer curve with fixed production

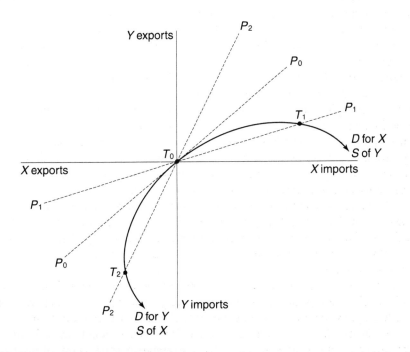

Fig. 4.8. Offer curve with variable production

be a supply of X for export and a demand for imports of Y as shown by point T_2 on the offer curve.

It should be emphasized that there is no new information in Figure 4.9 compared with Figure 4.4. The trading triangles of the previous figure which showed trade as a residual between production and consumption are now shown directly with respect to a trading origin. This is convenient for some purposes, although it entails a cost in that the level of production and consumption can no longer be seen. For convenience, the scale has been enlarged, and following convention, the relative price has been re-orientated so that it is a positive rather than a negative slope.

4.10   The world trading equilibrium

We can now consider the properties of a trading equilibrium between two countries that together constitute the whole world. It is assumed that there are no transport costs or other barriers to trade, so that the commodity price in equilibrium is the same in both countries. Equilibrium in the commodity markets requires that world demand equals world supply, i.e. that for each product the exports of one country are equal to the imports of the other country. These conditions, in conjunction with the neo-classical supply-and-demand analysis for each country, are sufficient to complete the model in the sense that the price, the volume of trade, and the volume of production and consumption and so on in each of the countries is determined. This is illustrated by the use of the offer curves of the two countries.

The diagrammatic trick is to show one country's demand for X and supply of Y in the same quadrant as we are showing the other country's supply of X and demand for Y. This is done in Figure 4.9.

If the two countries had identical offer curves, as would be the case if the supply and demand conditions were identical in each country, then the offer curves would be mirror images of each other in the opposing quadrants. They would never intersect, but they would be tangential at the origin. The world price would be the same as the no-trade price in each country, and there would be no trade. But in general demand and/or supply conditions will differ, and so will the offer curves. Then there will be an intersection in one or other of the quadrants. In Figure 4.9 we have arbitrarily drawn the offer curves so that there is an intersection in the North-East quadrant which shows country A's demand for X and supply of Y, and country B's demand for Y and supply of X. This is consistent with the slope of A's offer curve at the origin being steeper than B's offer curve, as would be the case if the no-trade price of X relative to Y in country A (slope P_A) is greater than in country B (slope P_B).

At the price P^* there is an intersection of the offer curves at point T^*. This represents an international price and volume of trade that satisfies all of the conditions for a world equilibrium. The price is the same in both countries, and the

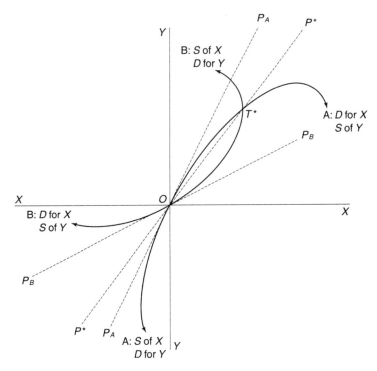

Fig. 4.9. Equilibrium of two trading economies

volume of exports of each good is equal to the volume of imports. We also know, from the way that we constructed the offer curves, that, at this price and volume of trade, consumers and producers in each country are in equilibrium, and that the value of trade is balanced for each country.

4.11 Uses of the offer curve

The offer-curve analysis has simplified the representation of each country's desire to trade, and has made it easy to show the conditions for an international trading equilibrium. This has been achieved at the cost of losing the direct representation of the conditions of domestic production, consumption, and welfare.[6]

Offer curves are used for several purposes. They will be used in Chapter 9 below in the discussion of an 'optimum tariff' to illustrate the effects of protection on the

---

[6] It is possible to construct 'trade indifference curves' from the conditions of domestic production and consumption that show directly the community welfare of a country associated with each volume of trade. This geometric construction was originally developed by James Meade in 1952.

terms of trade. We shall also be using them to discuss the effect of economic growth in one block of countries, such as the developed industrial countries, upon the desire to trade with other, possibly less developed countries. We now use the offer curves to discuss the stability of a trading equilibrium.

4.12 Stability of equilibrium

We have used the intersection of offer curves to represent the conditions of an international trading equilibrium. The question that now arises is whether that equilibrium is stable. First it should be realized that in Economics 'stability' has a rather narrower meaning than in general parlance. To describe an equilibrium as stable does not imply that it is immune from substantial and perhaps frequent changes. Changes in the equilibrium price and volume of trade will occur when there are changes to the conditions of production and demand that determine the countries' desire to trade; and these changes may be substantial and frequent. They do not indicate instability in the economic sense. Economists describe an equilibrium as being stable if small disturbances to that equilibrium at unchanged values of the underlying parameters are self-correcting, in the sense that the economy reverts to its initial position. Whether or not an equilibrium is stable in this sense will depend upon, among other things, how the markets respond to a disequilibrium situation.

In theoretical economics, tests for stability are usually formulated in mathematical terms; but the offer-curve diagram allows us a simple and intuitively clear test that can be related to the elasticities of the curves. In Figure 4.10 the equilibrium of

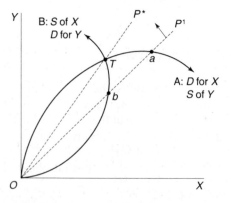

Fig. 4.10. Stable trading equilibrium

two trading economies is shown as the intersection of the two offer curves at T, and with the price represented by the slope of the line OP^* passing through T. At this price country A's demand for X is equal to country B's supply of X, and conversely for the good Y.

Now suppose that there is a small disturbance to the equilibrium price, so that it shifts to the line OP_1 with the price of X having fallen relative to that of Y. At this new price, country A will want to trade at the point a on its offer curve, whereas country B will want to trade at point b. Country A wants more trade than country B, and so there will be an excess demand for X and an excess supply of Y on the world market. In response to this disequilibrium, the normal market response will be a rise in the price of X relative to Y. The price line rotates back to its initial position and the disturbance has been corrected.

But now consider Figure 4.11.

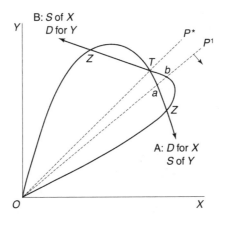

Fig. 4.11. Unstable trading equilibrium

In this diagram the offer curves have been drawn with considerably less elasticity than in the previous figure, so that they intersect from behind. Once again T represents the equilibrium volume of trade, and the slope of the line P^* represents the price. A fall in the price of X relative to Y is shown by the line OP_1. Once again the countries will want to trade at the points a and b respectively; but now country A wants less trade than does country B. There will be excess supply of X and excess demand for Y. In this case the normal market mechanism will cause the price of X relative to Y to fall further. This equilibrium is unstable. It can be seen that there are two other intersections of the offer curves at the points Z. It is left to the reader to confirm that these equilibria are stable.

The question now arises as to how inelastic the offer curves have to be in order to generate an unstable equilibrium. First it can be seen that, although both of the curves are inelastic, they have the normal sign in the sense that demand in each case is rising as the price falls.

We can use the diagrammatic representation of the elasticity of demand of an offer curve, which was illustrated in Figure 4.6, to calculate the elasticities in the borderline case where the disturbance is neither self correcting nor self reinforcing. This case is shown in Figure 4.12.

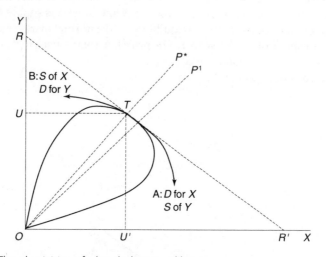

Fig. 4.12. The elasticities of a borderline equilibrium

In this figure the offer curves are tangent to each other in the region of the point T. A small disturbance to the price will generate neither an excess demand nor an excess supply of the product whose price has fallen, so there is no tendency for the price to return to its initial value nor for it to move further away. This is the borderline case between stability and instability. If the offer curves were more elastic then the equilibrium would be stable, but if they were less elastic it would be unstable. By extending the tangent through T to the two axes, the price elasticity of demand for X of country A's offer curve, e_A, can be shown as $-OU/OR$, and similarly country B's price elasticity of demand for Y, e_B, is $-OU'/OR'$. By the property of similar triangles, it can be seen that $OU/OR = R'T/RR'$, and $OU'/OR' = RT/RR$. These sum to unity, so the condition for the trading equilibrium to be stable can be expressed:

$$|e_A| + |e_B| > 1 \qquad (4.4)$$

where $|e_A|$ and $|e_B|$ are the numerical values of the elasticities of demand.

We conclude this discussion of stability with a few observations. First, students of open economy macroeconomics will have noticed the similarity of this condition with that for the stability of an exchange rate with respect to a change in the terms of trade (the Marshall-Lerner conditions). This similarity arises because the two cases are essentially different formulations of the same issue.

The second point is that under free-market conditions we are not likely to observe equilibria that are unstable in this technical sense, since their existence would be very short-lived. However, markets that are tightly controlled and regulated might be unstable since their prices might be maintained, albeit with difficulty, in spite of market pressures to change them. This is a reason why the conditions for stability, and the possibility of instability of the exchange rate, was such an important issue in the days of exchange controls and fixed exchange rates.

Thirdly, unstable markets are associated with perverse comparative static results. For example, consider the effect of a fall in the demand for X in country A. This will be reflected by a contraction of the offer curve. In the stable case this will result in a fall in the price of X, which sends out to the markets the appropriate signal to produce less and to consume more. But in the unstable case, the effect of the fall in demand for X is to increase its price, which sends the wrong signal to the producers and consumers.

Fourthly, and associated with the last point, even if markets are not technically unstable, they work better when elasticities are high.

Finally, the empirical question as to whether international trade elasticities are high or low is not easily answered. Elasticities of demand and supply depend, among other things, upon the time horizon that is being considered and upon the policy regime with respect to trade that is being implemented. For example, the elasticities of demand and supply of agricultural products of the European Union under the policies of the Common Agricultural Policy must be very low.

4.13 Bases of trade

In this chapter we have discussed how differences between countries in their desire to trade can generate a trading equilibrium that is beneficial to both of the countries. The offer-curve representation disguises the sources of these differences between countries; but they might arise from differences in conditions of domestic supply, or from a difference in tastes, or from both. In fact, much of international trade analysis examines possible sources of differences in production possibilities as giving rise to trade based on comparative advantage; and this is how we proceed in Chapter 5 of this book. It is possible to illustrate a trading equilibrium between two countries with different production possibilities and similar tastes by means of a diagram showing directly the production and consumption in the two countries, although we do not do so here. It should be apparent that, in these circumstances, trade allows the countries to become more specialized in production, and to become similar in their consumption. We could also envisage countries with identical production possibilities but with different tastes. In this case international trade will lead to similar production patterns between the countries, and more specialization in consumption. The classic diagrammatic representation of these cases and the illustration of the conditions for equilibrium trade is provided by Leontief (1933).

4.14 Summary

- Demand conditions in conjunction with supply determine international trade equilibria.
- A small country is a price-taker so it can expand its trade without affecting the terms of trade. An expansion of trade by a large country, however, is likely to worsen its terms of trade, thereby benefiting its trading partners.
- International trade expands the consumption possibilities of the trading economies. Consumers can benefit from the ability to consume combinations of goods different from those that are produced.
- High price elasticities facilitate the functioning of international markets.

5

FACTOR ENDOWMENTS

....

5.1 Introduction

This chapter considers differences in factor endowments between countries as one of the most important explanations of the causes of trade. In Chapter 4 it was emphasized that the differences between countries giving rise to trade might arise from differences in either demand or supply conditions in the countries. In fact, most of international trade theory has been concerned with differences in productive capacities as the determinants of comparative advantage and trade. In the neo-classical production model we have seen that the production possibilities are determined by technology (the production functions) and by factor endowments, so differences in either of these could be the basis for trade in that model. Trade might also arise because of some deviations from the assumptions of the neo-classical model, in particular because of increasing returns to scale and imperfect competition. This chapter uses the neo-classical model developed earlier to analyse how trade might be based upon differences in the availability of the factors of production. Other possible explanations are considered in subsequent chapters.

We shall discuss two related models that emphasize differences in the national endowments of the factors of production as the determinants of trade. The first of these is the Heckscher-Ohlin model. This is the neo-classical model discussed in Chapter 3, with the added assumption that countries are similar except with respect to the availability of the factors of production. The second is the Specific Factor model, sometimes known as the Ricardo-Viner model. This is similar to Heckscher-Ohlin, except that it departs from the basic neo-classical model by assuming that one factor of production is not mobile between the industries, but is in fixed supply to each of them, or is specific to one of them.

Both of these models attempt to answer the same questions:

1. Can differences in factor endowments alone lead to international trade, and what is the pattern of such trade?
2. What is the effect of trade and trade related policies upon the distribution of income (factor prices) within each country?
3. What is the effect of trade or trade-related policies upon factor prices internationally?

4.   How will changes in factor endowments in one country affect output and factor prices?

We shall examine these questions in some detail in the context of the Heckscher-Ohlin model, and rather more briefly in the Specific Factor model.

We shall see that both of these models are built upon extremely restrictive assumptions, and that they have limited explanatory or predictive power. Furthermore, the predictions concerning the determinants of trade are in some cases trivial; for example, the observation that Honduras exports bananas because it is well-endowed with banana trees is no doubt true, but it is not very interesting. Nevertheless, these models, particularly Heckscher-Ohlin, are very important in providing an understanding of how economic systems work by focusing attention on the interaction among certain economic variables. They should be seen in this light rather than as descriptions of reality. They certainly do not provide universal explanations of the patterns of international trade. The idea that trade is based on the availability of factors of production has considerable intuitive appeal. It is therefore interesting to see that the conditions under which standard economic theory predicts that this will be the case are quite restrictive.

5.2 The Heckscher-Ohlin model

The Heckscher-Ohlin model takes its name from two Swedish economists, Eli Heckscher (1919) and his pupil, Bertil Ohlin (1933). They emphasized the role of factor endowments in determining the pattern of trade, and promoted the discussion of the implications that such trade has for the earnings of the factors of production. The formulation of the model in the context of neo-classical production theory has to a considerable extent been the work of Paul Samuelson, and his name is sometimes added to those of Heckscher and Ohlin in designating the model.

It is useful to distinguish between the Heckscher-Ohlin *model*, which is the whole theoretical construction concerning trade and production based upon a difference between countries in their factor endowments, and four *hypotheses* or *propositions* which arise from the model, and which answer the four questions propounded above. These propositions are:

1.   The Heckscher-Ohlin hypothesis that each country will export products that are intensive in the use of that country's abundant factor of production, and will import products that are intensive in the use of the country's scarce factor of production.
2.   The factor price equalization proposition that international trade will equalize the real return to the factors of production throughout the world.
3.   The Stolper-Samuelson proposition that international trade benefits a country's abundant factor of production, but reduces the real return to its scarce factor of production.

4. The Rybczynski proposition that at unchanged terms of trade an increase in a country's endowment of just one factor of production will result in an increase in the output of the good that uses that factor intensively, and a fall in output of the other product.

These propositions were formulated independently at separate times, but all arise from the general Heckscher-Ohlin theoretical framework.

5.2.1 The assumptions

We shall now describe the assumptions of the model, and explain the purpose of these assumptions. We shall see that if the assumptions are not satisfied, one or more of the propositions may not hold, or may become unclear or even meaningless.

Dimension It is assumed that there are two countries, two products, and two factors of production. This allows us to have a diagrammatic representation of the model, and provides us with clear results. An expansion of these dimensions is necessary for empirical application, but generates problems which are considered later.

Factors of production These are homogeneous in the sense that they are of the same quality throughout the world. This assumption makes it possible to identify factor endowments by the quantity available alone.

It is also assumed, as in the neo-classical production model of Chapter 3, that the factors are in fixed supply to each country, but are mobile between the industries within each country. If the factors are not in fixed supply, the concept of factor endowments, which is fundamental to the model, becomes problematic. The assumption that both factors are mobile between the industries is abandoned in the Specific Factor model.

Technologies There are three assumptions concerning technologies. The first is that neo-classical production functions of the sort discussed in Chapter 3 relate the output of goods to the factor inputs. These are linear and homogeneous with constant returns to scale, and with positive but diminishing marginal productivity of the factors.

The second assumption concerning technology is that the production functions are the same throughout the world. Thus the isoquant representing the factor combinations that will yield a specific amount of a product will be identical in all countries. This assumption ensures that it is not differences in access to technology that are the bases of comparative advantage.

The third technological assumption is that products differ in their factor requirements, and that one product can always be identified as being intensive relative to the other product in the use of a particular factor of production. It is necessary to assume that there are no factor-intensity reversals if the Heckscher-Ohlin proposition is to be unambiguous or even meaningful.

Demand   Demand is homothetic, so that the proportion in which goods are consumed depends only upon prices and not upon income throughout the world. This assumption ensures that differences in tastes or in levels of income do not determine the pattern of trade. Notice that an implication of this assumption is that if international trade equalizes commodity prices throughout the world, then if a country has a given proportion of world income, it will consume that same proportion of each and every one of the world's goods and services.

Non-specialization   It is assumed that with free trade both countries will produce both goods. This assumption implies that the countries are not too different in their factor endowments, and is needed if the effect of trade on factor prices is to be complete.

Markets   It is assumed that there are no transport costs or other barriers to trade, so that commodity prices are equalized throughout the world. This assumption is necessary if the full results of the model are to be achieved.

It is further assumed that commodity and factor markets are perfectly competitive, and that economic agents (consumers and owners of the factors of production) are optimizing in these competitive markets. This is what was being assumed in the discussion of neo-classical production in Chapter 3.

Some of these assumptions have the purpose of isolating differences in factor endowments as the source of comparative advantage and international trade. Others are necessary if the full results of the model are to be achieved. They are not put forward as descriptions of reality. In fact, much of the use of the Heckscher-Ohlin model is as a framework of analysis when one or more of these assumptions are relaxed. For example, one of the assumptions listed above is that there are no tariffs, but one of the central propositions derived from the model (Stolper-Samuelson) concerns the effect of a tariff on the returns to the factors of production. Similarly, the model assumes that the factors are in fixed supply, but the Rybczynski proposition is concerned with what happens when there is an increase in factor endowment.

5.2.2   Factor prices and factor proportions

It is being assumed that for each product there is throughout the world a homogeneous production function with constant returns to scale, so that the physical marginal products of the factors depend only upon the proportion in which the factors are used. Competition in the factor markets and cost-minimizing behaviour by the producers will ensure that production takes place using the factors of production in proportions which equalize the marginal rate of substitution between the factors (the slope of the isoquants) to the relative price of the factors of production. As a result, there will be a monotonic relationship between factor prices and factor proportions for each industry, with a rise in the relative price of one factor being associated with a rise in the relative use of the other factor.

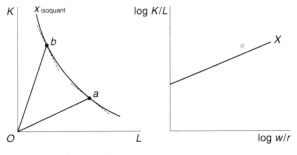

Fig. 5.1. Factor prices and proportions

The left panel of Figure 5.1 depicts an isoquant for the *X* industry using factors *K* (capital) and *L* (labour). At relative factor prices given by the slope of the isoquant at the point *a*, the factors will be used in the proportion of the ray *Oa*; but at higher prices of labour to capital, such as is shown by the slope of the isoquant at *b*, the *K/L* proportion will be higher (ray *Ob*). This relationship between the factor prices and factor proportions, which is derived from the production function, is shown in the right panel of Figure 5.1, where *w* and *r* are respectively the price of *L* and *K*. It is often convenient to show this relationship in logarithmic form, because then its slope has a direct economic interpretation. The elasticity of substitution between factors in an industry is the proportional change in factor proportions associated with a proportional change in factor prices. This can be defined as

$$\sigma = \frac{dK/L}{dw/r} \cdot \frac{w/r}{K/L} = \frac{d\log K/L}{d\log w/r} \tag{5.1}$$

which is the slope of the relationship between factor proportions and factor prices when plotted in logarithmic form, as in the Figure. The elasticity of substitution, which is a measure of the ease with which the factors can be substituted for each other in response to changes in factor prices, is a property of the production function. Special cases are (1) Cobb-Douglas production functions in which the elasticity of substitution is unity; (2) fixed coefficient production functions in which the elasticity of substitution is zero; and (3) perfect factor substitutability in which the elasticity of substitution is infinite. The isoquants and the corresponding factor proportions–factor prices relationships for these three cases are shown in Figure 5.2. (The Cobb-Douglas case may not be accurately drawn.)

A more general type of production function is the CES (constant elasticity of substitution). This has the property that the elasticity of substitution is constant at all factor proportions, but it can lie between zero and infinity. Cases (1), (2), and (3) are all special cases of CES production functions.

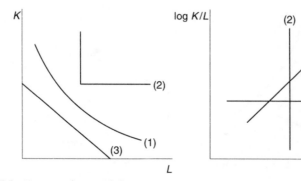

Fig. 5.2. Factor substitutability

5.2.3 Factor intensities

The relationship between factor proportions and factor prices for two or more commodities can be compared, and the relative factor intensities of the industries at particular prices can be identified.[1] If the industries have similar factor substitutability, one industry will be consistently intensive in the use of one factor in the sense that it will always use more of that factor relative to the other factor than will the other industry. Such a case is shown in Figure 5.3. At a low price of labour to capital (slopes at x' and y' in the left panel) X is capital-intensive and Y is labour-intensive. This remains the case at high prices of labour to capital (slopes at x'' and y'').

The right-hand panel shows Good X as having a higher capital–labour ratio than Y at all relative factor prices. However, if the industries differ in the degree to which the factors can be substituted for each other, there may be a factor-intensity reversal, with one industry being capital-intensive at some factor prices and labour-intensive at others. Such a case is shown in Figure 5.4.

In this Figure Y is a more flexible industry than is X. This is reflected in the relatively straight Y isoquant on the left side of the diagram, and by the steeper elasticity of substitution line on the right-hand side.

At a low price of labour relative to capital (slopes at x' and y') the X industry is capital intensive, but at a high price of labour to capital (slopes at x'' and y'') Y is capital intensive. At some factor price, $(w/r)_0$ in the right panel of Figure 5.4, both industries would use the factors in the same proportion. This is the point of factor-intensity reversal.

---

[1] The relative factor intensities can be defined in two ways: (1) At a given capital-labour ratio the isoquant of the labour-intensive product is steeper than that of the capital-intensive product, i.e. the marginal productivity of labour to capital is higher. (2) At a given relative factor price, the capital–labour ratio is higher in the capital-intensive industry than in the labour-intensive industry.

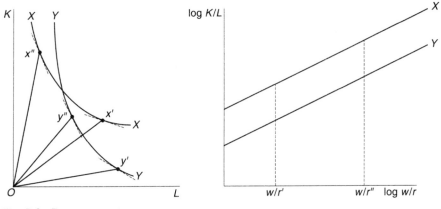

Fig. 5.3. Factor intensity

5.2.4 Factor endowment and feasible factor prices

A country's overall factor endowment will determine the range of feasible factor proportions for each industry and so will determine the range of feasible factor prices. A country with endowment E in Figure 5.5 could specialize in the production of commodity X, in which case the factor proportions in the X industry would, of course, be at E, and the corresponding factor prices would be at $(w/r)'$. If a very small amount of Y was also produced, the factor proportion in the Y industry would be approximately $(K/L)'$. If, on the other hand, the country specialized in Y, then the factor proportion E would have to be used in the Y industry and the factor prices would be at $(w/r)''$. If a small amount of X was also produced it would be at the factor proportions $(K/L)''$.

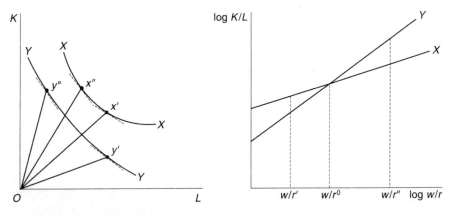

Fig. 5.4. Factor intensity reversal

These cases can also be illustrated with the box diagram in Figure 5.6. Specialization in X means that production is at the y origin on the contract curve; the factor prices would be the slope of the X isoquant at that origin, and the factor proportions in the X industry are the slope of the diagonal (overall endowment). A very small amount of Y could be produced at the factor proportions represented by the slope of the contract curve at y. Similarly, specialization in Y is depicted by the extreme point x on the contract curve.

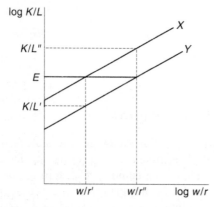

Fig. 5.5. Factor endowment and prices

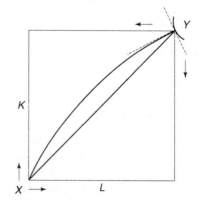

Fig. 5.6. Factor endowment and allocation

The possible range of factor prices in such a country would be $(w/r)'$ to $(w/r)''$ in Figure 5.5. The extent of this range depends upon the difference in the factor intensity of the two industries. If the industries used the factors in the same proportion, there would only be one factor proportion and factor price at which the goods could efficiently be produced, i.e. the contract curve would be the diagonal of the box diagram. But more generally, the industries will have different factor intensities so the factor proportion in each industry changes as the outputs of the two commodities change.

5.2.5 Factor prices and commodity prices

Factor prices determine the costs of production, so changes in relative factor prices will be associated with changes in relative commodity prices. When this relationship is shown in logarithmic form, its slope is the elasticity of the relative commodity prices with respect to the relative factor prices, that is, the proportional change in the commodity prices with respect to a proportional change in the factor prices:

$$\frac{dP_Y/P_X}{dw/r} \cdot \frac{w/r}{P_Y/P_X} = \frac{d\log P_Y/P_X}{d\log w/r} \tag{5.2}$$

where P_Y/P_X is the price of Y relative to that of X. This elasticity depends upon the relative factor intensities of the two industries. If the X industry uses only K and the Y industry uses only L, then a change in the price of L relative to K will be associated with an equal proportional change in the price of Y relative to the price of X, i.e.

$$\frac{d\log P_Y/P_X}{d\log w/r} = 1 \tag{5.3}$$

If Y used only K, and X used only L, then

$$\frac{d\log P_Y/P_X}{d\log w/r} = -1 \tag{5.4}$$

In general, when both commodities use some of both factors, a rise in the price of one factor relative to the other will be associated with a less-than-proportional rise in the relative price of the commodity that is intensive in the use of the factor whose price has risen. This is the 'magnification effect' discussed in Chapter 3. The rate of change in the elasticity of factor proportions with respect to factor prices will depend upon the relative substitutability of the factors in the two industries. If the industries have equal elasticities of factor substitution, then there will be no change in the relative factor intensities, and so the commodity price–factor price elasticity will be monotonic. This is illustrated in Figure 5.7.

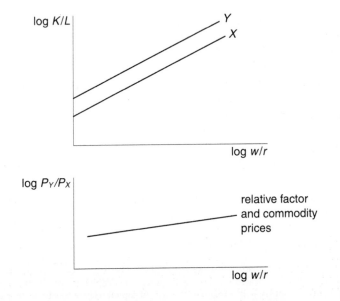

Fig. 5.7. Factor prices, factor proportions, and commodity prices

A contrasting case is shown in Figure 5.8. Here the elasticity of substitution in industry Y is higher than in X. At low prices of labour relative to capital, Y is labour-intensive, so a rise in wages relative to rent raises the price of Y relative to that of X; but since capital can be substituted for labour faster in the Y industry than in the X industry, the rate at which P_Y/P_X rises with a rise in w/r is diminishing. A point is reached where Y is no longer labour-intensive, so any further rise in w/r will be associated with a fall in P_Y/P_X.

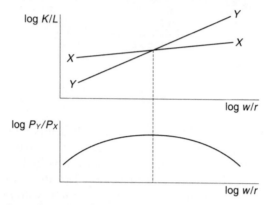

Fig. 5.8. Factor intensity reversal

5.2.6 Factor price equalization

Under the assumptions of the Heckscher-Ohlin model, countries have the same technologies; thus Figure 5.7 or Figure 5.8 could represent all countries, and the relationships between factor price, factor proportions, and commodity prices will be the same for all countries. It can now be seen what additional assumptions are necessary if trade is to result in an equalization of factor prices between countries. The importance of the assumption that there are no factor-intensity reversals can be seen by comparing Figures 5.7 and 5.8. With no factor-intensity reversals (as in Figure 5.7) there is only one relative factor price (and one set of factor proportions) associated with each relative commodity price. Thus, if the effect of international trade is to bring about equal commodity prices in the countries, then if both countries are to continue producing both commodities they must have the same factor prices, and in each industry the factors must be used in the same proportions in both countries. This is the 'factor-price equalization' proposition.[2]

---

[2] Note that factor price equalization does not imply that per capita income is equalized by international trade. $I = wL + rK$, where I is national income; so per capita income $I/L = w + rK/L$, which will be higher in the country with a high endowment of capital relative to labour. (For simplicity it is being assumed that population is equal to the labour force.)

5.2.7 Factor price equalization using the dual

The most direct way of showing the relationship between commodity prices and factor prices is in terms of the 'dual' using cost functions as was demonstrated in Chapter 3 above.

This also provides us with a simple demonstration of factor-price equalization. Figure 5.9 is a reproduction of Figure 3.9 from that Chapter.

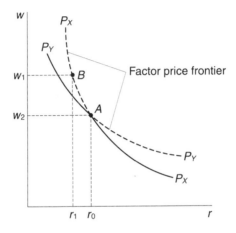

Fig. 5.9. Feasible factor prices

The isocost curves for each industry show the combination of factor prices that yield a given price for each good. Only at point A would the factor prices be consistent with the particular prices of both goods, and therefore allow the production of both goods at these prices. Under the assumptions of the Heckscher-Ohlin model, the prices and the isocost relationships for each industry are the same in both countries. Thus Figure 5.9 represents both countries, so the factor prices would have to be at the same point A in both countries if they are to produce both goods, and we have factor-price equalization.

The factor prices could differ if at least one of the countries produced only one of the goods. Thus, in Figure 5.9, one country could produce both of the goods at the factor prices shown at point A, whereas a second country could produce the good X at higher wages and a lower price of capital as shown at point B. It could not, however, produce the good Y at these prices.

5.2.8 Pattern of output: the Heckscher-Ohlin hypothesis

We have just demonstrated that, under the assumptions of the model, each product must be produced using the same factor proportions in each industry. How is

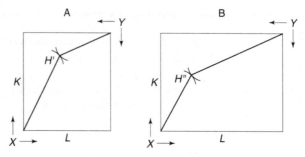

Fig. 5.10. Equalized factor proportions

this to be reconciled with the presumption that the countries have different over-all endowments? This is intuitively obvious, and is illustrated in the box diagrams of Figure 5.10 where the countries are producing at 'corresponding points'.

Countries A and B are using their inputs at combinations such as H' and H'' respectively. The line xH' is parallel to xH'', and yH' is parallel to yH''. This indicates that in each industry the factors are used in the same proportion in the two countries. The isoquants will have the same shape and slope in each country, so if H' is on country A's efficiency locus, H'' must be on that of country B, with the same marginal rate of substitution between the factors in both goods and both countries. It can easily be seen that at such corresponding points the proportion of factors going into the capital-intensive industry (X) relative to the labour-intensive industry (Y) must be higher in country A which is relatively well endowed with capital, than in country B, which is relatively capital-poor. Provided that tastes are not so dissimilar between countries as to offset this production pattern, each country will export the commodity that is intensive in the use of its relatively abundant factor. This is the Heckscher-Ohlin hypothesis.

5.2.9 Incomplete specialization

Note that if the overall endowments of the two countries are very different, their feasible factor prices and factor proportions may not overlap, or may only coincide over a narrow range. Under these circumstances it would be impossible or unlikely that the demand conditions would give a solution in which factor prices were equalized. One or both countries would be completely specialized in the production of one good. The corresponding points would lie outside one or both of the boxes. Trade would have brought about an incomplete movement towards factor price equalization, but the Heckscher-Ohlin pattern of trade would still hold.

5.2.10 Factor returns and endowments: the Stolper-Samuelson hypothesis

We are now in a position to link the effect of international trade on the earnings of the factors of production to a country's relative factor endowments. This is done in two stages: the first stage identifies a factor as gaining or losing from trade depending upon whether it is used intensively in the export or import competing industry; while the second stage uses the Heckscher-Ohlin hypothesis to identify the relatively abundant factor as the gainer from trade, and the relatively scarce factor as the loser.

The first stage has already been covered in the discussion of neo-classical production in Chapter 3 and in section 5.2.5 of this chapter. We have seen that the rise in the relative price of one good will be associated with an increase in the return to the factor of production that is used intensively in that good, and a fall in the earnings of the other factor. Since international trade increases the relative price of the exported good, it is the factor that is used intensively in the export industry that gains, and the factor that is used intensively in the import industry that loses from international trade. This is the weak version of the Stolper-Samuelson result, and it is independent of the Heckscher-Ohlin hypothesis.

The second stage invokes the Heckscher-Ohlin hypothesis to link the factor earnings to the pattern of trade, and thus to factor endowments. Since it is the abundant factor that is used intensively in a country's export industry, it is that factor that gains from trade. Conversely, it is the scarce factor that is used intensively in the import competing industry, and so loses from trade. This is the full, or strong, Stolper-Samuelson result.[3]

Stolper-Samuelson-type reasoning is a powerful motivation for European trade policy. The import of labour-intensive manufactured goods is believed to be detrimental to the earnings and employment prospects of European labour—particularly unskilled labour—and so is subject to pressure for protection. Stolper-Samuelson reasoning was explicitly used in the formulation of Australian tariff policy in the early postwar period, a purpose of the policy being to encourage immigration from Europe. Since Australia was land-abundant and labour-scarce relative to Europe, the policy of protecting the labour-intensive manufacturing industry was expected to rase the earnings of labour and to encourage immigration.

5.2.11 Factor intensity reversals

If the commodities differ significantly in their elasticities of substitution between the factors of production, and there are factor-intensity reversals as in Figure 5.8,

---

[3] In their original exposition, Stolper and Samuelson discussed the effect of a tariff on the earnings of the factors of production. The corollary of the effect of trade on factor earnings is that a tariff, by increasing the domestic price of the imported good, will benefit the scarce factor and harm the abundant factor.

then there is not just one relative factor price consistent with each relative commodity price. It is therefore possible for commodity prices to be the same in the two countries and for both countries to be producing these commodities with equal costs but with different factor prices and factor proportions. Consider two countries whose overall factor endowments lie on different sides of the reversal point, e.g. E_A and E_B in Figure 5.11. The after-trade commodity price in both countries could be $(P_Y/P_X)^0$, but the factor prices could be $(w/r)'$ in country A and $(w/r)''$ in country B.

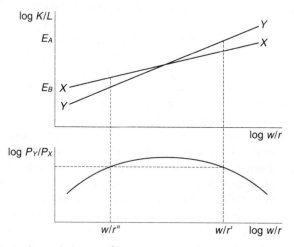

Fig. 5.11. Factor intensity reversal

Under these circumstances the model fails catastrophically, in the sense that its main hypotheses are no longer valid.

Trade will not have equalized factor prices and may not have brought them closer together. Commodity X is capital-intensive in country B but labour-intensive in A. More capital relative to labour is used in both industries in country A than in country B. This is illustrated by the box diagrams in Figure 5.12.

In Figure 5.12 commodity prices may have been equalized, but xQ' is steeper than xQ'', and yQ' is steeper than yQ''. No conclusion can be derived about the pattern of trade, so the Heckscher-Ohlin result does not hold. Indeed, it must be wrong for at least one of the countries, since if one country is exporting the product that is labour-intensive for that country, then the other country must also be exporting its labour-intensive product. But both countries cannot be labour abundant.

It remains the case that trade will be beneficial to the factor of production used intensively in the export industry of each country, and will be detrimental to the other factor; so the weak version of the Stolper-Samuelson hypothesis still holds.

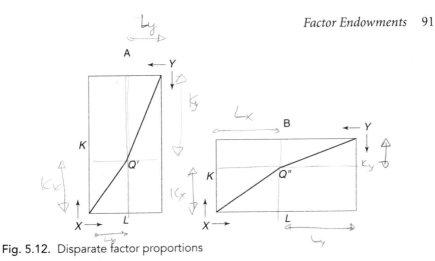

Fig. 5.12. Disparate factor proportions

But it is no longer possible to relate trade to factor abundance and scarcity, so the strong or full Stolper-Samuelson result fails.

It may help to give an example of a possible factor-intensity reversal. Consider two products, rice and textiles. Rice can be produced using very different factor proportions. In Bangladesh rice production is very labour-intensive, involving transplanting the seedlings by hand, very careful weeding, and so on. It is quite likely that in that country rice production is more labour-intensive than the production of textiles. But in the USA, rice is produced much more capital-intensively, using aeroplanes to distribute fertilizer and pesticides. It is rice that is capital-intensive and textiles that are labour-intensive in that country. Thus if the United States is exporting rice to Bangladesh and is importing textiles, then both countries are exporting their capital-intensive product. Under these circumstances the trade is beneficial to the owners of capital in both countries and is detrimental to labour. Note that the Heckscher-Ohlin proposition has to be wrong for one of the countries.

5.2.12 When will the Heckscher-Ohlin prediction about trade direction break down? A summary

It may be helpful to ask when and why the Heckscher-Ohlin (HO) prediction of a country's direction of trade breaks down. Let us answer this question for the case of two countries (A and B), trading two goods (x and y) that are produced with two factors (K and L). Let A be endowed with a higher ratio of K to L than B. The HO prediction is that A exports x if x uses a higher ratio of K to L than y in A. When can this be wrong?

There are essentially four cases when this prediction can be false. One is a *demand reversal*. Give all A's residents a strong taste bias towards x, compared with B's. For A, this will make x more expensive (relative to y) in autarky—dearer, in fact, than in B, if the taste bias is very pronounced. So A will import x, not export it.

The second case can arise when the two products differ greatly in flexibility. If x is highly flexible, its isoquants will be nearly linear, and its isoprice nearly *L*-shaped. Let y be highly inflexible, so that it needs K and L in nearly fixed proportions. With the two countries differing sharply in endowment ratios, most of what little L there is in A has to go to the inflexible industry y. In B it is K that is scarce, and most K will be employed making y. There is a *factor intensity reversal* here. Good x is relatively K-intensive in A, but relatively L-intensive in B. If the two countries trade, one of them will obey the HO prediction, but the other will disobey it.

Our third case of HO trade prediction breakdown is *technology reversal*. Give A's y-producers a very big technical lead over B's, while production functions for x are similar. If the technology difference is large enough, it should swamp the effect of factor endowments, and make A export y, rather than x.

Our fourth case is one of *multiple autarky equilibria*. Focus on A, which is well-endowed with K, the factor used intensively in x. Split A's residents into those who own K and those who own L. Give K-owners a big taste bias towards x. We can then generate two possible stable equilibria in A, when A is in autarky. In one, x is in low demand and supply, and cheap; demand for y is high because most of the national income goes to the L-owners. In the other, supply and price are high for x; K-owners get most of the national income; because they favour x in consumption, demand for x is high, too. Between these two stable equilibria there should exist an unstable equilibrium, with middling demand and supply levels for both goods. If A is suddenly allowed to trade, we might be at the dear-x stable equilibrium, that would tend to make x the importable; or we could be at the cheap-x stable equilibrium, where the HO prediction about trade direction was correct.

5.2.13 Why factor prices may not equalize: a summary

The conditions needed for international trade to lead to the equalization of factor prices between countries are highly restrictive. These conditions suggest several reasons why it may not occur. Many of these have already been identified in this chapter; but it is useful to state all of them at this point here.

First, there may be barriers to trade, such as tariffs or international transport costs. This will stop commodity prices from equalizing. So isoprices, and their intersection points, will differ across countries.

Second, we may not have perfect competition. Market imperfections tend to break the link between the prices and marginal products of factors, so that the isoprices can no longer be derived straight from production functions. Linked to the absence of perfect competition may be departures from the traditional assumption of constant returns to scale, which make for non-unique isoprices even if competition is perfect.

Third, there could be cross-country differences in technology for one (or more) of the products. A country with a technical lead in the production of x will have an x-isoprice further from the origin than in the other country. So isoprice intersection points are likely to differ between countries.

Fourth, we could have more internationally immobile factors than freely traded goods. This will normally lead to a problem of 'underdetermination'. There will be too few (equalized) commodity prices to pin down the unknowns (the prices of internationally immobile factors). Heterogeneities in factors, such as labour, and the difficulty of splitting human capital from labour, are relevant here: ideally we should insist on all factors being disaggregated down to levels where they are homogeneous. Much of the disparity in wages throughout the world can be associated with differences in human capital embodied in labour.

The fifth possibility is complete specialization. Recall that the gradient of the tangency to an isoprice, in w,r space, is minus the capital labour ratio in that sector. A country's capital–labour endowment ratio is a weighted average of the capital–labour ratios in its industries. An isoprice intersection point gives a feasible range for the economy's capital–labour endowment ratio. If the endowment ratio lies outside this range—say it is steeper than the gradient of the steeper isoprice at the point of intersection—we shall observe complete specialization in the capital-intensive product. The economy's wage rate will be lower than abroad, and its capital rental higher.

A sixth possible explanation is the existence of factors that are immobile between industries within countries. We shall see in Section 5.5 below that, if the relative endowment of 'specific' factors differs between countries, factor prices will not be equalized.

The seventh and final case of factor price non-equalization arises in the presence of a factor intensity reversal (fir) within the relevant range. A fir occurs when two industries differ in flexibility. The flexible sector's isoprice is more convex than the isoprice in the less flexible industry. Typically we now get two points of intersection, not one. If the two countries' capital–labour endowment ratios are far enough apart, the capital-rich country will gravitate towards the intersection where the wage rate is high; the other should move to the other intersection point, where it is the capital rental that is high and the wage rate low.

We know that trade actually fails to iron out factor price differences between countries. This is especially true of wage rates, when we compare rich and poor countries. In principle any of our six factors could explain this. In practice, the third—international technology differences—looks the likeliest culprit.

5.2.14 The Rybczynski proposition

The Rybczynski proposition is concerned with the effect of an increase in the endowment of just one of a country's factors of production upon the pattern of output if the relative price of the commodities (terms of trade) remains unchanged.

This proposition has implications which are interesting in the context of

economic growth and factor mobility. In one sense the proposition can be considered as a deviation from the main Heckscher-Ohlin model because one of the
central assumptions of that model—fixed factor endowments—is relaxed. But
analytically it can be seen as a special case of the Heckscher-Ohlin hypothesis. The
Heckscher-Ohlin hypothesis considers the pattern of output of two countries that
have the same commodity prices because of free trade, but that have different factor endowments. The Rybczynski proposition considers a country whose endowments have changed in a specified way, and whose commodity prices are
unchanged by assumption.

   In considering the effect of an increase in just one of a country's factors of
endowment, we can first note that the augmented factor could be used in the production of either of the goods without changing the inputs into the other one.
Thus the production possibility frontier expands in all dimensions. However, the
increase in the one factor will obviously facilitate the production of the good that
uses that factor intensively, so the expansion of the production possibility frontier
will be biased towards that good. This is shown in Figure 5.13, in which the
expansion of the production possibility frontier has been biased towards the good
X. This would be consistent with an increase in the factor of capital, with the good
X being capital-intensive.

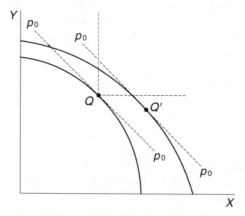

Fig. 5.13. Production possibilities with an increase in the factor used intensively in
the production of X

   In Figure 5.13 it is feasible to produce more of either or both of the goods, but
the Rybczynski proposition states that at unchanged terms of trade the output of
Y will fall. Production will shift from some point, like Q on the original production possibility frontier, to Q' on the augmented one. At Q' the slope of the production possibility frontier is the same as at Q, because by assumption the
commodity prices have not changed. It is to be demonstrated that Q' is below Q
reflecting the absolute fall in the output of good Y.

   That the output of Y must have fallen can be seen by using the box diagram.

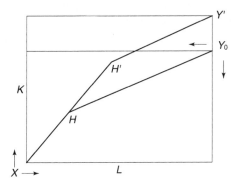

Fig. 5.14. Enhanced endowment of *K* but unchanged factor proportions

Figure 5.14 imposes the box with the enhanced endowment of the factor *K* upon the box representing the original endowments.

In this Figure, the input of the factors may initially have been at point *H* in the shorter box, with the factor inputs measured from the origins *x* and *y₀*. After the increase in the endowment of factor *K*, the inputs into *X* and *Y* will have to be at some point such as *H′* measured from the origins *x* and *y′* respectively. Because of the assumption of unchanged commodity prices, in conjunction with all of the other assumptions of the model, production after the increase in the one factor must be at unchanged factor proportions in each industry. In terms of the box diagram the inputs must be at 'corresponding points', with the slopes of the rays back to the relevant origins being unchanged, as shown in the Figure. It is readily seen that this requires a reduction of the inputs of both factors into the good *Y*.

The intuition of this result is straightforward. The expansion of the capital-intensive product *X* can absorb the extra capital. But although *X* is capital-intensive, it does require some of the other factor: labour. Where is this labour to come from? Its overall supply has not increased; and the assumption of unchanged terms of trade prevents the economizing on the use of labour by the adoption of less labour-intensive methods of production. The only way that the labour necessary for the expansion of *X* can be provided is by the reduction in the output of *Y*. Notice that cutting back on the production of *Y* will release some of both factors of production, but it will release relatively large amounts of labour. At the new equilibrium the expansion of the production of *X* will have absorbed not only the augmented capital but some of the original endowment of capital that has been released by the reduction of output of *Y*. Thus the Rybczynski proposition has very strong implications for the effect of a change in the supply of one factor of production on the pattern of output.

The Rybczynski proposition is often used in the discussion of the effect of economic growth upon a country's desire to trade. The basic proposition suggests that growth arising from the accumulation of just one factor of production will have either a strongly positive or a strongly negative impact on the desire to trade,

depending upon whether it is the factor of production that is used intensively in the export industry or the import competing industry that is increasing. This can be illustrated using the offer-curve analysis developed in Chapter 4. Figure 5.15 shows the offer curve, *OA*, of a country A that is supplying the good *X* and demanding the good *Y*.

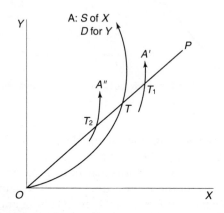

Fig. 5.15. Pro-trade or anti-trade growth

The initial equilibrium would be at point *T* if the price is as shown by the slope of the ray *OP*. The Rybczynski analysis tells us how the offer curve shifts along that ray. If the augmented factor is used intensively in the *Y* industry, the offer curve expands to *A'* so as to intersect the price ray further out at some point like T_1, but if it is used intensively in the import-competing industry *X*, then the offer curve will contract (*A"*) so that it is intersecting the price ray at some point like T_2.

This discussion provides an illustration of one of the purposes of assumptions in economic analysis. Suppose that the country we are discussing is a small one trading with a large world. Then that country will be a price-taker, and in effect the rest of the world's offer curve will be the perfectly elastic price ray *OP*, and the assumption of unchanged terms of trade is a reasonable one. If, however, the 'country' being considered is large, or is a block of countries such as the European Union, or such as the less developed countries in aggregate, then the assumption that the rest of the world's offer curve is perfectly elastic is unrealistic. It would better be represented by the offer curve *OB* in Figure 5.16.

In this case, the changing desire of country A to trade will affect the terms of trade, negating the initial assumption. This is an important result because it suggests a mechanism whereby pro-trade growth in one group of countries may benefit other countries by improving their terms of trade. Country A's offer curve in Figure 5.15 expands to *OA'* yielding a new equilibrium at T_1 with a higher price of good *X* relative to that of *Y* as shown by the slope of *OP'*. But the Rybczynski analysis makes us aware that the opposite can happen. An accumulation of the

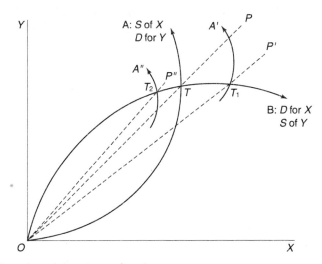

Fig. 5.16. Growth and the terms of trade

factor of production used intensively in the import competing industry will reduce the country's desire to trade, contracting the offer curve to OA'', yielding an equilibrium at T_2, and worsening the rest of the world's terms of trade to that shown by the slope OP''.

The point about the assumption of unchanging terms of trade in the large-country case is that it is made in order to shed light on the implications of that assumption, and thus to provide some insight into how the terms of trade might be expected to change under certain circumstances.

5.2.15 Increase in both factors

There are two straightforward variations of the Rybczynski proposition that are of interest. The first is concerned with what happens to output if the factors of production increase in proportion to the original endowment. Under these circumstances the production possibilities of the economy will expand to scale; and if prices are unchanged, the output of both the goods will increase in the same proportion. Provided that demand is homothetic, i.e. that there is unitary income elasticity of demand for both products, the offer curve of the economy is expanding in proportion to the growth of the factors. This is known as neutral growth.

The second variation of the Rybczynski proposition concerns the change in factor endowments that would, at unchanged commodity prices, leave the output of one of the commodities unchanged. This is simple. If capital and labour are both increased in the proportion in which they are used in the X industry, then the extra factors can be exactly absorbed in that industry without any change in factor proportions, and the output of the Y industry will be unchanged.

Conversely, if the factors are increased in proportion to their use in the *Y* industry, the output of *X* will be unchanged. Thus the factor intensities of the two industries form a cone defining the proportions within which a growth in the supply of both factors will yield an increase in the output of both products.

The Rybczynski method of analysing the effects of changes in factor endowments is a useful analytical tool. It is used in the discussion of economic growth in Chapter 12 below.

5.3 Testing the Heckscher-Ohlin proposition

The measuring of relationships between factor endowments and trade is discussed in Chapter 8 below. We will, however, at this stage discuss briefly the first and most famous attempt to test the Heckscher-Ohlin hypothesis, that of Leontief (1953), and some of the developments that have arisen from it. This test is of particular interest, not only because it cast doubt on a relationship that had generally been considered as self-evident, but because it engendered much theoretical and empirical research into the appropriate specification of the Heckscher-Ohlin model, and into alternative explanations of the determinants of trade based on deviations from the assumptions of that model.

Leontief had pioneered the use of input–output analysis. He used the matrix that he had developed for the United States for 1947 to examine the use of primary factors of production—labour and capital—in the exporting industries compared with import-competing industries. He measured the amount of capital and labour required to produce one million dollars' worth of exports and of import-competing goods. This yielded what is perhaps the most famous empirical result in the whole of economics:

Since the United States in 1947 was self-evidently capital-rich compared with the rest of the world, the anticipated result, in accordance with the Heckscher-Ohlin proposition, was that the United States would be exporting capital-intensive products. But these results—known as the Leontief paradox—suggest the opposite. To quote Leontief (1953):

an average million dollars' worth of our exports embodies considerably less capital and somewhat more labor than would be required to replace from domestic production an

Table 5.1. Factors required to produce $ million worth of exports and import replacement

Factors required to produce $ million worth of:		
	Exports	Import replacement
Capital		
(dollars in 1947 prices)	2.55 million	3.09 million
Labour (man-years)	182.3	170.0
Capital-labour ratio	$14 thousand per man-year	$18.2 thousand per man-year

equivalent amount of our competitive imports. America's participation in the international division of labor is based on its specialization on labor intensive, rather than capital intensive lines of production.

These results caused surprise and consternation in the economics profession. Leontief himself drew two conclusions: firstly, that the United States is characterized by a surplus of labour and shortage of capital compared with the rest of the world; and secondly, that protectionist policies in the United States benefit capital rather than labour. The first of these demonstrated Leontief's great faith in the Heckscher-Ohlin hypothesis, and the second is consistent with the Stolper-Samuelson proposition, if indeed the United States really is labour-abundant. Leontief reconciled his conclusion that the United States was labour-abundant with the apparent abundance of capital by suggesting that labour is not homogeneous, and that American labour needed to be augmented by a factor of three to account for its fundamental productivity. It is apparent that this is an *ad hoc* procedure, since it must be possible to find some multiplicative factor which, if applied to the American labour supply, would make that country labour-abundant. Nevertheless, Leontief's concept of the non-homogeneity of labour has proved fruitful when formulated in terms of the endowment of different types of labour or of human capital. This is discussed further below.

In the two decades following the publication of Leontief's results there were numerous other attempts to explain patterns of trade by the endowments of the basic factors of production, that is, labour and capital. Some of these involved studies of a single country's trade; others considered patterns of bilateral trade between pairs of countries. Overall the results have been very mixed, although they tend to improve when estimates of human capital are introduced. Nevertheless the impression remains that patterns of trade cannot generally be explained on the basis of the endowments of the broadly aggregated factors of production.[4]

The failure of the Heckscher-Ohlin model to provide a general explanation of patterns of trade has led to two separate approaches to the determinants of trade. The first involves explanations of trade based on deviations from the fundamental assumptions of the Heckscher-Ohlin model. Among the most important of these are trade based on imperfect competition and increasing returns to scale, and trade based upon differences between countries in the availability of technology. These are discussed in subsequent chapters. The second approach—described more fully in Chapter 8—is based upon a careful re-specification of the model. This usually involves an extension of the factors of production to include natural resources, different types of land, and labour with different levels of skills, as well as capital; and an extension of types of commodities corresponding to these factors. The extension of the dimension of the model involves theoretical complexities that are beyond the scope of this book; but the essence of the model is maintained in a formulation by Vanek (1968) which provides the basis for most

---

[4] Surveys and discussion of the early attempts to verify the Heckscher-Ohlin proposition are provided by Stern (1975) and Deardorff (1984).

modern attempts to estimate the relation between trade and factor endowments. The basic argument is as follows.

A particular country's factors of production are fully utilized either in the production of goods for domestic consumption or for export. Since tastes are assumed to be homothetic, and trade is assumed to have equalized commodity prices throughout the world, each country consumes a share of each commodity that is equal to that country's share in world income. But, under the assumptions of the model, all countries produce each good using the same factor proportions. Thus each country is indirectly consuming a share of the world's endowment of each factor of production that is equal to that country's share in world income. Therefore net trade has to account for the disparity in each country between its share of the world endowment of each factor and its share in world income. For example, the European Union might account for 20 per cent of world income. The implication of the model is that the EU will consume 20 per cent of coffee, wood products, consumer durables, and so on; and so will indirectly consume 20 per cent of the world's endowment of coffee bushes, trees, skilled labour, unskilled labour, capital, and so on. The EU's deficit relative to 20 per cent in endowment of trees, unskilled labour, and so on, and its surplus in endowment of skilled labour and capital, will be reflected in its net trade.

The link between net trade and factor endowments provides the basis for modern tests of the Heckscher-Ohlin model, but the results remain poor.[5] Leamer (1994) cites Bowen, Leamer and Sveikauskus (1987), 'The Heckscher-Ohlin model does poorly, but we do not have anything that does better.'

A fuller discussion of the modern empirical work, including a demonstration that the Leontief paradox itself is resolved by correct specification, is provided in Chapter 8 below.

5.4 Heckscher-Ohlin: concluding comments

We have seen that the Heckscher-Ohlin proposition does not stand up well to empirical verification; and it certainly does not provide a universal explanation of the pattern of world trade. This is not surprising, given the number of restrictive assumptions that are required for the proposition to be theoretically valid. The model does, however, provide insight into the relationship between patterns of output, factor endowments, factor prices, factor proportions, and commodity prices that are central to an understanding of international trade theory. Much of this theory and related empirical investigation is concerned with what happens when some of the restrictive assumptions are not satisfied. We have touched briefly upon some of these when we considered, for example, the implications of abandoning the assumption of no-factor-intensity reversal, or of incomplete specialization. Other parts of this book will consider the implications of differences

---

[5] See e.g. Bowen, Leamer, and Sveikauskus (1987).

in technology between countries, imperfect competition and increasing returns to scale, and non-homogeneity of the factors of production. The remainder of this chapter will discuss the specific factor model of international trade.

5.5 The specific factor model

We now consider a variation of the factor endowment approach to international trade in which—in contrast to the Heckscher-Ohlin model—some factors of production, for example fixed capital or natural resources, are not homogeneous and can only be used in, or are specific to, one industry. This approach—which is also known as the Ricardo-Viner model—can be seen as an extension of the Ricardian model, since it provides an explanation of differences in relative labour productivity between countries. It can also be seen as a short-run variation of the Heckscher-Ohlin model, since some factors which may be mobile between industries in the long run are fixed in the short run. This model provides rather obvious explanations of the pattern of trade, such as that Norway exports fish and oil because it has the appropriate natural resources (specific factors of production); but it has interesting implications for the effect of trade and trade-related policies upon the distribution of income, and it provides a useful framework for analysing a problem known as the Dutch Disease or de-industrialization, which concerns the detrimental impact of the development of a natural resource upon other sectors of an economy.

The basic model is quite simple, and is a variation of the neo-classical production model described in Chapter 3. There are two products, X and Y, each of which is produced using a specific factor (fixed capital or natural resource) which can only be used in one industry, and a homogeneous and mobile factor, labour, which is in fixed overall supply but is mobile between the industries. The specific factors are fully utilized in the industries in which they are fixed, and the labour is allocated so that the wage, which is the value of its marginal product, is the same in both industries. We are concerned with the same questions that were addressed in the context of the Heckscher-Ohlin model: the pattern of trade, whether or not trade causes the returns to the factors of production in the trading countries to converge, the effect of trade upon factor earnings within the countries, and the effect of an increase in the endowment of a factor of production upon output and factor prices.

5.5.1 Capital mobility: short vs. long run

We start by briefly noting the difference between production possibilities in the short run (when one factor is immobile) and the long run when all resources are mobile.

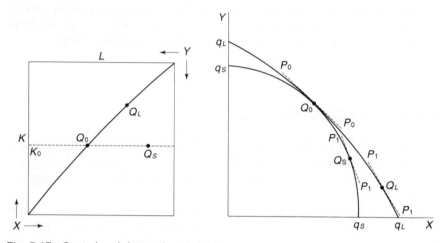

Fig. 5.17. Capital mobility and output: short vs. long run

The box diagram on the left panel of Figure 5.17 shows the endowments of capital and labour of an economy. In the long run both factors are mobile between the industries and can be allocated along the efficiency locus between points *x* and *y*, yielding a production possibility frontier $q_L q_L$, shown on the right side of the Figure. Suppose production is originally at the point Q_0 which is on the efficiency locus with a particular allocation of capital and labour. This is also a point on the long-run production-possibility frontier. But if capital is immobile in the short run, any change in production has to be achieved by the reallocation of labour only. The factor allocation line is horizontal through the original allocation point Q_0. This is clearly inferior to the long run allocation and involves greater increasing costs. Thus the short run production possibility frontier $q_s q_s$ lies inside that for the long run except at the original production point, and is more concave.

A rise in the relative price of *X*, from P_0 to P_1, will shift production from Q_0 to some point like Q_S in the short run, and then eventually to some greater supply response at Q_L as the allocation of capital adjusts in the long run. This is an illustration of the obvious point that elasticities (in this case a supply elasticity with respect to price) are higher in the long run than in the short run.[8]

This example also provides an illustration of how the pattern of trade can be determined by history or by the relative flexibility of countries. We can interpret these figures as representing two countries with similar factor endowments; but with one country having for some reason its capital stuck at some initial allocation, whereas the other country is a latecomer whose capital is uncommitted or is more flexible. It is the latter country that will be able to adjust most readily to a change in commodity prices, and this will be reflected in the pattern of trade. The

---

[8] There is likely to be an over-shooting in the short run adjustment of labour. The dynamics of such models are discussed in Neary (1978).

first-comer, or more rigid economy, is likely to find a higher proportion of its output in declining industries. This may be a problem that Western Europe is facing or will face relative to the rapidly growing and highly flexible economies of South-East Asia.

5.5.2 Production with one fixed and one variable factor

The standard neo-classical production function with constant returns to scale over two factors of production has positive but diminishing returns over one factor when the other is in fixed supply. This is shown in Figure 5.18.

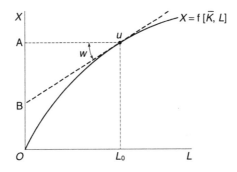

Fig. 5.18. Total output as a function of labour input

Total output of the product X when the capital is fixed is shown as a function of the input of the variable factor, that of labour. It can be seen that output increases but at a diminishing rate as the labour input increases; that is, the marginal product of labour is positive but diminishing. With labour input L_0, output of X will be OA. The marginal product of labour is shown by the slope of the tangency at U. On the standard assumption that labour is being paid its marginal product, this slope will equal the real wage w; and the total payment to labour will be $w.AU$, which is AB in the diagram. The rest of the output OB is therefore available as the total payment to the owners of the fixed factor K. An increase in the input of labour will be associated with an increase in output, a reduction in the wage rate (although the total wage payment might increase depending upon the specification of the production function), and an increase in the return to the owners of the fixed capital. The important point to understand in this model is that—as in the neo-classical model from which this is derived—the marginal productivity and thus the real wage of labour depends upon the availability of the other factor per unit of labour; and, conversely, the return to the fixed factor will depend upon the amount of labour with which it is being combined.

It should also be noted that a change in technology or a change in the availability of the fixed factor will give rise to a new total product curve. In particular, an increase in the endowment of the fixed factor will yield an increase in the total and marginal product of labour at any labour input.

We can derive a similar relationship for the output of the other good Y, which is assumed to be dependent upon the input of labour and of a specific factor T.

5.5.3 Equilibrium labour allocation

The standard diagrammatic treatment of the specific-factor model is to show the total labour endowment as the length of the horizontal axis, with the allocation of labour to each of the industries being measured from each end. The *value* of the marginal product of labour in each of the industries is shown as a function of the labour input on the vertical axis.

In Figure 5.19, allocation of the total available labour into the two industries is shown from the origins O_X and O_Y. The curves sloping down from each axis show the value of the marginal product of labour in each industry. It is important to note that the location of a curve could change either because of a change in the productivity of labour—perhaps because of a change in the endowment of the specific factor—or because of a change in the price of the commodity.

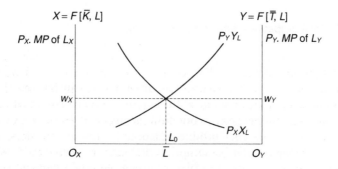

Fig. 5.19. Equilibrium labour allocation

It is being assumed that labour is mobile between the two sectors, and that it is being paid the value of its marginal product. Thus equilibrium allocation of labour requires that the value of the marginal product is the same in both industries. This occurs where the two value-of-marginal-product curves intersect. In the diagram, this is where the labour allocation is shown as L_0, and the wages w_X and w_Y are equalized.

We can use this basic diagram to derive the main results of the Specific Factor model.

5.5.4 Change in a commodity price

First, we consider what happens if there is some exogenously determined rise in the price of one of the commodities (Y). With unchanged endowment of the specific factor the physical product of labour relationship is unchanged, but the value of the marginal product of labour rises in proportion to the price increase. This is shown as an upward shift of the $P_Y Y_L$ curve in Figure 5.20.

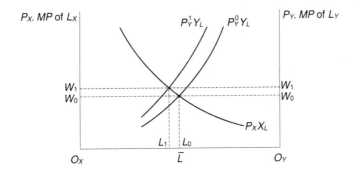

Fig. 5.20. An increase in the price of Y

At the initial labour allocation there would now be disequilibrium in the labour market, with the value of the marginal product of labour being less in the X industry than in the Y industry. This is corrected by a movement of labour from X into Y until equilibrium is restored at L_1. It is easy to see what has happened to wages from the diagram. They have risen in money terms from W_0 to W_1. This is an increase in terms of the product X whose price is unchanged, but it can be seen that it is less than the proportional shift in the yy curve, and so is less than the rise in the price of Y. Thus wages have fallen in terms of the product Y. The overall effect of the commodity price change on the return to the mobile factor is thus moderate, and depends upon the consumption pattern of the wage earners.

The effect of the commodity price change on the earnings of the specific factors is much stronger. Labour has moved away from the industry whose price has not changed. Thus the output of that product accruing to the owners of the factor of production specific to that industry has fallen; and since the price of Y has risen, the purchasing power of that income is further diminished. The owners of the factors of production specific to the industry whose price has risen, on the other hand, are doubly blessed. The returns in terms of the product accruing to the fixed factor has increased because the amount of labour working in that industry have increased. Furthermore, the price of that product has also increased, augmenting the purchasing power of the enhanced earnings. Thus the specific factor model has strong implications for the effect of a change of a commodity price on the returns to the specific factors, but a muted and ambiguous effect on the earnings of the mobile factor of production.

$$\hat{r}_y > \hat{P}_y > \hat{W} > \hat{P}_x > \hat{r}_x \tag{5.5}$$

Here the results are generalized. The circumflexes indicate the proportional changes, and r_x and r_y are the returns to the factors of production specific to the X and Y industries respectively.

5.5.5 Different endowments of a specific factor

It is apparent that a country that is relatively well endowed with the factor specific to a particular industry will have a comparative advantage in the production of that product. We illustrate this with a particular case which is used to demonstrate the 'Rybczynski' result, and which also shows that trade does not necessarily bring about an equalization of the prices of the factors of production.

Let us suppose that we have two countries, A and B, that have the same endowments of the mobile factor, labour, and of the factor K which is specific to the production of the good X; but that country B has a greater endowment than country A of the factor T which is specific to the production of the good Y. Furthermore, we are assuming that international trade has equalized the commodity prices in the two countries. We can then show the allocation of labour and the value of the marginal product of labour in the two countries on the same standard diagram. In Figure 5.21 the relationship between labour input and the marginal product of labour in the X industry is the same in both countries because they have the same endowment of the relevant specific factor. Thus the value of the marginal product of labour relationship for X is the same in both countries. In contrast, in the Y industry, the physical marginal product of labour in country B is greater than that in country A because the former country has a greater endowment of the

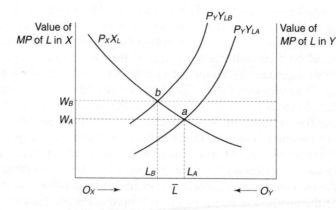

Fig. 5.21. An increase in the endowment of factor T

specific factor T. Thus the Y_{LB} curve showing the value of the marginal product of labour in the Y industry in country B lies above the Y_{LA} which shows the corresponding relationship in country A.

This figure looks the same as the preceding one; but there is an important difference in interpretation. In the previous diagram, the value of the marginal product of labour in the Y industry changed because the price of Y changed, with the factor endowment and the physical product of labour relationship being unchanged. In the present diagram, commodity prices are unchanged, whereas it is the physical productivity relationship that differs.

We can now interpret the result. Equilibrium in country A occurs at point a, with labour allocated at L_A, and with the wage W_A. Equilibrium in country B occurs at point b, with labour allocated at L_B, and with the wage W_B. The new pattern of output on the expanded production possibility frontier is shown in Figure 5.22 below.

5.5.6 Output and factor prices

In this particular case—in which we have fixed the scale of the example—the country well-endowed with the factor specific to the production of Y must be producing more of that product than does the other country, because it is utilizing more of both labour and of the specific factor in its production. On the other hand, it must be producing less of the product X because, although the application of the fixed factor is the same in the two countries, the allocation of labour to the production of X is less. If we relax the assumption that the countries are the same size with respect to endowment of capital and labour, we could generalize our result to the proposition that the country relatively well-endowed with a specific factor will produce relatively large amounts of the product that uses that factor. This generalization is left to the reader.

The particular case chosen is sufficient to demonstrate that, in contrast to the Heckscher-Ohlin model, the Specific factor model does not lead to an equalization of factor prices. From the figure we can see that wages are higher in both industries in country B than in country A. This is consistent with the better overall endowment of specific factors relative to that of labour in country B. The returns to the specific factor in the X industry will be higher in country A than in country B because there is more labour working in that industry per unit of the specific factor. The return per unit of the factor specific to the Y industry will be less in country B than in country A, because although the total amount of labour working in that industry is higher in country A, the amount of labour per unit of the specific factor will be less.

Although the full factor-price equalization does not occur in this model, we can use the results concerning the effects of a change in commodity prices derived above to identify the gainers and losers from trade, and also to see whether there is some partial convergence of the factor prices in the trading countries. Given similarity of demand conditions, the product relating to the abundant specific factor will be relatively cheap in each country in the absence of trade. International trade will therefore raise the price of the relevant product in each country, and will thereby raise the price of the relatively abundant specific factor. Thus trade causes some convergence internationally in the prices of the specific factors. The result that the abundant specific factor benefits and the scarce specific factor loses from trade is similar to the Stolper-Samuelson result derived in the discussion of the Heckscher-Ohlin model. But no such results can be determined for the mobile factor. We have seen that the effect of a commodity price change, and thus of trade, on wages (labour being the mobile factor) is indeterminate. Therefore nothing can be deduced about whether labour gains or loses, and there is no presumption that wages will come closer together internationally.

5.5.7 The Rybczynski result and de-industrialization

It will be recalled that the Rybczynski proposition concerns the effect of a change in the endowment of one of the factors of production, when the endowment of other factors and commodity prices remains unchanged. The case illustrated by Figure 5.21 that we have been discussing can be interpreted as such a situation. The country has had an increase in the endowment of the factor of production specific to the good *Y*, and this has resulted, at unchanged terms of trade, in an upward shift of the marginal product of labour curve. We have seen that this will result in an increase in the output of *Y*, and an absolute fall in the production of the other good. This is the Rybczynski result which is illustrated by a shift in the production possibility frontier in Figure 5.22.

The increase in the specific factor has increased the capacity to produce just the

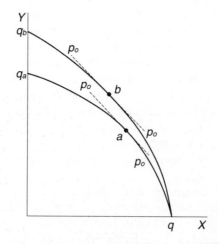

Fig. 5.22. Production possibilities with an increase in the factor specific to *Y*

good *Y*, so the production possibility frontier has expanded along the *Y* axis.[9] At unchanged commodity prices, represented by the constant slope of the tangents, production will shift from some point such as Q_a on qq_a to Q_b on qq_b where output of the good *X* has fallen. This corresponds to the shift in the equilibrium allocation of labour from point *a* to point *b* in Figure 5.22.

The effect of a change in the endowment of a specific factor on the pattern of output is very similar to that derived in the Heckscher-Ohlin model: the Rybczynski result holds. However, the implications for the returns to the factors of production are different. In the Heckscher-Ohlin case there is a one-to-one correspondence between factor and commodity prices, so that the assumption of unchanged terms of trade implies that there is no change in factor prices. But in the specific factor case we have seen that the increase in one specific factor will increase the returns to the mobile factor, and will reduce the returns to the specific factor that has not been augmented.

This model provides some insight into the de-industrialization or Dutch disease problem. Consider the implications of the development of North Sea oil in the United Kingdom during the early 1980s. This can be considered as an increase in a specific factor. The Rybczynski result predicts that mobile resources are drawn into the industry with the augmented specific factor, while output in the other sector declines. Of course, the North Sea oil case is more complex than our simple model. Among other considerations, there are a variety of factors of production, and unlike in the model, full employment was not maintained. Nevertheless, the impression of mobile resources of capital, management, and labour being attracted into the new sector while traditional industry declined is convincing. The model predicts that immobile factors stuck in declining sectors (such as manufacturing or coal) will face declining returns. In the case of the United Kingdom, the declining returns in the traditional sectors took the form of unemployment and unutilized capacity rather than falling factor prices; but here again, the general impression of deprivation for the fixed factors in the declining sectors is consistent with the model.

5.6 Summary

- If a country is relatively well-endowed with a certain factor of production, it will tend to export a good in which that factor is intensively employed. This prediction could be upset by reversals in demand, technology, or factor intensities.
- Under special conditions, international trade in goods could equalize the prices of factors across countries, but several considerations could prevent this.
- If a factor is immobile between a country's industries, its real reward is likely to differ between those industries. Trade raises the reward to a factor specific to exportables, and lowers the reward to a factor specific to importables.

[9] This is in contrast to the Heckscher-Ohlin case discussed above, where the increase in one factor increased the possibility of producing both goods, although that possibility was biased in favour of one of the goods.

6

TRADE AND TECHNOLOGY

....

6.1 Introduction

Technology has always been prominent in international trade theory. The Ricardian model of trade discussed in Chapter 2 can be interpreted as being based upon international differences in technology. Although the factor endowments model typically assumes that each country has access to the same technology, it can be fairly easily extended to allow for differences in technology. However, it has become apparent, particularly in the second half of the twentieth century, that technology is not static. Technological change can be incorporated into these models in the form of an increase in the efficiency of producing a given good. However, the implications of technological change are typically unclear. In the Ricardian model the effects hinge upon which sector experiences the technological improvement (see Chapter 2). What is important in the Heckscher-Ohlin model is not only the sector, but also whether the technological gain is capital-saving or labour-saving.

These models are, however, confined to considering once-and-for-all changes in technology. In this chapter we consider new theories of trade, developed in the 1960s and 1970s, which highlight the role of technology in creating *new* products and processes. These theories focus upon the dynamic, ongoing nature of technological change, and have helped to provide a link between the increasing expenditures on Research and Development (R&D) that were being observed in industrial countries and international trade. Expenditures on R&D in Europe and in other OECD countries have risen rapidly in real terms over the last three decades, and the shares of R&D in investment and GDP have increased.

In this chapter we discuss how differences in the rate of technological change across countries can give rise to trade, and why countries with a relatively high rate of technological progress will tend to export technology-intensive products. We then consider the effects of a widening or a narrowing in the technology gap between advanced and less-developed countries. An often-heard concern in Europe and other advanced industrial countries is that their technological lead over less advanced countries is diminishing, and that it is becoming increasingly difficult for firms in Europe to compete with lower-wage countries.

The vast majority of expenditure on R&D is undertaken in the advanced industrial countries: 96 per cent of the world total in 1990 (UNESCO 1993). Although new products and processes are often first produced in the innovating countries, the relevant technology may diffuse overseas, so that the location of production will shift to lower-cost locations. We consider models of this North-South product cycle, and show that there will be an incentive for the advanced, innovating countries to seek to reduce the diffusion of new technology to less-developed countries. This has been an important issue at the Uruguay Round of GATT negotiations. Economic theory, however, provides little support for the demand of the advanced countries, made during these trade negotiations, that there should be worldwide constraints on the diffusion of new ideas to the developing countries.

6.2 The technology gap model

The explicit treatment of technology as a factor determining trade flows was first made by Posner (1961). His technology-gap theory asserted that new products and processes are continually being developed, and that for a period of time the country which is host to a particular invention or innovation will have a technological lead over other countries. This country will be able to export the good concerned even though it may not have an apparent comparative advantage in terms of being well-endowed in the factors used intensively in the production of the good. Trade occurs because the time it takes before the new good is demanded in other countries (the demand gap) is less than the time it takes for the new technology to be implemented in production abroad (the imitation gap). The imitation gap will arise if patents protect the innovation or if it takes time to learn how to apply the new process or produce the new good.

   This theory thus predicts that trade will result from disparities between countries in the rate and nature of innovation. Countries which have a persistently fast rate of innovation will tend to export technologically advanced goods to countries with slower rates of innovation in return for more standardized, labour-intensive goods. Countries which have similar rates of innovation will also trade with each other, since the nature of innovations, the new goods and processes that are developed, will differ between countries. This provides an explanation for trade between countries with similar factor endowments and in similar products (intra-industry trade).

   Innovation results from R&D activities which are intensive in the use of skilled labour. Hence, countries relatively well-endowed in highly trained and educated labour will tend to be more innovative. Further, innovators may need to be aware of demand conditions and hence be close to the market into which the new product is first introduced. New products embodying the most recent technological advances will be more easily introduced into markets in wealthy countries. These considerations all suggest that rich, developed countries will exhibit the fastest rates of innovation.

A country with a rapid rate of innovation will exhibit a high technological intensity in their exports; rich countries will tend to export technologically advanced products. However, as Krugman (1986) stresses, it is important to recognize that causation runs from technological change to export structure. There is nothing in this theory to support the idea that actively promoting industries producing high-technology products, as policy-makers in Western countries are wont to do, will stimulate growth. The rising share of high-technology products in an advanced country's exports is, as Krugman says, 'a symptom of its progress, not a cause'.

Posner argued that technological leaders will always be in a favourable position to consolidate and extend their initial advantage. Innovations typically lead to further advances in technology. Hufbauer (1970) suggests, along similar lines, that the advantage may be preserved by consumer loyalty to the new product and lower production costs emanating from 'learning by doing'. This has led to the argument that trade based upon technological innovation may be relatively unfavourable to those countries which are the least technologically advanced.

However, an apparent feature of the recent development of the world economy has been the narrowing in the technological lead of the industrial countries. Krugman (1986) presents a formal model of trade based upon differences in technology. Assume that there is one factor of production, labour, and that for each good, z, there is a best-practice technique of production defined in terms of labour requirement, $a^*(z)$. With technological change these best practices are continually improving, so that $a^*(z)$ falls over time such that $a^*(z) = e^{-g(z)t}$. The rate of improvement in best-practice technique, $g(z)$, differs across industries, and goods can therefore be ranked by technological intensity.

Countries, too, can be ranked by their level of technology, in terms of the extent to which (uniformly across industries) they lag behind the best practice techniques. Let λ_I and λ_J be the technological lag in number of years of two countries, I and J, and let $\lambda_I < \lambda_J$. Thus, country I will be able to produce all goods with less labour input than country J since

$$a_I(z) = e^{-g(z)(t-\lambda_I)} < a_J(z) = e^{-g(z)(t-\lambda_J)} \tag{6.1}$$

for all z and t. Hence I, the more technologically advanced country, will have an absolute advantage in all products. However, I's comparative advantage will be in the goods with greater technological intensity, since the gap in technology between countries matters least for goods which experience slow technical progress.

So, in Krugman's model, there is a ladder of countries, with the more technologically advanced on the highest rungs, and a scale of goods, in which those higher on the scale experience faster technological progress. Countries further up the ladder will have higher wages; if a country with inferior technology had higher wages it would not have a cost advantage in the production of any products.

Assume for simplicity that there are just two countries, one technologically advanced and the other, country 2, relatively technologically backward. Assume also that there are identical Cobb-Douglas preferences in each country. This means that a constant proportion of expenditure will be spent on each good. Given a continuum of goods (z) there will be a marginal good (z^*) for which the costs of production are equal in both countries. Since country 1 is more technologically advanced, its labour will be more productive, and at the margin this productivity advantage will determine the wage rate

$$\frac{w_1}{w_2} = \frac{a_2(z^*)}{a_1(z^*)} \tag{6.2}$$

Thus country 1 will produce all goods $z > z^*$, and country 2 will produce goods $z < z^*$.

Now consider the effects of an exogenous improvement in the technology of the rich, advanced country. This increases the technological gap in all industries, but the consequent increase in productivity is greatest for goods with higher technology intensity. The relative wage of the rich country rises, and the number of products it produces increases, and hence the range of products produced by the less advanced country declines. The rich country unambiguously gains, the real wage rises in terms of all products; in terms of those products produced in country 1 because of the rise in productivity, in terms of those produced in country 2 because of the increase in the relative wage, and in terms of those previously produced in country 2 and now produced more cheaply in country 1 (these products would have become cheaper in terms of country 1's labour had their production remained abroad, because of the rise in the relative wage, but this is then further reinforced by the change to the lower-cost location).

The less technologically advanced country suffers from an adverse change in the relative wage, and becomes more specialized in the least technology-intensive goods. However, the country still gains, since there is a rise in purchasing power. The real wage in terms of products produced domestically is unchanged. However, the prices of goods traditionally purchased from country 1 fall. This arises because the increase in the relative wage for country 1 is less than the rise in the productivity of the marginal good z^*. As can be seen from equation 6.2, $a_1(z^*)$ rises but the number of goods produced by country 1 also increases, so that the new relative wage is determined by a product which is less than z^* on the scale of goods. Since the productivity increase is greater for all goods $z > z^*$, the prices of all goods traditionally produced by country 1 decline. In addition, those goods which country 2 previously produced can now be purchased more cheaply from abroad, and so the real wage must rise.

A narrowing of the technology gap in terms of an exogenous increase in the technological capability of the less advanced country benefits the latter country. The relative wage moves in its favour, and more goods of higher technology-intensity are produced. The rich country may, however, lose. The real wage in terms of goods whose production remains in country 1 is unchanged. The real wage rises for the goods previously produced in 1 but which are now available more cheaply from country 2. However, the ability to purchase goods traditionally produced in country 2 will fall. This occurs because the rise in the relative wage for country 2 will exceed the increase in its productivity. It is possible that, if the gap in technology is small, any further narrowing will lead to an overall decline in welfare for the advanced country; the gain from greater purchasing power over medium-technology products, those previously produced domestically, will be unable to cover the loss from lower purchasing power over the low-technology products typically imported from the less advanced country. This will encourage the advanced country to adopt policies to maintain its technological advantage, the stimulation of innovation, and possibly constraints upon the dissemination of technological information.

6.3 The product cycle theory

The technology-gap theory tells us why the rate of innovation is likely to be fastest in rich, developed countries. However, it cannot explain why production of the new good will take place, at least initially, in the innovating country. Why is the new innovation not exploited in the least-cost location? Hirsch (1967) and Vernon (1966) provided reasons as to why this may be so. Hirsch suggests that the development and initial production of new products requires large amounts of skilled labour, which are most likely to be found in the country in which the innovation originated. The product-cycle theory developed by Vernon starts from the assumption that all firms in advanced countries have access to the same technological know-how, but that the application of such knowledge requires entrepreneurs, who are not equally conscious of or responsive to the available opportunities. Vernon argued that awareness of and reaction to the possibilities of launching new products will be determined by ease of communication with the market, which is in turn a function of geographical proximity. Vernon also stressed the need for flexibility in the use of inputs in the initial production runs. Subsequent work has emphasized the importance of 'learning by doing' in the early stages of the life of a product, and that the innovating country is likely to have a comparative advantage in learning.

Thus, initial production of a new product will take place in the home economy, where close contact with consumers and specialist suppliers of inputs into the production process can be easily maintained. High-technology products will be first produced in high-income countries where the opportunities for their development will be most apparent. The new product is likely to be differentiated by consumers from existing goods in the market and hence will convey a degree of monopoly power to its producers. With weak competition, price may be set with little reference to the production costs of rival firms.

This first stage of the product cycle is illustrated in Figure 6.1 in terms of exports and imports. The product is introduced at time t_0, and initially the good is produced and sold only in the innovating country. Demand for the product in other countries of similar levels of income will soon emerge, and the innovating country will export the good. There may also be a demand for the product by wealthy individuals in less developed countries.

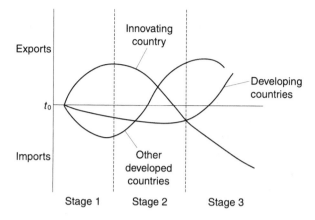

Fig. 6.1. The product cycle

As demand expands, the product becomes more standardized, making available economies of scale through mass production. Physical capital is likely to replace human capital as the most intensively used factor of production. This occurs during the second stage of the product cycle, and leads to heightened concern over production costs relative to rival firms. If factor price differences outweigh the costs of exporting to foreign markets an incentive may arise to exploit lower-cost, overseas locations. Since the factor input requirements will probably remain similar to those of production in the innovating country, output will be relocated to other developed countries but having lower factor prices. If the innovation is easily imitated, production may move overseas even in the absence of foreign investment, as local entrepreneurs become aware of the opportunities to commence production. Thus, as the use of physical capital in production rises, comparative advantage shifts away from the innovating country to other developed countries.

During stage 2, as shown in Figure 6.1, the volume of exports of the innovating country declines as production is established overseas. Eventually this country may become a net importer of the good, which now embodies a relatively high level of physical capital.

The final stage of the product cycle occurs if the technology used in production of the good becomes completely standardized. The importance of unskilled labour in the production process rises which, together with a more fierce competitive environment, leads to cost considerations being paramount. Firms in the innovating country may establish factories in low-wage developing countries. Again, if the technology is universally available, then activity may become centred on developing countries even in the absence of overseas investment by firms in developed countries. As shown in Figure 6.1, during this stage the developing countries may become net exporters of the product. It is probable that at some time during this stage, or earlier, a new product will be innovated and a new cycle will commence. In the product cycle the mix of inputs required to produce the product changes, from the intensive use of human capital in the first stage, to physical capital in the second stage, and to unskilled labour in the final stage. These changes in input requirements shift comparative advantage away from the original innovator to similar developed countries and thence to developing countries. In the final stage the pattern of trade would be consistent with that predicted by the Heckscher-Ohlin theory.

Vernon based his theory on the experience of the United States in the immediate postwar period, a time when there were significant differences in factor costs between the United States and the most advanced countries in Europe. Since that time these differences have narrowed markedly so that the basis for the second stage of the product cycle appears to have been removed.

Further, massive improvements in communications and the spread of global networks of multinational enterprises have reduced the need for close physical contact between engineers, plant managers, and salespersons. This, together with the ability of multinationals to scan the world to observe demand and cost conditions overseas, suggests that from the outset production of a new good by a multinational firm will be located in the country offering the most attractive factor prices. In this case trade is immediately consistent with a Heckscher-Ohlin explanation.

Vernon, in a later article (1979), discussed these developments but maintained that the theory could still be relevant to the process by which small firms move towards exporting and then investment in overseas production facilities. He also contended that the product cycle still has considerable power in explaining trade between developed and developing countries, often referred to as North-South trade.

In the context of trade between rich and poor countries, Krugman (1979b) formalized the product cycle in a simple one-factor (labour), two-region (North and South) general equilibrium model. The use of a formal model allows the welfare implications of technological innovation in developed countries and technology transfer to developing countries, the key features of the product cycle, to be clearly identified.

The assumption of a single factor of production in each region rules out Heckscher-Ohlin explanations of the determinants of trade. In addition, it is assumed that the cost conditions for the production of each of n goods are the same in each region, so that the Ricardian model of trade is not relevant. This allows attention to be focused upon technological change as the determinant of trade.

In this model, although there are many goods, they can be classified into two types, old and new. The technology used to produce old goods is universally available. Assuming wages are higher in the North, $(w_N > w_S)$ ensures that old goods will only be produced in the South. New goods will only be produced in the North for the reasons expounded by Vernon. Thus, n_N is the number of goods produced in the North, which is equivalent to the number of new goods, and n_S is the number of goods produced in the South or, equivalently, the number of old goods.

The utility function, identical for all consumers, is defined over both old and new goods and is of the Dixit-Stiglitz form

$$U = \left[\sum_{i=1}^{n} q_i^{\alpha} \right]^{\frac{1}{\alpha}} \tag{6.3}$$

where $0 < \alpha < 1$, q_i is the quantity of consumption of good i, and n is the total number of available goods ($n = n_N + n_S$). The key feature of this utility function is that, with given income, welfare will rise following an increase in the overall quantity of goods currently consumed and/or following an addition to the number of goods consumed. That is to say, the consumers like variety. Assuming that perfectly competitive conditions prevail, and normalizing so that a unit of labour produces one unit of a good, then the price of any good produced in the North or South will equal the wage rate in that region ($p_N = w_N$, $p_S = w_S$). All goods produced in the North will have the same price, and all Southern-produced goods will have the same price. The utility function implies that goods with the same price will be consumed in the same quantity, and so the model can be developed in terms of the representative Northern good and the representative Southern good.

The demand for new goods relative to that for old goods will be determined only by relative prices and hence relative wage-rates

$$\frac{q_N}{q_S} = \left(\frac{p_N}{p_S} \right)^{-\left(\frac{1}{1-\alpha} \right)} = \left(\frac{w_N}{w_S} \right)^{-\left(\frac{1}{1-\alpha} \right)} \tag{6.4}$$

where q_N and q_S are the consumption of any good produced in the North and South respectively. The demand for labour (l) in each region will be determined by the number of goods produced and the quantity of output of each good

$$\frac{l_N}{l_S} = \frac{n_N q_N}{n_S q_S} = \left(\frac{n_N}{n_S} \right) \left(\frac{w_N}{w_S} \right)^{-\left(\frac{1}{1-\alpha} \right)} \tag{6.5}$$

which upon rearrangement gives

$$\frac{w_N}{w_S} = \left(\frac{n_N}{n_S} \right)^{1-\alpha} \left(\frac{l_N}{l_S} \right)^{-(1-\alpha)} \tag{6.6}$$

showing that the wage in the rich North relative to that in the poorer South depends upon the number of new products that are introduced, which is determined by technological innovation, and the number of old products produced in the South, the result of technology transfer.

So, in this model technological innovation results entirely in an increase in the number of products (it does not raise the productivity of the production of existing goods), whilst technology transfer, the process by which new products become old products and amenable to production in the South, leaves the total number of products available unchanged. For simplicity assume that innovation (ι) is a constant proportion of the total number of goods currently produced

$$\Delta n = \iota n \tag{6.7}$$

where technology transfer (τ) is modelled as the average time it takes for imitation to occur, thus

$$\Delta n_S = \tau n_N \tag{6.8}$$

and therefore

$$\Delta n_N = \iota n - \tau n_N \tag{6.9}$$

In equilibrium in this model there will be a stable share of new products in the total number of goods

$$\frac{n_N}{n} = \frac{\iota}{\iota + \tau} \tag{6.10}$$

and so the number of products produced in the North relative to the number of products produced in the South, and given equation (4) the relative wage in the North, will be determined by the rate of innovation compared with the rate of technology transfer

$$\frac{n_N}{n_S} = \frac{\iota}{\tau} \tag{6.11}$$

Thus, the North always exports new, high-technology products in exchange for products produced in the lower-wage South with standardized technology. However, the composition of such trade is continually changing. Each good goes through a product cycle, being produced and exported first by the North and then, after technology diffusion, by the South.

A rise in innovation leads to an increase in the number of products being produced. A rise in technology transfer entails that goods previously produced in the high-wage North are now produced in the low-wage South; there is a saving of resources for the production of a given amount of goods. Hence an increase in either innovation or technology transfer will raise global economic efficiency; there is an increase in world output for a given amount of factor resources.

From a distributional point of view an increase in ι benefits the North; consumers benefit from the increase in the variety of goods available for consumption, and, because the ratio of new to old goods rises, there is an increase in the relative wage of Northern labour and a favourable movement in the terms of trade of the North. Consumers in the South also gain from the greater number of products, but this is offset by the adverse movement in the wage and, hence, terms of trade relative to the North. In Krugman's model the choice of utility function ensures that the overall effect of a rise in the rate of innovation is positive for the South. However, in a more general model it is quite possible that the effect on welfare in the South could be negative.

A rise in technology transfer has no effect upon the number of goods produced, but reduces the ratio of new goods to old goods with a corresponding fall in the wage of Northern labour relative to that of Southern labour. The terms of trade therefore move in favour of the South and against the North. The North may become worse off. Changes in the *rates* of innovation and technology transfer by changing the ratio of new goods to old goods will have analogous effects to those of once-and-for-all increases just described, a rise in the number of products produced in a region relative to the number produced elsewhere leads to an improvement in that region's terms of trade.

So, new products and new industries are continually emerging in the North as a result of technological innovation. The monopoly of the North in producing new products is reflected in relatively higher wages than in the South. At the same time this monopoly is continually eroded by technological transfer, with the result that industries in the North will always be disappearing due to the subsequent low-wage competition from the South. From a global efficiency point of view, this decline of industries in the North is beneficial. But, for a given rate of technology transfer, there must be constant innovation of new products in the North if living standards are to be maintained. Any acceleration in the rate at which new techniques pass from the North to the South may leave workers in the richer countries worse off in absolute terms. Thus, the two regions will take completely opposite views as to the desirability of technology diffusion.

Dollar (1986) extends this model by allowing the rate of technology transfer to depend upon the difference in production costs between the North and the South. There is also allowance for capital as an additional factor of production which is mobile between the North and South. In Krugman's model an increase in the size of the labour force in the South, by raising the demand for products produced in the North whilst leaving supply in the North unaltered, will improve the terms of trade for the North and the wages of Northern workers. In Dollar's model this effect occurs in the short run, but over the longer run the increase in relative production costs in the North leads to a faster rate of technology diffusion and the migration of capital to the South. This alters supply conditions in the North and leads to lower wages for Northern workers. Thus, increases in population in developing countries will lead eventually to a decline in the demand for labour in industrial countries by stimulating a faster flow of technology to low-wage countries.

This, Dollar argues, is consistent with recent experience. Population growth in developing countries in the 1960s initially led to greater demand for the products produced in rich countries. In the 1980s and 1990s industries in the North, such as steel, textiles, footwear, and cars have been unable to compete with products produced in low-wage developing countries. However, new products and new industries have not been generated at a pace fast enough to employ all of the workers displaced by the decline of old industries in the rich countries. This is typical of European countries, and provides one of the reasons for the consistently high unemployment rates that are observed. A commonly heard complaint in the EU (and the United States) is the perceived inability of European firms to compete with firms from low-wage economies.

Any attempt to maintain old industries in the North via further enforced cuts in wages relative to those in the South would not be successful in this model. As Dollar notes, innovation in the North is the factor that 'enables and in fact *requires* that workers in the North earn a premium over wages in the South'. The continual erosion of this wage premium would ultimately reverse the pattern of production, and lead to innovative activity shifting to the (former) South.

A common response in Europe to the issue of competition from low-wage economies has been the use of trade restrictions and industrial policies, such as sector-specific subsidies. The iron and steel industries, footwear, and textiles and clothing are typical in this respect. These policies have, in general, not been designed to facilitate the orderly adjustment of resources out of these industries, but rather, have attempted to support the existing level of activity. However, the models discussed here provide no support for the idea that intervention can provide conditions under which firms in a technologically mature industry in industrial countries can regain international competitiveness.

Traditionally, industrial and trade policies in Europe have been targeted at particular sectors. Under the implicit assumption that there is sufficient information to identify which products should be produced and how this should be done, industrial and trade policies have been formulated in terms of outputs, and have sought to channel resources into the favoured industries. The assumption of perfect knowledge cannot be supported when innovation is the principal source of comparative advantage. Now there is uncertainty about the outcomes, since it is impossible to predict which techniques and products will be introduced, let alone the firms that will produce them. In such an environment, 'targeting specific firms or even industries becomes increasingly wrought with danger' (Audretsch 1995). Rather, in these conditions policies should be aimed at the factors responsible for innovation and the generation of new ideas.

6.4 Trade related intellectual property rights

Countries in the North may also try to stem the diffusion of new technology overseas. In the models discussed above, the two regions will take diametrically opposite views of the desirability of technology diffusion. Indeed, the protection of intellectual property rights has been one of the 'new issues', together with trade in services and international investment, included in the recent Uruguay Round GATT agreement. 'Trade Related Intellectual Property' issues (TRIPs) were included in the round at the insistence of the richer countries, primarily the European Union, the US, and Japan. These countries were anxious to prevent products and processes developed domestically being copied by other countries, principally developing countries, who did not adhere to the same standards of intellectual property protection as in the richer countries. Imitation rather than overseas production by the Northern innovator has become the principal vehicle for the transfer of technology from North to South (Grossman and Helpman

1993). The wealthy countries even argued that it was also in the interests of developing countries themselves that they ensure the greater protection of the intellectual property rights of Northern firms and so reduce the rate of technology diffusion. As we shall see, there is, however, very little support from economic theory for such an assertion.

Innovation generates knowledge, something which is different from that previously available. Knowledge typically has the characteristics of a public good; once it has been produced it can be used by any individual or firm at a very low additional cost. Efficiency will be maximized by the widest dissemination of new ideas. Conflict arises, since the greater the diffusion of new ideas the smaller the benefits to the originators, and the lower the return to the investment in research and development which generates the new ideas in the form of new processes or products. Without some form of protection of intellectual property rights there will be little incentive to innovate. Such protection, in the form of patents, copyright, and trademarks, brings the benefit of a higher rate of innovation and thus a greater range of products and processes in the future. There is, however, a cost in terms of the granting of a monopoly to the innovating firm. For a new product this entails that consumption will not be at the optimum level; a smaller quantity will be sold at a higher price than if the new technology were more widely available and the market for the product more competitive.

Thus, there are benefits and costs of the protection of intellectual property. In many countries this is implicitly recognized by the granting of temporary protection to try to achieve a balance between the benefits to consumers from having access to new products and the incentives to generate these new products. In the European Union, for example, patent protection is granted for twenty years (twenty-five for pharmaceuticals).

In an international context there are also costs and benefits from extending the protection of intellectual property on a geographical basis. Assume that there is no innovative activity in the South, and that, in the absence of the protection of intellectual property rights, there will be a competitive supply of the product from Southern producers. These are not unreasonable assumptions. The costless diffusion of new technology to developing countries may dissuade investment in innovative activities in the developed countries, and so reduce the number of new products available to consumers in the South. But, on the other hand, intellectual property protection in Southern markets increases the market power of Northern firms in those markets. Southern consumers will enjoy a lower level of consumer surplus, since the quantity of consumption will be smaller than if the new product were not protected. This loss of consumer surplus will always exceed the increase in the Northern firm's profits, thus generating a deadweight loss, or inefficiency, for the world economy.

Deardorff (1990) shows that for new products there is no reason to expect that, from a global point of view, universal protection of intellectual property is optimal. The costs of extending such protection to all countries will exceed the benefits. This is because the marginal benefits of additional protection of intellectual property decline as the number of countries covered increases. The benefits from granting protection in an additional market emanate from the new inventions that are now produced that were not previously profitable to produce. The greater the size of the market already protected, the larger the number of products already invented and, since the most profitable inventions will be exploited first, the relatively less beneficial will be the remaining inventions.

The costs of protecting the additional market are given by the difference between the loss in consumer surplus from greater monopoly power over the protected goods and the increase in the firms' profits for these products. As more markets are covered by protection, and more inventions are made profitable, more products become subject to monopoly pricing and the size of the global deadweight loss will rise. So, if the number of inventions that have already been stimulated by protection of intellectual property is high, then it is likely that the overall effect on global welfare of extending such protection still further so as to encourage some less desirable inventions will be negative. Deardorff concludes that 'there is a strong presumption in favour of the optimal geographic scope for patent protection being something less than the entire world'.

But where should protection of intellectual property stop? Equity arguments suggest that the poorest countries should be excluded. As we have seen, patent protection by reducing consumer surplus and raising monopoly profits acts to transfer income from consumers in the protected market to the firms which introduce the invention, these typically being based in the rich, developed countries. Thus, welfare will be transferred from the poor to the rich if protection of intellectual property is extended to all countries. Deardorff states strongly that the poorest countries should be excluded.

Chin and Grossman (1990) come to a similar conclusion in the case of process innovations. In an explicit North-South model they show that, in general, welfare in the South will be higher in the absence of protection of the intellectual property rights of the Northern innovator. Only in the unlikely case of a market being dominated by demand in the South and substantial cost savings being generated by innovation will the protection of intellectual property potentially benefit the South. From a global point of view the effect of innovation on production costs is crucial. For innovations which greatly enhance productivity the protection of intellectual property in the South ensures a higher level of world welfare; the North could conceivably compensate the South for maintaining the protection of intellectual property and still be better off itself. For innovations which have small effects upon productivity, world welfare is higher when there is the fullest diffusion of technology.

Diwan and Rodrik (1991) argue that if the North and South have different technological needs then protection of intellectual property in the South may encourage innovations by Northern firms which are particularly appropriate to the South. When the two regions have similar preferences for technology, then again the South has no incentive to provide protection of intellectual property.

The TRIPs agreement will require developing countries to adopt minimum standards of protection of intellectual property. The way in which the agreement is enforced and therefore its effectiveness will not become immediately apparent, since there are long transitional arrangements for developing countries. The least-developed countries have eleven years from the entry into force of the World Trade Organization (WTO) to fully comply with the obligations of the TRIPs agreement. Nevertheless, the models discussed here suggest that the agreement will be to the detriment of welfare in the poorest countries and, because of its universal coverage, be economically harmful from the global perspective.

It has been argued that lack of protection of intellectual property discourages multinational firms from investing in developing countries. If this is the case, the TRIPs agreement will stimulate overseas investment in developing countries. There is, however, no strong evidence that the standard of protection of intellectual property has a significant effect upon foreign investment flows. Indeed, Ferrantino (1993) finds evidence to suggest that intra-firm trade tends to be higher for countries with weak protection of intellectual property. Multinational firms prefer to undertake foreign direct investment in countries with weak protection of intellectual property, rather than trade so as to maintain control over their technological information. In this case, a higher standard of protection of intellectual property in developing countries may reduce the incentives of multinationals to invest in these countries.

6.5 Conclusions

In this chapter we have considered how technology can determine the pattern of trade, and how the narrowing of technology gaps and the increasing diffusion of technology influence welfare in different parts of the world. Differences in the nature and the rate of innovation across countries generate scope for beneficial trade. Technologically advanced countries will export technology intensive goods in exchange for less sophisticated goods from technologically backward countries. Advanced countries may also trade amongst themselves, even though they have similar rates of innovation, because the nature of innovation, in terms of the products and processes that it generates, will vary between countries. An increase in the technology of advanced countries will lead to benefits for all countries. A reduction in the technology gap between rich and poor countries will benefit the latter, but may reduce real incomes in the advanced countries.

Technology also plays a central role in explaining how the location of production of a product can change during the product's lifetime. Rich, advanced countries are the source of innovations, and are the initial place of production, since skilled labour inputs and proximity to the market are crucial. As the product becomes standardized, and unskilled labour becomes more important, it may become amenable to production in low-cost locations. This shift in production is more likely to occur if the technology required is widely available.

Constraints upon the diffusion of technology to the low-wage, developing countries, by means of the protection of intellectual property rights, encourage innovation and increase the monopoly power of the innovating firms. This increase in monopoly power is to the detriment of consumers. There is a transfer of welfare from the poor South to the rich North and, under the most plausible of conditions, an overall loss to the world economy.

Within European countries there is a perception by some that low-wage competition from developing countries has been a principal cause of the historically high levels of unemployment experienced in most countries during the 1980s and 1990s. It is also believed that the transfer of Western technology and ideas has contributed to the ability of firms in these developing countries to out-compete rival European firms. This is an issue to which we shall return in Chapter 14, when we look at the links between trade and jobs and trade and wages. However, the analysis presented here suggests that the temptation to protect European firms in their home market should be avoided. Instead, the authorities should ensure that domestic conditions are most conducive to technological innovation and advance.

The models discussed in this chapter treat the rate of innovation as being exogenously determined. The rate of imitation is either taken to be exogenous or is determined in a rather *ad hoc* manner, as in Dollar's model. Recently, attention has focused upon the factors which influence the rate of innovation and the rate of technology transfer. Economic models have been developed which allow for the endogenous determination of innovation and imitation. These models, which are to be discussed in Chapter 12, show how the rate of innovation affects the rate of growth and international trade and also how trade performance may stimulate innovation and hence growth.

6.6 Summary

- Countries where innovation is rapid tend to export newly invented, capital-intensive products, importing standardized, older, labour-intensive products from countries where innovation is limited or absent.
- Given time, as a product ages, production may switch abroad to take advantage of lower labour costs. Technological gaps between advanced and developing countries may decline with imitation and diffusion, or widen with further learning.
- Protecting the intellectual property rights of innovating firms in rich 'northern' countries brings benefits and costs; allowing imitation by less advanced 'southern' firms need not lower northern growth.

INTERNATIONAL TRADE
AND IMPERFECT COMPETITION

7.1 Introduction

Recent years have witnessed a major intellectual revolution in economists' analysis of international trade. It had been customary for trade to be studied in a perfectly competitive framework. While it is true that international trade tends to make product markets *more* competitive, it does not follow that they will be perfectly competitive. Furthermore, the comparison between free trade and no trade must recognize the fact that autarky will inevitably display features of imperfect competition, even if free trade does not.

Economists have also observed that many countries both export and import the same kinds of goods. France exports cars and wine and steel and computers to Germany, and Germany exports these goods to France. In a Ricardian or Heckscher-Ohlin framework such a phenomenon is impossible. Imperfect competition could, however, help to explain it.

The organization of this chapter is as follows. Section 7.2 explores oligopoly in international trade. Oligopoly is one of the two major kinds of imperfect competition, which stresses the fewness of the number of producers, and their resulting interdependence. In Section 7.3 attention shifts to monopolistic competition, where the emphasis is on product differentiation. Monopolistic competition can arise in two forms: it may be that consumers enjoy the variety afforded by different commodities, or it may be consumers who are differentiated in their preferences between such goods. Section 7.3.1 looks at the first case, and Section 7.3.2 the second.

7.2 Oligopoly in trade

Let us begin with a domestic profit-maximizing monopolist, only selling into the home market. For simplicity, suppose that the domestic demand curve is linear and that the firm's marginal cost is horizontal, at a value of c. The price will lie halfway between c and the vertical intercept of the demand curve, which we can call a. The home firm will produce just half of the output that would be observed under perfect competition (when the price would equal c).

What can be said about social welfare at this point? The simplest, although not uncontroversial assumption to make is that this can be defined, for each product, as the sum of three elements: profits earned by the home firm (since marginal cost is horizontal, this is the only form of producers' surplus); domestic consumers' surplus; and net income, if any, received by the state as a result of tax policies. In our case, the third of these is zero. If output is x, profit for the home firm $= (p - c)x$ and the consumers' surplus equals $[(a - p)/2]\, x$. These are shown in Figure 7.1 by areas α and β respectively. Since $p = (a + c)/2$, α and β sum to $x\{[(a - c)/2] + [(a - c)/4]\} = 3x(a - c)/4$.

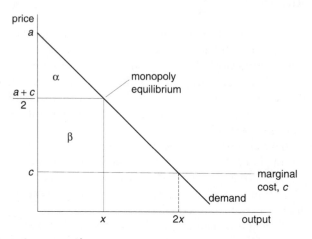

Fig. 7.1. Domestic monopoly

Now imagine that the home market is invaded by a foreign firm, which also has a marginal cost of c. To explore what happens next, we need to look at how they compete. There are various possibilities; we consider three.

The first is that they collude, to maximize joint profit, splitting the market between them. The argument in favour of this is that the two firms have a common interest in maximizing what the two of them can earn, and, since this is so, if profit is their aim, they ought to recognize and exploit this common interest to the full. In this collusion case, the price does not budge at all. Total output, of the two firms together, stays at x. The consumers do not benefit from any increase in surplus. But the home firm's profit halves. Since social welfare, by assumption, places no weight on profits earned by foreigners, this reduction in home profits (from $(p - c)x = [(a - c)/2]x$ to half that) cuts social welfare from $[3(x/4)](a - c)$ to $(x/2)(a - c)$. There is an unambiguous social welfare loss. Social welfare falls by one third.

The second possibility is that the two firms compete as vigorously as possible with each other. Each sets its price, let us suppose, to maximize its profit, taking the other's price as given. This is known as *Bertrand Competition*. What happens? Each firm has an incentive to undercut the other. Assuming that consumers are perfectly informed, and free to switch at no cost and at once, a firm can steal all its rival's profit and business by setting its price just a little bit below his. Of course, both can play this game. The end result, known as the Bertrand paradox, is that price drops down to marginal cost, c. It will not go below this, since no-one gains from selling at a loss; but price cannot survive above c because of the incentive to undercut.

Social welfare in this Bertrand case goes up sharply. Total output doubles, from x to $2x$, since the new price is marginal cost. There is no profit for either firm now. But consumers' surplus swells to $(a-c)x$. This represents a gain in social welfare, as far as this market is concerned, of one third. Previously social welfare, it will be recalled, was $[3(x/4)](a-c)$.

The third possibility we shall investigate is in many ways the most appealing. This is quantity-competition (as opposed to the price-competition idea of Bertrand). The original analysis was conducted by Cournot over 150 years ago. Cournot assumed that each firm would set its output to maximize its profits, taking rivals' output levels as given. Each firm thinks of itself as a monopolist in the market that remains, once its rival (or rivals) have set output.

In our example (as in Cournot's), market demand is linear and marginal costs are common and horizontal. Now the total (potential) market is $2x$, since this is what a perfectly competitive industry (or Bertrand duopoly) would produce. With monopoly, there is no rival, so the profit-maximizing output is half that, namely x. What will happen in this symmetrical Cournot duopoly? Let us assume that one of the firms sets its output at q in equilibrium. The other must produce half of the remaining market, that is $(2x-q)/2 = x - q/2$. But the two firms behave in exactly the same way. So $q = x - q/2$. That implies that $q = \frac{2}{3}x$. Each duopolist produces two-thirds of what a monopolist would produce, or one-third of the total (perfectly competitive, or Bertrand) market.

Together, the two firms expand output from x (under monopoly) to $4x/3$. That means that the price will come down. It will fall to two-thirds of the way down from a to c. Figure 7.2 illustrates. With price now equalling $(a + 2c)/3$, the consumers' surplus triangle enlarges. Previously, with monopoly, it was just $[(a-c)/4]x$. Now it will be $\{(4x/3)[a-(a+2c)/3]\}/2 = \frac{4}{9}x(a-c)$. This amounts to a rise of seven-ninths.

The upshot seems to be that social welfare must go up, but this is in fact wrong: it goes down. The reason for this is that the home firm's profit falls by a larger amount. Let us see what it will be. The price equals $(a + 2c)/3$, so the price-cost margin equals $(a-c)/3$. Previously it was $(a-c)/2$. The profit per unit of output has dropped by one third. That is not the end of the matter. Total profit for the home firm is the product of the price–cost margin and the level of its output. Output was x before the foreign firm arrived. Now it is only $2x/3$. So the home firm's profit has fallen from one half of $(a-c)x$ to only two-ninths of it.

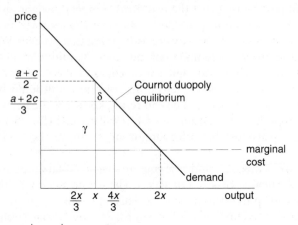

Fig. 7.2. Cournot duopoly

The foreign firm (since both behave alike) also earns a profit $\frac{2}{9}(a-c)$ in Cournot competition. But the point that matters for social welfare is that foreigners' profits do not count. So total social welfare for the home country is $\frac{4}{9}x(a-c)$ for consumers' surplus, plus $\frac{2}{9}x(a-c)$ for home profit. These sum to $\frac{2}{3}x(a-c)$. Under monopoly it was $\frac{3}{4}x(a-c)$, a fall of one-ninth. Geometrically, the transfer of profit from the home firm to the foreign firm (area γ in Figure 7.2) is greater than the triangle of net gain (area δ). Consumers gain more than δ—their rise in consumers' surplus is the sum of areas $\delta + \epsilon$—but ϵ is transferred from home profit. Our assumption on social welfare implies that this transfer is irrelevant. In fact, γ is not just larger than δ: we know that it has to be exactly *four times* larger.

The result that $\gamma = 4\delta$ can be seen from the fact that δ is a triangle and γ a rectangle, and from observing that although the bases of γ and δ are equal, the height of the γ rectangle is twice as large as the height of the triangle δ.

The net effect on home social welfare, then, of the arrival of the foreign firm, is:

1. loss of $\frac{3}{4}(a-c)$ under collusion;
2. gain of $\frac{3}{4}(a-c)$ under Bertrand Competition;
3. loss of $\frac{1}{12}(a-c)$ under Cournot Competition.

Only in case (2) does home social welfare go up. Foreign welfare, however, rises in both (1) and (3). In case (1), foreign welfare increases by the foreigner's share of total profit, that is $\frac{3}{4}(a-c)$. So if world welfare is just the sum of the two countries' national social welfare levels, it will be unchanged. That example of foreign trade is a 'zero-sum' game: the exporter gains what the importer loses.

But collusion is obviously a special case. In both (2) and (3), world welfare (defined in the above way) must rise. In (2), it rises by $\frac{3}{4}(a-c)$, since the foreign firm earns no profit in equilibrium. In case (3), it increases from $\frac{3}{4}(a-c)$, the old level, to $\frac{8}{9}x(a - c)$, once the foreign firm's profit is added in. So under both Bertrand and Cournot competition, this kind of international trade is not a zero-sum game. The total size of the surpluses, at the world level, can only go up.

It is noteworthy, though, that the home country is still a loser under Cournot Competition, under our assumptions. But there are many ways of enlarging or modifying our analysis that can reverse this disagreeable result. Here are a few of them.

One thing we can do is to introduce full symmetry. This means adding a *foreign* market to which our home firm gains access, and competes with the local incumbent there in a similar, Cournot fashion. With full symmetry, the home firm will earn profit of $\frac{2}{9}x(a - c)$ on its overseas sales. Adding this into social welfare cancels the effect of the foreign firm's domestic profit (area γ). So we are left with the little triangle δ, of pure gain.

Another idea would be to challenge our definition of social welfare, placing a higher weight on the surplus of consumers (who may, for example, be poorer than profit-recipients on average, and have a higher marginal utility of income) than on profit. Social welfare will now register a gain as a result of the transfer ϵ in Figure 7.2. Added to this is the fact that triangle δ now counts for more, per square centimetre, than area γ. By emphasizing consumers' surplus enough, we could tilt the net social-welfare change from negative to positive under Cournot duopoly.

A third point is to extend the story from duopoly—two firms—to a more general case of oligopoly, with two or more foreign firms in addition to the home one. Adding in a second foreign firm is, in fact, enough to create a net gain for home social welfare. Although the home firm's profit gets squeezed further, there is a large rise in consumers' surplus, some of it at the expense of the first foreign firm, and this effect is enough to generate a positive net effect on domestic welfare in comparison with no trade.

A fourth consideration is the fact that there is international diversification of shareholding. Some of the profits earned by the foreign firm could come back to home-country shareholders. If this effect is large enough (and if some home-firm profit gets paid abroad), we can transform a net home-welfare loss under Cournot duopoly into a net home gain.

All these points emphasize the possibility that international Cournot oligopoly can be beneficial for every country concerned. There is no doubt that consumers gain by foreign entry into domestic markets, and there are benefits to social welfare when all relevant parameters are symmetrical.

The main source of possible trouble for home welfare which international Cournot oligopoly could deliver is asymmetry. A country is likeliest to *lose* when:

1. it has a relatively high level of domestic demand;
2. it has a relatively small share in the worldwide number of firms competing worldwide;
3. its home firm has relatively high production costs.

The reasoning is as follows. On (1), a larger home market than foreign market, all else equal, means that the foreign firm will earn more profit on its exports than the home firm does on its overseas sales. On (2), the smaller the home country's share of world production, the larger the chance that the net flow of profits favours abroad. The significance of (3) is that, like the fewness of domestic firms, it implies a low home-country share in world profits.

One must be careful, though, to remember that our remarks about welfare have been based on purely partial-equilibrium concepts. The fact that there might be an adverse effect on one oligopolistic market (because net imports bit heavily into home profits) does not mean that the general equilibrium effects on potential social welfare need be unfavourable. Take case (3) above, where the home firm had relatively high costs. We would surely think of the good in question as a product where the home country lacked comparative advantage. There should be an efficiency gain when the resources released from this industry (as the home firm contracts under fire from lower-cost rivals abroad) are transferred into other industries where the country's relative cost position is stronger.

This issue of relative costs and net trade brings out some powerful parallels between international oligopoly trade of the kind we have been considering here, and the perfect competition analysis of earlier chapters. Whether a country is a net exporter of an international oligopoly product is influenced by relative costs. Cross-country technology differences matter. So, too, do factor abundance differences: it could be that the country's firm has a cost advantage conferred by the relative cheapness of a factor of production in which it is intensive. Demand is relevant as well. If demand at home is relatively weak for this product, that will be a consideration that will make for positive net exports, all else being equal.

The important insight that this suggests is that international oligopoly theory should not be seen as a *rival* to the traditional trade theories which stress international differences in tastes, technology, and factor endowments. Those three factors continue to apply, and all of them will play a role in helping to determine the country's net trade position for the product in question.

What international oligopoly adds, however, is three new phenomena that did not apply in the perfect competition stories. Consider these in turn.

1.   the significance of the *number of firms*;
2.   the significance of the *pure profit rents*;
3.   the idea of *reciprocal trade*.

Whether a country is a net exporter of a commodity produced under international oligopoly does not depend only on cross-country differences in technology, tastes, and factor endowments. The number of firms matters too. Suppose the world consists of two countries, alike in all respects except that there happen to be more home than foreign firms. That means that there will be more production at home than abroad, if the oligopoly game is played in similar ways by all the firms. Relatively higher production must entail net exports if other considerations are common. If there are two US wide-body jet producers (Boeing, and MacDonnell-Douglas) and one European one (Airbus), Europe should be a net importer of that product when the three firms' outputs and market sizes are equal.

Pure profit rents vanish under perfect competition. In imperfect competition, they need not. They will tend to, if entry into the industry is uninhibited by barriers. But in the presence of trade barriers, any profits earned are likely to persist—unless, that is, the firms in question compete vigorously over price, as they do in Bertrand's model. Cournot competition with entry barriers should typically generate persistent profit rents. This is an important point for policy, as we shall see later: it suggests new arguments in favour of protection.

Our third point concerns reciprocal trade. With international Cournot oligopoly we shall see the same product being exported and imported. Trade is two-way. The phenomenon is sometimes called 'cross-hauling' or 'reciprocal dumping'. This will occur under a wide variety of cases, including Bertrand as well as Cournot competition. It will even arise in the presence of (sufficiently modest) international transport costs. There is widespread evidence of two-way trade in many industrial products. Germany imports cars from France; France imports cars from Germany. If products are undifferentiated—as in standard oligopoly models—cross-hauling of this kind is precisely what the Cournot model predicts. Each country's firms invade foreign markets because, if they did not, valuable profit opportunities would be foregone.

We conclude this section with a brief look at what lessons international Cournot oligopoly might have from the standpoint of European integration.

The integration of Western Europe has had two main strands. First, there has been a progressive elimination of tariff barriers, stretching back for several decades. The original six members of the European Union had eliminated internal tariff barriers by 1963. By 1980 they had disappeared between the EU-6 and the new 1973 members, Denmark, Ireland, and the UK; by 1987 between the EU-9 and Greece; and six years later between the EU-10 and Portugal and Spain. The last tariff barriers between the EU-12 and the new members that joined in 1995, Austria, Finland, and Sweden, will also soon have disappeared.

Second, there has been more recent progress towards the elimination of non-tariff barriers, as a result of the Single European Market that came into being on 1st January 1993 throughout the EU-12 area. These barriers often restricted the volume of certain imports from EU partners, sometimes even prohibiting them.

Of the two types of trade restrictions, it is the quantitative, non-tariff barriers that have more pervasive effects in Cournot international oligopoly. A tariff barrier handicaps importers, reducing import volume and raising price somewhat. But a binding physical ceiling on imports that has similar effect on import volumes to a tariff raises market price much more. This is because the domestic firm—let us say there is just one of them—can now act as a true monopolist for the residual home demand that is left once imports have been subtracted. In comparison with the tariff, the non-tariff barrier squeezes consumers' surplus more, and generates higher profits. The net change in social welfare is likelier to be less adverse with the tariff.

There is another difference. An optimal tariff in Cournot oligopoly is not prohibitive. But if a quota is set by the home government to maximize home social welfare—in the absence of any retaliation—its 'optimum' level is, in fact, prohibitive. That way foreign profits in the home market are eliminated, and although domestic consumers suffer from a steep price rise, the sum of home firm profits and consumers' surplus is maximized at this point. In perfect competition, by contrast, if the home country lacks any power to influence world prices the optimum levels of tariffs and quotas are both zero.

This implies that quota and physical restriction removals in Western Europe will be highly favourable for consumers. Furthermore, if the number of European firms able to compete with each other is high, Cournot oligopoly will generate an equilibrium quite close to perfect competition.

7.3 Monopolistic competition and international trade

7.3.1 Liking for variety

There are two main families of theories about monopolistic competition, a market form where there are several firms producing good but imperfect substitutes. One of these differentiates consumers, by location or preference, so that all consumers of a certain type will opt to buy just one firm's product, and those of other types will buy elsewhere.

The second theory assumes that consumers are similar, but enjoy buying a variety of different goods that are available. In the first story, some people prefer Indian cooking to North African or Italian. So the population sorts itself out into regulars that always eat curries, regulars that consume pasta, and regulars who only eat couscous. In the second, everyone likes to vary his or her routine, and visit restaurants of all types periodically. We shall concentrate in the present section on monopolistic competition of the second kind; the first kind will be examined in Section 7.3.2. The variety theory of monopolistic competition that occupies here is often known as the Dixit-Stiglitz model after its inventors (Dixit and Stiglitz 1977).

We could think of numerous examples that fit the second sort of monopolistic competition which is under consideration here. Many people may not have a favourite cheese or flavoured yoghurt, but like the choice. Sometimes they buy Camembert, sometimes Cheddar, sometimes Gouda. Sometimes they eat apricot-flavoured yoghurt, sometimes strawberry. They enjoy having wardrobes with different-coloured dresses or shirts. One year they holiday in Rhodes, another year in Madeira or Skye.

It is usual in monopolistic competition to assume free entry. We shall adhere to this assumption here. The number of firms in the industry is therefore endogenous. It is determined by a break-even condition that profits vanish. Each firm in an industry is restricted to producing just one variant of the commodity in question. There are increasing returns, most easily captured by the existence of a fixed cost, the same for all producers, which is faced by anyone with a positive level of production.

Because no good is a perfect substitute for any other in the industry, firms within it face a downward-sloping demand curve. If price discrimination is precluded, this translates into negatively-sloped average revenue, which in turn means that marginal revenue lies below average revenue. The firms aim to maximize profit; so they charge a mark-up on marginal cost. The size of this mark-up is inversely proportional to the elasticity of the average revenue curve they face. The position of that average revenue curve also depends on the prices set by other firms: if other firms were to charge more, average revenue would increase. The easiest assumption to make is that each firm sets its own price independently, taking the other firms' prices as given.

When preferences are homothetic, and symmetrical between the different varieties, and we shall assume that this is so, the resulting price can be expressed as

$$(p - c)/p = 1/\{e - [e - 1]/n\} \qquad (7.1)$$

where n is the number of firms, c is marginal cost (assumed constant and uniform across the firms), and e, defined as a positive and constant parameter, is the elasticity of substitution between the different varieties of the product. When n is very large, $(p - c)/p$ tends to $1/e$, a standard monopoly result: clearly p declines as e rises. But if n is finite, the price–marginal-cost gap widens, and price always rises as the number of firms shrinks.

The next step is to endogenize the number of firms. Let I denote the aggregate income of all the residents of our economy, and a the fraction of their income they devote to this set of goods we are considering (if a is a given number, preferences are Cobb Douglas between this set of goods, and others, but CES—displaying a constant elasticity of substitution, e—between the different products of this industry).

Let F be the size of fixed costs. The output of a representative firm will therefore be aI/pn. We can then derive an expression for the firm's profit, using our equation for price, and then find the value of n at which profits vanish. The answer is

$$n = [e - 1 + aI/F]/e. \qquad (7.2)$$

We can then substitute this solution for n back into our price equation to find

$$p = ce/[(e - 1)(1 - F/aI)] \qquad (7.3)$$

Higher demand for our industry's products means more firms, more variety, and lower prices; higher demand could come from increased income, I, or an increased propensity to spend on them, a. So, in a sense, the industry's supply curve is downward sloping. Higher fixed costs (F), on the other hand, mean that price has to rise to keep profits constant at zero, and the number of firms and varieties will drop.

Let us now see what happens when this economy is opened up to free trade with other, similar countries that were previously isolated from each other. The main effects are very similar to an increase in aggregate income, I: the total number of varieties goes up (but less than in proportion to the rise in I, assuming that e exceeds one); and the price comes down.

Algebraically, these results are easily seen by inspecting our equations for the equilibrium values of n and p. Suppose there are m identical countries, each with income of Y. All we do is to replace aggregate income I in our formulae by mY, and take care to recall that n now refers to the total number of varieties available to consumers, and no longer the number of firms in the single economy with which we began.

Economic integration now has two effects. First, the widening of the total market means that there are more varieties on offer than before. This increases consumers' utilities directly, because they like wider choice, and experience an increase in the range of varieties that all of them buy. So this is the first benefit.

The second benefit comes from the drop in the price. More varieties means that the perceived elasticity of the average revenue of each firm in the expanded trading area goes up. So the profit-maximizing mark-up of price over marginal cost goes down. This, too, is welcome to consumers. As a consequence of the reduction in the prices of all the varieties, the total area's number of firms has to slip a little, to expand output of the survivors and keep profits for each of them unchanged at zero.

A numerical example may help. Suppose that $e = 3$ and aY/F equals 10. When the countries are all isolated, there will be room for four firms in each. Price will equal $5c/3$. So if there are four countries in all, there are sixteen firms, but each consumer gets to buy only four varieties (from his or her local firms). Now we integrate these four economies. The total number of firms falls from sixteen to fourteen, and the price falls to $20c/13$. Each consumer experiences a 250 per cent increase in the varieties he or she will buy.

So if c equals 78 German marks, for example, the price was 130 marks before the integration, and only 120 after it. These two results (more varieties, and lower prices) always ensue. It follows that consumer welfare must go up. And the absence of rents (recall that marginal costs were assumed horizontal, and free entry removed profits for firms) ensures that this translates unambiguously into increased welfare.

Up to now we assumed that our economies were identical in all respects. What happens if the marginal cost of production, c, is not the same in each? There could be two main possible reasons for this. International differences in technology are one. Inter-industry differences in factor intensities, and inter-country differences in factor endowments, provide the other. The first would be a Ricardian phenomenon, while the second corresponds to the Heckscher-Ohlin explanation for trade.

In either case, production in our industry will now concentrate exclusively in the country where marginal cost is lowest, once economic integration proceeds. The firms in higher-cost countries will vanish, or relocate, to take advantage of the superior technology or more favourable factor prices. So, in our numerical example, the fourteen firms there is room for will all produce in the country with the smallest marginal cost. This gives a third source of gain for the consumers in the other three countries. If 78 marks was the lowest marginal cost, and the other three countries' marginal costs were, say, common at a level of 90 marks, the pre-trade prices there will have been 150 marks, not 130. The price cut from 150 marks to 120, as local firms disappear after economic integration, is even larger than before.

It is worth stressing that this variety-based story of monopolistic competition across international boundaries should not be seen strictly as an *alternative* to the standard theories of trade (such as Ricardo's, or the Heckscher-Ohlin model) which have been traditionally based on perfect competition. Rather, it is better thought of as a possible extension or *enrichment* of them.

We still need to appeal to Ricardo or Heckscher-Ohlin (or possibly some other theory) to tell us why production-marginal cost ratios in different countries are not the same, if that is so. The monopolistic competition story sketched here does an appealing job at explaining why quite similar goods may be exported and imported by a particular country, as evidence amply testifies that many are. It is not the sole possible explanation, because our cross-hauling oligopoly model of Section 7.2 provides another.

But the general equilibrium structure of these economies, of which the imperfectly competitive industry we are studying forms part, also matters too. It is this that drives marginal cost ratios. It is this that may explain why production of such goods tends, as it so often does, to be much higher in some countries than others. So the variety model of monopolistic competition is essentially a valuable and highly realistic add-on to the old theories that concentrate upon technology, factor-intensities, and factor endowments. It is in no sense a rival to them.

What this add-on does is two things. First, it may help to explain the phenomenon of similar goods being exported by country A to B, and at the same time imported by A from B. It is not the only explanation for this, but it is an attractive one. Second, and more important, it provides new reasons for thinking that international trade is beneficial. The enhancement of varieties available to consumers that imports offer may well be a valuable good in its own right: many more exotic flavours for your yoghurt!

7.3.2 Monopolistic competition with differentiated consumers

In this section we shall assume that consumers are not all alike. They do not buy a little of everything, as they did in the previous section. Instead they buy a product, if at all, from just one supplier. The preferred supplier may be closer to them geographically, an important idea when transport costs are taken into account. So we may think of the present section in terms of location: consumers live in different places, and this affects whom they buy from, and the resulting structure of a monopolistically competitive industry.

Location may, however, be better thought of as a metaphor. Think of newspapers. Many people buy their local newspaper because they are more anxious to learn the details of events in their city or region than in others. They could perhaps buy the local newspaper of a neighbouring region at no extra cost; but it would be much less interesting for them. Better still, think of the differences between national newspapers. Some tell you all about the private lives of actors and footballers; others are serious providers of political information. But some of those may be somewhat slanted to the left or to the right. Some tell you more about events in America, or finance, or the arts world. Some readers like gossip. Others prefer serious reporting of news from a socialist standpoint, or a more conservative one. You buy the newspaper you do because it comes closest to telling you what you want to read.

A newspaper has to position itself in the market and decide which sets of readers it aims to satisfy most. Suppose readers can be placed on a single dimension, running from 'light gossip' at one end to 'heavy news' on the other. Let there be an equal number of potential readers, alike in every respect save their newspaper tastes, at each point along a continuum between these endpoints. Let the disutility suffered from reading a less-than-ideal paper from your personal standpoint be proportional to the distance from your ideal.

In a setting like this, Hotelling (1929) demonstrated that duopoly leads to minimum differentiation. This follows, at least, if the question of pricing is side-stepped or treated as predetermined. In Hotelling's equilibrium, both newspapers offer products that will be ideal to the median individual in the middle of the line.

In a social optimum, by contrast, one would want one moderately 'light' paper, one-quarter of the distance from the gossip end to the other, and one moderately heavy one, located three-quarters of the way to the heavy extreme at the other. This will also be the result if the two papers collude, or happen to be owned and controlled by the same company. Hotelling's argument for minimum differentiation rests on the fact that if one paper is located off-centre, the other will attract more business and profits by positioning itself slightly away from that point on the side of the median.

Now suppose that there are two countries (with a common language or with polyglot readers), and one paper in each. Initially trade is banned, giving each a local monopoly. Then we allow trade. Setting the issue of pricing on one side, it appears that Hotelling's argument suggests that trade does nothing, because each will stick to the median reader.

A very different result emerges from the research of d'Aspremont *et al.* (1979). These authors integrate the pricing and location decisions of the firms. They assume quadratic transport costs (so that your disutility with a certain product goes up with the square of your distance from it). They do this because Hotelling's case of linear transport costs gives no solution when pricing and location are determined simultaneously.

What d'Aspremont *et al.* find is that independent duopolists, setting price and location to maximize their own profits when the other's decisions are taken as given, can end up at the two extremes. This is not a social optimum either. Total transport costs are just as high as in the minimum-differentiation case. But international trade would, in our simple little case, at least have the merit of providing more choice and a more colourful outcome!

As both these theories limit the number of firms to two, and fix it at that number, it is interesting to explore models of monopolistic competition with differentiated consumers where the number of firms is a continuous variable determined by the free-entry condition that profits vanish, as in Section 7.3.1. One such model has been constructed by Salop (1979), which lends itself straightforwardly to multi-country application.

The Salop model, in essence, is this. All firms that produce a particular good choose where to locate (metaphorically) on a circle. The circle's circumference is one. There are equal numbers of consumers, for convenience one in each economy, for whom 12 o'clock, 6 o'clock, or any other point on the circle, is their ideal. Apart from their varying notion of the ideal, consumers are homogeneous. A consumer buys at most one unit of the good, and only from the supplier that suits best (that is, the cheapest taking the monetary equivalent of the disutility of 'transport costs' into account).

If there are to be n firms in this market, they will position themselves evenly along the circle, reflecting the d'Aspremont principle of maximum differentiation, rather than the Hotelling one of minimum. So the distance between adjacent suppliers is $1/n$. Let a consumer's distance be x from one nearby supplier A who charges P, and $(1/n) - x$ from the other, B, who charges p. Denote by t the consumer's transport cost per unit distance (linear, as with Hotelling, rather than quadratic, as in the d'Aspremont case). The consumer's full price, gross of transport cost, is $P + tx$ if she opts to buy from A, and $p + t/n - tx$ if from B. If she is indifferent between buying from A and from B, then

$$x = \{p - P + t/n\}/2t \qquad (7.4)$$

Firm A has a neighbour on her other side, call him C, who will charge p by symmetry. As in the variety-model of Section 7.3.1, all the firms have common, horizontal, marginal cost of c and fixed cost of F, and set their own price to maximize their profit taking other firms' prices as given.

Firm A's profit will therefore be $-F + 2x(P - c)$. This is so because x defines the outer boundary of her market, and there are, of course, outer boundaries on both sides (one with B and one with C). So $2x$ is her output; and $P - c$ is her profit per unit. Using our expression for x, then maximizing with respect to P treating p as given, and finally setting $P = p$ by symmetry, implies

$$p = P = c + t/n$$

and the equilibrium value of the number of firms, n, is found by setting profits to vanish.

The resulting levels of n and $p - c$ are $\sqrt{[t/F]}$ and $\sqrt{[tF]}$ respectively. Higher t makes for more firms because that means consumers are fussier and firms are inclined to charge more. Higher F means more overhead costs, so each firm's market has to expand, and its price go up, to balance the books: the number of firms dwindles and the price rises. With both t and F trivial, the number of firms is very large, and we approach perfect competition in the limit. What is going to give us something close to perfect competition is the combination of our Bertrand pricing assumption (firms set their own price to maximize profit, taking the prices of other firms as given), together with the fact that, with t and F trivial, the distance between neighbouring firms becomes very small.

This is how Salop's story works for a closed economy. Now let us see when a number of similar economies are allowed to trade with each other. Let us keep c, t, and F, and our assumptions about the consumers and behaviour of producers the same, and just assume that m identical economies are now amalgamated. We keep n to mean the total number of firms, now for the whole enlarged market.

Our equation for price ($p = c + t/n$) remains unchanged. But because each firm's output expands from $2x$ to $2mx$, the break-even condition that profits vanish tells us that the equilibrium total number of firms selling into any of the markets goes up to $\sqrt{[mt/F]}$. So price, net of marginal cost c, drops to $\sqrt{[tF/m]}$. So most consumers, at least, get a firm that comes closer to meeting their ideal version of the product. Total transport costs come down. So does the price of the product. And while there are more suppliers in each market, the total number of firms drops, resulting in a saving of fixed costs. This brings nothing but gain, in other words.

Suppose m is 4, as in our example in the variety case in Section 7.3.1. There are four integrated economies now, instead of four isolated ones. The number of sellers in each of the markets doubles: three-quarters of them are now foreign firms. The total number of firms in the four economies, taken together, halves. The gap between price and marginal cost halves. Another thing that halves is the deadweight welfare loss, which equals (for each of the economies) the sum of the total fixed costs of its firms, plus the psychological transport costs borne by its consumers. Consumers' surplus in its traditional sense plays no direct role in welfare in this model, because consumers' demand curves are vertical.

Had our economies differed in their firms' marginal costs, we should expect to see the entire market taken over by suppliers from the economy where these were lowest. This would bring further benefits to consumers in the other countries (although not to those living in the supplying country).

The conclusion we reach is that Salop's model of monopolistic competition with differentiated consumers carries highly optimistic implications for an open economy. International economic integration brings benefits in the form of lower prices, widened choice, and a saving in real resources (those fixed costs). These favourable results are quite similar in character to those that we found to spring from the variety model of Section 7.3.1.

There are one or two notes of caution that we should observe, however. We have taken transport costs to be purely metaphorical. They represent the psychological cost to a consumer of having to make do with a product that has a less-than-ideal placing on the clockface, or circle, from her standpoint.

Suppose instead that we take transport costs literally, and look at the geographical interpretation of the model, it seems that allowing international trade will have next to no effects, save perhaps on border regions, where there are consumers closer to foreign than to domestic suppliers. Furthermore, the empirical success of the gravity model of trade warns us against thinking that there are always going to be large gains from expanding opportunities to trade between countries which are geographically far apart.

A further qualification is that the firms are modelled here, and in Section 7.3.1 as well, as Bertrand price-setters. They might not be: they could collude with neighbours, for example. In that case the model has to be amended by assuming that each consumer will buy not just one unit of the good (so long as it is cheap enough) but a varying quantity, depending on the price plus transport costs. Provided that transport costs are metaphorical, it turns out that exploring this idea complicates the analysis, and modifies the results in certain details, but continues to deliver not dissimilar conclusions about the benefits of widening markets.

7.4 Market imperfections and the possibility of damaging trade

Trade is usually beneficial. Not everyone benefits from it, of course. Even under perfect competition, there are individuals who stand to lose from it. Examples include, firstly, owners of scarce factors, used intensively in a country's importable industry; secondly, owners of factors specific to importables industries; and thirdly, people with mixed incomes and tastes strongly biased towards exportable goods. The first group loses because of the Samuelson-Stolper effect studied in Chapter 3, section 3.7: the contraction of importable production to which the advent of trade leads cuts the real price, in terms of all products, of the factor used intensively there. The second group suffers because the rent for a specific factor must fall when the industry to which it is specific cuts back production. In the case of the third group, the problem is that trade raises the price of exportables, not in terms of all factor prices but at least relative to some average of them. But under perfect competition there is at least the opportunity for transfer payments, to ensure that there are no losers, only gainers, within an economy that switches from autarky to free trade. 'Potential welfare' can only go up with trade.

Introduce market imperfections, and this last proposition starts to become doubtful. It is possible that a society's potential welfare falls. One instance of this is an idea first put forward by Graham (1923). Suppose there are two industries, one blessed with increasing returns, and the other with decreasing returns. Call them *x* and *y* respectively. Let there be two countries, A and B. Before trade occurs, both economies will produce both goods. With trade, one country may become the exclusive producer of *x*, while the other switches its resources into *y*, where there are decreasing returns. Graham argued that the former will gain and the latter lose.

There are two ways this could arise. We could see producers of *x* and *y* as perfectly competitive, in the sense that they are numerous and are all price-takers, but the economies of scale (and diseconomies) could be external to the firms and internal to the industries. The *y*-industry could be fishing, for example. That is a prime case of a decreasing-returns industry: as the number of fisherman and fishing trips expands, the average size of catch goes down. The average cost per fish rises to reflect increased congestion in the fishing-grounds. The *y*-industry suffers from a 'tragedy of the commons'—overcrowding and excessive exploitation of a mispriced resource. The x-industry displays beneficial externalities, on the other hand: computer hardware and software producers could be a case in point. As the computer industry expands, there are induced inventions and improvements that serve to lower average costs all round.

Sweden and Finland joined the European Union on 1 January 1995. Suppose this leads to a big expansion in these economies' fishing industries. Finland and Sweden abandon computer production, and the rest of the European Union stops fishing. In such a case, Graham argued, Finland and Sweden could be better off in autarky.

The other type of increasing/decreasing-returns effect could be internal to the firm. Then we would see the increasing returns industry concentrated in few firms—indeed, perhaps in just one. The producer or producers might, however, be forced to price at average cost (just like the computer companies with the external economies of scale). But the mechanism in this case, if it was present, would turn on the threat of entry by a hypothetical competitor that enjoyed similar technology. This would make the industry 'perfectly contestable' if a set of rather restrictive conditions were fulfilled.

The possible welfare loss from trade for the country that contracted output of x and transferred resources into y would only arise, however, *if inappropriate fiscal or industrial policies were applied.* In sector x, with its increasing returns, true marginal cost is below average cost (and price). In y, the opposite is true. Optimal policies would call for subsidies on x and taxes on y. What the two countries could achieve in isolation, even with such policies, would be less efficient than if they traded freely (and set optimal policies). With optimal policy, potential welfare should rise in both countries, though this would presumably require a net transfer from the x-importer to the y-exporter, too.

There are a few still more intriguing cases, where it is possible for trade to lower potential welfare in *both or all* countries. We shall touch on three of them.

The first example was constructed by Brander and Krugman (1983). Consider the case of cross-hauling oligopolies in two countries, with which this chapter began. We get the same good exported from A to B and exported from B to A in a Cournot duopoly with similar marginal costs. There is nothing wrong here, so long as international transport costs are trivial: the Cournot duopoly reduces the prices consumers pay in both countries, and the extra surplus for consumers more than outweighs the loss of profits the two firms face, in comparison with the state of affairs under autarky (when each would be a monopolist in its own market).

But now bring in sizeable international transport costs. We shall still see some two-way trade, so long as the monopoly price exceeds marginal cost plus transport cost. But the to-ing and fro-ing of the product will give rise to the possibility that consumers' surplus gains fall short of profit losses (including the extra transport costs). If this is so, and all other types of trade in other products are negligible, we may conclude that trade has harmed potential welfare in both countries.

Another case of welfare-reducing trade was put forward by Newbery and Stiglitz (1984). Newbery and Stiglitz looked at a pair of economies which produces two goods (call them *x* and *y* again) where *x* was a 'safe' product and *y* a 'risky' one. Good *y* is an agricultural product, with output highly sensitive to the weather. Rain makes for large output; drought the reverse. Assume that if it rains in economy A, it rains equally on all the *y*-producers there, and it does not rain anywhere in B. Under autarky, country A's *y*-producers will enjoy large output but low prices when it rains; and, when there is drought, low output but high prices. If preferences are Cobb-Douglas, the demand for *y* will be unit-elastic, and the incomes of the *y*-producers will be independent of the weather there. So autarky could provide perfect income-insurance. If producers are risk-averse, that could be very valuable to them.

Now let the two Newbery-Stiglitz economies trade with each other. The price of *y* will be common (barring international transport costs). A drought in one country will be accompanied by rain in the other. The incomes of *y*-producers will suddenly become destabilized and highly variable. If they are risk-averse, both economies will display shifts of resources out of *y* into the safe product, *x*. This introduces inefficiency. If this inefficiency is serious enough, it could lower not just the utility of producers, but that of consumers, too, and, of course, in both countries.

A third example of trade that could harm welfare in all countries is due to Sinclair (1995). Here there are a number of goods produced under increasing returns. Under autarky, each economy will produce all such goods, in inefficiently small amounts, and under conditions of monopoly. Monopolies are assumed to be owned by local residents, whose utilities the firms set out to maximize in their pricing decisions. In autarky, this could lead to such goods being priced at marginal cost (assuming that all citizens are alike in their preferences and share-holdings).

Introduce trade, and each good is now produced by just one firm and in only one country (a different country for each, it is assumed). The surviving monopolies gain from scale increases that lower marginal and average cost. They continue to price at (now lowered) marginal cost in *home* markets. But in overseas markets, assuming the ability to price-discriminate, they price to maximize profits, as there are no foreign shareholders' utilities to take into account. The end result will be lower utility in every country, the benefits of cheaper exportables being more than offset by higher prices on other goods, now delivered by overcharging foreign monopolies.

What these three cases have in common is that it is not really trade that lowers welfare *per se*: it is the accompanying market imperfection that is really responsible for the trouble. In the Brander-Krugman case, a policy of optimal regulation (or specific-subsidy-cum-*ad-valorem* tax) could enforce price at marginal cost in each country, avoiding the need for wasteful cross-hauling. In the Newbery-Stiglitz case, access to a complete set of futures or insurance markets would get rid of the problem, and replicate the advantage conferred, accidentally, by autarky. Finally, in the Sinclair case, regulation or taxation could prevent monopolists from overcharging in foreign markets (as could a removal on restrictions on shareholding, so that each surviving monopolist priced to maximize the utilities of an internationally diversified set of stockholders).

7.5 Summary

- International oligopoly may cause two-way trade in goods. A high price in one country attracts imports from the other. Consumers benefit in both countries; trade will be balanced if demand and cost conditions, and number of firms, are the same.
- Two-way international trade may also arise in monopolistic competition. Trade enlarges the varieties available to consumers, typically widening the gains from trade.
- The welfare effects of international oligopoly are ambiguous if international transport costs are large. Trade could also be welfare-reducing in other special cases, such as the absence of a complete set of markets in which agents can insure themselves against all eventualities.

TESTING TRADE THEORIES

8.1 Introduction

An important part of the appraisal of theoretical economic models is their ability to explain observed behaviour in the form of economic data. Despite the title of this chapter, there has not been and never will be a proper and conclusive test of any of the trade theories we have discussed. Indeed, as argued by Leamer and Levinsohn (1994), the purpose of empirical analysis is not to test whether a particular theory is valid or not, but rather to assess the extent to which the theory provides a useful approximation to actual economic activity. Taken literally, all trade theories can be rejected as a perfect explanation of the real world without the need for any analysis of data. In all cases the assumptions needed to make the theories tractable are often clearly at odds with reality. No theory can be exactly correct. With regard to the Heckscher-Ohlin model, the assumptions of perfect competition, identical technology, and so on are easily rejected by casual empiricism, without the need for complicated statistical procedures. Similarly, the assumption of identical endowments of factors of production which underlies many of the models of trade under imperfect competition is untenable. The point is that the former theory more clearly highlights the impact of differences in endowments by neutralizing the effects of imperfect competition; whilst the modern trade theories can more easily illuminate the way imperfect competition determines trade flows by having identical endowments or identical factor intensities.

The standard approach to testing in economics assesses a particular theory against a well-specified alternative. This is not possible with regard to trade theories, since it is not feasible to specify and estimate a complete general model of trade and then test the restrictions implied by the various theories, such as the Heckscher-Ohlin model. The general model would be vast, and would include factor endowments, scale economies, differences in technology, non-homothetic demand, imperfect competition, and so on. The role of empirical analysis in international trade is to evaluate the accuracy of a theory, often bearing in mind that the theory will have a limited range of applicability. Thus, we should expect the Heckscher-Ohlin model to be strong in explaining trade between countries which are very different, whilst theories of trade under imperfect competition should perform well for trade between more similar countries. However, the decision of whether a theory exhibits sufficient accuracy will be one of judgement; but, in general, if a theory is found to have little power in explaining actual data we should be wary of using it for policy prescriptions.

In this chapter we consider studies which have sought to assess the accuracy of various trade theories. We commence with studies of the Heckscher-Ohlin theory, and show that the Leontief Paradox, which stimulated so much theoretical and empirical work to explain it, was in fact based upon a conceptual misunderstanding of the underlying model. In fact Leontief's results have been shown to be compatible with the US being capital-abundant. This highlights the need for a clear conceptual framework in defining a theory in terms of an empirical model. We then proceed to discuss empirical analysis of more recent trade theories which incorporate economies of scale and imperfect competition.

8.2 Empirical studies of the Heckscher-Ohlin model

This section continues the analysis of Chapter 5, which described the factor-endowments model of trade. We commence by closely following Leamer (1984) in showing how one can carefully specify an empirical model on the basis of the Heckscher-Ohlin theorem. Most previous empirical studies have not been based upon a fully articulated version of the underlying theory and so, most notably in the case of Leontief, have produced possibly erroneous results. We start with the simple two-factor, two-commodity world in which the propositions of the theory are most easily derived. This generates the 'commodity version' of the HO theorem; the labour-abundant country will export the labour-intensive good. However, it becomes impossible to state the HO theorem in this simple form when the number of goods and factors exceeds two. Thus we then proceed to the many-factor, many-commodity extension in the Heckscher-Ohlin-Vanek (HOV) model which has formed the basis of most empirical work. This provides us with the 'factor content version' of the HO theorem; a country will tend to export the services of its abundant factor, as embodied in the factor content of the goods it exchanges internationally.

We start with the factor intensity or input-output matrix

$$A = \begin{bmatrix} a_{K1} & a_{K2} \\ a_{L1} & a_{L2} \end{bmatrix} \tag{8.1}$$

where the a_{ij} are the factor input intensities, a_{K1}, for example, being the input of capital required to produce a unit of output of good 1. Assuming factor-price equalization and identical technology, then the factor intensities will be identical in all countries. Good 1 is defined as capital-intensive relative to good 2 if

$$a_{K1}/a_{L1} > a_{K2}/a_{L2} \tag{8.2}$$

whilst a country, say A, is capital-abundant if

$$K/K_W > L/L_W \text{ or } K/L > K_W/L_W \tag{8.3}$$

where the subscript W refers to the world. The amount of output of each good, X_1 and X_2, multiplied by the factor input intensities, gives the total demand for each factor; whilst V, the vector of endowments, shows factor supply. Equating factor supply to factor demand gives

$$V = AX, \; V = [K\,L]', \; X = [X_1\,X_2]' \tag{8.4}$$

or alternatively

$$X = A^{-1}V \tag{8.5}$$

and by extension

$$X_W = A^{-1}V_W \tag{8.6}$$

Now free international trade ensures that all countries face the same relative price ratio for the two goods, therefore, given the assumption of identical demand (consumers in both countries maximize the same homothetic utility function), each country consumes the two goods in the same proportion. Thus, the amount of the two goods consumed in a country, represented by the vector C, will be given by the country's share of world expenditure, the scalar s, and the value of world output of the two goods

$$C = sX_W \tag{8.7}$$

For balanced trade, each country's expenditure must equal its factor income, and s will be the ratio of the country's GNP to world GNP. The net trade of a particular country is the difference between its production and consumption

$$T = X - C = A^{-1}V - sA^{-1}V_W = A^{-1}(V - sV_W) \tag{8.8}$$

where

$$V - sV_W = \begin{bmatrix} K - sK_W \\ L - sL_W \end{bmatrix} \tag{8.9}$$

represents the vector of excess factor supplies, which has signs $(+, -)$ for a capital-abundant country. It can also be shown that if X_1 is the capital-intensive good then the inverse of the input–output matrix must have the following pattern

$$A^{-1} = \begin{bmatrix} + & - \\ - & + \end{bmatrix} \tag{8.10}$$

So that

$$T = \begin{bmatrix} + & - \\ - & + \end{bmatrix} \begin{bmatrix} + \\ - \end{bmatrix} = \begin{bmatrix} + \\ - \end{bmatrix} \tag{8.11}$$

Thus, as was shown in a less technical way in Chapter 5, a capital-abundant country will have positive net exports of the capital-intensive good.

When, for the sake of reality, the number of factors and the number of commodities is extended beyond two it is no longer possible to state the HO theorem in this straightforward way. In higher dimensions the sign pattern of the inverse of the factor-intensity matrix becomes much more complicated to deduce and

interpret, so that there is no simple way to relate the signs of the excess factor supply vector to the net trade vector. In other words, it is no longer clear which goods
a country will export and which goods it will import.

Vanek (1968) provides a useful restatement of the theory for the multidimen-
sional case by rearranging equation (8.8) as

$$AT = V - sV_W \qquad (8.12)$$

where AT shows factors embodied in net exports. Defining a capital-abundant
country to be one where the ratio of capital in that country to the world endowment of capital exceeds the ratio of the country's GNP to world GNP (the ratio s).
The HOV theorem then states that a country will export the services of its abundant factors and import the services of factors which are scarce. The core of the
HO model is thus a simple linear relationship between a country's trade and the
difference between its resources of capital and labour (V) and the amounts of capital and labour it would have had if it had the same composition of resources as
the world (sV_W). It is this specification of the factor-endowments theory which
has formed the background to most empirical work on explaining international
trade flows.

Ideally estimation of such a relationship would be based upon observations of
trade, factor intensities, and endowments of factors of production. However,
until recently, most studies have used observations on two of these sets of variables and then used the theory to deduce the third. Three types of such studies
can be identified:

1. Factor content studies which use measured trade (T) and factor intensities
    (A) to infer factor abundance ($V - sV_W$).
2. Cross-commodity regression analysis for a given country, again using T and
    A to deduce factor abundance.
3. Cross-country regression analysis using data on trade and endowments to
    obtain the factor intensities.

8.3 Factor content studies

The most famous of studies in this category is that of Leontief. As shown in
Chapter 5, Leontief compared the amounts of capital and labour embodied in US
exports and import-competing substitutes, and found the ratio of capital to
labour embodied in exports to be less than that embodied in import substitutes.
This contradicted the widely held belief that the US was abundant in capital.
Much of the response to this 'paradox' concentrated on the restrictiveness of the
assumptions underlying the HO model. Much attention has been focused upon
the limitations imposed in Leontief's analysis by assuming only two factors of
production. A large body of theoretical and empirical work has highlighted the
importance of allowing for different types of labour in terms of their level of skill.
Leontief himself believed that the answer to the 'paradox' lay in the greater pro-

ductivity of US labour relative to labour in other countries. Much emphasis has been placed upon the potential role of human capital, in terms of education and training, in determining the pattern of trade. The possible influence on trade flows of differences in the structure of consumer demand between countries, variations in technology, increasing returns, and imperfect competition have all been investigated. Such work is clearly valuable in its own right. However, it turns out that the initial stimulus to this research may have been false. Leamer (1980) has shown that the statistical basis for the Leontief 'paradox' is unfounded.

Firstly we should note that the specification of the HOV theorem above assumes that trade is balanced. Leamer highlights that if a country runs, say, a balance of trade deficit so that it currently consumes more than its share of world GDP, then even if it is capital abundant the country may import the services of capital. In other words, a country may be a net importer of both capital and labour services. The proposition adopted by Leontief that if capital embodied in exports is less than the amount of capital embodied in import substitutes then the country must be relatively abundant in labour is only correct if the net export of capital services has the opposite sign to the net export of labour services. Using Leontief's data for 1947, Leamer found that the US was a net exporter of both capital and labour services. In this case the amount of capital embodied in net exports should be compared with the amount of capital embodied in consumption. This calculation reveals the US to be capital-abundant in 1947. There is no paradox!

To show this we specify separately the HOV equations in (8.12)

$$K_T = K - sK_W, \quad L_T = L - sL_W \tag{8.13}$$

where K_T and L_T are the amounts of capital and labour embodied in net exports. Following Leamer (1980), these can be rewritten as

$$\frac{K}{K_W} = \frac{sK}{K - K_T}, \quad \frac{L}{L_W} = \frac{sL}{L - L_T} \tag{8.14}$$

From equation (8.3) it follows that a country will be capital-abundant if

$$\frac{K}{K - K_T} > \frac{L}{L - L_T} \tag{8.15}$$

This equation in turn can be manipulated to give

$$-KL_T > -LK_T \tag{8.16}$$

which shows clearly that if the net export of capital services has the opposite sign to the net export of labour services then trade will reveal the factor with positive net exports to be the relatively abundant factor. That is, equation (8.16) will be satisfied if $K_T > 0$ and $L_T < 0$. If $L_T > 0$ and $K_T < 0$ then the country will be revealed to be labour-abundant.

This highlights the importance of considering net exports when evaluating the HOV theorem. Leontief, however, considered exports separately from imports, and identified capital abundance when the amount of capital per worker embodied in exports exceeded that embodied in imports. Leamer shows that this approach, too, requires that K_T and L_T have opposite signs. In fact, the US in 1947 was a net exporter of both capital and labour services, so that Leontief's approach was invalid. In this case, if the number of commodities is greater than two, then the relative amounts of factors embodied in exports and imports will not give an unambiguous indication of relative factor abundance. A country which exhibits a higher level of capital per worker in imports may not necessarily be relatively abundant in labour.

Leamer shows that if $K_T > 0$ and $L_T > 0$ then the country will be revealed to be capital-abundant only if $K_T/L_T > K/L$, that is, if the ratio of capital to labour in trade exceeds that of production. Using Leontief's data, this was in fact the case in 1947, so that the US was revealed by trade to be capital-abundant.

8.4 Cross-commodity regression analysis

A second approach to the empirical assessment of the HO model has been to consider the relationship between trade and factor inputs for a range of industries within a particular country. Typically, a measure of trade performance for each industry is regressed upon indicators of the input requirements of different factors used in that industry, the sign of the estimated parameters being interpreted as exhibiting factor abundance or scarcity. For example, Baldwin (1971) found that US net exports were negatively related to the capital intensity of production, thus also suggesting a Leontief paradox.

Leamer and Bowen (1981), however, have shown that the interpretation of the regression coefficients in these studies is incorrect. In general there can be no presumption that the sign of these estimates will only reflect factor abundance, so that a negative sign on the capital-intensity variable will only indicate capital scarcity under very special circumstances.

8.5 Cross-country regression analysis

An additional method used to assess the HO model has been to investigate the relationship between the net exports of a particular commodity for a range of countries and the factor endowments of those countries. So again, information on two of the sets of variables in the HOV equations, net trade and endowments, are used to infer the third variable, factor intensities. The key piece of work in this category is that of Leamer (1984), who shows that the HO theorem implies a linear relationship between trade and resource endowments.

Leamer estimates the relationship between ten broadly defined traded commodities, such as raw materials and capital-intensive manufactures, and eleven types of factor endowment. In general the estimated equations appear to explain an important element of the variation in the data, suggesting that factor endowments are a significant determinant of comparative advantage. Leamer concludes that 'the Heckscher-Ohlin theory comes out looking rather well'. However, this approach, and those discussed above, are weakened by considering only two of the sets of variables in the HOV equations. Leamer (1984) assesses the weaker hypothesis that there is a linear relationship between the structure of trade and resource endowments. A correct approach must consider the relationship between the three sets of variables, factor endowments, factor inputs, and trade. We now discuss a factor content study which adopts such an approach.

An interesting study by Balassa and Bauwens (1988) combines both the cross-country and cross-commodity approaches in seeking to explain the determination of intra-European trade in manufactures. They examine net trade between pairs of European countries for around 150 different commodities. The explanatory variables are factor intensities (industry characteristics) and factor endowments (country characteristics). As we have seen above, a correct specification of the factor-endowments theory entails assessing net trade. However, although the theory is concerned with total trade of each type of product, it says nothing about bilateral trade between any two countries.

The empirical results highlight that for bilateral trade within Europe there is a (highly significant) positive correlation between relative factor endowments and the relative factor intensity of trade; the more capital-abundant a country the more capital-intensive its exports tend to be. It is concluded that these results provide some support for the factor-endowments theory of trade.

8.6 Conceptually correct studies of the Heckscher-Ohlin theorem

With unbalanced trade, the share of world consumption denoted by s will be equal to

$$s' = s - \frac{B}{GNP_W}$$

where B is the trade balance. Countries with a negative trade balance, for example, will consume an amount which exceeds their share of world income. The correct formulation of the HOV theorem then becomes

$$AT = V - \left(\frac{GNP - B}{GNP_W}\right)V_W \qquad (8.17)$$

However, to make inferences about the HOV theory it is necessary to manipulate these equations to take account of the trade balance. Following Bowen *et al.* (1987), we define the adjusted factor content of trade as

$$F^A = AT - \left(\frac{B}{GNP_W}\right)V_W = V - \left(\frac{GNP}{GNP_W}\right)V_W \qquad (8.18)$$

For each element (factor) of this equation (for simplicity we continue here with just two factors) we can divide by the world endowment of the factor and then further divide by the share of world income to get

$$Z_K = \frac{F_K^A}{K_W} \Big/ \frac{GNP}{GNP_W} = \frac{K}{K_W} \Big/ \frac{GNP}{GNP_W} - 1$$

$$Z_L = \frac{F_L^A}{L_W} \Big/ \frac{GNP}{GNP_W} = \frac{L}{L_W} \Big/ \frac{GNP}{GNP_W} - 1 \qquad (8.19)$$

where $F_K^A = K_T - K_W(B/GNP_W)$ and similarly for labour. The left-hand side of these equations contains the amounts of each factor embodied in net exports, adjusted for any imbalance in trade, as a proportion of the total domestic endowment of that factor. The right-hand side of the equations provides a measure of factor abundance; the ratio of the share of the world endowment of the factor to the share of world income. Thus, if these equations are reliable, the factor content of trade will provide an indirect measure of factor abundance.

The equations in (8.19) can be used to assess the HO theorem that factor abundance determines the sign of net exports (which commodities are exported and which are imported) in two ways. Firstly, the signs of the terms on either side of equations (8.19) should match. To show this note that the income share is equal to an earnings-weighted average of all factor endowment ratios. In the simple two-factor case

$$\frac{GNP}{GNP_W} = \frac{p_K K + p_L L}{p_K K_W + p_L L_W} = \frac{p_K K_W (K/K_W) + p_L L_W (L/L_W)}{p_K K_W + p_L L_W} \qquad (8.20)$$

where p_K, p_L are the world price of capital and labour. Thus, the sign of the net trade in the services of a particular factor, adjusted for trade imbalance, will show whether that factor is abundant or scarce relative to the average of all other resources. This can then be compared with actual data on resource endowments.

Secondly, equations (8.19) imply that if $Z_K > Z_L$ then the country must be more abundant in capital than in labour. Further, if Z_K for, say, country i is greater than for country j, then i must be more abundant in capital than j. A general test then compares the ranking of net trade, adjusted for trade imbalance, for each country and each factor with the ranking of factors according to data which directly measure endowments.

Table 8.1 lists the Z terms computed by Bowen *et al.* (1987) using data for 1966 and 1967 for a number of European countries, the US, and Japan. The importance of this research lies in the fact that data on all three sets of the variables in the HOV equations, trade, factor intensities, and factor endowments, are used to assess the theory. This compares with previous studies which are incomplete by using data on two of the variables to infer information about the third. The first two rows of the table show the adjusted net trade relative to national endowment for capital and labour. Looking at the values for the US shows that $Z_K > Z_L$ so that there is no 'Leontief Paradox' to undermine the HO theory. These data suggest that all European countries with the exception of Finland are labour-abundant.

Table 8.1. Ratio of net trade to national endowment (*100) for various factors of production

Country	Cap.	Lab.	Prof.	Manag.	Cleric.	Sales	Serv.	Agric.	Prod.	Arable	Forest	Past.
Austria	-2.0	3.0	2.7	5.6	2.9	3.8	3.2	3.1	2.6	-80.7	13.5	24.4
Bel–Lux	-2.4	1.8	0.9	1.8	1.9	1.4	2.4	-4.3	2.8	-364.3	-922.5	53.3
Denmark	-4.9	5.8	2.4	8.7	4.3	5.1	4.5	24.6	1.2	33.6	803.7	1763.4
Finland	4.7	2.1	0.5	4.2	1.8	1.9	1.9	1.3	3.2	-24.4	30.5	434.7
France	-4.1	0.8	0.7	1.2	1.0	0.9	1.1	0.2	1.0	-21.3	-198.7	1.8
Germany	-1.1	-0.4	1.0	1.3	0.5	-1.1	-1.1	-11.9	2.1	-323.6	-377.6	-124.8
Greece	-5.5	2.9	4.5	15.0	5.4	4.5	4.7	2.2	2.0	46.9	-61.2	1.1
Ireland	-1.9	6.7	4.5	13.8	7.2	6.1	8.1	10.6	2.7	17.3	-130.0	72.7
Italy	-7.0	0.7	1.3	4.7	1.4	0.4	1.3	-1.7	1.9	-39.9	-431.7	-131.9
Neth'ds	-4.6	4.6	3.5	6.4	3.7	4.7	5.5	22.8	1.4	82.7	-719.9	330.9
Norway	-5.5	5.6	3.8	6.2	8.0	10.2	10.6	14.6	-0.1	-125.5	106.0	660.4
Portgal	-10.3	1.9	3.9	10.9	3.8	2.8	2.7	0.6	2.5	-28.5	24.8	12.0
Spain	-6.2	3.0	4.6	13.9	4.4	4.1	3.9	2.5	2.2	-2.7	-12.0	4.9
Sweden	0.8	1.4	0.6	2.3	1.1	1.1	1.4	-0.7	2.2	-67.2	30.9	48.0
Switz'd	-5.8	3.4	4.5	11.6	3.5	5.4	4.1	-0.8	3.0	-863.0	-352.4	-12.3
UK	-12.9	0.6	1.8	2.0	1.4	1.3	1.3	-18.6	1.1	-313.4	-2574.0	-91.9
Japan	-5.5	0.1	0.4	0.5	0.3	-0.1	-0.0	-1.5	1.2	-341.4	-268.6	-1999.0
US	0.1	-0.3	0.2	-0.1	-0.2	-1.1	-0.7	1.5	-0.3	19.5	-23.8	-1.6

Source: Bowen et al. (1987)

Definitions: Cap.: capital; Lab.: labour; which is also subdivided into Prof.: professional/technical; Manag.: managerial; Cleric.: Clerical; Sales: sales; Serv.: service; Agric.: agriculture; Prod.: production; there are also three types of land, Arable, Forest and Pasture.

In addition, Finland is revealed by trade as the most capital-abundant country in Europe, with Ireland the most labour-abundant.

The remaining columns of the table show allowance for different types of labour as factors of production and three categories of land inputs. These figures suggest that the UK is relatively abundant in skilled labour (managerial and professional and technical) but scarce in land and capital. Germany is abundant in production workers and managerial labour and also scarce in land. There are some strange entries in the table. A number of countries appear to export more than 100 per cent of the services of certain of their factors, such as Denmark and pastureland. Greece, Ireland, and Spain appear to be better endowed with skilled labour than other European countries. These potential peculiarities may reflect the inapplicability of applying factor intensities derived from the US input–output table to all countries. There is some suggestion, contrary to the assumption of the Heckscher-Ohlin model, that these intensities are not common across countries.

Formal tests of the sign and rank propositions derived from equations (8.19) by Bowen *et al.*, based upon data for 27 countries and the 12 factors presented in Table 8.1, provide little support for the HO theory. The hypothesis that the sign of the factor content of trade and the sign of the excess factor share are independent could be rejected by only one factor, arable land. Similarly, with regard to the rank test, the hypothesis of a zero-rank correlation is rejected by only four factors, and the proportion of correct orderings by factor or by country rarely exceeds 50 per cent. In the majority of cases, therefore, the ranking by factor content of trade was inconsistent with the ranking by factor abundance.

As we mentioned earlier, proper empirical assessment of an economic theory requires an alternative to test against it. Bowen *et al.* (1987) test the equality between the factor content of net trade and factor supplies, as implied by the HOV equations (8.12), against a number of alternatives. These allow for deviations from homothetic preferences, variations between countries in technology in terms of (proportionally) different factor input coefficients, and for errors in the measurement of the data. It is found that the assumption of homotheticity cannot be rejected by the data. This result conflicts with other studies which find little support for the assumption that, in the absence of changes in relative prices, expenditure on all goods rises in proportion with expenditure (see, for example, Hunter and Markusen 1988). Bowen *et al.* find that the HOV hypothesis is rejected against alternatives which allow for errors of measurement in trade and factor endowments and for differences in technological coefficients. However, the model with technology differences does not provide plausible estimates; for a number of countries including, for example, Mexico and the Philippines, factors appeared to be more productive than those in the US. For a group of other countries factors produce negative outputs! Bowen *et al.* conclude that the Heckscher-Ohlin theorem finds little empirical support, yet the alternatives are not at all plausible.

Trefler (1993) examines in more detail the importance of differences in technology in explaining the apparent poor empirical performance of the HOV model and the observed absence of factor-price equalization. Trefler's approach is to measure the endowment of each country in terms of productivity-equivalent units of service. Differences in factor prices between countries are shown to be proportional to international differences in factor productivities. The test of the theory is formulated by deriving the productivity differences that are necessary to make the model fit the data perfectly and then examining whether these are compatible with actual differences in factor prices. For example, if it is necessary to assume that the ratio of German to Spanish productivity is two for the model to fit perfectly, then the ratio of German to Spanish wages should also be around two. Trefler's results suggest that once this modification for productivity differences is made, the HOV model explains much of the factor content of trade.

These results suggest that it is too early to completely abandon the factor endowments model of trade. A number of authors have suggested that, whilst it is difficult to accept the model as a general explanation of trade, it still has considerable power in explaining trade in particular types of goods, those manufactures with standardized technology and no specific factors, such as textiles and footwear. An alternative theory which has been subjected to a high degree of theoretical activity is that which allows for imperfect competition and economies of scale. The empirical analysis of such models is still in its infancy. Again the approach is to compare the predictions of the model against the data rather than test the theory against a strict alternative.

8.7 Empirical studies of trade under monopolistic competition

Much of the stimulus to the development of theories of trade with monopolistic competition stemmed from empirical analysis and specifically the demonstration of the importance of intra-industry trade. For a period empirical studies were therefore undertaken in the absence of a fully developed theory. This contributed to a 'kitchen sink' attitude (Leamer and Levinsohn 1994) to the choice of variables which ought to be included in estimating equations to explain the level of intra-industry trade between two countries.

Following the development of a theoretical structure to explain trade under monopolistic competition, initiated by Krugman (1979) and discussed in Chapter 7, there have recently been several attempts to use properly specified empirical models. The principal piece of work is that of Helpman (1987). The HOV theorem is concerned with identifying which products a country will trade, and says little about how much trade a country will undertake and who it will trade most intensively with. However, as a general observation, the volume of trade appears to be higher between countries with high incomes. This is strongly supported by the gravity model which we shall discuss below. Thus casual empiricism suggests some relationship between country size and the volume of trade. Helpman (1987) shows how the theory of trade under monopolistic competition can provide a basis for such a relationship and can be used to derive models which enable a statistical assessment of its importance in the data.

Before considering monopolistic competition we first highlight the unimportance of country size in the traditional model. In the standard two-country, two-factor, two-commodity model with homogeneous products, constant returns to scale and identical homothetic preferences the volume of trade between the countries is given by

$$V = p_X (X_A - s_A X_W) + p_Y (Y_B - s_B Y_W) \qquad (8.21)$$

where $X_W = X_A + X_B$ is world production of good X, and similarly for Y_W, X_A being output in country A and s_A the share of country A in world GDP. Assuming that country A has comparative advantage in the production of good X and country B in good Y then the equation shows that the volume of trade is the difference between the value of output and the value of consumption of both goods. With balanced trade this reduces to

$$V = 2p_X (X_A - s_A X_W) \qquad (8.22)$$

and relative country size has no particular effect upon the volume of trade.

We may now assume that X and Y are differentiated products, each variety of which is produced under increasing returns to scale. There is monopolistic competition, so that there will be a large number of firms each producing one variety of a product and making zero profits in the long run. In this case, unlike in the traditional model, the number of firms plays an important role. The volume of output of, say good X, in each country will be determined by output per variety x and the number of firms, n

$$X_A = x n_X^A, X_B = x n_X^B, X_W = x (n_X^A + n_X^B) \qquad (8.23)$$

and similarly for good Y. If preferences are homothetic and all consumers have a utility function of the Dixit-Stiglitz type, in which greater variety generates higher utility, then with sufficiently low transport costs every variety of both goods will be demanded in each country. Thus there will be intra-industry trade, since some varieties will only be available from abroad. In fact, in this simple model, all trade will be intra-industry trade.

The value of exports by country A will be equal to

$$s_B p_X n_X^A x + s_B p_Y n_Y^A y \qquad (8.24)$$

and the volume of trade will be given by

$$V = s_B p_X n_X^A x + s_B p_Y n_Y^A y + s_A p_X n_X^B x + s_A p_Y n_Y^B y \qquad (8.25)$$

which given equation (8.23) reduces to

$$V = s_B (p_X X_A + p_Y Y_A) + s_A (p_X X_B + p_Y Y_B) \qquad (8.26)$$

The terms in brackets give the value of total output, and hence GDP, in each country. With balanced trade the volume of trade becomes

$$V = 2 s_A s_B GDP_W \qquad (8.27)$$

where GDP_W is the combined GDP of the two-countries or world GDP. The volume of trade with differentiated products therefore depends upon the shares of both countries in global GDP and so upon relative country size. The volume of trade will be greater, the smaller the difference between s_A and s_B.

Intra-industry trade is most prominent amongst a subset of the world's economies: the high-income industrial countries in Western Europe, North America, and Japan. The theory of trade under monopolistic competition is likely to be most relevant for exchange between such rich countries. One would not expect the theory to have great power in explaining trade between poorer, developing countries. To assess empirically the relationship postulated in equation (8.27) Helpman extends the analysis to trade within a group of countries. Denote the group by I so that the combined GDP is given by

$$GNP^I = \sum_{j \in I} GDP_j \tag{8.28}$$

and the share of an individual country, j, in group GDP is

$$s_j^I = \frac{GDP_j}{GDP^I} \tag{8.29}$$

and the share of group I in world GDP is

$$s^I = \frac{GDP^I}{GDP_W} \tag{8.30}$$

From equation (8.27) the volume of trade between members of group I will be

$$V^I = \sum_{j \in I} \sum_{k \in I} s_j GDP_k \tag{8.31}$$

for all k not $= j$, where, as before, s_j is the share of country j in world GDP. By using equation (8.29)

$$V^I = \sum_{j \in I} \sum_{k \in I} s_j s_j^I GDP^I = GDP^I \sum_{j \in I} s_j(1 - s_j^I) \tag{8.32}$$

If there is balanced trade then the share of country j in world GDP will be equal to the product of its share of group GDP, and the share of the group in world GDP, that is

$$s_j = \frac{s_j^I GDP^I}{GDP_W} = s_j^I s^I \tag{8.33}$$

The substitution of equation (8.32) into equation (8.30) gives

$$\frac{V^I}{GDP_W} = s^I \sum_{j \in I} s_j^I(1 - s_j^I) = s^I \left[1 - \sum_{j \in I} (s_j^I)^2 \right] \tag{8.34}$$

The term in square brackets is a measure of the dispersion of country size within the group. It reaches its maximum value when the countries are all of identical size in terms of GDP. This equation shows that the volume of intra-group trade relative to world GDP will increase as the share of the group in world GDP rises and as the members of the group become increasingly similar in terms of size. The final equation should be adjusted to allow for imbalance in trade, although in practice it turns out that this makes little difference to the empirical results (see Helpman 1987 for specific details).

Equation (8.34) provides for an empirical assessment of the importance of theories of trade under monopolistic competition in explaining actual trade flows. Helpman considered data for 14 OECD countries for the period between 1956 and 1981. A clear positive relationship was found between the ratio of intra-group trade to global GDP and the dispersion of country size. This supports the proposition derived from the theory that as countries become more similar in terms of size the volume of trade amongst them increases.

Helpman used simple graphical techniques to assess this relationship. Hummels and Levinsohn (1993) applied standard econometric techniques to regression equations representing Helpman's model. Their estimates, using similar data for OECD countries, provide further strong support for a positive relationship between trade volume and size dispersion. To check the robustness of this result, Hummels and Levinsohn applied the model to data for a number of non-OECD countries. Again they find much support for the theory. This is, however, rather damning, since the countries in the second data set (for example, the Congo and Paraguay) were chosen, *ex ante*, as likely to provide cases inconsistent with a model of monopolistic competition. The fact that the empirical model appears to be successful when applied to both appropriate and inappropriate data suggests that factors outside of the model of trade under monopolistic competition are important determinants of the volume of trade.

The tests discussed above are based upon the assumption that all trade is intra-industry trade. Helpman also derives equations to explain the share of intra-industry trade in total trade. In other words, he allows for trade due to monopolistic competition and trade generated by differences in endowments. When two countries are similarly endowed with factors of production then the share of intra-industry trade in total trade will tend to be high. Countries with significantly different endowments are expected to primarily undertake inter-industry trade.

Helpman assumes that differences in factor endowments can be approximated by differences in per capita income, and then tests the hypothesis that the share of intra-industry trade in trade between two countries should be higher for countries with a similar income per head. He estimates the following equation:

$$\frac{Intra_{ij}}{Intra_{ij}+Interi_{ij}} = \alpha_0 + \alpha_1 \log\left|\frac{GDP_i}{POP_i} - \frac{GDP_j}{POP_j}\right| + \alpha_2 \min(\log GDP_{iy} \log GDP_j)$$

$$+\alpha_3 \max(\log GDP_{iy} \log GDP_j) \tag{8.35}$$

where POP represents population. As explained above, the sign of α_1 was expected to be negative. The minimum and maximum levels of GDP were included to control for the effects of relative size. The share of intra-industry trade was expected to be positively related to the level of GDP of the smaller country and negatively related to the income level of the larger country. Helpman's statistical results suggested a significant negative relation between differences in income per head and the importance of intra-industry trade in total trade between two countries, although the strength of this relationship appeared to have declined over the sample period of 1970 to 1981. Similarly, the signs of α_2 and α_3 were found to be as expected. These results are argued to provide support for hypotheses about trade derived from a model with product differentiation and monopolistic competition.

Doubts over the validity of these results are, again, cast by Hummels and Levinsohn (1993). They highlight two problems from using the difference in income per capita to approximate differing factor endowments. Firstly, the approximation will only be correct if there are just two factors of production and all goods are traded. Since this is not what we observe, we need to know just how good a proxy dissimilarity of per capita incomes is for differences in factor endowments, and whether alternative measures would undermine the principal results.

Secondly, there is uncertainty as to whether per capita income reflects demand determinants of trade, as suggested by Linder, or supply determinants, that is, factor endowments. Linder argued that countries with comparable demand structures, reflected by similarity of per capita income, would tend to produce and trade similar goods. Hummels and Levinsohn estimate an equation similar to (8.35), but instead of using differences in income per head they use differences in capital per worker to measure differing factor endowments. Their results show that using data on actual factor intensities changes the conclusions from this type of analysis. The coefficient with regard to differences in capital per worker was found to be statistically insignificant in all bar one of the twenty-two observations, implying that except for this single year the hypothesis of no relationship between differences in factor endowments and the share of intra-industry trade could not be rejected. Hummels and Levinsohn also find that using a different estimation technique to exploit the panel nature of the data undermines the support for the theory. They suggest that much of the variation in the share of intra-industry trade in bilateral trade-flows between OECD countries is due to factors specific to pairs of countries, which casts doubt on the possibility for a general theory which can explain intra-industry trade.

So, despite an initially favourable empirical assessment, recent tests have generated scepticism about the usefulness of models of trade under monopolistic competition in explaining actual levels of intra-industry trade. There are alternative theories of intra-industry trade, such as those derived from reciprocal dumping in oligopolistic markets. However, the empirical assessment of these models is not well developed. Research in this area is constrained by the lack of data by which to test the underlying theories, and the sensitivity of the predictions of the model to underlying assumptions. For example, we know that the nature of the competition in such markets is important, yet there is no simple way of accurately measuring how firms interact. As we shall see in the chapter on strategic trade policy, the use of simulation models is all that has been possible so far. These models have highlighted the important role that economies of scale and the nature of competition *can* play in determining trade flows, but they cannot be used as a basis by which to test the *actual* empirical significance of these variables and so the validity of the underlying theory.

To summarize so far, then, the most rigorous tests of the Heckscher-Ohlin theorem find little statistical support for the posited relationship between the factor content of trade and factor supplies. There is, however, a large volume of at least circumstantial evidence that factor endowments play an important role in explaining international trade flows in certain commodities. The theory cannot explain some of the major developments in world trade in the postwar period, and in particular the increasing exchange of similar products between industrialized countries. Other theories have been developed which relax some of the assumptions underlying the Heckscher-Ohlin model, allowing for differences in technology, increasing returns, and imperfect competition. The problem is that none of these theories finds strong support in the data, although, again, they appear to be useful in explaining certain types of trade. Clearly more needs to be done on both the theoretical and empirical front. We are left without a general theory which can explain the source of all international trade, and are unlikely to find one. Finally we discuss an issue which all of the theories so far discussed tend to ignore, the importance of distance between countries in determining trade between them.

8.8   Gravity models and the importance of distance

Deardorff (1984) suggests that there are three questions upon which a theory of trade should be expected to give an answer. Which goods do countries trade? With whom do countries trade? How much do countries trade? As we have seen above, the theory of trade under conditions of monopolistic competition has provided for the empirical assessment of the volume of trade between two countries. This research is, however, still very much in its infancy. Traditional trade models have been confined to considering only the first of these questions. In part this follows from the constraints imposed by simplifying assumptions. In many models there are only two countries, so that the issue of bilateral trade does not arise. In multi-country models, goods are typically assumed to be identical, and the source of a country's imports and the destination of its exports are indeterminable. One way of removing this indeterminacy of trade partners is to introduce transport costs and, in effect, treat relative proximity as an additional source of comparative advantage. However, transport costs are generally not taken into account in trade theory, and so the pattern of bilateral trade flows is not considered. Similarly ignoring transport costs means that the models are unable to predict accurately the volume of trade.

Although theoretical work has concentrated upon the questions of why countries trade and which goods they exchange, a branch of empirical analysis has concentrated on explaining the volume of trade between pairs of countries. Such analysis explicitly includes transport costs, typically approximated by the distance between countries, as a primary determinant of the level of bilateral trade. Countries which are in close proximity are expected, other things being equal, to trade more intensively than countries which are far apart. The particular empirical model is known as the gravity model.

The standard gravity model, developed in the 1960s by Linnemann (1966), describes the trade flow from a particular source country i to a particular destination country j in terms of the following relationship:

$$lnX_{ij} = \alpha + \beta_1 lnGDP_i + \beta_2 lnPOP_i + \beta_3 lnGDP_j + \beta_4 lnPOP_j$$
$$+ \beta_5 lnDIST_{ij} + \Sigma\gamma_k D_{kij} \qquad (8.36)$$

where X_{ij} is the value of the trade flow from country i (exporter) to country j (importer), GDP_i is the Gross Domestic Product of country i, POP_i is the population of country i, $DIST_{ij}$ is the distance between countries i and j, D_{kij} are dummy variables representing the adjacency of i and j (*ADJ*) and preference relationships between i and j, and α, β_i and γ_k are parameters to be estimated.

The volume of trade between any pair of countries is explained primarily by their incomes (to proxy demand and supply) and the distance between them (to proxy transportation costs). Population is included to reflect the fact that larger, more populous countries tend to be more self-sufficient and so indulge less actively in trade. Additional variables are included to take account of artificial trade barriers and the fact that adjacent countries tend to trade more intensively.

Brenton and Gros (1995) estimate such a relationship, using 1992 data, for sixteen Western European countries, six Eastern European countries, and Canada, the US, and Japan. A summary of the results, which are typical of those of previous studies using this model, is provided in Table 8.2. The signs of the estimated parameters are consistent with theoretical expectation: trade increases with income in the importer and the exporter, and decreases with population and distance. The parameter on exporter GDP is greater than one suggesting that the value of exports rises more than proportionately with income. The elasticity of trade with respect to distance is –0.6. Leamer and Levinsohn (1994) note that the value of this distance elasticity appears to have remained constant over time. Thus, the explanation for the increase in trade in the second half of this century is not that the world is getting smaller. Rather, it is that world income has become more dispersed, so that the economic mass of Europe and Asia has grown relative to that of North America.

The gravity model has proved to be a very successful empirical model. It typically explains a high proportion of the variance in bilateral trade data. Almost 90

Table 8.2. Estimates of the gravity model using data for 25 countries for 1992

C	GDP_i	POP_i	GDP_j	POP_j	DIST	ADJ	EUEFTA	R^2
1.38	1.01	–0.24	0.89	–0.14	–0.64	0.75	0.52	0.88

Source: Brenton and Gros (1995).

per cent of the variation in trade flows between the countries studied by Brenton and Gros (1995) was explained by the gravity model. This follows from the ability to allow for the key developments in trade relations during the past five decades: intra-industry trade, the tendency for countries with high income per head to trade more intensively with similar rich countries, and the tendency for trade to grow faster than income.

In an interesting application, McCallum (1995) uses data on trade between Canadian provinces (i.e. intra-Canadian exchange), and between these provinces and individual states in the US, to estimate the gravity model. The results suggest that, on average, trade between Canadian provinces is twenty-two times greater than trade between provinces and US states. This suggests that despite all the discussion of the increasing internationalization of economies, exchanges within an economy are far more important than trade between different countries so that clearly 'national borders matter'.

The problem with the gravity model is that it cannot be clearly derived from a well-developed model of trade. There is thus no strong theoretical background with which to appraise the results of the empirical model. As Deardorff (1984) concludes, the gravity models 'tell us something important about what happens in international trade, even if they do not tell us why'. The bridging of this gap between the empirical success of the gravity model and trade theory is a matter for continuing research.

One of the early uses of the gravity model was to assess the economic effects of the EEC (Aitken 1973). The results of Brenton and Gros (1995) suggest that being a member of the EU or EFTA (EUEFTA) raises trade with partners by about 70 per cent. A more recent application of the gravity model has been to assess the potential impact upon trade flows of the transformation of the formerly centrally planned economies in Eastern and Central Europe into market-based economies. The previous system led to a bias towards trade amongst the former COMECON members and against trade with Western countries. Transformation is therefore expected to lead to a large increase in trade with the West.

Using the estimated parameters from the gravity model and applying them to data on GDP, population and distance for Russia and her trading partners provides a prediction of the pattern of Russian trade, on the assumption that such trade will be determined by the same factors which currently influence trade between market economies.

The gravity model predictions shown in Table 8.3, based upon current GDP, suggest that there will be a substantial reorientation of trade towards the West, and in particular towards the EU. The importance of the CIS countries, the Baltics, and Eastern Europe in Russian trade declines considerably. It could be argued that current GDP does not provide a useful measure of purchasing power in Russia upon which to make predictions about the long-term structure of Russian trade. The recent falls in GDP may be quickly reversed as liberalization proceeds and some catch-up in levels of GDP should be expected. Thus, the final two columns of the table present predictions based upon the assumption that over the next ten years GDP in the West grows at an annual rate of 2.5 per cent,

Table 8.3. The actual and predicted distribution of Russian trade using the gravity model

	Actual shares (first half of 1994)		Predicted shares at current GDP		Predicted shares with income catch-up	
	Exports	Imports	Exports	Imports	Exports	Imports
CIS	22.6	25.3	5.8	4.5	7.0	5.6
EU	29.7	30.6	42.1	43.7	41.1	42.8
France	3.2	3.5	7.3	6.9	7.1	6.7
Germany	15.7	8.9	12.9	12.1	12.6	11.8
Italy	3.9	5.8	6.8	6.5	6.7	6.4
UK	1.8	2.3	2.6	5.7	2.6	5.6
Other EU	6.0	9.1	14.0	10.8	13.7	10.6
EFTA	8.9	9.1	15.3	15.7	14.9	15.4
E. Europe	9.6	8.2	2.6	2.0	3.2	2.5
Baltics	3.1	1.9	0.8	0.6	0.9	0.7
China	5.1	2.8	2.6	1.8	2.5	1.8
Japan	3.2	3.3	7.3	8.1	8.5	7.9
USA	6.1	6.1	8.8	9.6	8.5	9.4

Source: Brenton and Gros (1995).

whilst in the CIS countries and in Eastern Europe GDP grows at an annual average of 5 per cent.

8.9 Conclusions

Empirical assessment is crucial to the development and reformulation of economic theories. International trade theory is no exception. There has been a large volume of empirical work on the ability of the standard Heckscher-Ohlin model to explain actual trade flows, much of this work having been stimulated by the presentation by Leontief of the apparent paradox that in 1947 the US had a comparative advantage in labour-intensive commodities. Subsequently, the methodological basis for this finding has been shown to be incorrect. Proper examination of the theory requires that the relationship between the factor content of net trade, factor endowments, and factor input intensities be investigated. Many studies use observations on only two of these sets of variables to infer the values of the third.

Conceptually correct tests of the theory find little support for the HOV theory. This is not surprising, given the restrictiveness of many of the assumptions underlying the model. Some of these assumptions, which reflect convenience in specifying the theory, can be relaxed for empirical analysis without destroying the fundamental link in the theory between factor endowments and trade. There is some evidence that once account is taken of differences between countries in technology, the HOV model is more powerful in explaining the pattern of international trade. Nevertheless, the ability of the model to act as a general theory of international trade has been undermined by recent changes in the nature of trade flows, and in particular the increase in intensity of trade between similar countries.

This empirical observation stimulated the search for new theories of trade based upon imperfect competition, product differentiation, and economies of scale. Confrontation with the data has lagged behind the theoretical developments. However, initial studies suggest doubts about the ability of such theories to provide an adequate explanation of trade between industrial countries. Further statistical analysis to improve our understanding of the empirical basis of trade relations is therefore of the utmost importance.

In Europe it is important to understand the determinants of trade flows to be able to assess the implications of trade liberalization. Different theories of trade imply differences in the distribution of the benefits of trade liberalization and the costs of adjustment. If the principal stimulant to trade is differences in factor endowments, then trade liberalization will encourage inter-industry specialization. In rich countries in the EU, the relative price of labour-intensive commodities will decline, which in turn will reduce the real wage of unskilled labour and the return to factors specific to those industries. Resources will have to move from labour-intensive to capital- and human-capital-intensive industries. For labour this may require retraining, which carries an economic cost. Thus, there will be strong incentives for lobbies to form to oppose trade liberalization.

If trade is primarily conducted in an environment of imperfect competition and economies of scale, then trade liberalization will tend to promote intra-industry specialization. Factors will have to adjust within industries. Trade will reduce the rents earned by certain factors in particular industries. For a particular industry, the removal of trade barriers will tend to increase the exports of a country, hence enhancing producer surplus. At the same time increasing import penetration will benefit consumers, as prices fall and variety increases, but will displace some local production. Thus the overall effect for producers and the country as a whole is unclear, and will depend upon the extent to which competition is enhanced and the degree of unexploited economies of scale. However, adjustment is generally held to be easier when trade liberalization generates intra-industry specialization.

The recently concluded Europe Agreements between the EU and Bulgaria, the Czech Republic, Hungary, Poland, Romania, and Slovakia incorporated a much slower pace of trade liberalization for labour-intensive, 'sensitive' sectors. Initial indications suggest that these agreements have caused little adjustment difficulties in the EU, and have led to a significant increase in the level of intra-industry trade between the EU and each of these countries.

8.10 Summary

- Empirical tests of the Heckscher-Ohlin model produce a mixed verdict at best. Leontief's paradox may be explained by unbalanced trade.
- Tests should ideally employ independent data on trade, factor intensities and factor endowments; a major study that does this finds little support for Heckscher-Ohlin.
- Tests of monopolistic competition models and the idea that trade between countries rises as they become more similar in size are unconvincing.
- Evidence reveals that trade is favoured by geographical proximity.

9

THEORY OF TRADE POLICY

9.1 Introduction

In this chapter we shall be considering the basic theory of trade policy. This concerns the effects that trade and trade-related instruments might be expected to have upon various economic parameters and upon welfare. Some applications of European trade policy will be discussed in Chapters 17 and 18 below.

The discussion in this chapter will be both positive and normative. It will be positive because the analysis of such issues as the effect of a tariff upon the volume of production, consumption, imports, and upon the price of a good can be carried out in the context of economic theory independently of any consideration of the desirability of that tariff. It will be normative, because we shall be making welfare judgements. In particular we do want to establish criteria by which a policy can be assessed as welfare-improving, and by which various policies can—at least in principle—be evaluated and ranked. We shall start the discussion by considering once again the normative concept of the gains from trade.

autarky-

9.2 The gains from trade and compensation

We have previously described how the classical and neo-classical economists have seen trade as making available consumption possibilities that are not available in autarky. This is illustrated in Figure 9.1, which shows that, in the absence of trade, consumption will be restricted to the production possibility frontier of the economy, and will be at some point such as A where the slope of that frontier is equal to the non-trade price, P_A. In contrast, under idealized circumstances, free trade at some international price, P_W, different from the autarky price and represented by the slope of the production possibility frontier at the point Q, would give rise to the production combination represented by Q, and would permit consumption along the budget line associated with that income and the international price.

In Chapter 4 we associated the shift from one indifference curve to a higher one, such as from A to C in the diagram, as representing the gains from trade.

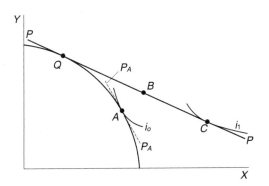

Fig. 9.1. Gains from trade

There were two problems which we noted, both associated with the change in income distribution which may arise as a result of the change from autarky to trade. The first is that a unique set of indifference curves may not exist. We evaded this problem by assuming that all consumers have the same tastes, and that these tastes are homothetic in the sense that the proportion of income spent on each good depends only upon prices and not upon the level of that income. This is an undesirable restriction, since in some contexts—particularly in the consideration of less-developed countries—the relationship between the pattern of demand and income distribution is an important issue. The second problem is that—as we have seen in the discussion of the Stolper-Samuelson model—some people may be worse off as a result of a change from autarky to trade. This raises the difficult problem as to how one policy can be assessed as superior to another when the welfare of some has deteriorated. This is, of course, an issue that is much broader than an evaluation of trade policy. The way that most economists explicitly or implicitly handle this problem is through the concept of compensation. Referring again to Figure 9.1, we can see that the consumption possibility curve associated with trade lies outside that associated with no trade except at the point where the international price is the same as the domestic relative cost of production, and that it never lies inside the production possibility frontier. The implication of this is that trade permits all the consumption possibilities available in the absence of trade, and makes available some additional ones. If society chooses a pattern of consumption different from the no-trade pattern, it is in some sense showing a revealed preference for that pattern. Furthermore, it is in principle feasible for the gainers to compensate the losers from the move to trade. This can be seen by noting that the trade consumption possibility curve passes outside of the autarky consumption point, indicating that the economy could consume at points such as *B*, where there are more of all goods compared to the no-trade situation. In the absence of administrative costs, and assuming that transfers can be made in a way that does not distort production and consumption, it will be possible for the enhanced bundle of goods to be distributed so that everyone has more of everything. In this sense there are potential gains from trade. It should be noted that trade may yield a combination of goods such as at C where there is more of one good and less of the other consumed than under autarky. It may not be possible to make everyone better off from this particular bundle of goods. For example, it might be the case that the trade solution is associated with an uneven distribution of income under which many luxury goods are consumed. The more even distribution of income associated with the payment of compensation could yield a pattern of demand in which more non-luxuries and fewer luxuries are demanded. This possibility does not negate the possibility of compensation. The payment of compensation under these circumstances would shift demand from point C along the budget line towards B, where there is sufficient of the non-luxury good to accommodate the changed demand conditions. It should be noted that this possible compensation criterion is not dependent upon the restrictive assumptions discussed in Chapter 4 that were necessary in order to derive the community indifference curves. All that is required is that consumption possibilities available with trade include all of those available without trade plus some additional ones. In terms of Figure 9.1, the trade budget line must lie partially outside, and never be inside, the production possibility frontier (Samuelson 1962).

More serious reservations about the compensation principle arise when the authorities lack either the administrative capability or the will to pay compensation. Under these circumstances, the assessment of a situation in which there are potentially more of all goods available as being superior to one in which there are less goods but a different income distribution is dubious. This is particularly a problem if the regime is undemocratic, since then there is no basis for assuming that it is implementing social preferences. Nevertheless, this is the criterion which we, in common with most economists, will be using.[1,2]

A final point is that the discussion above, and particularly Figure 9.1, assumed that the country could trade as much as it wanted at given international terms of trade. This 'small country' assumption was reflected in the straight budget line in the diagram. The case for trade—although not that for free trade—does not require this assumption. The terms of trade of a large country may not be perfectly elastic, but are likely to deteriorate as the volume of trade increases, in which case the budget curve reflecting the consumption possibility curve will be concave. Provided that the elasticity is not so low that the budget line is more concave than the production possibility curve, trade will still provide consumption

---

[1] Other criteria can be used. For example, the social philosopher John Rawls (1972) argues that it is the welfare of the poorest group in society that is relevant in evaluating policies.

[2] An interesting application of the principle and practice of compensation occurred in the United Kingdom in 1994. The Government, on grounds of economic efficiency and to raise revenue, attempted to raise the rate of the value added tax VAT on domestic fuel to 17.5% in line with that on most other products. It was recognized that expenditure on fuel constituted a relatively high proportion of the budgets of the poor, particularly the elderly, so the Government stated that pensions and welfare payments would be adjusted to compensate the vulnerable for the tax rise. There was, however, so much scepticism as to whether the compensation would be sufficient that the Government found it expedient to withdraw the proposal.

possibilities that are not available under autarky, and will be superior according to the potential compensation criterion.[3]

9.3 The case for free trade

We now consider, in rather general terms, the case for free trade or, conversely, the case for policy intervention. We start by following Corden (1974) in identifying three stages of thought. This leads to a comparison of some of the main trade-related instruments, and a discussion of their effectiveness in achieving various objectives.

9.3.1 Free trade as an extension of *laissez-faire*

The first stage of thought is in the classical tradition which saw free trade as being an extension of *laissez-faire*. The economic rationale of this position is that under certain circumstances *laissez-faire* including free trade is Pareto-optimal. This is shown in Figure 9.1 above. Implicitly, in this diagram, the perfect functioning of the commodity and factor markets has led to production at point Q which is on the production possibility frontier, with the relative cost of production equal to the world price. Production at this point maximizes income at this price. Free trade allows consumers to maximize their welfare by consuming at point C. Any other combination of production and consumption would be inferior. At this optimum certain marginal conditions are being satisfied. In particular, the relative marginal cost of production (the slope of the production possibility curve) is equal to the relative marginal cost of obtaining the goods through international trade (the slope of the perfectly elastic international price line) which is equal to the marginal rate of substitution between the goods in consumption (the slope of the indifference curve). Following terminology and notation developed by Bhagwati (1971), the domestic rate of transformation (DRT) is equal to the foreign rate of transformation (FRT), which is equal to the domestic rate of substitution (DRS). Furthermore, if all countries were following free trade under these idealized conditions, there would be a world economic optimum, with marginal costs of production and marginal rates of substitution being equalized throughout the world.[4]

---

[3] Whether or not the terms of trade are perfectly elastic is of considerable importance in evaluating free trade relative to restricted trade, as we shall discuss in the context of the 'optimum tariff' below.

[4] This discussion and the diagram is in the context of a two-commodity world, but these results can be generalized to many products.

9.3.2 Distortions and the theory of the second best

The second stage of thought is the recognition that the onerous conditions for *laissez-faire* to be Pareto-optimal will never be met. These conditions require not only that all markets function perfectly without externalities, but also that the markets for factors and commodities including all contingencies are complete, and that all the participants have complete knowledge of all these markets. Since these conditions are never satisfied, the general presumption in favour of *laissez-faire* cannot be maintained. This is clearly damaging for the case for free trade based upon the extension of *laissez-faire*. Thus many arguments for intervention in trade have been put forward upon the grounds that some market failures make free trade inappropriate. For example, the infant-industry case for protection is based on the grounds that, due to failures in the markets for capital, and particularly human capital, industries that will be viable in the long run will never get established in the face of international competition. Therefore, it is argued, such industries should receive temporary protection in order to allow them time to acquire the necessary capital, skills, and scales of production to become competitive. This stage of thought was predominant in the early post-Second-World-War period, and seemed to receive theoretical support from the 'Theory of the Second Best' (Lancaster and Lipsey 1956). This theory demonstrates that if a general equilibrium has several requirements for Pareto optimality, and if, due to some distortions or constraints, one or more of the conditions for optimality cannot be achieved, then in general there is no presumption that the constrained (second-best) optimum requires that the other conditions be satisfied. It may be helpful to consider a non-economic example: Suppose that the optimal tyre pressure on an automobile is 30 lbs per square inch on all the wheels. But if, due to some constraint, only 20 lbs per square inch can be maintained on one of the tyres, then it cannot be presumed that the second-best solution will require the other wheels to have a tyre pressure of 30 lbs per square inch. A well-known economic application—dating from before the formalization of the theory—is Viner's demonstration that it cannot be presumed that in a world of tariffs it is optimal for some subset of countries to remove their tariffs against each other and form a customs union. The relevance of the theory of the Second Best to the case for free trade is that it demonstrates that in a world of distortions and constraints it cannot be presumed that free trade is optimal. Many arguments for protection or for export subsidies are based upon the presumption that the trade intervention will offset the effects of distortions that prevail in any economic system.

9.3.3 Ranking of policies

The third stage of thought that most economists would accept today is the recognition that, although in a distorted world there is no presumption that *laissez-*

faire is optimal, neither is there any presumption that trade intervention is appropriate.

There is a recognition that some policies may be able to counteract some of the undesirable effects of distortions, but it is also realized that the policy instruments themselves create distortions. Policy intervention, then, requires knowledge about the distortions that are being corrected, and the distortions that are being created by the policy instruments. Some progress, however, has been made in developing general criteria for the evaluation of policies. This has been the work of economists such as H. G. Johnson and J. Bhagwati, who have developed what is described as the theory of distortions and welfare, and of M. Corden in particular, who has done much to illuminate the relevance and the applicability of the theory to those engaged in the formulation and evaluation of economic policy. The general principle of the theory of distortions and welfare is simple. Policies should be directed as closely as possible at the distortions that they are trying to correct. The more remote is the policy instrument from its objective, the more probable is it that the undesired side effects arising from the implementation of the policy will outweigh the benefits achieved. The implication of this principle for trade policy is that, normally, trade intervention is an inappropriate policy instrument to correct a distortion within the domestic economy, because the trade instrument is too remote from the distortion. An instrument that focuses more directly upon the distortion should be used instead. Thus, in the case for protection of an infant industry mentioned above, if the cause of the problem is a failure in the markets for capital or human capital, then the appropriate policy instruments should be directed at those markets, not at international trade. The effect of import restrictions will be to distort consumer choice, and to give the economy an undesirable bias against production for export. This approach restores the presumption that free trade is optimal, and places upon advocates of trade intervention the burden of demonstrating that the trade instrument is the one of all the feasible instruments that focuses most directly upon the objective, and that the costs of the use of that instrument will not outweigh the benefits.

This principle will be illustrated in the context of a comparison of tariffs and production subsidies; but first it is necessary to see how these instruments work.

9.4 Instruments of protection

We shall concentrate the discussion upon tariffs and production subsidies, with a briefer consideration of import quotas. Although the policy instruments are generally used in a world that is known to be Pareto-imperfect, in this discussion we shall—to facilitate the exposition—assume that they are introduced into a system that is initially Pareto-optimal. This implies that there must be costs associated with the instruments that we shall identify. We are thus assuming that any objectives are 'non-economic' in the sense that they are not reflected in the welfare functions of the economic agents identified in the models.

We shall be using both partial and general equilibrium techniques of analysis. This is because both are widely used to discuss trade policy; but also because it is illuminating to understand the relationship between these methods, and why their results sometimes differ.

9.4.1 Tariffs vs. subsidies: partial equilibrium

Figure 9.2 represents the demand and supply conditions of a small country that can import a product at a perfectly elastic world price P_W. The demand and supply curves, D and S, properly reflect the marginal social benefit of consuming the good, and the marginal social cost of producing it domestically. With free trade the price will be P_W, with domestic production q_0, consumption c_0, and imports of $q_0 c_0$. We are assuming that there are no distortions, so this is Pareto-optimal. Note, using Bhagwati's terminology, that the domestic rate of transformation, DRT (the marginal cost of producing the good domestically) is equal to the foreign rate of transformation, FRT (the marginal cost of importing the good), which is equal to the domestic rate of substitution, DRS (the marginal value of the good in consumption).

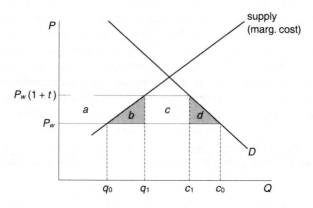

Fig. 9.2. Tariff: partial equilibrium

We now introduce an import tariff at rate t. This raises the domestic price to $P_W(1 + t)$. Domestic production expands to q_1, consumption falls to c_1, and imports fall to $q_1 c_1$. This is the standard diagram of the partial equilibrium representation of the effects of a tariff. Obviously we have departed from Pareto optimality. Using Bhagwati's notation, DRT = DRS > FRT.

This diagram allows us to identify the distributional effects of the tariff. Using the area between the price and the demand curve as a measure of consumer surplus, we can see that consumer surplus has fallen by the areas $a + b + c + d$. Some of this loss is matched by a gain to the producers: the change in the area between the supply curve and the price, area *a*. Some has been transferred to the government in the form of tariff revenue: this is the tariff times the volume of imports, the area *c*. But this leaves the two shaded triangles, areas *b* and *d*, as net losses to the economy. It is important to understand the nature of these losses. The area *b* represents the cost of the additional domestic production over the international supply that it has replaced. Notice that the extra cost of the first unit of extra production permitted by the tariff is low, since the marginal cost of that production is only slightly above the world price; but the cost of the last unit of domestic production made possible by the tariff is the full amount of the tariff. The area *d* is the loss experienced by the consumers who were previously enjoying consumer surplus on the product, but who have now given up consuming it. Here again, we get a triangular shape loss because some of the consumers were previously enjoying consumer surplus close to the amount of the tariff, whereas others valued the product at little above the world price, and so were not enjoying much consumer surplus. Notice that there is no terms of trade effect here, because it is being assumed that the world supply is perfectly elastic.

9.4.2 Production subsidy: partial equilibrium

Now consider the effect of a production subsidy of the value *s* per unit of output. The effective supply curve shifts down by the amount of the subsidy to S' (an increase in supply at any price). The amount received by the producers rises to $P_W(1 + s)$, but the imports continue to enter the economy, and are purchased by consumers at the price P_W. The effects are shown in Figure 9.3.

The critical difference between this diagram and the one representing the effects of the tariff is that consumers are still able to purchase the product at the

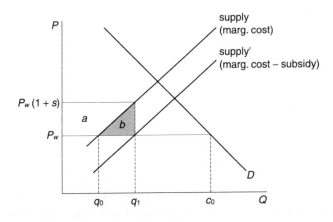

Fig. 9.3. Production subsidy: partial equilibrium

world price, and so maintain consumption at c_0. Domestic production rises to q_1, and imports fall to $q_1 c_0$. The distribution of the costs is quite different. The government has to pay the subsidy to all producers and so loses (incurs expenditure) the rectangle consisting of the areas $a + b$, whereas the producers gain the area a. The consumers (except in their role as direct taxpayers) are unaffected. There is a production loss as in the case of the tariff of the triangle b, but there is no consumption loss.

Comparing the policies, we can see that the costs of a production subsidy are less than those of an equivalent tariff, because there is no direct effect upon the consumers. If the purpose of the policy is to expand domestic production or to increase producer income, the production subsidy is a lower-cost instrument than the equivalent tariff because it focuses more directly upon the objective and avoids the undesirable side-effect of creating a consumption distortion.

Suppose, however, that the 'non-economic' objective is to reduce the dependence upon international trade. This is a trade-related objective, so a trade-related instrument is appropriate. It would require a higher production subsidy than a tariff to achieve a given reduction in imports, so the tariff would be preferable even though the tariff distorts the consumers' choice. This is illustrated in Figure 9.4, which shows the production subsidy compared to the tariff to achieve complete self-sufficiency.

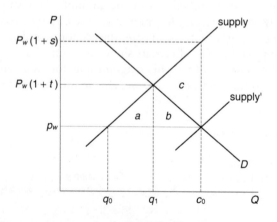

Fig. 9.4. Tariff vs. production subsidy for self-sufficiency

A tariff of t per cent raising the domestic price to $P_W(1 + t)$ will achieve self-sufficiency by expanding domestic production and constraining consumption to the quantity q_1. The cost of this policy is the triangle a which constitutes the production cost, plus the triangle b which is the consumption cost. The production subsidy needed to expand the domestic production to satisfy the level of demand, c_0, consistent with the world price is much higher than the tariff. This is shown as

$P_W(1 + s)$ in the diagram, and it generates a net cost of $a + b + c$. This is a production cost only, but it is unambiguously higher than the combined production and consumption costs of the tariff. This is an illustration of an additional point: that it is usually preferable to have several small distortions than a few big ones. In this case the two moderate distortions created by the tariff are preferable to the one big distortion imposed by the very high production subsidy needed to achieve self-sufficiency. For this reason economists often advocate the desirability of eliminating the most severe distortions at an early stage in implementing trade liberalization.

9.4.3 Tariffs vs. subsidies: general equilibrium

We now carry out the comparison of tariffs with production subsidies using simple general equilibrium analysis. Once again a policy distortion is introduced into a system that is initially Pareto-optimal. In addition to illustrating the effects of the policy instruments upon production, consumption, and trade, the general equilibrium diagram enables us to identify the national income accounting aspects of the policies. This is useful in that it enables us to fully identify the distribution of national income between the producers, the payers of tax or the recipients of redistributed revenue, and the government. In Figure 9.5 we start with free trade at a world price of X in terms of Y, (P_W), given by the slope of Q^*C^*. Production is at Q^*, and consumption is at C^* where the indifference curve i^* is tangent to the budget line. The value of national income in terms of Y is Y^*. Initially there is no government revenue or expenditure, so all of national income is distributed between the producers, with OA being received by the producers of Y, and with the rest, AY^*, being received by the producers of X.

9.4.4 Production subsidy

We now introduce a subsidy on the production of X which raises the return per unit of output received by producers to $P_W(1 + S)$. Production shifts to Q_1. The value of national income at world prices falls to OY_1, but gross factor income before tax rises to OY_2. This consists of OB to the producers of Y and BY_2 to the producers of X. The income of the producers of X is composed of BY_1, from the market price of the product, plus Y_2Y_1, which is the value of the subsidy. The government expenditure on the subsidy is Y_2Y_1, so if the budget is to be balanced, the government will have to tax factor income by Y_2Y_1, thereby reducing disposable income to OY_1 and permitting consumption at C_1 where an indifference curve i_1 is tangent to the budget line. Note that at C_1 the value of consumption is equal to national income at world prices. The production subsidy does not distort consumers' choice (the marginal rate of substitution in consumption is equal to the price); but in contrast to the partial equilibrium analysis, it should be noted that

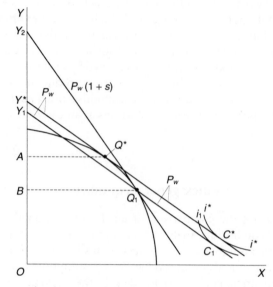

Fig. 9.5. Production subsidy: general equilibrium

consumption of X falls. This is because there is a fall in real income, and it is assumed that X is a normal good.[5]

9.4.5 Tariff

We now consider the effect of a tariff imposed at the same rate as the subsidy in the preceding discussion.

The tariff changes the domestic price to $P_W(1 + t)$. Production is at Q_1, so at world prices national income is Y_1. Consumption is at C_2, a point where trade is balanced at world prices, and where the marginal rate of substitution in consumption is equal to the tariff-distorted price. This is shown by the indifference curve i_2 having at c_2 a slope equal to the tariff-distorted price, $P_W(1 + t)$. The value of factor income is OY_2, and the value of consumption at the tariff-distorted prices is OY_3. Y_2Y_3 is the tariff revenue collected on the imports. It is redistributed to the citizens, thereby maintaining a balanced government budget. The tariff-revenue redistribution raises disposable income to Y_3, enabling the consumption

---

[5] The ceteris paribus assumption implicit in the partial equilibrium analysis is that national income is unaffected by the imposition of the tariff or subsidy, so the only effect on consumption arises through changes in the price. This assumption is reasonable if we are considering a product that constitutes only a small proportion of national income, e.g. honey, so that the income effect can be ignored. However, if the product is important, e.g. the whole class of importable goods as in the two-good general-equilibrium model, then the income effects are important and should be made explicit.

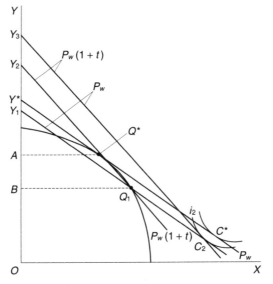

Fig. 9.6. Tariff: general equilibrium

at C_2 to be maintained. Notice that consumption constrained by the tariff on indifference curve i_2 in Figure 9.6 is inferior to that with the equivalent subsidy, which is on indifference curve i_1 in Figure 9.5. This reflects the higher cost of the tariff.

It may be helpful to provide a numerical example of the effects of a tariff that can be related to this diagram.

Choose units of measurement of the goods so that the free trade price of both X and Y is unity, such as £1. Now we impose a 20 per cent tariff upon the import of X, raising its domestic price to £1.20. The post-tariff production will be at Q_1, where the slope of the production possibility frontier is 1.2. Suppose that output at this point is 80 units of X and 100 units of Y. Then national income measured at world prices is £180, Y_1 in the diagram, whereas measured at domestic prices it is £196 or Y_2. Consumption with balanced trade must be on the world price budget line passing through Q_1, at a point where the slope of the indifference curve is equal to the tariff-distorted price of X in terms of Y (1.2). Let us suppose that this point C_2 is where 40 units of Y are exported for 40 units of X, so consumption is $120X$ and $60Y$, and tariff revenue is £8. At world prices, the value of consumption is £180, which is equal to the value of output shown at Y_1. But at domestic prices the value of consumption is £204, shown at Y_3. This level of expenditure is sustained by the value of production, Y_2, plus the redistributed tariff revenue, Y_2Y_3.

In comparing the subsidy with the tariff in this analysis, the most important points to note are as follows. Firstly, the tariff imposes a consumption distortion, whereas the production subsidy does not. Thus a lower level of welfare is achieved with the tariff than with the equivalent subsidy, as can be seen by noting that the point C_2 in Figure 9.6 is on a lower indifference curve than point C_1 in Figure 9.5. Therefore the production subsidy is the more efficient instrument to achieve the objective of raising domestic production of a particular good. This is an application of the general principle that the most effective instrument is the one that is most closely directed at the objective.

Secondly, the implications for government financing are different, since the subsidy requires government expenditure that has to be raised from taxation, whereas the tariff is an indirect tax which raises revenue for the government which in the analysis is then redistributed back to the citizens. In the event of the government not being able to collect taxes without cost and without creating additional distortions, the simple policy conclusions of the analysis have to be reassessed.[6]

9.4.6 The equivalence of export taxes and tariffs

The general equilibrium analysis makes it clear that, under the assumptions of this trading model, an export tax is equivalent to an import tariff. It is the relative price of the commodities that determines the pattern of consumption, production, and trade; and a tax on exports reduces the domestic price of exports below the world price, and so raises the domestic price of importables relative to exportables in the same way as does the tariff. This analysis, with its assumptions of two commodities, full employment, and balanced trade, may seem remote from the real world. Nevertheless, the concept that a tax on imports is an explicit tax on exports is an important one, and is of much wider relevance than in the context of this model. In general, protection of the import-competing sector of an economy reduces the competitiveness of the export sector in world markets.

9.4.7 Quotas

We now briefly compare the effects of a quota with those of a tariff. We shall be demonstrating that, in a static sense, an import quota can be equivalent to a tariff; but we shall see, firstly, that the income distribution effects are likely to be different, and secondly, that the quota is a much more rigid instrument, so that the response of the economy to change is likely to be different under a regime where protection is by means of quotas rather than tariffs. A very important aspect of

---

[6] The Common Agricultural Policy of the European Union, which is discussed in Ch. 18 below, provides an important application of the ranking of trade controls v. income support measures. In 1971–2, prior to joining the CAP, the United Kingdom changed the basis of its agricultural support from income subsidies for producers to import tariffs and controls. On the criterion of directing instruments at objectives, this was clearly a retrograde step. The Conservative government of the time, however, believed that the level of direct taxation was distorting incentives, so that the move from direct to indirect taxation associated with the policy switch was anticipated to stimulate economic effort and enterprise.

the rigidity of the quota is that it confers more monopoly power upon potential domestic monopolists than does the 'equivalent' tariff. This last point will be developed in the discussion of trade and monopoly below.

We limit the discussion to partial equilibrium analysis, and we refer the reader back to Figure 9.2 above, which shows the partial equilibrium effects of a tariff. A quota might take the form of a limit in the value of a product that can be imported, or it might be expressed as a maximum market share. For ease of exposition, we shall treat a quota as a limit on the quantity of a good that can be imported.

In Figure 9.2, free trade at the world price P_W will generate imports of the quantity $q_0 c_0$. Now suppose that an import quota of the volume $q_1 c_1$ is imposed. There is now excess demand for the product at the world price. This will be eliminated by a rise in the domestic price of the product to $P_W(1 + t)$ in the diagram, with a rise in domestic production to q_1 and a fall in consumption to c_1. Thus this quota has had the same impact upon consumption, production, and trade as the equivalent tariff. The net cost is, as before, the areas b and d. The income distribution is, however, in one respect different. The area c, which represented the tariff revenue of the government, is now a rent accruing to the holders of the quota. These have the right to buy the good at the world price and to sell it at the higher domestic price. It is possible, in principle, for the government to auction off the quotas and thereby capture this rent; but in practice this never happens. The quotas may be allocated to domestic residents, in which case the rent is maintained within the economy; but they may—as under 'voluntary export restraints' widely imposed by the European Union on its trading partners—be allocated to the foreign suppliers, in which case the quota rents are lost to the economy. More generally, real resources may be used up in the attempt to acquire the quota rents, thereby dissipating those rents. A further problem with quotas, in common with other measures of administrative control, is that they are liable to be allocated corruptly by the administrators in exchange for political, financial, or other favours. Quotas are less transparent than tariffs in various respects, one of these being with respect to the beneficiaries of the quota rents compared with tariff revenues. These issues are discussed more fully in Chapter 15 below.

The second important difference between the tariff and the quota is the rigidity of the latter. This makes the dynamic effects of the instruments quite different. Suppose that there is an increase in the world productivity in the imported good, so that the world supply price falls. Under a tariff the domestic price would fall by the same proportion, so the consumers would benefit from the change and the domestic producers would be under pressure to increase their productivity. But, with a quota, the domestic price does not change. All that happens is that there is an increase in the quota rents. The tariff sets a specified limit on the amount by which the domestic price can exceed the international price. The quota sets no such limit. This is another respect in which the tariff is more transparent than the quota: in the extent of protection provided.

Another feature of the rigidity of quotas compared with tariffs is that the former tend to make the effective demand facing domestic producers less elastic, so enhancing the potential monopoly power of these producers. This is discussed more fully in Section 9.8.

The brevity of this discussion of quotas is not intended to reflect their importance. Quotas and other quantitative restrictions (generally known as NTBs—non-tariff barriers) are now far more important as restrictions of world and European trade than are tariffs. The reasons for this, and its implications for trade policy reform, are discussed in subsequent chapters.

9.5 Trade policy and economic distortions

In the previous section we induced economic distortions by applying a policy instrument in a situation that was initially Pareto-optimal. This necessarily imposed a loss of welfare upon our economy. In this section we invert the discussion by considering the more relevant case, where the policy is introduced in order to correct some existing distortion. We shall see that the analysis is very similar, except that now there is a potential gain for the economy from the elimination or reduction of the distortion; and the problem is to identify the instruments that maximize this gain net of any losses arising from their distortionary side effects. The general principle remains the same: instruments can be ranked on the basis of how closely they are directed at the policy objective they are intended to achieve. We shall also note, as before, that it is generally possible to improve welfare by reducing or replacing a severe distortion with smaller ones. We shall first illustrate these principles by using partial and general equilibrium analysis to compare the effects of a tariff and a subsidy to correct a distortion within the domestic economy. Then, in Section 9.6, we consider the situation where the distortion arises within the trading sector because of the inelasticity of the rest of the world's demand and supply for our economy's exports and imports.

9.5.1 Production externality: partial equilibrium

Let us suppose that there is some production externality that causes the social cost of producing the import competing good to be less than the private or market cost. This is shown in Figure 9.7 by the social supply curve, S_S, showing the true cost of producing the good, lying below the market supply curve, S_M. Once again we have a demand curve D that properly represents the social benefit from consuming the product, and a perfectly elastic supply of the good at the world price P_W.

Laissez-faire will yield production at q_0 and consumption at c_0. This is suboptimal, because the marginal social cost of producing the good at q_0 is below both the cost of importing it and the marginal benefit from consuming it. Using Bhagwati's notation, this can be expressed as DRT < FRT = DRS. Production needs to be increased to q_1 where the social marginal cost of domestic production

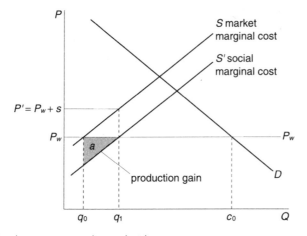

Fig. 9.7. Production externality: subsidy

equals the cost of an import. This can be achieved by raising the effective return to producers to P', which could be implemented by a production subsidy such that $P_W(1 + s) = P'$. This is the instrument that exactly focuses on the distortion and yields Pareto optimality. Now, DRT = FRT = DRS. The gain to the economy is the hatched area a which represents the reduction in costs from replacing imports by the lower-social-cost domestic production.

Suppose the production subsidy instrument is not available, perhaps because the authorities are not able to collect tax revenue. Will a tariff do the job? Clearly, the production can be increased by imposing a tariff that raises the price to P' so that $P' = P_W(1 + t)$. This raises production to q_1, yielding the production gain area a as before. Now, however, the price facing the consumers has risen, so consumption falls to c_1, as is shown in Figure 9.8.

We have now replaced one distortion by another. Now, DRS > DRT = FRT. This consumption distortion causes a net consumption loss of the area b. We cannot tell, without precise information about the costs and demand conditions, whether the tariff solution is better or worse than the *laissez-faire* production distortion it was intended to correct. The tariff instrument is clearly inferior to the production subsidy, because it does not focus so closely on the target distortion, and so creates undesirable side-effect distortions.

It can be seen, however, that a small tariff, although not 'first-best', will help. This is because there is considerable gain in production efficiency per unit of marginal production arising from a small increase in production, whereas there are only small losses of consumer welfare associated with marginal losses of consumption arising from a small tariff. We can consider a 'second-best' tariff t^* (less than t) which equates the marginal gain from production to the marginal consumption loss. In this case we have two distortions, DRT < FRT < DRS, but neither is as great as the uncorrected production externality, or as the consumption distortion caused by the fully offsetting tariff.

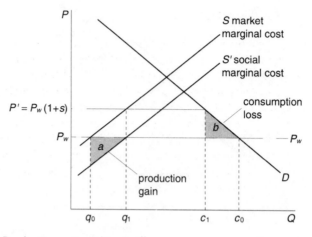

Fig. 9.8. Production externality: tariff

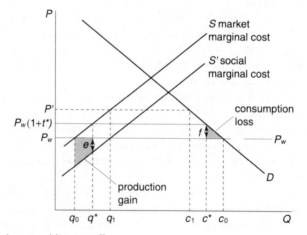

Fig. 9.9. A second-best tariff

In Figure 9.9 the second best tariff t^* yields a level of production q^* and a level of consumption c^* at which the gap (vertical distance e) between the social supply curve and the world price (showing the social benefit of the marginal unit of output made possible by the tariff) is just equal to the gap (vertical distance f) between the world price and the tariff-augmented price (showing the loss of consumer welfare of the marginal unit of consumption foregone because of the tariff).

9.5.2 Factor market distortions

We have limited discussion to cases in which the market failure caused a less-than-optimal pattern of output, but did not prevent the economy from functioning on its production possibility frontier. Many domestic distortions will cause sub-optimal levels as well as patterns of output. Factor market distortions which cause factor prices to differ between sectors are important examples of these. Suppose the wage in the import competing sector of an economy is higher than in the exporting sector. This distortion will have two effects. Firstly, it will shrink the production possibility frontier, except at the extreme points of specialization; and secondly, it will cause the social cost of producing the import competing good to be below its market cost or world price.

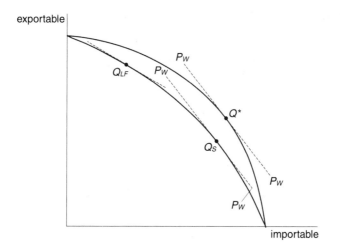

Fig. 9.10. Factor market distortion

This is shown in Figure 9.10. Optimal production would be at Q^*, which is on the undistorted production possibility frontier with the true cost of production equal to the world price. But with *laissez-faire* the economy will be producing on the diminished production possibility frontier at a point such as Q_{LF}, at which too little of the import competing good is being produced, because the social cost of production (slope of the diminished production possibility frontier) is below the market cost and world price. Here we have a hierarchy of policies. First best will be a factor market instrument, a subsidy on the use of labour in the import-competing sector. This will completely correct the distortion, allowing production to shift to Q^*. Second best could be a subsidy on production in the import competing sector. This will correct the disparity between the social cost and world price of the products, and thereby encourage an appropriate adjustment of production, but it will do nothing to correct the inappropriate factor intensity of production. Output will therefore shift to the point Q_S, which remains on the diminished production possibility frontier. Third best, and clearly inferior to the production subsidy, will be a tariff (not shown on the diagram). This will have the same effects on production as the subsidy, but will introduce an additional distortion on consumption. A small tariff can still help under these circumstances; but, in general, the further the instrument is from the distortion it is intended to correct, the lower is the level at which it can appropriately be applied, and so the lesser is the correction that can be made to the target distortion.[7]

9.6 Optimal tariff and the terms of trade

We now consider a case where the distortion is external to the domestic sector, so that a trade-related instrument is appropriate from the perspective of the country.

We no longer assume that the country is a price-taker in world markets faced with perfectly elastic terms of trade; but rather, that the country is a large one which can affect world prices. Under these circumstances the country can, by restricting the volume of trade, improve its terms of trade. This generates a gain for the economy to set against the losses arising from the distortion of production and consumption. This is illustrated in Figure 9.11.

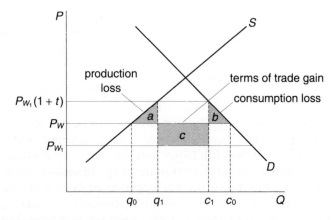

Fig. 9.11. Tariff with a terms of trade gain

---

[7] Corden (1974) provides a comprehensive discussion of the hierarchy of instruments to correct economic distortions.

The world price is initially P_{W0} with production at q_0, and consumption at c_0. It is now being assumed that this world supply is less than perfectly elastic with respect to price, so a tariff at rate t could, by reducing demand for imports, reduce the world price to some point such as P_{W1}, while raising the domestic price to $P_{W1}(1 + t)$. Production has risen to q_1, and consumption has fallen to c_1. This has created production and consumption costs shown by the triangular areas a and b respectively, and is the same as the analysis shown in Figure 9.2 above. The new consideration is that the foreign supply price has now fallen so that the remaining imports q_1c_1 are now being obtained for the economy at a lower cost. This terms of trade gain is simply the imports multiplied by the fall in their supply price, which is the rectangle c. It can be seen that if the tariff is too low, there will not be much of a terms of trade effect to generate a gain; however, if the tariff is too high the distortionary production and consumption costs become high, whereas imports fall, squeezing the base on which the terms of trade gain is based.

The 'optimum' tariff or export tax is one which, from the perspective of the country imposing the tax, maximizes the gain from an improvement in the terms of trade relative to the losses arising from the distortion of production and consumption. The case for the tariff or the tax arises because the country faces a less than perfectly elastic foreign demand for its exports and supply of its imports. Because of this inelasticity the marginal cost of imports or the marginal revenue from exports will not be equal to their prices, and so *laissez-faire* will not be optimal. The optimum tariff or tax is one that corrects this distortion. Note that the analysis assumes no retaliation on the part of the trading partners.

9.6.1 Optimum export tax: partial equilibrium

Consider a country facing a less than perfectly elastic demand curve for its exports, $D_{foreign}$ in Figure 9.12, with marginal costs as shown.

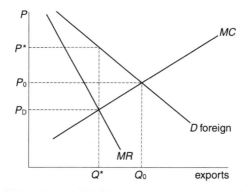

Fig. 9.12. Optimum exports

If the industry is competitively organized, the marginal cost curve will be the supply curve. *Laissez-faire* will yield exports of Q_0 at a price of P_0. This is sub-optimal, because the marginal cost of supplying the exports exceeds their marginal revenue. The country is not exploiting its potential monopoly power. Optimal would be to provide Q^* at a price P^*. This could be achieved by an export tax that created a wedge between the price paid by foreigners (P_F) and the domestic price (P_D) received by producers such that the domestic price equals the marginal cost.

In general an export tax can be defined $t = (P_F - P_D)/P_D$. This tax is optimal when the domestic price equals marginal revenue. Thus

$$t^* = (P - MR)/MR \tag{9.1}$$

where P is the price and MR is the marginal revenue. Thus the optimal export tax is identical to the mark up that a monopolist will charge over marginal cost. Using the relationship $e = P/(MR - P)$ where e is the price elasticity of the foreign demand curve yields

$$t^* = 1/(-e - 1) \text{ or } t^* = 1/(|e| - 1) \tag{9.2}$$

A monopolist will maximize profit by restricting output. The problem here is that the industry is competitively organized, so that the individual firms treat the price as exogenous and expand exports until their marginal cost is equal to the price.

The purpose of the optimum tax is to make the individual firms act collectively, as if they were a monopolist. The same result could, in principle, be achieved by the government nationalizing the industry and restricting supply, or by imposing export quotas aggregating to the optimum supply.

This discussion has been formulated in the context of an export tax rather than a tariff. This is because it is more likely that a country has monopoly power in one of its exports than in one of its imports, and because the analysis then becomes closely analogous with elementary monopoly theory. We have previously referred to the general equilibrium equivalence of tariffs and export taxes; and, as can be seen in the following paragraphs, it makes no difference whether a tax is imposed on exports or a tariff on imports. The optimal tax or tariff depends only upon the foreign elasticity of demand (or supply).

9.6.2 Optimum tariff: general equilibrium

We now derive the same result using a general equilibrium model on which, for simplicity, it is assumed that there is no production of the imported good Z. The country under consideration produces a given amount of Y, some of which it trades for Z under conditions of less than perfectly elastic demand and supply. This is illustrated in Figure 9.13, in which OA is the fixed output of Y, and the curve AD is the foreign demand for Y and supply of Z offer curve.[8]

[8] The optimal tariff is usually derived by using offer curves for the more general case in which the production of both goods varies with the tariff. However, the loss of generality from assuming that only one good is produced domestically does not significantly affect the argument, and allows production, consumption, and trade to be seen on the same diagram.

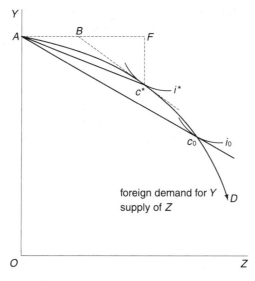

Fig. 9.13. Optimum tariff

Optimal for this country would be trade at c^*, at which point the marginal cost of Z in terms of Y through trade equals the marginal rate of substitution between the goods in consumption. This is illustrated by the tangency of the indifference curve 1^* to the foreign offer curve at this point (both having the slope of Bc^*). *Laissez-faire* will give a solution at c_0 which is on the foreign offer curve; but with the marginal rate of substitution between the goods in consumption equal to the average cost or price (slope of the line Ac_0) rather than to the marginal cost (slope of the offer curve). The optimal tariff (or export tax) confronts the domestic consumers with the price of Z represented by the slope of the offer curve at c^* (slope of Bc^*), whereas the foreigners receive the price shown by the slope AC^*. The tariff that achieves this is $t^* = AB/BF$. Since the price elasticity of the foreign demand for Y is $|e| = AF/AB$, it can be seen by manipulation of the diagram that $t^* = 1/(|e| - 1)$.

The optimum tariff analysis is useful for illustrating the point about relating instruments to distortions. The policy applications are strictly limited. The most dramatic example of countries improving their terms of trade by means of trade controls was the raising of the price of oil by OPEC during the 1970s. This was possible because of the low elasticity of demand of the rest of the world for OPEC's oil, and because of the ability (for a while) of OPEC to discipline its members to act collectively, like a monopolist. The tripling of the price of oil in 1973 can be related to the formula for the optimum tariff. Let us suppose that the price was initially the competitive price: then a markup of 200 per cent would have been optimal if the price elasticity of demand was 1.5. This seems plausible in the short run, but the long-run elasticity is clearly much higher. The rising elasticity

of demand facing OPEC provides one of several reasons for the subsequent difficulties of OPEC in maintaining the price of oil.

Perhaps the most successful long running cartel has been that for diamonds,
managed by the De Beers company. This has been maintained by the strict control over the marketing of diamonds made possible by De Beers' monopoly of
South African supply, and by the willingness of Russia—the other major producer—to sell its diamonds to De Beers. It is interesting to note that this cartel is
under pressure at the present time, because Russia's urgent need for revenue is
encouraging it to bypass De Beers and market its diamonds directly.

Attempts by other producers of primary commodities to raise the price of their
exports by restricting output have generally proved unsuccessful.

Improving the terms of trade is one of the few possible arguments for
protection that is not commonly advocated by policymakers in the industrial
market economies. Perhaps this is because, for most countries, the price elasticity of demand for industrial exports is too high to make the terms of trade effect
of protection significant, particularly in the face of probable retaliation. The possibility of major trading blocs engaging in competitive optimum tariff behaviour
and the implications that this would have for world welfare are considered in
Chapter 13.

9.6.3 Optimum tariffs with duality: a two-country framework

This section shows how a country's trade can be derived from income and cost
functions, and how these in turn generate offer curves. Offer curves are then
deployed to discuss a trading equilibrium in a two-country world, where each
applies its 'optimum' tariff.

In what follows, we shall assume there are two countries, Home and Abroad.
Abroad's variables will be denoted by a star (*). Both countries produce and consume two goods under perfect competition. There are no distortions. Everyone in
Home has identical incomes and identical, homothetic preferences; the same is
true of Abroad.

We shall begin by using the duality income and cost functions (introduced in
Chapter 1) to depict autarkic and free-trade equilibria. From the income and cost
functions we shall derive offer curves for the two countries. The next task will be
to show that, if one of them is so small that it cannot influence its terms of trade,
its optimum export tax or import tariff is zero. Then we shall illustrate the optimum, necessarily non-zero, export tax or import tariff for a country large enough
to influence its terms of trade. Finally, we shall show what can happen if both
Home and Abroad apply their optimal trade taxes.

Autarkic equilibrium is characterized by the condition that home demand
equals home supply for each of the two goods. As we saw in Chapter 1, what this
implies geometrically is tangency of the income function to the cost function that
applies under autarky utility. The slope of the tangent to the former, in Figure
9.14, is the home supply of good x; the slope of the tangent to the latter is the

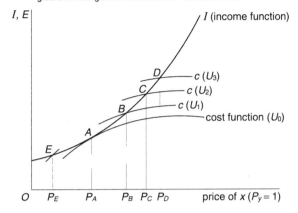

gradient of tangent to income function = output of x;
gradient of tangent to cost function = demand for x

Fig. 9.14. The autarkic equilibrium at A, with production of x exceeding demand for x at higher prices

(compensated) home demand for x. At point A, these are equal. So the (relative) price of x at which this occurs, P_A, is the autarkic equilibrium price.

Now consider a higher price, P_B. The income function is steeper here, at B, so the home supply of x rises. The slope of the tangent to the cost function passing through B gives us home demand for x. The difference between the gradients of these two tangents is the excess supply of x. This is the country's supply of exports.

We then repeat the exercise for other prices, such as P_C, P_D, and P_E. We trace out the supply of exports for each price. Notice that at P_E, which is well below P_A, the country opts to be a net *importer* of good x. To the right of P_A, it will be an exporter. Exports first rise as P increases; after some point, they may fall.

Assuming that trade is always balanced, we know that the value of the country's excess supply of x will equal the value of its excess demand for y. This tells us that we can plot its preferred volumes of exports of x and imports of y for all possible prices. The result is the home country's *offer curve* which we have already encountered in Chapter 4. This is depicted in Figure 9.15. Repeating the exercise for the other country gives its offer curve, too. Equilibrium under free trade, assuming no international transport costs, is given by the point at which these offer curves intersect.[9] This is shown in Figure 9.16. The gradient of the ray from the origin, O, to point D gives the terms of trade in free trade equilibrium. The steeper that ray, the better the terms of trade will be for Home (whose offer curve is OC), and the worse for Abroad (whose offer curve is OC^*). Figure 9.17 shows the domestic equilibria for Home and Abroad corresponding to point D in Figure 9.16.

---

[9] A pair of countries' offer curves will always intersect at least twice: once at the origin, and once in the positive quadrant. They could intersect more than once in the positive quadrant, as in Fig. 9.18. In that diagram, the equilibria D and F are stable; between them lies an unstable equilibrium E.

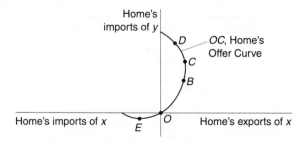

Fig. 9.15. Home's preferred exports and imports, at different relative prices: the Offer Curve for Home

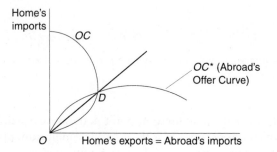

Fig. 9.16. The free trade equilibrium at D

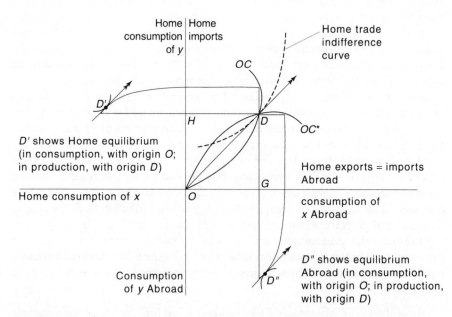

Fig. 9.17. The free trade equilibrium at D, with consumption and production equilibria in each country

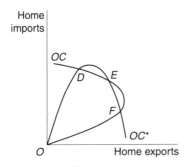

Fig. 9.18. Multiple intersection of offer curves

At the price P_D, Home's supply of exports is G, and its demand for imports will be H. Point D in Figure 9.16 gives the country's optimal volumes of exports and imports at the price P_D. Every other point along the ray OD will correspond to less attractive levels of trade. Point D is therefore a point of tangency between the ray OD and a *trade indifference curve*. This trade indifference curve gives the locus of all trading points that offer Home's residents the same indirect utility as at D. The offer curve OC is in fact the locus of all price-ray/trade-indifference-curve tangencies (see Figure 9.19): there will be not just one trade indifference curve, but a whole map of them.

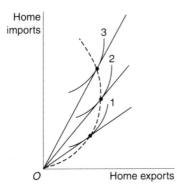

Fig. 9.19. The offer curve for Home (dashed), and trade indifference curves (labelled 1, 2, 3)

Now suppose Home is small, so small that it cannot affect the world relative price of x, P. This means that Abroad's offer curve which it faces is *linear*. Point D is therefore not just the optimal point of trade along the ray OD—it is the optimal trading point, given Abroad's offer curve, OC^* (Figure 9.20).

How can we depict the effects of a tariff levied by Home on its imports of y (or a tax on its exports, x)? The domestic price of x, in terms of y, will have to fall by

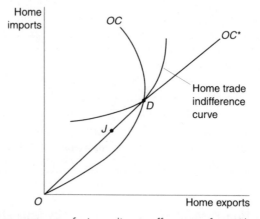

Fig. 9.20. The home country facing a linear offer curve from Abroad: a tariff lowers Home 's potential welfare

the full amount of the trade tax. Production of y will fall; resources will switch, instead, into higher domestic production of x.

   The new domestic equilibrium will be at a point such as J in Figures 9.19 and 9.21. The gradient of the tangent to the income function at the price P_J gives the new, lower volume of production of x in Home. Home's government collects revenue from its export tax or import tariff, equal to distance LM (in units of the numeraire good, y). Let us assume this is handed back to domestic residents as an equal lump-sum. This means that domestic residents' income rises by LM; and the gradient of the tangent to the cost function passing through point J gives us the resulting level of Home's demand for x, and, indirectly, the utility associated with this new equilibrium. The key point is that, despite the trade tax income,

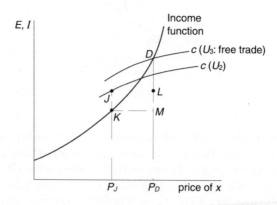

Fig. 9.21. Effects of a tariff levied by Home, when it faces a linear offer curve

Home's representative resident's indirect utility is *unambiguously lower than it was under free trade.* So the trade tax is welfare-reducing. This is true no matter how large or small the export tax (import tariff) rate is: hence our finding that a price-taking country's optimal trade tax is necessarily zero.

When the home country is not small, however, this finding disappears. Abroad's offer curve is not a ray from the origin now; it is like the concave curve depicted in Figure 9.22. Home can, of course, trade freely at point D. *But it can do better than this.* If it restricts its trade a little, what it loses on reduced trade volume will be more than offset by the welfare gain from improved terms of trade. Because Abroad's offer curve is concave, not linear, cutting trade will bring Home a rise in the relating price of *x*: the buying power of each unit of its exports of *x*, in units of *y*, will rise.

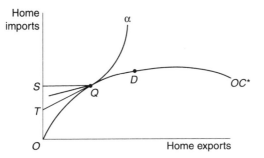

Fig. 9.22. Home facing a concave offer curve, restricting its trade optimally to Q

Home does best by restricting its trade to point Q. At Q, Abroad's offer curve is tangent to Home's highest attainable trade indifference curve (labelled α). The external relative price of *x* increases, to the gradient of OQ.

Home can cut its trade by an export tax or an import tariff. Either will lower its excess demand for *y* and its excess supply of *x*. We can infer how high the trade tax has to be to achieve point Q. The gradient of the double tangent to Abroad's offer curve and Home's trade indifference curve α at Q gives the *domestic*, internal price of *x* in terms of *y*. A comparison of this with the gradient of OQ tells us the gap between internal and external relative prices—and hence the size of the trade tax. The ratio of the former to the latter is $1 + \bar{t}$, where $\bar{t}$ is defined, here, as the (optimum) value of the tariff or export tax rate.

At Q, Home is applying its *optimal* tariff (or export tax). A lower rate would still achieve net benefit; but monopoly power would not be exploited to the optimum extent. If the tariff rate exceeded, $\bar{t}$, Home would have cut back its trade too far. At Q, Home optimizes (see Heffernan and Sinclair, 1990, for a diagrammatic account of the duality approach to optimum tariffs).

The size of the optimum tariff, $\bar{t}$, is given by the formula $\bar{t} = 1/(e-1)$ where *e* is the elasticity of Abroad's offer curve. The value of *e* at point Q is found by

drawing a perpendicular to the vertical axis (*S*) and producing the tangent to *OC**
to that axis (giving point *T*): $e = 0S/0T$ (the ratio of the vertical distances from the
origin to *S* and *T* respectively).

If Home is better off at *Q* than at *D*, what of welfare in the other country?
Abroad is worse off, far worse off. It has suffered from a reduced volume of trade.
On top of this, it is injured by a deterioration in its terms of trade, too. The world
has not gained from Home's import tariff (export tax). Indeed, in an important
sense, the new equilibrium at *Q* is less efficient than at *D*. Consumers in Home
and Abroad now face different relative prices of the goods. The same is true of
producers. As we shall see, this contravenes conditions for efficient resource allocation at the world level.

For the present, however, let us see if Abroad can do better for itself than free
trade. The answer is a qualified yes. If Home is not vastly larger than Abroad,
Home's offer curve confronting Abroad will not be linear, but curved. That means
that Abroad can also improve its terms of trade by restricting its trade volume by
an export tax or import tariff. It too can apply an optimum tariff.

Figure 9.23 presents a double-tariff-ridden equilibrium where both Home and
Abroad are applying their optimal import tariffs (or export taxes). Both countries

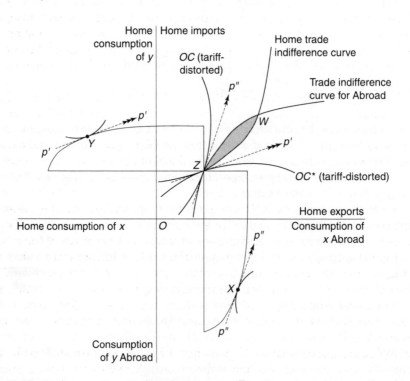

Fig. 9.23. Both countries set their optimum tariffs, taking the other's tariff as given
(Nash equilibrium)

pull their offer curves inwards; they intersect at Z. The gradient of OZ gives the terms of trade. That of the double tangent to OC^* and Home's trade indifference curve is the internal price ratio inside Home, p'. The slope of the steep tangent to OC and Abroad's trade indifference curve at Z gives the internal price ratio, p'', inside Abroad's domestic economy.

Point O represents the origin for trade (depicted in the upper right quadrant). It is also the origin for consumption in both economies. Abroad's consumption of the two goods (Home's exportable on the horizontal axis, its importable on the vertical) is shown in the bottom right quadrant. The upper left quadrant presents Home's consumption of these two goods (its importables vertical).

Point Z is the origin for *production* in the two economies. Home's production possibility set is shown upwards and leftwards of Z. Point Y is the equilibrium inside Home's economy. Here its producers and consumers optimize, facing the flat internal price ratio p'. The vector from O to Y shows Home's pattern of consumption. That from Z to Y gives its pattern of production. Point X, similarly, depicts equilibrium in consumption (*vis-à-vis* O) and production (*vis-à-vis* Z) inside Abroad's economy. In Abroad, the steep domestic price ratio p'' applies.

The inefficiency of this double-optimum-tariff equilibrium can be shown from the fact that the two internal price ratios, p' and p'', are unequal. The condition for efficiency in exchange between a pair of consumers is that their marginal rates of substitution be equal. If it is not, allowing them to trade with each other will lead to the possibility of mutual benefit. The Pareto efficiency condition for exchange between consumers in the two countries is clearly violated. Permitting a Home resident to give up some y for some extra x, and an Abroad resident to do the opposite, could make both better off.

There is production efficiency at the world level too. Production is efficiently organized between two economies (each operating on their production possibility frontier) *when the marginal rates of transformation are equal.* These two rates are obviously unequal at X and Y. By getting Home to produce more x and less y, and Abroad to produce more y and less x, the world as a whole—and therefore, in principle, everyone everywhere—could enjoy more of both goods. The two panels of Figure 9.24 illustrate.

The efficiency of the double-optimum tariff equilibrium can be shown in another way. Consider Figure 9.23, where both countries are applying their optimum tariffs and trading at Z. Because each trades at a point where the other's offer curve is tangent to its highest attainable trade indifference curve, the two trade indifference curves are not tangent to each other. They intersect at Z. They also intersect at W. Now consider the striped lozenge-shaped area of which Z and W are the south-west and north-east corners. This set of trading points offers higher potential welfare for both Home and Abroad than the tariff-ridden equilibrium at Z.

Both Home and Abroad could gain, then, by increasing their trade with each other. That can be said about any trading point where either or both countries have restricted their trade. Only free trade is best in this sense. Free trade represents a cooperative equilibrium. Restricted trade is inferior to it; at least one of the

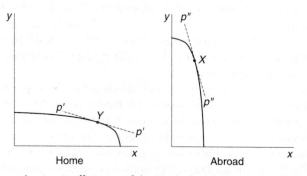

Fig. 9.24. The production inefficiency of the Nash double optimum-tariff equilibrium

parties must benefit from moving to free trade, and, if side-payments between the countries are allowed, it must be possible for both to do so.

The double optimum-tariff point, shown at Z in Figure 9.23, is a Nash equilibrium. Each is doing as well as it can for itself, *taking the other's trade policy as given*. We have encountered a Prisoner's Dilemma. Tariffs on imports, or taxes on exports, dominate free trade for a country that faces a non-linear offer curve from the rest of the world: whatever the other party or parties do, it is better off restricting its trade than trading freely. Yet the Nash equilibrium is inferior to the cooperative equilibrium in the sense that both could be better off trading freely (if needs be with side-payments).

There are two further points to note. One is that although at least one country must be worse off in the Nash equilibrium than under free trade, it is not always true that both or all must be. Consider Figure 9.25. Here the bargaining power of the two countries is very different. Home's offer curve is almost linear, while Abroad's displays pronounced curvature. This means that Home's optimum tariff is quite large, while Abroad's is negligible. If both apply their optimal tariffs,

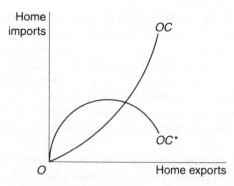

Fig. 9.25. Free trade, when Home's optimum tariff would be very much larger than Abroad's

Abroad will of course be worse off than under free trade. But Home is likely to be better off.

The disparity in offer curve elasticities here—Abroad's offer curve is not very elastic, while Home's is almost infinitely elastic—is the key reason for this result. Home's offer curve may be much more elastic in the relevant range simply because it is a very *much larger economy*. Alternatively, what may make its offer curve so much more elastic than Abroad's is *greater flexibility*. Home's production possibility frontier and community indifference curves could display much more substitution in production and consumption than Abroad's.

The final point to note is that the Nash equilibrium in a 'one-shot' game may not be selected when the game is continuously repeated. Suppose each country expects the other to retaliate to a trade tax by imposing a punitive trade restriction in the next period or periods. A potential trade-taxer now has to weigh up its immediate benefit from imposing a tariff against the loss it thinks will follow from subsequent retaliation. If the retaliation is sufficiently speedy, painful and/or protracted, and the potential trade-taxer does not discount its future benefits and losses too highly, it will choose to adhere to free trade. To make this argument watertight, we need to assume that the injured party will indeed retaliate when it is confronted with a tariff.

9.7 Immiserizing growth

Since the nineteenth century economists have been concerned that economies could become worse off as a result of economic growth. The possibility of such 'immiserizing growth' was initially analysed in the context of a growing country turning the terms of trade against itself to such an extent that its welfare deteriorated. In particular, this has been a concern of development economists and policy makers in primary-product-exporting countries who have feared that an expansion of production in conjunction with low income and price elasticities of demand for primary products could generate this perverse result. Indeed, such fears were a major motivation in the emphasis on commodity agreements during the debates concerning the 'New International Economic Order' during the 1960s and 1970s.

Immiserizing growth resulting from deteriorating terms of trade is a possibility. Necessary conditions for this are, firstly, that the growth is so biased towards the production of exports that the production of import competing goods falls, and secondly that an inelastic demand for exports is not being countered by an optimum tariff or tax. We have seen, in the discussion of the Rybczynski proposition in Chapter 5, that growth in the form of an expansion in the supply of the factor of production used intensively in the exportable industry could result in a fall in the output of the import competing good; and it is quite difficult for primary-producing countries individually or collectively to implement optimum-tariff policies. Nevertheless, most countries have some diversification of exports, and their terms of trade cannot be crudely identified with the price of a particular commodity; so although deteriorating terms of trade may have been eroding the gains from economic growth for some primary exporting countries, it is unlikely that this has been to such an extent as to make that growth immiserizing.

9.7.1 Immiserizing growth and domestic distortions

Immiserizing growth is a possibility whenever there is an uncorrected distortion in an economy (see Bhagwati 1968). Some domestic distortions are much more severe than any that are likely to arise from less-than-perfectly elastic demand for exports or supply of imports, so most incidents of immiserizing growth are likely to be found in economies that are maintaining such severe distortions. We illustrate this diagrammatically and with some examples.

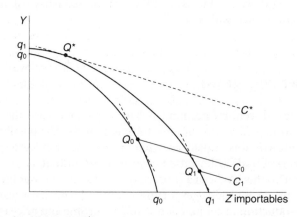

Fig. 9.26. Immiserizing growth

In Figure 9.26 we have an economy with an initial production possibility frontier shown by q_0q_0. The distortion is that the relative price to producers of the importable good Z (the slope of q_0q_0 at the point Q_0) is significantly higher than the relative international price (shown by the slope of the budget line Q_0C_0).

Initially production is at Q_0, permitting consumption along the budget line Q_0C_0. We now have unambiguous growth shown by the expansion of the production possibility frontier in all dimensions to q_1q_1. But this growth has been biased towards the importable good Z to such an extent that, at unchanged domestic prices, the production is at point Q_1 where the output of the other good has fallen. The budget line at unchanged world prices is now Q_1C_1, which lies below the original budget line, indicating that growth has been immiserizing. Note that this is only possible because of the conjunction of the distortion and the biased growth. In the absence of the distortion, the after-growth production would be at Q^*, yielding the budget line Q^*C^*, which is superior to any obtainable before the growth. It is also worth noting that the degree of distortion has not got any worse in this example: the relationship between the international and the domestic prices is unchanged. What has happened is that the biased growth has drawn resources away from the product that was already being under-produced, thus making the effect of the distortion worse.

Immiserizing growth can be illustrated by a simple numerical example. Suppose the international price of both Y and Z is 1, whereas the domestic price of Y is 1 and of Z is 2. (The currency units are irrelevant.) Then suppose output is initially 100 units of both Y and Z. Thus national income at domestic prices is 300, and at world prices it is 200. Now suppose production changes to 75 units of Y and 120 units of Z. National income at domestic prices has risen to 315, so the national-income accountants and the government would be congratulating themselves upon the 5 per cent economic growth. But at world prices, national income has fallen by 2.5 per cent to 195. That the apparent growth is spurious can be seen by noting that the extra 20 units of Z could have been obtained through trade from the original output at a cost of 20 units of Y instead of at the cost of 25 units of Y resulting from growth.

Apparently in Poland before liberalization, oil was being subsidized to such an extent that it was profitable to grow tropical flowers in heated greenhouses and to export them to Germany, even though the value of the flowers was less at world prices than the oil required to grow them. Under such circumstances it is easy to believe that an accumulation of capital could have facilitated the production of even more flowers at even greater loss.

Within the European Union the most obvious severe distortion is excessive agricultural protection. It is plausible that improved agricultural productivity would be immiserizing.

9.7.2 Too many pigs

A striking example of excessive production and possible immiserization in European agriculture is provided by pig production in the Netherlands. Pigs are reared intensively in the Netherlands, but there is a serious problem in disposing of the ever-increasing output of excrement that is now threatening to pollute the water supply. The government has not been able to find satisfactory methods of disposing of this undesirable by-product; and the Dutch farmers are proving very resistant to any suggestions that they should limit their pig production. The problem is that the cost in the form of smell and water pollution is mainly external to the producers, so we have a straightforward case of the social cost exceeding the market cost of production. The resulting excess production and the possibility of immiserizing growth are illustrated in the partial equilibrium diagram, Figure 9.27. In this diagram it is being assumed that at low levels of production the externality is negligible, so that the market and social-marginal cost curves coincide;

but as production increases the external cost becomes serious, so that the social cost rises relative to the market cost. This is shown by the curves SC_0 and MC_0 in the diagram. (The social cost curve includes both the market cost and the externality.) We assume that the European Union fixes a price, P_{EU}, which provides a perfectly elastic demand for the pigs at that price. We also assume, for simplicity, that the Netherlands pays a negligible proportion of the cost of maintaining the price, so that the price represents the social benefit of the product. It is assumed, however, that all of the external costs fall upon the Netherlands (ignoring the fact that under some climatic conditions the pig by-products can be smelt in Eastern England).

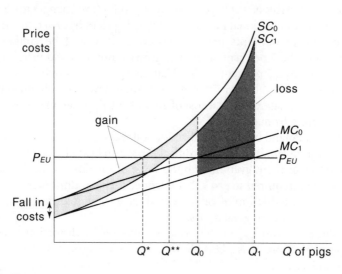

Fig. 9.27. Too many pigs

In the diagram, production is initially at Q_0 where the market cost MC_0 is equal to the price. This is more than optimal production, which is at Q^* where the social cost is equal to the price. Now suppose that there is some technical innovation which reduces the market cost of production by some fixed amount per pig. This will be reflected in a flat-rate fall in both the market and social cost curves, to MC_1 and SC_1 respectively. Optimal production expands to Q^{**}, but actual production expands to Q_1. There is a gain associated with the reduced cost of the original production. This is the area between the old and the new social cost curves up to the point Q_0. But there is a loss on all of the expanded pig production equal to the excess of the new social cost curve over price from Q_0 to Q_1. These gains and losses are marked on the diagram; and it can be seen that the loss from the economic growth might exceed the gain, so growth could be immiserizing. It should also be noted that technical progress would have yielded a gain if pig production was optimal.

9.8 Trade policy and domestic monopoly

Trade or potential trade deprives a domestic monopolist of some or all of its monopoly power. The pro-competitive gains from trade are an important feature of most of the theoretical models of intra-industry trade, as we have discussed in Chapter 7, and increasingly they are included in empirical estimates of gains and losses associated with various trade policies.

The diagrams use standard partial equilibrium monopoly analysis to compare monopoly behaviour with and without international trade.

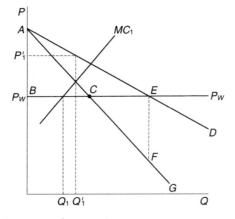

Fig. 9.28. Domestic monopoly: case 1

In the diagram, domestic demand is AD, and the associated marginal revenue curve is AG. The monopolist, in the absence of international competition, will choose the output that will equate marginal cost to marginal revenue in the standard way.

But suppose there is a perfectly elastic international supply at price P_W. Then the effective demand curve facing the domestic supplier becomes BED, and the associated marginal revenue curve is $BEFG$. Demand is now more elastic and the monopoly power has been eliminated or reduced.

The comparison of free trade with autarky depends upon the cost structure. In Case 1, the marginal cost curve passes between B and C, as in Figure 9.28. This is a high cost producer. If there is free trade, price will be P_W and output will be Q_1. Note that this is the same as if the industry was competitively organized. But if trade is prohibited, domestic output will rise to Q_1' and price will be P_1. In case 2, the marginal cost curve passes between C and E, as shown in Figure 9.29.

If there is free trade, price will be P_W and output will be Q_2. But if trade is prohibited, domestic output will fall to Q_2' and price will be P_2'. A point to note in this case is that domestic output falls as a result of protection. In Case 3 we

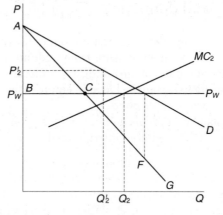

Fig. 9.29. Domestic monopoly: case 2

consider a low cost producer (exporter). The marginal cost passes between E and D, as in Figure 9.30.

If the industry was competitive, Q^* would be produced, with Q_H being supplied to the domestic market and the rest being exported. This is the best that the monopolist can do if trade (re-import) is allowed. But if re-imports are prohibited the market is segmented, and the monopolist will supply each market so as to equate marginal revenue with marginal cost ($MR_{home} = MR_{foreign} = MC$). This is achieved by producing at Q^*, but only supplying Q_M to the domestic market at the price P'_3, with the rest being exported: a case of dumping because the monopolist is selling the product at a lower price abroad than at home. The important point about this case is that it is potential trade that deprives the monopolist of

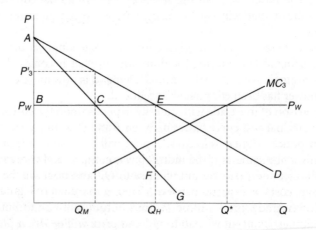

Fig. 9.30. Domestic monopoly: case 3

power. With free trade, any attempt by the domestic producer to impose discriminatory pricing will be thwarted by the re-importing of the product at the world price.

9.8.1 Potential monopoly; quotas vs. tariffs

The discussion of free versus prohibited trade can be considered as a special case, in which a zero tariff is being compared with a prohibitive (zero) quota. In general, because a quota is more rigid than a tariff with respect to the volume of permitted imports, the quota will confer more monopoly power upon the domestic producers than will a tariff. This can be seen by comparing the quota that would, under conditions of perfect competition, allow the same volume of imports as a tariff. In the relevant price range (at or above the world price plus tariff) the effective demand curve facing the domestic producers protected by a tariff is perfectly elastic at the tariff-augmented price; so the producers have no monopoly power. In contrast, the effective demand curve faced by domestic producers protected by a fixed quota is the domestic demand less the quota. This will have the elasticity of the domestic demand curve, and so will confer monopoly power on the domestic producers depending upon the inelasticity of that demand curve.

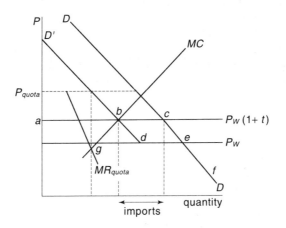

Fig. 9.31. Effective demand: tariff vs. quota

Given the domestic demand curve *DD* in Figure 9.31 and a perfectly elastic international supply at price P_W, a tariff at rate t will confront the domestic producers with an effective demand curve *acf*. Then if marginal cost is *MC*, domestic production will be *ab* and imports will be *bc*. Now suppose that the industry is protected by an 'equivalent' quota of *bc* instead of the tariff. The effective demand curve facing the domestic producers is the combination of lines passing through $D' def$ in the figure. This is less than perfectly elastic, and will be associated with a marginal revenue curve MR_{quota} over the relevant range. If the industry is competitively organized, the marginal cost curve will be the supply curve of the domestic industry, so we shall get the same output and price as under the tariff. However, if the industry is monopolistic, output will be constrained to the quantity corresponding to point g, and the price will be P_{quota}. The quota has allowed the domestic producer to exploit its potential monopoly power, whereas the tariff has not.

9.9 Summary

- There are gains from trade in the sense that the gainers from trade could compensate the losers.
- Policy instruments to correct market failure are likely to have undesirable side effects, so they should be focussed as closely as possible at the failure that they are intended to correct. Trade taxes are generally not optional except where the distortion being corrected is in the international trade sector.
- Large countries can improve their terms of trade by taxing their imports or exports. There is an 'optimum' tariff that maximizes their gains from improved terms of trade net of their losses from reduced volume of trade. Tariffs to improve terms of trade are not optimal from world perspective.
- In the presence of uncorrected distortions economic growth can be immiserizing.
- International trade limits the monopoly power of potential domestic monopolists. Quotas and other non-tariff barriers are generally more rigid than tariffs and so afford domestic producers more monopoly power.

10

STRATEGIC TRADE POLICY

10.1 Introduction

In Chapter 9 we saw that, in the theoretical world of perfect competition and no domestic distortions, the policy of free trade is superior for a country. Intervention to affect the level of trade will unambiguously reduce welfare in the domestic economy. The exception to this is where distortions emanate from international trade, for example, where the domestic economy is large enough relative to the world market that by altering the quantities it can influence in its favour the prices at which it trades.

Allowing for distortions in the domestic economy does not undermine the basic presumption towards free trade: at the most, trade policy is a second-best policy, to offset the effects of a domestic distortion, and there will always be an alternative policy, such as a production subsidy, which is superior. Although the policy prescription that comes from this analysis is clear, its usefulness is limited by the failure to take account of conditions which actually prevail in many markets, increasing returns to scale and imperfect competition. Recently economists have reconsidered the role of trade policy in an environment in which the world market is subject to distortions.

When returns to scale are internal to the firm, then the assumption of perfect competition is no longer tenable; markets subject to increasing returns to scale can only support a finite number of firms. In such a situation firms will recognize that their own actions will affect the market price. A further reflection of imperfect competition is that, in equilibrium, price will exceed marginal cost, but from societies' point of view an increase in output will be beneficial, since the benefit derived from the next unit of the good (as measured by its price) will exceed the cost of producing it. It is in this sense that imperfect competition leads to a second-best outcome, and, as we shall see, this can lead to trade policy interventions raising welfare in the domestic economy.

Initially, however, we should suspect that greater openness to international trade should help to undermine the monopoly power of domestic firms; removing trade barriers stimulates greater competition from abroad. In the first sections of this chapter we expand on this issue, and consider whether imports are an important means of 'disciplining' domestic firms earning excess profits.

If competition on the world market is characterized by a small number of firms earning excess profits, then although removing trade barriers will increase competition, the nature of this competition may be such that benefits from greater trade cannot be guaranteed. Thus in this situation it is possible for trade intervention to raise domestic welfare. Policies which raise the output of domestic firms will entail a greater share of the profits in the industry being appropriated to the home economy at the expense of foreign rivals. This has been termed strategic trade policy, since intervention by the government changes the nature of the strategic relationship between rival firms in different countries in favour of the domestic economy. At first sight the basis for such arguments appears to undermine the traditional case for free trade. However, as we shall see, there are a number of reasons to be very sceptical of this reasoning for trade policy, and so as a general rule no intervention into international trade still appears to be the best premise from which to base discussions of trade policy in Europe.

10.2   Imports as a discipline

In general, in imperfectly competitive markets there is a negative relationship between market share and the mark-up of price over marginal cost (profit). The more concentrated an industry (the greater the share of output provided by a given number of firms) the higher the level of excess profit for each firm. Thus any policy which serves to increase the number of firms competing in a particular market will have a beneficial impact for consumers in terms of lower prices relative to costs. This could be achieved via competition policy, seeking to break down artificial barriers to entry and other anti-competitive practices. An alternative would be to reduce trade barriers to permit greater external competition. Competition between firms in oligopolistic industries can, at least in theory, take many different forms. As we have seen above, firms can treat quantities as the strategic variable over which to make decisions, or they could compete in terms of prices. However, with very few exceptions, it can be shown that tariffs and quotas will raise the mark-up of price over marginal cost. This issue has received much attention in the industrial economics literature under the so-called 'Structure-Conduct-Performance' (SCP) hypothesis. Empirical research has generally found that the level of concentration among domestic firms has a smaller effect upon the profits of those firms, the larger is the share of domestic demand supplied by imports.

In an interesting extension to this idea, Jacquemin and Sapir (1992) have suggested that in European markets imports from outside the EU will have a stronger disciplining effect upon profits than intra-EU imports. There are two reasons why this effect is postulated:

1.   Collusive agreements, dominant positions and other restrictive practices which limit competition may be easier to arrange and impose within the European Union than on firms based in geographically distant countries.

2. The nature of imports from the rest of the world is different to that of trade between members of the Union. The degree of product differentiation, as reflected by the level of intra-industry trade, in intra-EU trade is higher than in extra-EU imports. Product differentiation tends to constrain the disciplinary effect of imports.

Econometric analysis, using data for a range of manufacturing industries in France, Germany, Italy, and the UK, has provided some statistical evidence that imports from outside the EU have a significant negative effect upon the profits of EU firms, while trade between these EU members has no significant effect. Artificial barriers both to trade within the EU and to trade from outside the Union were found to raise the profits of domestic firms. Thus, the removal of barriers which have constrained competition within Europe to enable the completion of the Single European Market should have depressed the margin of price over cost. One possible response of firms to greater competition from European rivals is to limit its effects via collusive agreements or through mergers. This analysis suggests that external liberalization by the EU will be complementary to the removal of internal barriers; the reduction of barriers to trade from countries outside the EU will help to ensure that the potential gains to the EU consumer from the Single European Market are fully realized.

The empirical analysis used to support the imports as a discipline hypothesis has typically come from industry studies. However, the hypothesis is really concerned with firm behaviour. Levinsohn (1993) investigated the effects of the 1984 Import Program in Turkey, which implemented a significant liberalization of imports, using detailed data on individual firms. The reduction in import protection was found to have reduced price–cost markups, lending support to the imports as a discipline hypothesis. So, when a domestic industry is dominated by a small number of firms who earn excess profits, external trade liberalization may provide a useful way of limiting the exploitation of monopoly power by these firms in the home market to the benefit of consumers in that market.[1]

10.3 Strategic trade policy

The defining characteristic of competition amongst a small number of firms (at least two) is interdependence: the outcome for any one firm (profits) depends upon the actions of the other firms (for example, output). The firms themselves recognize this mutuality. This arises because, unlike perfect competition, each firm through its own actions has an influence upon the market quantity and price. Thus, each firm when making its own decisions over a particular action has to take a view about the possible response of rival firms (the conjectural variation). It is in this way that the analysis of small-group oligopolies is more

---

[1] If the industry is dominated by a small number of foreign firms, then competition policy may be required to increase the degree of competition in the domestic market.

complicated than the analysis of perfect competition or monopoly. Further, there is no body of empirical evidence to suggest how firms compete in such markets; for example, is it price or output over which each firm decides? Nor do we know the precise nature of conjectural variations. This, as we shall see, makes policy recommendations for oligopolistic industries very fragile.

10.3.1 The Brander and Spencer model

One of the earliest and simplest, and probably most widely cited and influential of models of strategic trade policy was introduced by Brander and Spencer (1985). The model is highly simplified, but highlights clearly the key issues raised by strategic trade policy.

The model is one of duopoly, with each firm being located in a different country (A and B). Each firm sells a homogeneous good only in third markets. There is therefore no domestic consumption, and so changes in consumers' welfare can be ignored when considering changes in national welfare in countries A and B; only changes in producers' surplus (profits) need to be considered. The analysis is partial equilibrium, so it is implicitly assumed that changes in the industry under consideration have no effect upon factor prices and production in other industries.

The simplest, and most commonly made, assumption about the interdependence between firms is that each firm assumes that there will be no response from its rival. Brander and Spencer adopt the Cournot assumption whereby output is the strategic variable: each firm sets its own output so as to maximize its profits, in the belief that competitors will not change their output in response. In the Cournot model the outputs of the two firms are strategic substitutes (in the terminology of Bulow, Geanakopolous, and Klemperer 1985) in the sense that each firm's marginal revenue declines as the output of its rival rises. This gives rise to an important feature of the Cournot model that, given the equilibrium that occurs in the market, it is always possible for each firm to make more profits if only it could somehow persuade its rival to reduce its output. However, there is no mechanism by which the firm itself can induce this response from its rival.

The Cournot equilibrium is a Nash equilibrium, which means that, given the output of the rival, neither firm has an incentive to change its own output. However, government intervention, via the provision of an export subsidy, changes the nature of the game that the firms are playing. The threat of an expansion of output by the subsidized firm becomes credible, and the best response for the rival is to contract output. The result is that profits are shifted from the rival in the foreign country to the domestic subsidized firm.

We may highlight these issues by using a more formal representation of the Brander and Spencer model. We start with an inverse demand function which specifies market price as a function of the total quantity brought to the market, which is in turn the sum of the outputs of the two firms, A and B

$$p = p(q_A + q_B) \tag{10.1}$$

The profits of each firm are given by total revenue (price multiplied by the quantity produced by the firm) minus total cost, which is in turn a function of output

$$\pi_A = q_A p(q_A + q_B) - c(q_A)$$
$$\pi_B = q_B p(q_A + q_B) - c(q_B) \tag{10.2}$$

The first-order conditions for the maximization of profits (marginal revenue equals marginal cost) are

$$\frac{\partial \pi_A}{\partial q_A} = p + q_A \frac{\partial p}{\partial q_A} - \frac{\partial c}{\partial q_A}$$

$$\frac{\partial \pi_B}{\partial q_B} = p + q_B \frac{\partial p}{\partial q_B} - \frac{\partial c}{\partial q_B} \tag{10.3}$$

where the last term on the right of the equation gives marginal cost and the first two terms on the right give marginal revenue. If, say, firm A produces an extra unit it will generate additional revenue equal to the price that the unit is sold for (the first term) but that extra unit, by raising total quantity, will depress the market price ($\partial p / \partial q_A < 0$, $\partial p / \partial q_B < 0$) thus reducing the revenue on all existing units sold. In a more general model there would be an additional multiplicative term reflecting how the total quantity in the market changes following the additional unit of output by firm A. This would incorporate the conjectural variation, the assumption that firm A makes about the response of its rival to the extra unit. In the Cournot model no response from the rival is expected, so that the change in total quantity is equal to the change in output of firm A—this additional term is equal to unity.

Assuming that the relevant second-order conditions for a maximum hold, then equations (10.3) can be solved for q_A and q_B, known as the reaction or best-response function, showing the optimal profit-maximizing output for any given level of output from the rival. This relationship can be depicted graphically as in Figure 10.1. Underlying the reaction function are a series of iso-profit curves, such as $\Pi_A{}^1$, each representing a given level of profit for the firm. Iso-profit curves closer to the axis denote higher levels of profit. The highest level of profit for firm A is when the output of its rival, firm B, is zero and it acts as a monopolist.

The shape of the iso-profit curves for A can be best explained for a given output of firm B, for example as shown by the horizontal line through $q_B{}^1$. Where this line is a tangent to the lowest iso-profit curve for A gives the profit-maximizing output, $q_A{}^1$, given the output of B. For any point to the left of $q_A{}^1$, firm A could increase output and increase profits (and hence move to a lower iso-profit curve). This is because the positive effect on profits of selling an extra unit exceeds the negative effect on profits, which arises from the additional unit reducing the price received on all units sold. If firm A were to raise output above $q_A{}^1$ then the negative effect arising from the fall in market price would outweigh the gains from selling more units, and hence there would be a move to a higher iso-profit curve.

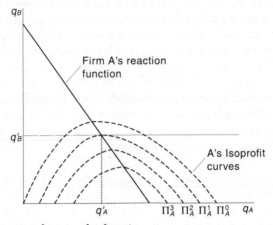

Fig. 10.1. The reaction function for firm A

For each possible output of B there is a unique profit-maximizing output for A, and the reaction function represents all these outputs.

The reaction function for B is derived in exactly the same way and, as shown in Figure 10.2, where the two curves cross gives the Cournot equilibrium. The curves have a negative slope, since an increase in output by the rival reduces the firm's marginal revenue and so marginal profits are negative and the best response is for the firm to reduce its sales.

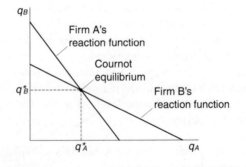

Fig. 10.2. Cournot equilibrium

The Cournot equilibrium is stable in the sense that any movement away from this equilibrium invokes behaviour which eventually leads to the initial equilibrium point being returned to. Thus, either firm acting by itself cannot raise its profits beyond those attainable at the Cournot equilibrium. Each firm has an incentive to raise sales because at the Cournot equilibrium the return from selling an extra unit (the price of the good) exceeds the cost of producing that unit.

But, in practice, an increase in output by a firm, given the optimal response of the rival, will reduce profits. This is because the market price falls, so that the revenue generated from the new output is more than offset by the lower revenue from existing sales. Profits can only be increased if the rival can be induced to reduce its output. In the Cournot game there is no mechanism to achieve this.

Government intervention, however, can change the nature of the game. The provision of a subsidy (a production subsidy and an export subsidy are equivalent in this model of selling to a third market only) by the government of, say, country A reduces the cost of producing each level of output for firm A. This implies that the reaction function for firm A will shift outwards to R'_A, as in Figure 10.3. Firm A will find it profitable to produce a higher level of output than at the Cournot equilibrium and the rival, firm B, will find that its best response is to accommodate the increase in output by A and reduce its own output. The profits of firm A will be higher and those of firm B lower than at the Cournot equilibrium. The optimal subsidy, that which raises the profits by the greatest amount, is that which raises the output of firm A to the level where B's reaction function just touches, is tangent to, the lowest isoprofit curve for firm A. This is known as the Stackelberg leader-follower equilibrium.

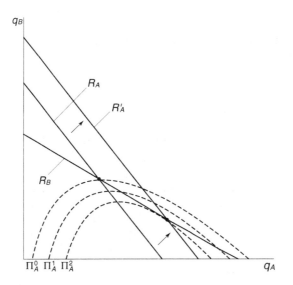

Fig. 10.3. Rent shifting in the Cournot model

The key result from this model is that the intervening country as a whole benefits from the policy. There is therefore a rationale for government intervention. The subsidy is simply a transfer from taxpayers in country A to the owners of firm A. The profits of the firm rise, but they increase by more than the value of the subsidy. This arises because the subsidy encourages the domestic firm to act more aggressively towards its foreign rival, while the rival, in response, produces less. This reaction is the 'strategic effect', since it derives from the strategic interaction between firms in an oligopolistic market. So, economic welfare in country A rises, but this is entirely at the expense of lower welfare in country B due to the lower profits for firm B. The use of a subsidy is a predatory policy as profits are shifted from country B to country A.

Another important feature of the model is that the welfare of consumers in the rest of the world rises, since the price of the product falls. The reaction function of firm A is more steeply sloped than that of firm B (this is necessary for a stable equilibrium in the Cournot model) so that the decline in the output of B is less than the increase in the output of A after the subsidy. Thus, total quantity rises after the subsidy and the price falls. The combined positive effects for country A and the rest of the world exceed the loss for country B. The subsidy by stimulating greater industry output, to an extent, offsets the distortion caused by the exploitation of monopoly power in the initial situation. The duopoly constrained supply so as to keep prices high.

The traditional view of an export subsidy is that it is detrimental to the domestic economy because of the negative terms of trade effect; the effect of the subsidy is to reduce the world price of the home country's exports. In this duopoly model the subsidy also leads to a terms-of-trade loss for the domestic economy, but this is more than offset by the profit-shifting effect. So profit-shifting appears to provide an incentive for trade policy distinct from the usual terms of trade arguments (Brander 1995).

10.3.2 Generalization of the Brander and Spencer model

The Brander and Spencer model is a particularly abstract view of the world; two firms in different countries selling only in third markets. We now see if there is a case for strategic trade intervention in more elaborate models. We firstly consider a situation in which the duopolists, in addition to serving third markets, also sell to consumers in the domestic market. In this case the effects of a production subsidy are no longer equivalent to those of an export subsidy. An export subsidy will encourage the domestic firm to divert sales to overseas markets. Quantity in the home market will decline, and price will rise. Thus, consumers in the country imposing the export subsidy will lose welfare which may more than offset the rise in profits for the domestic firm, as profits are shifted from the rival. Thus, there can be no guarantee that the domestic economy will benefit from the export subsidy, and no presumption that welfare in the global economy will be higher.

A production subsidy, on the other hand, will lead to an unambiguous gain for the country in which it is levied, and in the world as a whole, since the price in both the domestic economy and export market will fall. Thus, trade policy is no longer a useful tool. The appropriate means of offsetting the monopoly power in the industry is the traditional policy of a subsidy to production.

10.3.3 Import protection as export promotion

If we also consider markets where economies of scale in production are important, the effects of policy intervention are likely to be more pronounced. By facilitating an expansion of output, policy will reduce the costs of the domestic firm. This is the basis for the argument that import protection can lead to export promotion (Krugman 1984). The analysis is based upon the 'reciprocal dumping' model, in which two firms sell in each other's markets as well as the rest of the world, but the various markets are 'segmented' so that the price of a particular good may vary between locations. This model is modified so that instead of facing constant marginal costs each firm faces a downward-sloping marginal cost curve. Now if, say, the government of firm A imposes trade restrictions (tariffs or quotas) upon imports from firm B, then firm A will expand sales and firm B will sell less. The cost of an additional unit of output by firm A will decline, whilst that of firm B will increase. Thus, the trade restriction not only allows firm A to expand sales in its domestic market, but also facilitates an expansion of overseas sales as the marginal cost of serving all markets declines. There is a positive feedback from output to cost to output.

This academic idea very much appeals to businessmen facing strong competition from abroad; if only they could have protection in their home market they could become more efficient and eventually be competitive on world markets and therefore raise exports. However, although it is clear that producers would gain from such protection, the overall welfare effect for both the home country and the foreign countries is ambiguous. The fall in marginal cost acts in the same way as a production subsidy, shifting the reaction function to the right. However, in this case the rise in marginal cost of the rival firm leads to an inward shift of its reaction function. This means that the welfare effect in overseas markets will be indeterminate, and the effect on price and quantity can go either way. In the home market the effect of intervention will also be unclear. Producers will gain as profits rise, but protection will more than likely raise prices in the home market and so consumers will lose. The overall global effect of the policy will also therefore be uncertain.

10.3.4 Free entry and exit

So far we have considered imperfectly competitive markets where there are excess profits. The rationale for government intervention appears to lie in shifting profits from the foreign firm to the domestic firm. This requires that there is a fixed number of firms in the industry, so that there is no entry of new firms to compete for the excess profits being made. If entry into the market is possible then excess profits will be zero in the long run. Is a case for strategic trade policy confined to the relatively small number of industries which appear to be characterized by lack of entry of new firms? Venables (1985) provides an example of trade intervention which raises domestic welfare even when firms can freely enter the industry in the long run.

Venables uses a reciprocal dumping model with economies of scale; marginal costs are assumed to be constant, but each firm incurs some fixed costs, so that average costs fall throughout the range of output. The presence of fixed costs ensures that, although new firms are free to enter, there will be a finite number of firms in the industry and there will be imperfect competition. Cournot conjectures are assumed.

Now consider the effects of trade policy in the form of an import tariff or an export subsidy. The tariff will increase the demand for the output of domestic producers and reduce the demand for imports. As the output of domestic firms increases because of the economies of scale their average costs fall. Conversely, the average costs of foreign suppliers rise. Entry into the industry in the domestic market ensures that excess profits cannot be made, and implies that firms must set a price equal to average cost. So, provided that the greater proportion of domestic demand is satisfied by domestic firms (which will occur if there are transport costs), then the imposition of the tariff will reduce prices in the home market! This is completely counter to traditional theory. There will be an increase in consumers' surplus, and some tariff revenue for the government. Thus, with no change in profits (they are always normal), national welfare must rise. In the foreign market, prices will rise and welfare will fall. Again, the policy is predatory. The argument regarding the effect of an export subsidy is very similar; the subsidy stimulates output and leads to domestic firms operating at lower average costs.

The gains from intervention in both Krugman and Venables arise from the presence of economies of scale. Krugman allows for declining marginal costs, whilst Venables has the probably more empirically realistic assumption of fixed costs and fairly constant marginal costs. In Krugman's model the number of firms is fixed, so that the benefits from intervention by the domestic government arise in the form of greater excess profits for the home firm. However, domestic prices may rise so that there is no guarantee that overall welfare will increase. In the model of Venables the gains from intervention accrue to consumers in the form of lower prices. With no change in profits welfare must rise. The results of both Krugman and Venables are predicated on the assumption that international markets are 'segmented'. The price of a given good can vary between different markets, and the effect of policy intervention is that higher prices in the foreign country effectively subsidize lower prices in the home country.

Horstmann and Markusen (1986) have shown that if markets are 'integrated' so that price differences cannot persist, except for the effect of transport costs, then the case for strategic trade policy disappears. For a range of possible cases regarding demand and cost conditions, trade policy may reduce welfare. This arises because intervention stimulates inefficient entry into the domestic industry, leading to a lower level of output per firm and a higher level of average cost. In reality, for a number of reasons, price differences for a given good do exist between different national markets. On the other hand, perfect price discrimination between markets seems untenable. The most realistic structure for international markets is somewhere between the extremes of integrated and segmented markets.

10.4   Strategic trade policy: an evaluation

The literature on strategic trade policy led Krugman (1987) to assert that 'the case for free trade is currently more in doubt than at any time since the 1817 publication of Ricardo's Principles of Political Economy'. The profit shifting arguments of Brander and Spencer, and Krugman's import protection as export promotion, gained a wide audience and were perceived by some businessmen, administrators, and politicians as providing academic support for the intervention and protectionism they were seeking. The ideas behind strategic trade policy also received much attention from the academic community. The subsequent theoretical and empirical analysis has tended to show that the case for strategic intervention is rather weak.

All economic models are necessarily abstractions from reality. Therefore, for the prescriptions of a particular model or theory to have practical relevance they must be robust, in the sense that minor changes to the assumptions underlying the model leave the basic implications for policy unchanged. Further, we should expect our theory to be consistent with observed economic behaviour and to be of empirical significance. As we shall now show, strategic trade policy appears to fail these tests. We continue by considering the theoretical robustness of the models. We concentrate on the Brander and Spencer model because of its simplicity and popularity, although many of the criticisms equally apply to the reciprocal dumping models.

10.4.1   The nature of competition

The Brander and Spencer model uses the Cournot assumption to model the interaction between firms. This is, however, just one possible representation of the nature of competition in imperfectly competitive markets. Now consider another: Bertrand competition, where price is the strategic variable. Each firm sets its profit-maximizing price on the assumption that the price of the rival remains unchanged. First we must note that if the products of the different firms are homogeneous then the Bertrand equilibrium will be equivalent to the competitive equilibrium. Each firm, by slightly undercutting its rival, can capture the whole of the market. The incentive for such behaviour will remain until both firms set price as equal to marginal cost, when further undercutting would lead to losses. In this case there are no excess profits, and no role for strategic trade policy.

Hence, we consider two firms A and B selling different varieties of a good in a third market. Under the Bertrand model the best responses of each firm to a given price of the rival define upward-sloping reaction functions with underlying convex iso-profit curves (see Figure 10.4). Iso-profit curves further from the axis denote higher levels of profit. A stable equilibrium will arise where the price set by each firm is the optimal response to the price set by the rival, that is, where the reaction functions cross.

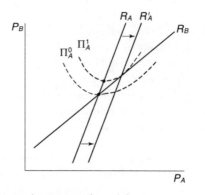

Fig. 10.4. Rent shifting in the Bertrand model

In this case if, say, firm A seeks to increase its profits it can only do so by charging a higher price and encouraging its rival to do likewise. Acting alone, firm A does not have a credible threat to raise its price; if it did so the rival could raise sales and profits by slightly undercutting A's price and eventually the original Bertrand equilibrium would be restored. Again, government intervention can make a higher price by firm A credible and ensure that the optimal response of firm B is to raise its price. However, the relevant policy, which shifts the reaction curve of firm A to the right, is an export tax, not an export subsidy! Intervening with an export subsidy would be detrimental to national welfare.

In the Cournot and Bertrand models firms make inconsistent conjectures; each firm continually makes mistakes in its assumption about how the rival will react, yet it never learns from these errors. So firms are naïve and irrational in not using all the information available to them in making their conjectures. In this environment government intervention can be effective if it corrects for the errors being made in the game by the home firm. Under Cournot the domestic firm believes that if it increases its own sales the rival will not change its own output, whereas the rival will actually respond by reducing its output. In effect the home firm makes its decisions believing the market is more competitive than it actually is. From the country's point of view it produces too little so that a subsidy will be beneficial. With Bertrand the home firm assumes that if it reduces its own price, and therefore increases sales, the rival will not change its own price, implying that the foreign firm will reduce output. What actually will happen is that the rival will reduce price, and therefore increase its sales. So, here, the home firm treats the market as being less competitive than it really is, and produces too much. A tax on the home firm is the relevant policy.

It was Eaton and Grossman (1986) who first argued that strategic trade policy is likely to be of little use in practice since the underlying models are not robust, and the particular policy prescription is dependent upon the nature of the model. Cournot and Bertrand are two, perhaps unrealistic, extreme assumptions about competition; in between there is a range of more plausible assumptions that can be made about the conjectures of each firm.

A further case is where firms hold 'consistent conjectures', such as in the Stackelberg model. We saw earlier that the optimal degree of intervention will lead to the Stackelberg outcome. Thus, on the face of it, if the home firm is already the Stackelberg leader in the market then intervention appears inappropriate; any government policy would move the firm away from the Stackelberg point and reduce profits. Consistent conjectures occur when each firm's assumption about the response of its rival is equal to the actual response and the conjectures about the slope of the rival's reaction curve are correct. However, it turns out that even with consistent conjectures the optimal degree of intervention is not zero. The reaction function of the rival foreign firm incorporates that firms conjecture about the reaction function of the home firm. Thus the home government could deliberately distort the reaction function of its domestic firm through a tax or subsidy, knowing that this will influence the conjectures of the foreign firm, although the optimal policy is generally very difficult to ascertain.

The general point from this discussion is that we know very little about the nature of competition that actually exists in particular industries. Now, since the policy prescription varies with the nature of competition, and we cannot be sure of the form competition takes, we cannot be confident in the policy prescription. In such an environment it can be argued that the most appropriate advice to give to policy makers is that the general rule of no intervention is likely to be the best course of action.

10.4.2 Strategic trade policy with many imperfectly competitive industries

The models which provide a case for strategic trade policy are all set in a partial equilibrium framework. A single industry is considered which is small enough so that changes in its output have no effect upon other industries and the prices of factors of production. General equilibrium considerations cast further doubt over the case for intervention. First note that if we allow for many industries, but all, bar the specific industry under consideration, are perfectly competitive, then the standard arguments for intervention follow through. This is because government intervention leads to resources being attracted into the imperfectly competitive sector where they earn a higher return than in the competitive sectors of the economy.

Difficulties arise if there are a number of imperfectly competitive industries, and in particular if these industries draw on a common pool of resources, some of which are scarce, that is, fixed, or relatively inelastic in supply in the short run. High-technology, R&D-intensive industries are generally believed to possess the properties which are likely to generate gains from strategic trade policy: imperfect competition and economies of scale. Such industries typically require the input of highly skilled scientists and engineers, the supply of which is unlikely to be able to respond quickly to policy-induced changes in output.

If a certain industry is chosen to receive an export or production subsidy then its output will rise and profits will be shifted from the foreign competitor. However, as this industry expands it will have to compete for the scarce factors of production with other industries. The price of these factors will be bid up and the costs of production of the other, non-supported, industries will rise. Domestic firms in these industries will have to reduce output, permitting foreign firms to raise their sales and snatch profits. So, although the profits of the targeted firm will rise, this gain will be offset by the loss of rents in the other imperfectly competitive sectors.

If all these industries are essentially identical in that they face similar demand and production conditions and similar degrees of foreign competition—in this case the industries are referred to as being symmetric—then the gains to any one (or more) subsidized industries will not outweigh the losses in profits in the non-targeted industries. So no intervention would be the best policy. If the imperfectly competitive industries are not symmetric, then net welfare gains from intervention are possible. The problem is, which industries to target?

Dixit and Grossman (1986) show that the information required to target industries successfully is immense. The industries which should be selected are not necessarily those which generate the greatest increase in profits, but rather, it should be those which shift the greatest amount of profit per unit of the scarce resource. This will depend upon production technologies both at home and abroad, the substitutability in demand between the home and foreign firms products, the market-price elasticity of demand, and the nature of competition. In practice much of this information will be subject to a high degree of uncertainty or will even be unavailable.

A simple alternative, which requires little information, would be to subsidize all high-technology industries. However, the effect of a uniform subsidy is to simply transfer rents from profits to scientists (the scarce resource). In the case of symmetric industries, individual industry outputs will be unaltered and total welfare unchanged. If industries are not identical, the rise in the price of scientists will have differential effects, and a net gain will only arise if those industries which are least affected by the rise in the price of the scarce resource are those most able to shift profits from the foreign firm per unit of this resource. There is no reason why this should be the case. So the analysis of strategic trade policy in a general equilibrium framework shows that there is a real danger that by trying to pick 'winners' the government may subvert other industries to the detriment of the country as a whole.

10.4.3 Identifying industries with excess profits

Trade policy in the Brander and Spencer model is successful because of the presence of excess profits, but how do we know if excess profits are being earned? High profits do not necessarily mean excess profits: they may reflect the return required to cover an earlier, risky investment. The large expenditures on R&D which characterize many high-technology industries will only be undertaken if the expected return (the return if innovation is successful multiplied by the probability of success) exceeds the cost of the investment. Thus, in these industries, there may be a stage of competition prior to that in the final product market, in which firms compete in terms of R&D expenditures and in which many firms fail. Thus, when looking at profits being made in the final product market, it is important to include the losses of those who failed in the earlier round of competition when seeking to assess excess profits.

10.4.4 Retaliation

The Brander and Spencer model also assumes that only one government intervenes. If, however, we simply extend the analysis to allow for the government of the country in which the rival firm is located also to be active, then there will be an incentive for both governments to provide export subsidies. In this case the governments face a prisoners' dilemma; there is an incentive for unilateral intervention, but both countries will be worse off following intervention than under free trade.

10.4.5 The number of domestic firms

The basic model for strategic trade policy is one of duopoly, with a single firm in each country. If there are a number of domestic firms, an export subsidy may reduce welfare. This is because the firms fail to take into account the effect of their own actions on the profits of other domestic firms. Exports may be higher and price lower than is socially optimal for the country. If firms were to coordinate their actions they would be able to raise joint profits.

Intervention in the form of an export subsidy would exacerbate the oversupply of exports; hence the relevant policy would be an export tax, as this would reduce exports and encourage less aggressive behaviour between domestic firms. Government intervention may be beneficial to ensure that national monopoly power is exploited when firms do not do so themselves because they are too small. So with imperfectly competitive industries, the greater the number of firms the more likely it is that an export tax rather than an export subsidy will be relevant. The precise number of firms in the industry necessary to change the policy prescription from subsidy to tax cannot be determined a priori, and depends upon industry conditions. In specific cases it could be as few as two.

Thus, there are a number of reasons to be sceptical about the case for strategic trade policy. Although it is perfectly possible that certain industries may offer opportunities for welfare-increasing government intervention, the information required to identify such industries successfully is formidable, if not impossible to obtain. Given such uncertainty and the negative welfare effects of incorrect intervention, for example, providing an export subsidy when an export tax is relevant, there appears to be little basis for an active trade policy in imperfectly competitive markets. This view is reinforced by the empirical evaluation of strategic trade policy. Before this is discussed, however, we take a slight detour to consider how, in practice, trade policies may lead to less competitive market outcomes.

10.5 Quantitative trade restrictions as facilitating practices

A further important issue highlighted by recent work on trade in imperfectly competitive markets is that trade restrictions in oligopolistic markets may have surprising or unexpected effects. In perfectly competitive markets tariffs and quotas are nominally equivalent; a quota level can always be found to replicate the effects of a particular tariff. We have already seen that this is not necessarily true in the presence of monopoly in the domestic market with competitive suppliers of imports. A quota permits the greater exploitation of market power in the domestic economy, because the home firm realizes that it can increase its price without there being an increase in the quantity of imports.

Harris (1985) and Krishna (1989) have shown how quantitative trade restrictions, and in particular VERs (voluntary export restraints), can affect the nature of competition between firms in oligopolistic markets. They show that such a policy can lead to a less competitive solution in which both domestic and foreign firms have higher profits at the expense of domestic consumers. The firms acting alone are unable to achieve such a market outcome, and so in this sense the VER acts to facilitate collusion.

Krishna shows that a VER imposed in a Bertrand duopoly at the free-trade level, which would have no effect under competitive conditions, leads to both firms raising their prices. This clearly highlights that quantitative restrictions and tariffs which generate the same level of imports will not have the same effects in such a market. At the free-trade Bertrand equilibrium the home firm, assuming that the price of the rival will remain unchanged, perceives that if it raises its price it will lose sales and the rival will gain sales. The VER signals to the home firm that the foreign rival cannot sell more, so that an increase in the home firm's price will lead to fewer lost sales than in the absence of the VER. The VER creates an incentive for the home firm to raise its price. However, given the upward-sloping reaction function for the foreign firm, its optimal response to this increase in price of the home firm is to raise its own price. So the VER leads to both firms increasing their price and therefore their profits.

Thus the use of a VER, or indeed any trade policy instrument, may change the nature of the rivalry between firms in imperfectly competitive industries, leading to a less competitive solution. This reinforces the negative effects of such intervention for the country using it. An increasing volume of empirical evidence is emphasizing the importance of such effects. We discuss below how trade restrictions on imports of cars from Japan into the EU may have led to a more collusive outcome in the EU market, to the detriment of consumers in EU countries. But first we provide an overview of the empirical assessment of strategic trade policy.

10.6 Empirical studies of strategic trade policy

In addition to assessing its theoretical robustness economists should refrain from using a particular theory to make strong policy recommendations until it has been thoroughly tested against observed economic behaviour. There is little point using a theory to advise those in government if its basic arguments are empirically irrelevant. This point is all the more important since the analysis of strategic trade policy is based in a second-best environment. Empirical studies are crucial to determine whether the conditions necessary for welfare improvement actually exist in the real world.

The normal approach to empirical analysis in economics is to specify a model representing the underlying theory and then econometrically estimate the parameters which define the relationships between the variables in the model using the available data. This approach provides for a range of statistical information by which to assess the empirical importance of particular variables and the ability of the model to explain the processes that are apparent in the data.

In general this approach has not been followed in the empirical assessment of strategic trade policy. Although the theoretical models are quite simple, their empirical application is very demanding of information some of which is difficult to find over many years or industries, such as expenditures on R&D. Other data may be unreliable. For example, information on production costs at the level of the firm is often required, leading to problems of confidentiality and accuracy, if, for example, the firms providing information are seeking support from the government. Thus, lack of information precludes econometric estimation of the parameters in the model. An alternative approach has been adopted using the method of calibration.

The basic model is assumed to be correct and the parameter values are taken from external sources, typically previous econometric studies or engineers' reports. These parameter values are then constrained to be consistent with a single observation (either data for one year or the average of a small number of years) under the assumption that this observation reflects an equilibrium outcome of the model. If (when) these parameter values are found to be inconsistent with the data, one or more are adjusted until a consistent set is obtained. A variant of this procedure, which has been extensively used in quantitative models of

trade under imperfect competition, is to use external estimates for all the parameters except one and then derive or calibrate the value of this parameter as that
which exactly ensures the model is consistent with the data.

In the Appendix to this chapter we consider in more detail studies of the
European car industry which, on the basis of its characteristics, satisfies the criterion for potentially beneficial strategic trade policy. Here we concentrate on summarizing the results from the more important empirical studies; more detailed
surveys have been provided by Richardson (1989) and Helpman and Krugman
(1989: ch. 8). There appear to be three basic conclusions from the variety of
empirical studies that has been undertaken using calibrated models:

1. Optimal trade policies under imperfect competition, in the absence of retali-
    ation, are generally non-zero. Such policies may imply large changes in trade
    flows and production but overall the relative magnitudes of the welfare gains
    from intervention are typically small. For example, Venables (1994) in a
    study of nine European industries finds that on average an import tariff of 20
    per cent would raise welfare by only about 1 per cent of the value of con-
    sumption in the base year. Export subsidies have even smaller welfare effects.
    There is no empirical support for large gains from import protection or
    export subsidies.
2. The gains from strategic trade policy are largest in the presence of economies
    of scale with free entry and exit of firms and when markets are integrated so
    that firms cannot charge different prices in different national markets.
3. The potential welfare losses if foreign governments retaliate and there is a
    trade war are much larger under imperfect competition. This then implies, as
    also supported by empirical studies, that the gains from trade liberalization
    will be greater than would be expected under the assumption of competitive
    markets. There is nothing to suggest that imperfectly competitive behaviour
    will reverse the gains from trade; rather, it amplifies them. The gains pre-
    dicted by Smith and Venables (1988) from removing internal barriers to
    trade within the EU so as to complete the Single Market are much larger than
    would be forecast by models based upon competitive behaviour.

Thus the results from these models are not particularly supportive of the case for
intervention, and even when positive effects are found they tend to be very small.
Further, there are a number of reasons to be sceptical over the results emanating
from this empirical work. Calibrated models cannot be subjected to the normal
range of statistical tests that are applied in econometric work; thus there is no
means of measuring how well the models explain the data. Also, the external
parameter values have an associated standard error, and so there is a degree of
uncertainty about their precise magnitude. This in turn should translate into
uncertainty concerning the predictions of the model. This can be partly addressed
by undertaking sensitivity analysis; varying one parameter at a time, recomput-
ing the model, and assessing the implications for the principal results. However,
as noted by Levinsohn (1994), this is not entirely satisfactory given the multiplicative nature of probabilities. The results from these models may be subject to

very large standard errors and hence great uncertainty. Overall this suggests that the results from calibrated models should be interpreted as simulating the theory for a particular set of parameter values, and that the results are not driven by data. This is not to deny the usefulness of these exercises, as they have certainly shed light on the key processes within the underlying theory. However, there should be considerable doubt over the extent to which they show the importance of strategic trade policy in the real world.

Finally, we discuss a study which does confront the idea of strategic trade policy with real data. Dick (1994) tests whether import protection targeted to specific industries in the US has promoted the exports of those industries. It is postulated that for a particular industry the share of exports by the US in total industrial country exports will be a function of whether the US has a comparative advantage in that industry, the extent of import protection granted to US firms, and the relative size of the domestic market. The latter variable is included since governments may also affect export performance by manipulating the size of the domestic market available to home firms via, for example, government procurement policies biased towards home companies. Dick then tests whether protection and relative market size are positively correlated with export performance. However, observed or revealed comparative advantage is potentially affected by past import protection, and the extent of current protection may be influenced by past export performance; thus, these variables are first normalized to give a measure of free trade comparative advantage and the relative targeted tariff and non-tariff rate.

The econometric results show that, as expected, free-trade comparative advantage has a positive and significant impact upon export performance. Relative targeted non-tariff protection and relative market size, however, are estimated to have a significant but negative effect upon export shares. The relative targeted tariff variable enters negatively, but is not statistically significant.

Thus, there is no evidence that industries in the US which have been subject to high levels of protection from imports or which have had access to large domestic markets are, on average, more successful in export markets. In fact, this study suggests that such industries tend to have smaller export shares than less protected industries. This result is confirmed even when the sample of industries is limited to those where increasing returns are strongest, industries where the potential for export promotion is supposedly greatest.

10.7 Conclusions

In the 1960s, 1970s and 1980s a commonly heard view, particularly from businessmen seeking protection from imports, has been that the traditional prescription of international trade theory against intervention is invalid because of the patent lack of realism of the assumptions underlying the theory. We have since seen a great deal of academic activity in evaluating trade policy in models which relax these strict assumptions, and in particular those of constant returns to scale and perfect competition.

To many this analysis, most simply captured in the Brander and Spencer model, appeared to provide a case for an active trade policy. However, it is now apparent that even though a case for unilateral intervention can be found, the practical difficulties of implementing the relevant policies are immense. The case for strategic trade policy is not robust as regards changes in the structure of the underlying models, and the notion that a government can pick winners in international trade runs the high risk that it will simply end up by supporting losers to the detriment of national welfare.

This scepticism regarding strategic trade policy is reinforced by empirical analysis which suggests that, even when intervention is beneficial, the effects on welfare are very small. In a number of cases which appear to provide the ideal environment for strategic trade policy, such as the car market in the EU, no strategic benefits can be found. In fact, trade policy in imperfectly competitive markets may well lead to more collusive outcomes to the detriment of the intervening country.

To many this analysis has strengthened rather than undermined the case against trade policy intervention. It has now been shown that relaxing assumptions to allow for increasing returns to scale and imperfect competition provides little support activism in trade. Rather, the general predisposition that welfare in the domestic economy will be most enhanced with liberal trade policies remains.

10.8 Summary

- Imports can act to discipline domestic monopolists.
- When a third market is supplied by one firm from each of two countries, an exporting country can gain by subsidizing its exports to divert profits from the foreign to the home firm.
- Opportunities to shift rent from overseas to home firms provide some case for strategic trade policy. If the firms' marginal cost curves slope down, import protection acts to promote exports. But the argument for strategic trade policy is not robust: it vanishes if firms compete in prices for example, and production subsidies are often superior when they are output-setters.

APPENDIX: THE CAR INDUSTRY IN EUROPE: A CASE FOR STRATEGIC TRADE POLICY?

On the face of it the car industry in Europe has the characteristics which proponents of strategic trade policy claim will make intervention effective. A number of studies have indicated scope for further exploitation of economies of scale, whilst the concentration of European sales amongst a relatively small number of suppliers is suggestive of imperfect competition. The six largest firms currently account for over 75 per cent of total car sales in the EU. Further, the car industry is an interesting case because of its importance in terms of output and employment in Europe, and the fact that it has been subject to a range of trade policies culminating recently in the replacement of a number of bilateral VERs affecting imports from Japan with an EU-wide VER.

The car industry has been extensively analysed in calibrated simulation models by Alistair Smith and Anthony Venables. Here we concentrate on two papers, Smith and Venables (1991) and Smith (1994). The basic model used allows for product differentiation with consumers having a love of variety, as represented by the Dixit-Stiglitz utility function (referred to in Chapter 7), and firms producing several different models of car. The demand for an individual model is a function of the price of that model and the overall price of cars. Firms' costs functions are such that there are economies of scale in terms of output per model and economies of scope in the number of models produced.

A key feature of the development of the market for cars in the EU since the early 1970s has been the increasing share of imports from Japan. This resulted, in addition to the common external tariff, in imports from Japan being subject to trade restrictions in a number of EU countries. The UK, France, Italy, Portugal, and Spain have all had VERs or quotas on imports from Japan, whilst on the other hand, the remaining markets have been free of non-tariff barriers.

Japanese sales in the UK were restricted between 1977 and 1991 to 11 per cent of the market; in France the Japanese market share has been constrained to 3 per cent. In the unrestricted German market, imports from Japan comprise around 16 per cent of sales and in the rest of the EU the share of the Japanese suppliers is over 25 per cent. The maintenance of these differing national restrictions required border checks between EU members to prevent trade deflection: that is, for example, Japanese cars being freely imported into Germany and then sold in the French market circumventing the trade barrier. In 1991, in preparation for the completion of the Single European Market which required the abolition of all border controls, these national constraints were replaced with an EU-wide VER. This agreement is referred to as a 'consensus' with the Japanese.

A feature of Smith (1994) is that the number of models per firm is endogenous, so that trade policy can influence the number of models produced not only by domestic firms but also firms in other countries. The change in the number of models per firm then has an effect upon a second stage of competition, where firms, under the Cournot assumption, choose output per model. Thus, this effect can be thought of as the strategic trade policy effect. Trade policy alters the nature of the competitive game between domestic and foreign firms. To try and identify the importance of the strategic trade policy effect of the national car restrictions in the EU, Smith simulates the effects of the national VERs with and without the number of models per firm fixed. Holding model numbers fixed eliminates strategic trade policy effects.

The results suggest that, for the EU as a whole, the gains from the VERs to producers in terms of higher profits are less than the loss of consumer surplus. Importantly, the gains to producers are lower when model numbers are variable rather than fixed. This implies that these trade barriers had no strategic trade policy effect. Even for an individual country, France, the VER reduces national welfare and has no strategic benefits. In this case the VER reduces the number of models produced by Japanese firms, but leads to a greater model range for a German, not a French producer. Thus, this analysis shows that one country's strategic trade policy may benefit another country's producer, and may overall appear to undermine the case for strategic trade policy.

As we have seen earlier, quantitative restrictions can facilitate anti-competitive behaviour. Smith and Venables (1991) highlight the potential presence and magnitude of such effects in the EU car market. First they compute that the net annual welfare effect of the national arrangements in place at the end of the 1980s was a loss of about 5 billion ecu, equivalent to over 3 per cent of the value of consumption in 1988. The effect of replacing the national restrictions with a EU-wide VER which constrains Japanese suppliers to their existing share of 8.8 per cent of the EU market as a whole is then considered. Such a switch has little effect on overall welfare in the EU, but leads to a more even distribution across EU markets of the effects of the trade restriction. So the costs to the EU of a community VER are very similar to those of the national constraints.

The effects of the EU-wide VER are then compared with a tariff, the magnitude of which is sufficient to maintain the total output of EU producers at the same level as under the VER. The effect of this policy switch is to reduce the prices and profits of all car manufacturers, both Japanese and European. The gain in consumer surplus from the lower prices exceeds the losses to EU producers. Once tariff revenue is taken into account, the net gain from replacing the VER with a tariff is over 3.5 billion ecu, and this figure can be viewed as the anti-competitive element of the 5-billion-ecu cost of the VER. Such anti-competitive effects of VERs make them a very inefficient form of intervention. This example also demonstrates the lack of equivalence between VERs and tariffs in imperfectly competitive markets.

This study highlights an issue which has, to date, been relatively neglected by trade economists: that of the interaction between trade and competition policies. This conflict can arise in both the importing and the exporting markets. For example, the 1991 consensus commits the Japanese authorities to 'monitor total exports from Japan to the EC and they will also monitor exports to France, Italy, Portugal, Spain and the United Kingdom, through twice-yearly bilateral consultations on current export trends and future forecasts for the following year'. This monitoring takes place within the framework of a 'forecast' of imports from Japan of 1.23 million cars in 1999 with total EU demand of 15.1 million cars, implying a share of the EU market of 8.15 per cent. There are also individual national targets for France (5.26 per cent), Italy (5.31 per cent), Spain (5.36 per cent), Portugal (8.36 per cent), and the UK (7.04 per cent) for 1999. Thus, although there is now an EU-wide trade restriction, there are, in effect, still national sub-quotas. The agreement states that the output of Japanese-owned plants operating in the EU will be able to circulate freely within the EU. However, the fact that the target for the UK is less than that in the national agreement prior to 1991 presumably reflects, at least in part, the implicit treatment of Japanese cars produced in the UK as imports into the EU.

Holmes and Smith (1995) argue that an important element of the regular negotiations will be the state of the car market in the EU. Since the European capacity of Japanese car firms is now an important component of the EU market, the output of Japanese plants in Europe is likely to be included in the import 'forecasts'. In this way the agreement may evolve into a series of market-sharing arrangements which are clearly contrary to the aims of competition policy in the EU. If competition policy were to be strictly applied it would undermine the trade policy with regard to Japanese cars.

Further, the import restrictions on cars are implemented by the Japanese authorities. This acts as a barrier to the entry of new firms, and in effect makes them enforce an export cartel. This clearly has anti-competitive effects in the EU market, and brings the agreement into conflict with Japan's own competition legislation. So, on the one hand, the EU is obliging the Japanese to enforce anti-competitive practices on its firms, whilst on the other it criticizes Japan for lack of action in implementing competition law.

INTERNATIONAL FACTOR MIGRATION

11.1 Introduction

Until now we have been assuming that factors of production, such as capital or labour, may be free to move between different sectors in a nation's economy, but not across international boundaries. It is the central aim of this chapter to see what can happen when this assumption is relaxed.

11.2 Evidence from Europe and other countries

11.2.1 International factor migration: the institutional aspects

The structure of this chapter is as follows. Section 11.2 examines the phenomenon of international migration in an institutional and historical setting, with a primary focus on Europe. In Section 11.3, we explore the comparative statics of international capital migration, and this analysis is extended to labour movements in Section 11.4. Section 11.5 investigates longer-run issues of capital movements in a dynamic setting.

Land cannot move between countries, although an upstream dam of a long river can enhance its productivity in one country and impoverish it in another. Capital and labour can and do migrate. What leads the owner of a factor to move it from country A to country B is the attraction of a higher prospective return in B than A. If there are no obstacles to international movement, expected returns should be equalized everywhere.

Barriers to international factor migration often prevent this, however. For labour there are the fixed costs of transactions in the housing market, for example, that can impede domestic as well as international migration. There may be costs, pecuniary and psychic, associated with learning a new language, gaining new qualifications, and leaving family and friends. Then there are regulations. The country the worker seeks to leave may disallow it. Those who tried to move from the former German Democratic Republic (East Germany) to the Federal Republic (West Germany) in the years before German reunification in 1990 risked life and limb. Many died doing so. The government of the intending migrant's country of destination may prohibit or restrict immigration, too. Such restrictions vary in their severity and effectiveness: up to ten million of today's residents in the United States, for example, are estimated to have entered the country illegally, many of them from Mexico.

Private costs are much less important in the case of international capital migration. The key barriers here are legal. Sometimes it is the destination country that tries to limit capital movement. Switzerland attempted to repel capital inflows in 1978 by imposing a negative rate of interest on non-residents' holdings of Swiss Franc bank deposits, for example. Swiss law still prohibits foreign interests from acquiring control of Swiss companies. For nearly twenty years Canada had a Foreign Investment Review Agency which sought to screen, and often prevent, take-overs of Canadian businesses by overseas investors. But more often it is capital exports by domestic residents that are subject to restriction. Britain imposed foreign-exchange control regulations against capital exports until 1979; similar restrictions applied by the governments of France, Italy, Spain, and Portugal lasted into the late 1980s and early 1990s.

The 1957 Treaty of Rome, which led to the founding of the European Economic Community linking Belgium, France, Italy, Luxembourg, the Netherlands, and West Germany, enshrined the principle of unfettered movement of capital and labour as well as goods between these six countries. In practice, however, some official barriers to intra-EEC labour and capital migration remained. These were only finally swept away by the provisions of the 1987 Single European Act which came into force throughout the enlarged, twelve-member European Community on 1 January 1993. By 1995 any resident of the fifteen-country European Union could be employed without official restriction anywhere in the Union. Member countries are required to grant mutual recognition to equivalent professional qualifications. Employment permits are required, and may be withheld, for residents of other countries. Norway and Iceland are exceptions: they, and the newly-enlarged fifteen-member European Union, constitute the European Economic Area (EEA) which respects the principle of complete labour mobility.

Historically, there has been relatively little migration of labour between the rich economies of West Europe. Religious and ethnic minorities did sporadically migrate as a result of political pressures: the flight of many Huguenots (Protestants) from seventeenth-century France, to Britain, Holland, and other destinations is one instance. Spain expelled her Jews (or at least those who would not convert to Catholicism) during the Inquisition in the sixteenth century, many moving to Holland. There was a large efflux of Jews from Nazi Germany in the 1930s. Religion was also to play a major part in the early settlement of North America: Puritans from England colonized New England; and many German immigrants to America, from the seventeenth century to the nineteenth, moved partly for religious reasons; then there was heavy Jewish emigration from Russia in the late nineteenth century, mostly to the United States. Whether motivated primarily by economic considerations or not, West European migration overwhelmingly took the form of emigration to other continents, rather than from one European state to another. It was the pull of cheap land, in Australia, Canada, New Zealand, Argentina, Southern Africa, and above all the United States which must have been decisive in many cases, right up to the late nineteenth century and beyond. In Ireland's case, the potato famines of the 1840s were the major force behind a spectacular population collapse, and heavy emigration, partly to Britain but predominantly to the New World. The combination of push and pull—the attraction of higher income prospects abroad and depressed conditions at home—were important in leading to substantial emigration from Italy in the years after 1945, most of it to the United States and to South America.

When West European states have attracted immigrants since the Second World War, it has not been, in the main, from each other. France, Germany, and the UK each added over three million to the labour forces between 1950 and 1990 as a result of immigration from outside Western Europe. France's immigrants came largely from Algeria and other ex-French North African territories. Britain's were attracted from former colonies in the Caribbean and southern Asia, while Germany's immigrants were mainly Turkish and Yugoslav in origin.

International capital movements have a long history. From the thirteenth century to the fifteenth, Florentine banks were major financiers to many European monarchies and governments. Florence, Genoa, Augsburg, the Flemish cities and, later, Amsterdam, funded construction projects, public works, wars, voyages of discovery, and capital outlays associated with international trade, first within Europe and then increasingly beyond it. Earlier, freebooting merchants will have played similar roles in Rome's expansion throughout the Mediterranean, and in the development of Viking trading empires stretching from Russia to eastern North America. The process continued with the Portuguese, Spanish, Dutch, and French in the sixteenth and seventeenth centuries. It was to reach its apogee with Britain. By 1914, British overseas investments, largely concentrated in the Americas, Australia, India, and southern Africa, had an estimated capital value double that of annual GDP. Outflows of new foreign investment, and inflows of income from foreign capital, both touched 10 per cent of national income in some years.

In the late nineteenth and early twentieth centuries, Britain was the world's leading capital exporter. But she was not alone. The world's largest ever investment project, the construction of the Trans-Siberian Railway, was mainly financed on the Berlin and Paris bourses. There were massive flows of capital from Belgium and the Netherlands to the Congo and the East Indies. The United States attracted capital from all the main financial centres of Western Europe.

This world ended in 1914. Capital outflows dried up. Europe's belligerent powers sold off much of their residents' overseas assets in wars. In the inter-war years most governments restricted capital exports to a trickle in order to protect foreign exchange reserves. After 1945, many West European countries borrowed heavily from the United States to finance reconstruction and balance external payments. A number of factors combined to keep capital exports from Europe low in the early post-war decades. One of these was macroeconomic policy. This came to be influenced by Keynesian doctrines, which emphasized the importance of keeping domestic investment high and regulating external financial transactions. By the 1950s and 1960s decolonization was breaking the links, furthermore, between many third-world countries and their main European suppliers of capital, making some lenders wary of possible expropriation. Much of Western Europe outpaced Australasia and North and South America in rates of growth and investment requirements. There was little room left for capital exports.

While most West European countries' balance-of-payments positions have kept capital exports low or negative for most of the post-war period, there are exceptions. West Germany is the most important. She has displayed a strong tendency towards trade surpluses, which were climbing to 5 per cent or more of national income by the late 1960s, and averaged close to this level in the next two decades. These trade surpluses were largely translated into capital exports. After German reunification in 1990, the West's capital exports were redirected to the former east Germany, and therefore vanished from the newly defined national accounts. From 1980 to 1985 Britain briefly regained her status as a leading capital exporter. The exploitation of North Sea oil, at a time when real oil prices were high, allowed her to earn large current account surpluses which were invested abroad. The ratio of Britain's net overseas assets to its national income jumped from approximately one-tenth to one-third in this brief period. In the second half of the 1980s, however, Britain and Spain were to vie for the position of the continent's leading capital importer. Overseas capital was attracted to Spain by a high rate of return, relatively low wages, and accession, in 1986, to the European Community; in Britain's case, there was a private-sector consumption boom fuelled by easy credit, tax cuts, and rising house prices.

West Germany aside, Europe has not regained the status as a major source of capital for the rest of the world that it enjoyed before 1914. But in another sense, the Europe of the 1990s differs dramatically from the Europe of the 1930s, 1940s, and 1950s. In these earlier decades, a forest of regulatory controls allowed most European countries to divorce domestic interest rates almost completely from interest rates prevailing in other countries. With the coming of full currency convertibility for non-residents in December 1958, and the progressive elimination of restrictions on national residents' access to foreign-exchange markets in later decades, international capital mobility has increased to the point where the gap between many countries' short-term interest rates is often vanishingly small. In general, one country's one-year interest rate on government bonds will differ from another's only by a margin that matches foreign-exchange-market participants' expectations of a change, over the year, in the exchange rate between them. If the one-year rate in French francs in Paris is 1 per cent higher than the equivalent Dmark rate in Frankfurt, the forward exchange rate will reveal an offsetting 1 per cent discount on French francs for delivery in a year's time against marks, relative to the spot rate—so if the spot rate is 3.6 francs per mark, the twelve-month forward rate will be 3.636.

The implication of this is that capital markets are now closely integrated between the main West European economies. Real interest rates on financial assets tend to equalize. And this can happen without necessarily provoking large or continuing international flows of capital. The integration is by no means limited to Western Europe. A single, global market for capital embraces the United States and Japan as well as a host of smaller countries. The United States was the main source of capital for the rest of the world, much of it paupered and shattered by war, in the mid-twentieth-century years. By the 1980s it was borrowing heavily from the rest of the world. That decade saw the United States swing from being the world's largest creditor to its greatest debtor: some of the borrowing came from Western Europe, and more from Japan.

In the first half of the 1990s, the transition of previously communist to market economies in Eastern Europe and much of Asia has led to additional pressures on world capital markets. Most of these countries have a chronic shortage of capital, resulting from a long history of centralized planning that had placed priority on traditional heavy industry, such as steel, and armaments. Commerce, light industry, and service sectors had received low priority in these economies, and a large backlog of valuable investment opportunities had built up. Much of West Germany's traditional surplus for capital exports to the outside world was diverted to meet the capital requirements of the former German Democratic Republic, which joined the Federal Republic in 1990. World real-interest rates stayed at historically high levels in the early 1990s, largely as a result of this development, and continuing if somewhat smaller demands for foreign capital from other formerly communist countries.

11.3 A comparative static approach to international capital movements

This section aims to present the main effects of international capital movements in a simplified setting. We begin by laying out a number of assumptions that enable us to get some direct results. Complications that can arise when these assumptions are relaxed are postponed until later.

We start by assuming that there are two countries, A and B. Each produces just one good. Output depends partly upon capital and partly on labour. The labour force is taken to be given in both economies. There are positive but diminishing marginal products of each factor, and constant returns to scale. A rise in the local capital stock employed in economy A will therefore raise output and the marginal product of labour there. But the marginal product of capital in A will decline as the capital stock increases.

We shall ignore taxation for the moment, and assume that there is none. There is perfect competition in the fullest sense: no monopoly or oligopoly issues; perfect flexibility of prices to clear markets; factors priced at their marginal products; and perfect information, about the present and the future. There are no externalities or technological changes. There is no depreciation. The cost of moving a factor from one country to another is assumed to be negligible. Portfolio holders aim for the highest return they can get. Governments adopt either of two policies: a total ban on international factor movements (which we take to be effectively enforced), or complete freedom for capital to move across international borders. Lastly, social welfare is defined as national income in each country.

Let us now see what happens when the two governments remove a long-standing ban on international capital movements.

There is one case in which nothing happens. This arises when rates of profit in the two countries are already equal. This would, of course, be a fluke. It is much likelier that A and B will display different rates of profit at the moment the ban on cross-country capital movement is taken away. Let us suppose it is higher in A than in B. Our assumptions about the behaviour of portfolio holders, and the absence of tax or migration costs, mean that capital will flow from B to A in search of higher return. The process continues until rates of profit are equalized. Domestic output will fall in B and rise in A. There will be upward pressure on wage rates in A, as its capital stock rises, and downward in B, where the opposite happens. So it seems that the capital-importing country, A, gains a great deal, and that B is in some sense a loser.

That impression is in fact false. We need to remember that the residents of B who own the capital they move over to A will earn profits on it. The flow of profit income from A to B will more than wipe out the loss of domestic output in B. B's national product, which is defined as its domestic product plus net receipts of profit income from abroad, goes up. In A, national product (or income) also rises, but obviously by not nearly as much as its domestic income, because of the out-flow of profit income.

Both countries experience a rise in national income, therefore, when restrictions on international capital movements are abolished. The size of what they gain is approximately proportional to the square of the profit-rate gap ruling previously. In the limiting case where this gap was zero, the national income gains vanish, too, because no capital will migrate.

Our assumption that each country's social welfare is defined as equal to its national income ensures that international capital movements must raise welfare, both from and for the capital-importer. In fact, if the marginal product of capital happens to be a similar linear function of the stock of capital in each country, these welfare gains will be evenly split between them.

These results can be shown geometrically. Fig 11.1 illustrates. Rates of profit appear on the vertical axis. K_B denotes the capital stock in economy B. This is measured rightwards, along the horizontal axis from the origin O. Country A's capital stock, K_A, is shown on the horizontal left-hand axis.

When the ban on capital movements was in place, stocks of capital in the two economies were K_A^0 and K_B^0. The forces of perfect competition established rates of profit of r_0^A and r_0^B. Capital was scarcer in A than B, since r_0^A exceeds r_0^B. Output in the two economies is shown by the areas under the countries' marginal-product-of-capital curves, between the origin and K_A^0 for A, and between O and K_B^0 for B.

The removal of the ban on capital movement leads to an equalization of profit rates at $\bar{r}$. Domestic output jumps in A by $a + c$. In B it falls, by the smaller area

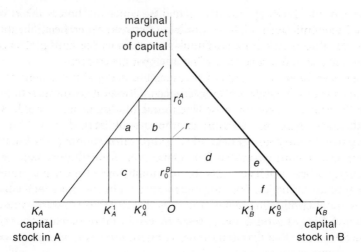

Fig. 11.1. The effects of capital migrating from country B to country A

$e + f$. (Our assumption of costless migration ensures that none of the capital gets lost in passage: the horizontal distances from K_A^0 to K_A^1, and K_B^0 to K_B^1, are equal).

The area c is paid over to the owners of $K_1^A - K_0^A$, who live in B, so A's national product rises by a. In B, it rises by $c - e - f$, which is positive (and equal to area a if, as drawn, the two marginal productivity curves are linear). Total wages in A rise by areas a and b. A's domestic capitalists suffer an income loss equal to b, which is transferred to its other factor, labour. But labour's gain $(a + b)$ exceeds this, by area a.

In B, it is workers who lose. They are worse off by areas $e + d$. B's capitalists gain $e + d$, plus the excess of area c over $e + f$. So their gain is $d + c - f$. In the diagram, it is clear that they are the biggest beneficiaries, followed by A's workers.

Within the terms of our assumptions, then, we can conclude that abolishing restrictions on international capital movements is beneficial for the countries involved (although not, of course, for everyone inside them, unless everyone derives income from holding capital and labour in reasonably similar proportions, which is possible but not likely).

At the world level, there is also an efficiency gain to be had. Suppose we ask how capital stocks should be allocated across the world, so as to maximize the total output they can produce. The answer is to shift capital between countries until its marginal product is equalized everywhere. This is a first-order condition for maximum efficiency. The second-order condition, to ensure that we get maximum rather than minimum world output, is fulfilled if the marginal productivities of capital are diminishing. One of our assumptions has stipulated this.

Allowing capital to migrate whithersoever it will, in search of the highest return, will achieve our maximum world-efficiency condition of equalized marginal products. We observe a happy coincidence between the ideal outcome for world economic efficiency, and the actual outcome of choices taken by self-interested economic agents. This equivalence between general equilibrium in all markets, and Pareto-efficiency, is a familiar result under idealized perfect competition, and it should not surprise us that we encounter it here.

Having established the merits of permitting unfettered movement of capital across international boundaries under ideal conditions, it is now time to consider some of the problems that can arise when these conditions fail to hold. We shall now look at what happens when our assumptions are relaxed.

We began with two countries, A and B. Adding other countries does nothing to upset our general conclusion that free international capital movement can only be beneficial. World efficiency calls for an equilibrium of marginal products of capital across all countries. Bringing extra countries in will not violate our result that free capital movements achieve this. Nor does it matter that we confined the number of factors of production to two. We can bring in as many factors as we like. The one point to note is that, under constant returns to scale, with positive but diminishing marginal product for each factor, a rise (fall) in capital could lower (raise) the marginal product of another factor once we go to three or more factors of production. So labour in A could lose, and land gain, when foreign capital enters the country. If the production function displays a certain degree of symmetry, however, all other factors in A will gain (and all other factors in B, which exports capital, will lose). The restriction that each country produces just one good is equally innocuous: adding extra products only serves to complicate the geometry, nothing else.

There is however, one important qualification to make about this last point. Suppose there are two goods and two countries, A and B, which have been trading freely with each other. That will equalize the relative prices of those goods in the absence of transport costs. We saw in earlier chapters that there are conditions in which free trade in goods can equalize factor prices across countries. These conditions are: identical constant-returns to scale production functions for any good in every country; incomplete specialization in production; no factor-intensity reversals; and, in addition to perfect competition, the existence of at least as many freely traded goods as there are internationally immobile factors of production. It follows that if this highly restrictive set of conditions happens to hold in full, rates of profit on capital will be driven to equality between countries. Removing a ban on the international migration of capital will have no effect.

The assumption that each factor's marginal product is positive but diminishing is not unduly restrictive, either. It holds few horrors. The reason for this is that perfectly competitive firms can never be in equilibrium in their choices of factors, in a region where this condition fails to hold. It is when we come to the issue of taxation that matters start to become more interesting. Suppose that both countries' governments tax all profit and wage income earned in their country at similar, positive rates. Let them also give full tax credit on overseas profit income that has been taxed in the host country: this is not unrealistic. Presumably B's capitalists will not care which government they pay tax to. The introduction of taxation will not upset our conclusion that pre-tax rates of profit are driven towards equality by free international capital mobility—provided that the tax rates are equal.

Country B's government will suffer a large revenue loss when capital is exported, however. Some of the rectangle c will remain with A's government. That means that B's national product could actually fall. This is bound to happen if the rate of tax exceeds the ratio of $c - e - f$ to c. So we now find a good reason why B's government may be highly reluctant to let its residents export capital abroad. From A's standpoint, however, allowing capital imports is even more beneficial than before. A's benefits from capital exports can, of course, be restored by assuming that income is taxed according to its recipient's residence rather than in the jurisdiction where it was earned.

If the two countries were to tax income at different rates—and we return to the previous idea of taxing income at geographical source—it will cease to be true that free-capital movements lead to an equalization of marginal products of capital worldwide. What is equalized is *after-tax* rates of profit. When tax rates differ, common after-tax profit rates imply different pre-tax profit rates. That is inefficient. Capital will no longer be allocated between countries to earn the highest (pre-tax) return.

The question of how countries' governments will set tax rates on non-residents' capital incomes is an intriguing one. They may set them unilaterally; or they may try to coordinate their decisions with foreign governments.

If they take the former course, and set their own tax rate treating other governments' tax rate decisions as given, we encounter a remarkable result. Under suitably simple conditions, the only equilibrium in this game is for these tax rates to be zero. Essentially there is always an incentive to undercut tax rates set elsewhere.

If governments understand this, they may react in various ways. One is to raise tax rates on other types of income, or on spending, to compensate. So the geographically immobile factor (labour? land?) has to bear a higher fiscal burden in a world of internationally mobile capital than when capital migration across world borders is disallowed. If capital tends to be owned by the rich and labour by the poor, international capital mobility is a force for economic inequality. On the other hand, it may be efficient that capital should be free from tax: Lucas (1990) demonstrates the truth of this in a model of dynamic behaviour that makes the long-run supply of capital infinitely elastic to the post-tax rate of interest. Efficiency and fairness may therefore point in opposite directions.

Another policy response by governments could be to coordinate their decisions about taxing capital. If all countries participated, these decisions could be made to stick. If only some did, non-participating governments would gain by undercutting, and we could ultimately return to the zero-tax result.

A third reaction might be to impose controls on capital movements, and go back, perhaps, to our initial starting-point of a total and effective ban. Local capital would be trapped, and taxed at will. This might look attractive, especially to a cash-strapped government in a potentially capital-exporting country. Yet there are efficiency-based arguments against this: not just the comparative static gains from allocating capital at the world level, nor the national income gains that would have to accrue to at least some countries, but also the Lucas-type long-run efficiency arguments, too. If capital really ought to be exempt from tax, to ensure an appropriate trade-off between jam today and jam tomorrow, then inter-government cooperation or capital export controls that serve to yield positive tax rates on capital can only be damaging in the long run.

The next assumption we made was to impose perfect competition in the fullest sense. There are four aspects to this. First, perfect competition drives factor rewards to equality with their marginal products. Second, perfect competition entails that prices equal marginal costs in factor markets. The third aspect to idealized perfect competition is perfect flexibility in the prices of goods and factors, which ensures that all markets clear. Then, hidden behind perfect competition, is a fourth feature, perfect information, and not just about the present and the past, but about the future, too.

Let us investigate the first two aspects of perfect competition first. Let us think of capital and labour as factors of production, hired by entrepreneurs. The entrepreneur's profit is what he keeps after he has paid out wages to his employees and capital rental charges to the people who have lent him his capital. Under perfect competition and a constant returns to scale production function, there is nothing left as surplus for the entrepreneur: perfectly competitive factor-rewards exhaust the product completely. But now make our entrepreneur a monopolist. Suppose his aim is to maximize his profit, and suppose also that he cannot price-discriminate in his product market and faces no risk of entry. What he will do now is to hire labour, and capital, up to the point where their rewards—assuming he cannot influence these—equal their *marginal revenue products*. The marginal revenue product of a factor is its marginal product, multiplied by the marginal revenue the employer gets from that last unit of output. He is a monopolist, so his marginal revenue is less than the price of the good he charges. In fact, marginal revenue MR will be given by

$$MR = P\left(1 - \frac{1}{e}\right) < P \qquad (11.1)$$

where e, a positive number, is the elasticity of his average revenue curve. Under perfect competition, $e \to \infty$, so $MR = P$. In monopoly, $e < \infty$ and so $MR < P$. Our conclusion is that monopoly will lead to too low a level of output, from the standpoint of economic efficiency. Too little labour and capital will be employed; alternatively, they will be paid too little, less than the values of their marginal products.

Capital and labour will be paid less than the value of their marginal products in other forms of imperfect competition, such as monopolistic competition, and, except in special cases (such as Bertrand equilibrium), in oligopoly, too. This result also holds when the entrepreneur believes he faces an upward sloping supply curve for one (or both) of the factors of production he hires, assuming that there is no discrimination in what he pays these factors. An upward-sloping supply curve for capital means that the entrepreneur faces a high marginal cost of renting capital: another unit of capital is not just more expensive in its own right, as he has to raise what he pays the other units of capital more, too.

The implication of this kind of departure from perfect competition for our purposes is this. Capital would flow from B to A when it earns less in B than A. But its low initial reward in B could reflect market imperfections there. The value of capital's marginal product in B could be much higher—higher, even, than in A. If that were so, world economic efficiency would prescribe that capital migrate from A to B!

More generally, giving entrepreneurs some degree of monopoly power in their product market, or monopsony power (an upward-sloping factor supply curve) in their factor market, will drive a wedge between the reward a factor earns and the value of its marginal product. The pattern of international factor migration, which will surely respond to international differences in rewards, will be distorted. The capital-exporting country may well experience a fall in its national income as a result. What it loses in domestic product, at the margin, will be given by the value of capital's marginal product there; this could indeed be much higher than what the migrating capital receives in its new home abroad. Market imperfections could, on the other hand, mean that the capital-importing country A gains a good deal more out of it than Fig. 11.1 suggests.

The third feature of perfect competition was its characteristic of perfect price flexibility. Let us now suppose that real wage rates paid to labour are sticky downwards, at least in the short run.

This will not be a matter of concern to country A, the capital importer. In the two factor case, at least, we saw that A's extra capital must tend to bid up labour's marginal product. So the pressure on wage rates there should be positive. In B, the capital-exporting country, the opposite is true. Wage rates will drop in B, if free to fall. What happens if something stops them falling there?

The answer is that B will experience unemployment. Some of B's labour will lose its jobs. Domestic output will fall in B by more than it would have done with wage-flexibility. It is not just the emigration that pulls domestic output down: this effect is reinforced by the resulting drop in the demand for labour, which translates directly into less employment because the wage rate is fixed. Suppose there is a third factor of production in B, land, which is fixed in supply and earns a perfectly flexible reward. This third factor will then ensure that B's output does not collapse completely. But output and employment fall by a common proportion, which is somewhat less than the shrinkage in B's capital stock. In practice, the process of capital emigration may, of course, take many years to be complete, and the unemployment we have been describing will take the form of workers in B losing their jobs in response to abnormally low levels of capital formation there.

Let us now turn to the issue of information. Idealized perfect competition assumes this is perfect, and this includes perfect foreknowledge. What happens if we introduce information deficiencies?

One possibility is that B's residents who send their capital off to A in the hope of higher returns are disappointed. The projects, some of them at least, turn out unprofitable. The flow of income from them is cut back, and could dry up. B's national income will rise less if this is so, and could fall. But A, at least, has the benefit of higher capital, which should yield some output even if it fails to deliver expected yields to its overseas owners. Alternatively, these investments could turn out more profitable than their owners had expected.

Introducing uncertainty could mean, if B's capital-exporters are averse to risk, that they underinvest in A. They may demand a higher mean expected return to offset anticipated risks. But this need not follow. B's capital-owners presumably face risks on their local investments, too. That implies that they will be concerned not just with the relative magnitude of risks on investments in the two countries—variances, let us say—but also on the *correlation* between those risks. It could be that bad news in B is good news in A, and vice versa. If anticipated returns are poorly correlated in the two countries, capital exports provide a welcome method of diversifying risks. If the correlation is negative, as it could be, they will tend to *overinvest* in A by the criterion of expected return.

The situation could be complicated further by the phenomenon of 'asymmetric' information. Suppose that someone selling shares in his business to attract extra capital knows more about his future prospects than the investor. This is not atypical. The investor must now be on his guard. He must ask, 'What does the seller know that I don't? Am I being offered a bad buy? Why does he want to sell?'

Informational asymmetries of this kind bedevil credit and equity markets. They are likely to imply that both credit and equity are scarcer and dearer than they would otherwise have been. Yet the supplier of capital has to be careful not to charge too much: that could induce adverse selection (sound equity sellers drop out, leaving the worse ones). It could also lead to moral hazard (the managers of the firm with outside debt and equity-holders could be tempted to slack, or to gamble).

Asymmetric information may have a geographical dimension. Potential local investors may know a little more about the quality of assets on offer than overseas ones. The dire difficulties faced by Lloyds of London, traditionally the world's largest wholesale insurer, owe much to their syndicates' acquisition during the 1980s of pollution reinsurance business from US companies that could have known more about very expensive claims in the pipeline. Ferranti, a distinguished armaments supplier, was recently driven into receivership after acquiring International Signal, a US company that had boosted its balance sheet by what turned out to be a large spurious export order. Imperial Tobacco had to lose its independence after paying too much for Howard Johnson, an American hotel and restaurant chain. Midland, once Europe's largest retail bank, absorbed vast losses after acquiring Crocker, a Californian bank with large problem loans it was prevented from checking; the ensuing haemorrhage to profits was ultimately to force Midland to sell itself to the Hong Kong and Shanghai Bank. A much earlier, celebrated example of spectacularly unsuccessful overseas investment was the North Sea Bubble that occurred in Britain in 1755. History is replete, then, with examples of capital exports that proved disastrous, and informational asymmetries undoubtedly played their part in these.

Our initial model also assumed that countries' social welfare functions were defined simply as national income. This is tantamount to saying that the societies in question were indifferent to the distribution of income between their residents. It is time to examine what happens when that uncomfortably restrictive assumption is relaxed.

The capital exporter, B, experiences a large transfer of income from labour to capital. Capital-owners tend often—not always—to be richer than those whose income comes largely or exclusively from the ownership of labour. Certainly this is true on the average. If we assume that individuals have a diminishing marginal utility of income, and utility functions in terms of income that are broadly similar, we may conclude that B's social welfare reacts unfavourably to this redistribution. If so, country B may regard its capital exports as a welfare-reducing phenomenon that its government would do well to obstruct.

Country A, on the other hand, is a recipient of capital. There the redistribution of income is from capital to labour. If A's government places a higher social-welfare weight on the income of capitalists than of workers, it too may view international capital movements askance.

The final qualification that merits mention relates to our initial assumption that each country takes the overseas interest rate as given. This may not be so; in a two-country world it is particularly implausible. The capital-exporter may perceive that it will earn a higher return on its residents' overseas investments if it restricts its exports of capital. Similarly, a large borrower can recognize that the rate of interest it has to pay to its foreign creditors will be lowered if it borrows less. There is an analogy here with international trade in goods. A small country cannot affect its terms of trade, so its optimal tariff on imports (or tax on exports) is zero, at least under idealized conditions. But a large country can improve its terms of trade (at its trading partners' expense) by restricting its trade through tariffs or export taxes, and its optimal taxes on trade are typically positive for this reason. Similarly, a large capital-exporter will have an advantage in taxing its capital exports to raise its return on them, and a large capital-importer will gain by taxing the imports of capital that its residents would otherwise undertake.

11.4 Labour migration

The analysis of international labour migration follows very similar lines to that of capital.

Let us start by stipulating the same set of assumptions that underpinned our treatment of capital movements, with just one difference: we replace capital by labour throughout. So there are our same two countries, one good, perfect competition, and no tax. We impose a social welfare function for each country that just adds the incomes of its initial residents. Capital movements are banned, and so, to start with, is international migration of labour. Then we abolish the restriction on labour movements. The initial wage rate is higher in B than in A. Migration then occurs. In the absence of any mobility barriers, migration presumably continues until wage rates are equalized. Labour flows, of course, from A to B.

The reduction in A's labour force leads to a fall in its domestic output. The wage rate rises, reflecting labour's increasing scarcity. The rate of profit there falls. The opposite happens in B. Those who gain are therefore A's emigrants themselves, the workers who remain in A, and B's capitalists. B's workers and A's capitalists lose. National income rises in both countries, however, if we count the wages earned by B's immigrants as part of the national income in A. The immigrants may well remit some of their wages back to family members who remain in A. World income rises, because we have reallocated labour so as to equalize its marginal product in each country.

These results constitute the basic liberal case for permitting labour to move across international boundaries. They also suggest one or two reasons why political obstacles may be set up to prevent it, and more reasons emerge when our assumptions are relaxed.

Resistance to immigration into B may be expected by the representatives of its labour force. The new arrivals serve to lower the equilibrium wage there, if they enter in anything but infinitesimal amounts. B's employers, on the other hand, can be expected to take a different view. If B's social welfare function, as reflected ·in its political processes, places a much higher weight on wages than on profits, and the immigrants are treated as outsiders in political terms, B's social welfare may be deemed to fall with immigration. And if social welfare in A weighs profits there more heavily than wages, resistance to the migration may arise in A's political system too.

Modifying our assumptions further, we can see that unemployment in A may exert pressure to emigrate, while unemployment in B provides both a disincentive to enter its labour market and an added argument for the political forces in B hostile to immigration to oppose it. If A's labour markets display widespread unemployment and B's labour markets are tight, A's unemployed will be encouraged to emigrate to B even if prevailing wage rates there, for those in work, are lower. So we need to be careful not to limit the driving force behind migration to a comparison of average wage rates in the source and destination countries. Furthermore, labour markets are segmented: doctors and chefs may move from an economy where average wages are higher to one where they are lower, because pay comparisons for medics or cooks display the opposite pattern.

Labour migration across international boundaries may also be triggered by international differences in tax systems. It is after-tax pay that will be compared, not pre-tax pay. A country with a relatively generous system of income support for the poor, and correspondingly higher rates of tax on those with larger incomes, is liable to lose its top earners and attract those with low ability to earn. This consideration may make governments wary of adopting a highly progressive fiscal structure, or at least a more progressive one than others, even if they might otherwise have sought to do so. The phenomenon of migration, actual or potential, is a factor that serves to limit a government's scope for redistribution through its tax system.

For centuries, the United States, Canada, and Australia have been the favoured destinations for European emigrants. It is noteworthy that these countries tend to employ immigration as a macroeconomic stabilizer: targets are lowered in recessions when unemployment is high, and raised when the demand for labour is strong. The receiving countries encourage immigrants with key skills, high earning-power, or significant wealth that they plan to repatriate. Applicants with more limited income prospects may be turned down.

11.5 The dynamic effects of international capital movements

In this section we shall explore the dynamic effects of international capital movements on the capital-exporter and recipient.

As always, it helps to simplify. There are two countries, A and B. In both, population is constant. Technical progress and depreciation are both negligible. Governments levy no taxes. Labour supply is exogenous. Just one good is produced, under perfect competition, with a positive but diminishing marginal product. Levels of technology, population, and labour supply in the two economies are the same. There is just one respect in which the two countries differ: everyone in country A discounts future utility at a higher rate than everyone in B. A's residents are more impatient than B's. Within each economy, everyone has similar preferences and endowments.

We start by assuming that there has been a fully watertight ban on international capital movements since time immemorial. Our assumption about the difference in impatience in the two economies means that both countries will have settled down, eventually, to long-run steady states with different rates of interest. The interest rate in A, where everyone is less patient, will be higher than in B. In both countries, adjustments in capital stocks will have ceased in the steady state; so income will equal consumption in both countries.

The similarities in technology, labour, and population mean that A will have a lower capital stock than B. This is a consequence of the fact that the marginal product of capital in B, which must equal its residents' impatience rate in the steady state, will be lower than in A. B's superior stock of capital translates into higher long-run values of output and consumption, too.

Now let us withdraw the ban on international capital migration. Capital shifts from B to A where (initially) it earns more. The process of capital migration drives interest rates together. So capital and domestic output rise in A and fall in B, until they are equal in both.

A's residents do more than just attract extra capital: they also borrow to finance extra consumption. This is so because their rate of impatience now exceeds the rate of interest they face (capital markets are perfect in this story). A's residents throw a big party. The psychological incentive to advance consumption from the future to the present exceeds the interest rate, which is their financial incentive to do the opposite.

In B, however, consumption immediately goes down, because interest now exceeds impatience there. This sudden fall in consumption in B is what provides A's residents, in essence, with the wherewithal for their extra consumption.

Now roll the clock forward. Consumption in A will be slipping now. In B, by contrast, it will be rising. The mounting debt charges on what A's residents have borrowed to finance their initial consumption splurge begin to mount. At some point they become so large that A is converted from being an immature debtor country (which runs a trade deficit in response to its heavy consumption) into a mature debtor country. A mature debtor runs a trade surplus, so that interest payments start to exceed fresh borrowing. At the switchover point, B metamorphoses from the status of an immature creditor (still running a trade surplus) to a mature creditor (with a trade deficit).

Eventually a new steady state will be reached, where investment ceases and consumption becomes trendless in both countries. The horrid difficulty we face, however, is that it seems as if the residents of the less impatient, more far-sighted country will in the end come to own all the world's assets. The spendthrifts in A, so it seems, will end up with nothing.

This ugly state of affairs may well materialize. But there are a number of ways of preventing it. The standard assumption is to suppose that discount rates are endogenous, climbing, let us say, in response to past consumption. If we follow this path, we can expect B's residents eventually to become less patient, and A's (who have to make do with less and less consumption in the medium term) to become more so. This way we can ultimately end up with an equalization of impatience rates, or at least some mechanism for stopping the poor people in A from starving.

This endogenous-discount-rate assumption is mathematically messy, however, and open to objections: why should people become more far-sighted as they get poorer? An alternative escape route, and in our view a more attractive one, is to assume that the rates at which the two countries' residents discount future utility are unchanging (and hence permanently different), but to relate the utility they get in any period not just to what they consume then, but also to their assets at that point. There is no logical reason why my utility today cannot vary with my wealth as well as my consumption.

Take an example. Suppose that the (undiscounted) marginal utilities of consumption and wealth, at any date, are inversely proportional to the levels of consumption and wealth respectively. That makes undiscounted utility expressible as some weighted average of the logarithms of consumption and wealth. Suppose that everyone in a society chooses a plan for optimum consumption, capital, and wealth, stretching out into the indefinite future, to maximize the discounted stream of utility, subject to a budget restraint at every point in time. This budget restraint states that, at every date, national income be devoted to consumption plus accumulation of wealth. Suppose this is true of everyone in A and everyone in B, with the single difference that A's residents discount future utility more highly than B's.

National income in the budget restraint is just as it has been defined earlier in this chapter: domestic output, plus net income on overseas assets. Overseas assets are the excess of wealth over local capital, which can of course be positive or negative. In our two country world, it is either, by fluke, zero for both, or, more generally, positive for one and negative for the other.

In the long run, when consumption has settled down to trendlessness in each economy, we find that there is a negative linear relationship between the rate of interest, r, the local discount rate δ, and the local ratio of consumption to wealth in each country:

$$r = \delta_A - \beta\, c_A/a_A \tag{11.2}$$

$$= \delta_B - \beta\, c_B/a_B \tag{11.3}$$

These equations are shown as the downward-sloping lines in Fig 11.2, with vertical intercepts on the interest rate axis of δ_A for country A and δ_B for country B. (The gradient of the line for country B in the negative quadrant is actually positive.) There is a common interest rate in the two countries, reflecting the absence of restriction on international capital movements. In our equation, c/a denotes the ratio of consumption to assets for each country. The term β is a common parameter in both countries, which reflects the relative weights placed on wealth and consumption in the utility function.

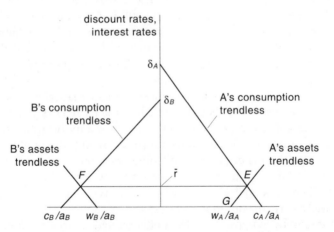

Fig. 11.2. The steady-state effects of international capital migration, when capital stocks are endogenous

It is not just consumption that is trendless in a steady state. The same is true of assets, too. Trendlessness in assets implies, from our budget constraints, another linear relationship linking r to the c/a ratio in each country:

$$\frac{c_A}{a_A} = r + \frac{w_A}{a_A} \tag{11.4}$$

$$\frac{c_B}{a_B} = r + \frac{w_B}{a_B} \tag{11.5}$$

These equations can be found by rearranging the budget restraints to make consumption the subject on the left hand side, setting asset accumulation to zero, and dividing through by assets. Here, w_A and w_B represent the wage rates in A and B.

Country A's trendless-asset equation is shown as the upward-sloping line in the right-hand quadrant. H has a horizontal intercept of w_A/a_A. The similar equation for B appears in the left-hand quadrant. Where the trendless-asset and trendless-consumption curves cut, at point E for country A and at F for B, determines the worldwide interest rate, $\bar{r}$, and also the consumption/assets ratios for the two countries.

We can go further. Our assumption of common production functions, technology levels, populations, and labour supplies yields the prediction that a common rate of interest equalizes not just capital marginal products, but also capital stocks, output levels, and wage levels in the two countries. That means that we can read off the ratio of a_A to a_B: it will equal the ratio of the distance OH to the distance OG. Country A owns less wealth than B, but their capital stocks are equal; so A is in debt, and B in credit.

Figure 11.3 illustrates the levels of capital and wealth for the two countries. It is a square: the sum of the two capital stocks, $k_A + k_B$, has to equal the sum of the two asset stocks, $a_A + a_B$. (A and B are the only two countries we are considering.) The bottom left corner gives the origin for country A, and the top right B's. The length of the square denotes assets, the height capital. The equal allocation of capital splits the box horizontally across the middle. But the long run asset allocation is off-centre at J, because A's residents, with their higher impatience rate, will be in debt to B's.

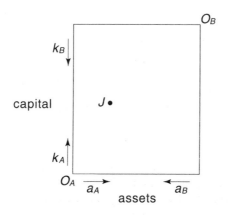

Fig. 11.3. Long run capital and asset positions for countries A and B

In the final steady state, of course, B's residents enjoy higher utility in any period than A's. This is because they are richer, and also because they will consume more by that stage, too. But we should be wary of inferring that the process of capital movement has been detrimental to A. It has not. Before this long-run steady state was reached A's residents enjoyed higher consumption, and B's less. They chose to do this because of the difference in their impatience rates. So our sympathy for A's residents must be tempered by the fact that their long-run indebtedness, and relative poverty, is explained by their relatively—and absolutely—high levels of consumption in earlier periods, something they opted to enjoy. The streams of utility, capitalized by their respective discount rates, will have higher initial present values in both countries than they could have achieved without the capital movements.

In the previous steady state, before the ban on capital movements was removed, A will have had a higher rate of interest than B, and therefore lower capital, output, and consumption. A numerical example may help at this point.

Let us suppose that output, in each country, equals the square root of the capital stock there; that $\beta = 1/5$ and that $\delta_A = 0.048$ and $\delta_B = 0.04$. The old steady state, before capital was allowed to move between the two countries, will have set the interest rate at 3⅔ per cent in A and 2⅔ per cent in B. Consumption per head will have been 175/12 in A and 17½ in B.

Allowing capital to move across international boundaries gives rise, eventually, to a new steady state where the rate of interest is common at 3 per cent. A's residents own one-quarter of the world's capital stock, or half their own. The remaining three-quarters is owned by the citizens of B. Steady-state consumption per head rises to 20⅚ in B. In A it slips back to 12.5. Aggregate consumption increases, to reflect the output gains to be had from reallocating the world's capital stocks to a more efficient equilibrium where their marginal products are equal. The world's capital stock is also higher in the new steady state than in the old. And although A's residents end up with less steady-state consumption than they had initially, before international capital migration was permitted, there will have been a long period where they enjoyed consumption of much more than the 175/12 they had previously, let alone the 12.5 figure they eventually reach.

Typical time-paths of consumption, interest rates, wealth, and capital for the two economies are presented in Figure 11.4. The period of time that needs to elapse between the initial removal of the international capital migration ban, and getting to within, say, 1 per cent of the final steady state must not be underestimated. It is indeed very protracted. With plausible numerical parameters, it may exceed 100 years.

The model we have discussed here may be thought of as a launching-pad for considering more complex cases. It is simple to introduce more general production and utility functions (although we need to be careful to retain the idea that utility depends on assets as well as consumption, or some other device, to prevent the patient-takes-all result). Depreciation, population growth, and (Harrod-neutral) technological progress can all be brought in. So, too, can governments, and taxation, as well as endogenous labour, and indeed money. Extra countries

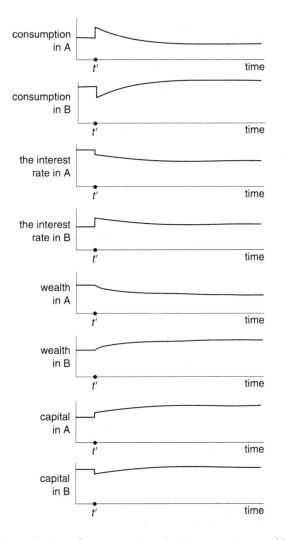

Fig. 11.4. The evolution of consumption, the interest rate, wealth, and capital in countries A and B, following capital–market integration at time t'

can enter the picture with little difficulty. But space prevents us from accomplishing these extensions here. We should note, however, that departures from perfect competition and information, and introducing issues of externalities and taxation, may set off alarm bells that should severely qualify the rosy view we might otherwise obtain about the merits of international capital movements, particularly from the standpoint of the capital exporter.

11.6 Summary

- In simple cases, international capital migration from country A to B should raise national income in A and B. Wages fall in A, however, and profits fall in B. Labour migration from B to A may have similar effects.
- Under various conditions, capital-exporting countries may gain from restricting their capital exports.
- International capital movements allow countries' residents to trade consumption claims across time. If A's residents discount utility from future consumption more highly than B's, they borrow.

12

TRADE AND GROWTH

12.1 Introduction

This chapter is concerned with the interrelationships of trade and growth. The trade effects of growth (as a result of factor accumulation, or technical progress) are examined in Section 12.2. In Section 12.3 we turn attention to the growth effects of trade.

12.2 The effects of growth on trade

Let us consider a world where there is perfect competition and free trade, and each country has given endowments of two factors of production, capital and labour. There are just two goods that can be produced, x and y. A is the home country, and B the rest of the world. B may consist of just one other country, or many.

Suppose we wish to explore all the effects of growth in country A. Let us imagine that growth is confined to A. This growth can take either of two forms. It may result from an enlargement of A's endowments of either or both factors of production. Alternatively, it may take the form of an advance in technology, confined to just one of A's two industries, or in both of them.

Take the factor accumulation first. Suppose, initially, that A is small, so small that it faces exogenously given prices for the two goods it trades. If A experiences an equiproportionate rise in both capital and labour endowments, its production of the two goods will go up by that same proportion. Since there has been no change in technology, and the smallness of A means that the price ratio of y to x is fixed, factor prices in A cannot change. If nothing happens to disturb the community's preferences, and it is hard to see why it should, we can conclude that the absolute volume of exports and imports rises by the same proportion as the rise in factor endowments. Country A is simply 'bigger' in all respects. A doubling of its endowments of capital and labour doubles its output and consumption of each good. So its exports and imports double, too.

Now suppose A is large, large enough to influence world prices of goods. What would have led to a doubling of exports and imports at the old terms of trade must now lead to a worsening in those terms of trade. The world price of A's exportable falls in terms of its importable. In A and B, producers react by switching production away from the cheaper good towards the now-dearer one. Countries A and B will both experience a rise in the real reward to the factor used intensively in A's importable industry, since this is the good which becomes scarcer. The volume of A's exports goes up; but its volume of imports may rise or fall. It rises if B's offer curve is elastic, but with an inelastic offer curve for B, B will actually supply less of A's imports than before.

These are the effects when A experiences the same proportionate rise in both its factor endowments. Now suppose it sees its labour endowment go up, with no change in its stock of capital. Let us begin, as before, by assuming that A is small and, therefore, a terms-of-trade taker.

The fact that commodity prices and technology are unchanged means that there is no reason for factor prices to alter. With both of A's industries enjoying constant returns to scale—a natural state of affairs under perfect competition— we now encounter a rather odd result. There has to be an absolute fall in the output of A's capital-intensive good, while the level of output of its labour-intensive good goes up. This is known as the Rybczynski effect.

The reason is that firms in both of A's industries will employ unchanged ratios of capital to labour. The only way that the additional labour can be put to work is for the labour-intensive sector, call it x, to expand production. To keep its capital–labour ratio unchanged, x must attract capital from the other sector y. If y is to release capital, and yet keep its capital–labour ratio unchanged, the output of y has to drop.

The new pattern of production, more x and less y, leads to an increase in A's trade with B if x is A's exportable. But if A imports x, its exports of y have to shrink. So A could well end up a less open economy than before. It is even possible for A's direction of trade to reverse: it could end up exporting x, rather than importing it, if the jump in A's labour endowment is large enough.

When A is a large country, its terms of trade will alter. Since the output of x rises at a given price, we infer that the price of x will now fall everywhere. Since y has become scarcer, the pattern of production will shift in both A and B towards y. The price of the factor used intensively in y, and this is capital, will be bid up. The reward to labour will go down, in both A and B. Country A's terms of trade will improve if it exports y, and worsen if it imports it. Note the difference from the case where A gained an equiproportionate rise in both its capital and labour endowments: in that case, we found that A's terms of trade would worsen for sure if it was large enough to influence world commodity prices. Here, where it is only A's labour endowment that has risen, whether A benefits from a terms of trade improvement or suffers from a deterioration depends on whether it imports or exports the labour-intensive good.

The algebra of the Rybczynski effect can be put simply. There are constant returns to scale, and the fact that factor prices are given means that capital–labour ratios (call these c_x and c_y in sectors x and y) are given too. Let Q_x (Q_y), K_x (K_y), and N_x (N_y) denote output, capital, and labour in sector x (in sector y). Denote proportionate changes by lower case letters, so that n_x means the proportionate change in N_x for example. We keep the total capital stock, $\bar{K} = K_x + K_y$, fixed, so that $dK_x = -dK_y$. The total labour endowment, $\bar{N}$, goes up, so that $-dN_x + dN_y = d\bar{N}$.

Because $k_x = q_x = n_x$, and $k_y = q_y = n_y$, we can write $dK_x = -dK_y$ as $K_x q_x = -K_y q_y$. We can also write $dN_x + dN_y = d\bar{N}$. Combining these to substitute for q_y we get

$$q_x \left(N_x - \frac{N_y K_x}{K_y} \right) = d\bar{N}$$

or

$$q_x(1 - c_x/c_y) = d\bar{N}/N_x \qquad (12.1)$$

Now $d\bar{N}$ is positive, because the economy's labour endowment has gone up. Equation (12.1) shows that q_x is positive—implying a rise in the output of x—if and only if $c_y > c_x$. In other words, when x is the labour-intensive sector (so that $c_x < c_y$), the output of x rises; but if x is the capital-intensive sector ($c_x > c_y$), the output of x must fall.

So much for changes in A's factor endowments. We saw that there was another possible cause of economic growth in A: no increase in its endowments of factors of production, but an advance in the technology that translates inputs into outputs for one or both of A's industries.

Technological advance may be characterized in various ways. It could be exogenous, resulting from an accidental discovery of a new, superior method of production. Or it may result from invention or innovation ensuing from deliberate choices, R&D decisions for example, by producers in one or both of the industries. We may also classify technological advances by their effects. If an advance raises the marginal products of the factors of production by the same proportion, it is said to be Hicks-neutral. Hicks-neutral technical change has the fortunate consequence of not altering the appearance of isoquant maps for the industry where they occur. The isoquant curves are not repositioned: they are simply relabelled, with each curve denoting higher output than before. Technical change may also be Hicks-biased, in which case it increases the marginal product of one factor by a higher proportion than that of another factor.

Let us suppose that there is a Hicks-neutral, exogenous technological advance that occurs in both of A's industries, and at the same rate. A is (initially) a small country, facing given world prices for x and y. Let us suppose that the preferences of A's residents can be aggregated into a uniquely defined social indifference map, and that these preferences are homothetic. (Homothetic tastes, it will be recalled, imply unit-elastic demands to income for each of the goods.) What happens?

Since world prices are given, A's output of both x and y rises by the same proportion as the advance in technology. If the technology index doubles for both products, output doubles. The prices of both factors of production double in A (while in B, where there has been no technical change, they remain the same). Because social preferences in A are given and homothetic, demand for both x and *y* doubles there. This means that A's exports and imports also double. Abroad, nothing changes, because B, the rest of the world, is so very much larger than A that it can absorb A's extra exports and supply her extra imports with no alteration in their relative price.

Quite a different set of consequences ensues if A is a large country. We can infer for sure that A's terms of trade will worsen in that case. The volume of A's exports goes up, of course. But the volume of her imports could drop. Fall they will, if B's offer curve is inelastic. When B's offer curve is elastic, A's extra exports, and additional import demand, can be accommodated with a relatively modest terms of trade deterioration.

The price of A's exportable now falls in terms of its importable. In A and B, production patterns switch in favour of the now-dearer product. That drives up the relative price of the factor used intensively in them, and this relative factor price change will occur in both A and B. Consumers in both countries react by substituting into the good that has become cheaper—A's exportable.

In this most general, neutral case of technological change in both of A's industries at the same rate, we therefore reach the conclusion that the rest of the world, as a whole, gains from it so long as the technological progress occurs in a country large enough to disturb world goods prices. But we must be careful to stress that not everyone benefits. Residents of B who own the factor used intensively in the production of the good imported from A will suffer an absolute reduction in their real income (assuming this is their sole or major income source). Furthermore, the rest of the world may well be an amalgam of many countries, some of which could export the same good as A. Such countries would suffer from the same terms of trade deterioration as A, and without the compensation that A enjoys in the form of superior technology.

These were the effects of Hicks-neutral technological advance, at a common rate, in both of A's industries. Now suppose the advance is confined to industry *x*. Let us begin, once again, by assuming that A is very small. A is a terms-of-trade taker. The world prices of *x* and *y* are given.

What happens to the pattern of production in A? There will be an increase in the output of *x* in A, for sure. But there is an absolute decline in the output of *y*. The effect is not quite the same as in the Rybczynski case of factor accumulation, but the qualitative results are quite similar. The reasoning is the same. Sector *x* bids for extra capital and labour, which reinforces the output-enhancing effect of the technological change. So sector *y* has to yield up resources, and suffer a drop in production.

The geometry of both economy-wide and sector-confined Hicks-neutral technical advances is portrayed in Figures 12.1 and 12.2. In Figure 12.1 there is an equiproportionate radial (or 'homothetic') expansion of the production possibility frontier (PPF). When country A is small the pattern of production changes from *C* to *C'*, with no further repercussions. If A is large enough to affect its terms of trade, however, and *x* is its exportable, the world price of *x* will have to decline, and the final pattern of production will be at a point such as *C"*. Figure 12.2 reveals Hicks-neutral technological progress confined to industry *x*. The PPF's

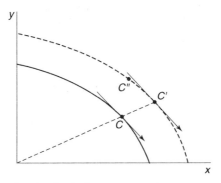

Fig. 12.1. Hicks-neutral technological progress at the same rate in both sectors: output effects

y-intercept cannot change. But its *x*-intercept increases substantially. If A is a small country, and hence a terms-of-trade taker, the new pattern of production will be at D'. When D' and D are compared it is clear that the output of *x* has risen while that of *y* has gone down. If A is a large country the world price of *x* falls, leading to some north-eastward movement along the new PPF from D' to a point such as D''.

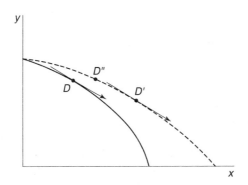
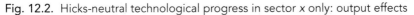

Fig. 12.2. Hicks-neutral technological progress in sector x only: output effects

12.2.1 Some qualifications and extensions

Our analysis up to now has rested on a number of simplifying assumptions. These may not hold. What follows is a brief account of what could happen if they do not.

Take the case of an addition to a country's factor endowments first. One of the assumptions with which we have been working is the premise of perfect competition and full domestic factor mobility. We looked at the effects of an addition to an economy's endowment of labour under this condition, and saw how it would then translate into a rise in the output of its labour-intensive sector and a contraction in its capital-intensive sector.

Suppose the other factor, capital, is temporarily frozen in its sectoral allocation. Capital, for the time being at least, is sector-specific and fixed. What will now happen is that wages, if free to change, will fall. The extra labour is absorbed, but at lower pay in both sectors. The rental rates on capital in both sectors go up. The output of both industries is raised. If wage rates are sticky, the extra labour will simply remain unemployed, and there will be no gains in employment or output. Time is often needed for factors to migrate between sectors, and for wages to react to labour-market shocks: so these very different consequences are quite a likely short-run response to labour supply changes.

An interesting European example of this is provided by Portugal after 1975. She granted independence in that year to her various African colonies. Two of these, Angola and Mozambique, had larger settler populations. Most of them returned to Portugal quickly, raising the country's adult population by over half a million. Many of these 'retornados' took a year or more to find work. Few of them repatriated much capital. Portugal is a small country, unable to affect the world prices of any products (except perhaps port and madeira wines). So Rybczynski's theorem would have predicted a large expansion in Portugal's labour-intensive traded-goods industries, and a cut in her capital-intensive ones. Neither happened, at least in the short term. Short-run capital specificity and wage stickiness prevented Rybczynski's effects from being demonstrated.

From the mid-1950s onwards, West Germany attracted over three million 'guest-workers', many from Turkey. Similar numbers of immigrants moved to Britain from the Caribbean and the Indian sub-continent at this time, and from North Africa to France. Most of these migrants brought little, if any, capital with them. We would predict, on the basis of the Heckscher-Ohlin Theory, that Britain, France, and West Germany—all presumably relatively well-endowed with capital compared with most other countries—would react by contracting trade. It would be their importables industries that should have been relatively labour-intensive. Yet the 1960s and 1970s witnessed a great expansion of trade in these three countries; all of them, especially West Germany, saw large and continuing rises in the ratios of exports to national income. Other forces may well have been at work here. Barriers were reduced or cut out, particularly intra-European trade, at much the same time; and domestic capital stocks were also growing fast, which would exert a strong pro-trade effect according to the Heckscher-Ohlin model. But this immigration experience makes one cautious about taking the Rybczynski arguments too far.

Turning to technological progress, there are a number of qualifications we should consider. We have taken the case of Hicks-neutral technical progress, either confined to one industry or economy-wide at a uniform pace. There is no reason for thinking that technological change has to be Hicks-neutral.

Hicks-biased technical progress raises one factor's marginal product by a higher proportion than another's. This repositions isoquants where it occurs. The economy's PPF does not move outward in the straightforward fashion depicted in Figures 12.1 and 12.2. We can identify two possible effects which Hicks-biased progress induces; let us assume that it occurs only in sector x. One effect could be to bring the two sectors' capital–labour ratios closer together. That would tend to make the PPF less curved. The new PPF will be closer to displaying linearity than the old one. If the gap in capital–labour ratios were eliminated, the PPF would actually become linear.

In such a case, the pattern of output changes one would expect for a small open economy (higher x, less y) would be reinforced. There would be a bigger pro-trade repercussion if x is exportable, and a bigger reduction in trade if it were y that was exported.

Were the technical progress to draw the two sectors' capital–labour ratios further apart, however, the new PPF would be more curved than the old one. At unchanged commodity prices the increase in x would be smaller than before, and it is just possible that the output of y could go up. So the trade effects become potentially ambiguous.

The idea that technical progress may be Hicks-biased is actually quite plausible. It makes sense to think of firms tilting their R and D activity towards saving the factor of production that has recently struck them as particularly expensive. The large wage hikes of the 1960s and early 1970s may have induced firms to undertake research into potential innovations that economized on labour. Some of these projects will have led to nothing, and those that came to fruition may have taken many years to produce results. It is possible that the marked weakening in labour demand displayed in much of Western Europe in the late 1970s and 1980s was a lagged response to labour-saving technical research programmes encouraged by the earlier jump in labour costs. Similarly, dear oil in the later 1970s and early 1980s may have imparted an oil-saving bias into the new technologies adopted subsequently. The high perceived cost of capital during the 1980s and early 1990s may exert a capital-saving bias to technological changes early in the next millennium.

There are other qualifications to note about technological progress, too. If importables are a luxury, and at least in the British case research suggests that they are, it becomes likelier that this type of growth is pro-trade biased. A big country becomes likelier to suffer a deterioration in its terms of trade; and the rest of the world, treated as a bloc, stands a greater chance of gain.

When a large country faces an inelastic demand for its exportable in the rest of the world, technical progress confined to its export industry could not merely benefit the rest of the world: it could actually lead to a reduction in domestic potential welfare. This case is known as 'immiserizing growth'. The phenomenon was first identified as a theoretical possibility by Bhagwati (1958). The reasoning is that the home country's export proceeds fall when increased supply confronts inelastic foreign demand. The chance of this occurring is highest when the home country has a low marginal propensity to spend on its exportable.[1]

---

[1] Immiserizing growth can also sometimes occur if technical progress takes place in an economy suffering from a distortion such as a harmful externality or trade restriction.

European countries are not in that kind of position. What they export is often a good substitute for the more sophisticated manufactures and tradeable services produced in North America or the Far East (and, of course, by their European neighbours). So rest-of-world demand is typically quite elastic, not inelastic. Nevertheless, the 'immiserizing growth' concept may have been influential in suggesting to the governments of advanced countries that there were large potential benefits in stimulating new technology that economized on key importables. The development of sugar beet and synthetic rubber, for example, has depressed world prices of cane sugar and natural rubber, which Europe and North America had long imported from the tropics. The long process of miniaturization in machinery and capital goods, most of it spontaneous perhaps, yet clearly not obstructed by Western governments, will have exerted similar long-term effects on a wide range of basic metals, and oil, which those countries typically imported.

12.3 The effects of trade on growth

So far, this chapter has explored some of the effects of growth, whether due to increased factor endowments or technological advance, on an economy's trade position. It is now time to see how changes in trade can affect growth.

In almost all circumstances, a movement from no trade to free trade enhances a country's aggregate real income or welfare. There could well be individuals who suffer, such as owners of factors employed intensively in, or specific to, the country's importables sector. But in aggregate the gains of gainers should exceed what losers lose. There are only a few cases where this may not be so, one of them being the rent-shifting case studied in Chapter 15.

A comparative static, once-and-for-all jump in real income is not really all that is meant by growth, however. Growth refers to a dynamic process of income increases spread over a long period. How can the opening of an economy affect growth in this sense?

Corden (1971) has constructed an interesting model that sheds much light on this question. He is considering an economy where growth takes the form of continuing increases in its stocks of capital and labour. There is no technological progress. Labour grows a given rate, n. The stock of capital ultimately grows at that rate, too, but this is true only in a very long-run, steady state. In the shorter run what drives the growth of capital is savings and the price of capital goods. The growth of total real income is the weighted average of the growth rates of capital and labour.

In Corden's story, there are two intermediate goods that can (in principle) be traded internationally. Their production uses capital and labour, very possibly in different proportions. The two intermediate products are inputs into the production of final goods, consumption, and investment goods. The two final sectors may employ different mixes of the intermediate goods.

When an economy shifts suddenly from no trade to free trade, nothing happens if the home pre-trade price ratio of the intermediate products is the same as that prevailing in the rest of the world. If the two price ratios differ, however, as differ they are likely to do, one of the intermediate sectors (importables) will cut production, and the other (exportables) expands. There is an expansion in the feasible set of exportables and importables that the two final sectors can buy. This is the familiar comparative-static jump in real income.

But that is not the end of the story. Typically some fraction of the additional real income will be saved. That means, at least for a while, that the growth rate of capital should go up. This effect is reinforced if exportables are capital-intensive and profit-recipients save a higher fraction of their income than wage-earners do. It is also reinforced if investment goods are intensive in that importable intermediate product, for that will imply that the switch from autarky to free trade cuts the price of investment goods and enlarges the volume of new capital that savings will buy. If exportables are labour-intensive, or investment goods are exportables-intensive, the boost to the growth of capital will be stunted somewhat.

It is a straightforward matter to apply Corden's model to the issue of changes in tariffs. A small economy that reduces its trade barriers will experience the same kind of dynamic effects as one which goes directly from no trade to free trade. The only difference is in degree. But a large economy that unilaterally cuts a tariff which was previously set at or below an optimal level should experience a comparative-static *fall* in real income. There is a presumption that savings will drop, and with it the ensuing growth of capital, although that last result may not follow if exportables are labour-intensive (with a higher savings propensity out of profits than wages) and investment goods are exportables-intensive. When the rest of the world also lowers its tariffs, however, at the same time, there is likely to be a gain, not a loss, in domestic real income, some of which is saved, with likelier-than-not positive effects on the subsequent growth of capital.

The primary mechanism in Corden's model is the link between once-only real-income changes generated by alterations in trade policy, and the induced effect on capital growth via savings. A favourable change in real income should add to savings; all else equal, higher savings imply a permanently enlarged absolute, and temporarily raised proportionate, growth in the capital-stock. An immediate implication is that the 'dynamic' income effects of trade policy are likely to have the same sign as the 'static' effects. The engine of growth in Corden's model is capital in the short to medium run, although the rate of output growth is ultimately set by, and equal to, the growth rate of labour. Technological progress is absent (although it is a simple matter to bring it in, in the form of an exogenous rate of growth of the 'quality' of labour—all Corden's results about the growth effects of trade would carry over, with minimal changes). Corden's story amounts to the extension to an open economy of a multi-sector version of the neo-classical growth model pioneered by Solow (1956). Paradoxically, the Solow growth-model family is really not an account or theory of growth. The growth rate, in the very long run, is assumed given, by the sum of an exogenous rate of population growth and an exogenous growth rate for the quality of labour. Technological progress, if present, is assumed to be 'Harrod-neutral'. It simply keeps raising the efficiency of labour. Harrod-neutral technological progress is equivalent to Hicks-neutral progress in the special case where the production function is Cobb-Douglas. (That means that output is a weighted geometric average of capital on the one side, and labour multiplied by an efficiency parameter on the other; the elasticity of substitution between capital and labour along an isoquant is constant and unitary.)

In recent years several economists have sought to build models of 'endogenous' growth. These theories aim to explain the rate of long-run growth, rather than, as in the Solow family of models, to treat it as an exogenous constant. Endogenous growth models of particular interest include those constructed by Romer (1986), Lucas (1988), Becker *et al.* (1990), and Aghion and Howitt (1992). In the Romer (1986) model, there are favourable externalities between capital stocks in different sectors that make aggregate output display constant returns to aggregate capital. This constant returns feature is also present in Lucas's model of training, the Becker model of endogenous fertility and education, and the Aghion-Howitt model of R&D spending.

Perhaps the most influential endogenous growth model, however, is presented in a second paper by Romer (1990), with interesting implications for international economic integration. The key idea is that the output of inventors is proportional to the stock of knowledge accumulated from previous inventions (the constant-returns assumption, again). New inventions are available for free to all inventors; but the right to turn a new invention, or blueprint, into a specific new type of capital good is privately appropriable. A new blueprint is purchased from designers, and then used by their purchaser to construct the unique, new capital good that will be rented out to the producers of final output. Capital does not depreciate. Patent lives are infinite, and 100 per cent effective against imitators. There is a positive, diminishing marginal product for each type of capital, but the return on one type of capital is unaffected by introduction of others. Each machine producer is a monopolistic competitor, and charges a profit-maximizing rental rate. The capitalized value of these profits is inversely proportional to the rate of interest.

The higher the rate of interest, the lower the present value of the stream of profits the machine monopolist will earn, and the less he will bid at auction for the design to which it relates. A lower price of new designs means less income for inventors. Potential inventors form part of a society's supply, assumed given, of 'human capital'. This factor is also valuable in final production. The allocation of human capital between inventing and employment in final output is struck where rates of reward are equalized. We can think of scientists choosing between careers as design engineers (inventing) and production engineers (service in the final-output sector). A higher rate of interest, then, means more production engineers and fewer inventors. Fewer inventors means fewer inventions, slower expansion in the range of capital-goods types in production, and therefore a slower rate of economic growth.

The model is closed by assuming that households plan their consumption programme by maximizing the discounted stream of utility provided by consumption at different dates. Utility from consumption therefore displays 'impatience'. There are two forces at work that govern the time-trend of consumption: these are the rate of interest, and the rate of impatience. When these two rates are equal, consumption is trendless. If interest exceeds impatience the reward from deferring consumption dominates its psychological cost, and consumption starts low and keeps growing. The higher the rate of interest, the faster consumption grows.

Romer's model concentrates on steady states, where key ratios, such as the ratio of consumption to income, are constant. That means that higher interest implies faster income growth, since income and consumption have to grow at a common speed in a steady state. This positive link between interest and growth, derived from inter-temporal optimization by consumers, is then combined with the negative interest-growth link derived from the blueprint auction price and the equilibrium allocation of human capital between inventing and service in final output production.

The result, then, is a co-determination of rates of interest and growth. If both links between interest and growth have to hold, equilibrium occurs where the two curves cut. Figure 12.3 illustrates this. The positive growth–interest relation, which comes from consumer optimization, is labelled the Ramsey curve after Frank Ramsey, who first proposed the idea in a famous paper in 1928. This is the upward-sloping curve in Figure 12.3. The downward-sloping curve I call the Romer curve, since it depicts the negative relation between the interest rate, and hence the pay and number of inventors, first set out in Romer's 1990 paper. The intersection at *E* determines the equilibrium long-run rates of interest and growth.

Romer's analysis relates essentially to a closed economy; but he concludes his paper with some intriguing remarks about how it can be applied to an open one. Suppose two previously isolated and otherwise identical economies suddenly permit full access to their own stock of previous discoveries to the

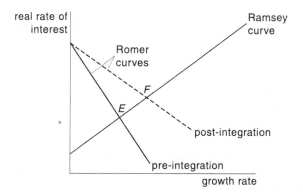

Fig. 12.3. Codetermination of the rates of growth and interest in Romer's 1990 model of endogenous growth

other's inventors. Suppose, too, that each economy's previous inventions are all different from previous discoveries in the other. Access to the stock of foreign knowledge leads to a doubling in the rate of invention. (Recall that the output of new designs is proportional to the stock of previous designs available for free to current inventors.) This means that each economy's Romer curve then pivots counter-clockwise around its vertical intercept. There would now be twice as much growth at an unchanged interest rate. But that cannot happen: the Ramsey curve slopes up, and will not change position. So the equilibrium interest rate goes up, and with it the growth rate.

The new steady-state equilibrium for both economies will then be reached at *F*. The Romer curve swings from the old, solid line to the new dashed one. Both the interest rate and the growth rate are higher at *F* than at *E*. How far the Romer curve moves out depends on how dissimilar the two economies' previous inventions are: had they been really identical, and if they remain identical, it will not change. Any dissimilarity, however, implies some outward movement of the Romer curve. How the Romer-curve shift is resolved into faster growth on the one side, and higher interest on the other, depends on the gradient of the Ramsey curve, which equals the elasticity of substitution in inter-temporal consumption. If this elasticity is low, so that people treat consumption in different periods as complementary, and the marginal utility of consumption in any period falls steeply as consumption rises then the Ramsey curve will be steep. In that case the primary effect of international economic integration in knowledge will be to put up the rate of interest, and the benefits in faster growth will be modest. If there is high substitution between consumption at different dates, the Ramsey curve will be quite flat. International economic integration will exert a large effect on the growth rate, and the interest rate will go up little.

It bears emphasis that what is being traded across international boundaries in this open-economy interpretation of the Romer model is not final output but ideas, and possibly also the distinct types of capital good that are constructed on the basis of them. To get the full benefit of the ideas they must be translated into the physical types of machinery or investment good that propels the economy's final output upwards. But the machine relating to an idea developed in Country A could, of course, be produced in B, as well as being rented out and employed there. So it may only be the blueprints that travel between countries.

International extensions of this model (and related variants) are discussed by Romer and Rivera-Batiz (1991) and Rebelo (1992). The interested reader is urged to consult them for further details. Within the European context, they also form the basis of Baldwin's analysis (1989) of the European Commission's '1992' programme. Baldwin argues that the Single European Act, and the consequent integration of European Union economies, may lead to dynamic gains in the form of permanently faster growth. These, he maintains, could ultimately dwarf the European Commission's estimates of the short-run real-income gains of about 5 per cent (Cecchini 1988).

The sceptic could retort, however, that European (and American or Japanese) inventors have long enjoyed some access to each others' discoveries. It is hard to

see how the removal of certain previous restrictions on intra-EU trade would necessarily generate additional flows of technical knowledge between different
countries. It could also be that different countries have stumbled on very similar
discoveries, so that the gains from pooling French and German stocks of knowledge—even assuming that the 1992 programme leads to this—would actually
make little difference to the productivity of either country's research sector.

International growth rate comparisons reveal some interesting characteristics.
Western Europe has displayed some tendency towards convergence, at least in levels of GDP per head. From 1980 to 1995 the two largest economies, West
Germany and France, have grown, on average, nearly 1 per cent per year more
slowly than the next three largest, Italy, the UK, and Spain, where income per
head was lower. The three economies where income per head was highest in
1945—Switzerland, Sweden, and Britain—grew more slowly than most of their
neighbours in the ensuing two decades. There have been exceptions; yet most of
the gaps in income per head across West European countries do appear to be
falling slowly, in relative terms, as time proceeds.

This process of convergence has been studied at a world level by Barro (1991),
Barro and Sala-i-Martin (1992), and several other authors. While Barro identifies
an unmistakeable general tendency towards convergence, others are more critical:
Bliss (1996) explores the implications of random shocks in modifying the
phenomenon, and Quah (1996a, 1996b) finds intriguing evidence that the international distribution of mean income per head has 'twin peaks'. For Quah there
seems to be a clutch of rich countries close to one end of the spectrum, with a
larger group centred round a much lower value towards the other.

'Catching-up' is clearly a complex process. There could even be cases of
'catching-down', where a country's income per head slips, at least relatively,
towards those of its neighbours or largest trading partners.

A central issue is the role played by trade in such growth patterns. Export
growth and output growth are closely correlated at the level of individual countries. Two key questions are: which way does causality run; and how is the direct
bilateral correlation affected when other variables are introduced? On the first
question, the balance of evidence suggests that the causal link from output to
exports is at least as strong as, and probably stronger than, the causal link from
exports to output. On the second, closer scrutiny of other variables suggests much
robuster links between 'openness' and the investment share of income, and
between the investment share and growth, than between openness (the ratio of
exports or imports or their sum to income) and growth. This, at least, is the conclusion of a powerful recent study by Levine and Renelt (1992).

If expanding trade is somewhat better seen as a consequence of growth than its
cause—or if expanding trade and expanding income are primarily associated
through other variables—we must still ask why it is that one country's growth is
interdependent with the growth of others. Foreign trade is not the only conduit
between economies that can generate such growth interdependencies. Others
include direct foreign investment, portfolio capital movements, and intellectual
transfers of ideas and technology across international boundaries.

If it is just a lack of domestic capital that is holding a country's income per head down and nothing else, the process of domestic investment should lead to a convergence eventually. But a country in this position could jump to higher output immediately through capital imports. Interest charges on those debts would keep its consumption and national income below the others, but the output gap could close very quickly. So international capital movements could be crucial. This point is stressed by Rebelo (1992). Rebelo also shows that this conclusion need not follow if consumers' preferences are modified in a way that differs from how they are usually modelled.

It is likely that technology, and not just domestic capital, inhibits income in poorer countries. Foreign direct investment may be particularly valuable, because it can transfer technological know-how as well as physical assets. Technological backwardness may also be remedied, or need remedying, through other mechanisms, such as research and development spending on innovation or imitation, and human capital development by education or training. Technology has many different dimensions.

The roles of imitation by poorer 'Southern' countries, and innovation in advanced, 'Northern' ones has been examined in detail by Grossman and Helpman (1991), among others. Although the North-South distinction is traditionally applied at the world level, it may also hold within Europe. Here 'South' will refer to the formerly communist countries in Central and Eastern Europe, and presumably also to Greece, Portugal, and at least certain regions of Spain and Italy. The Grossman-Helpman analysis looks at a host of questions, such as the determination of a steady state where the rich North and poorer South grow in parallel, and at the roles for tariffs and other policy instruments in modifying the growth processes in the various countries. Currie *et al.* (1996) have extended the Grossman-Helpman analysis to the case where a Southern country may at some point switch from pure imitation to a mix of innovation and imitation, and then progress later to pure innovation. If and when the third stage can be reached, the ultimate destination is complete convergence in income per head with the North. The key parameters controlling this progress are the gradual build-up of its speed of learning, and the relative costs of imitation and innovation.

In much of the discussion on these issues, it is assumed that faster growth is always beneficial. This may not always be true. Getting growth in the first place is initially costly (sacrificing consumption to education, R&D, or investment). There is an optimum balance between jam today and jam tomorrow. But the point that faster growth is not equivalent to higher welfare goes deeper. Aghion and Howitt's (1992) model of endogenous growth emphasizes that new technologies and new goods have a negative aspect, over and above the costs involved in creating them: they may lead to the wholesale displacement (and economic destruction) of existing assets and goods. Just as a firm may do 'too much' R&D from a social standpoint, due to the attraction of diverting other firms' profits to itself, so a society can advance its technology too rapidly as well.

If our conclusions on the links between growth and trade are inevitably rather complex, we should at least recall what can happen if a country chooses to cut its foreign trade towards vanishing point. One European country did this, progressively, between the late 1940s and the 1970s. The country was Albania. Albania was never rich, but its slide towards grinding poverty was remorseless and precipitous. However trade and growth are linked, at least one point seems to emerge from the Albanian example: complete economic isolation means no growth.

12.4 Summary

- Balanced, Hicks-neutral technological progress in a large country will change factor prices everywhere, and worsen its terms of trade, bringing overall gain to countries importing from it.
- The small general presumption that growth in one (large) country is likelier than not to help others, will be overturned if it is restricted to its import-competing industries.
- Trade liberalization is likelier than not to raise a country's growth rate, at least temporarily. Under suitable conditions, international economic integration could raise growth rates permanently in all countries.

TRADE BLOCS

13.1 Introduction

This chapter begins with the analysis of Free Trade Areas (Section 13.2), and moves on to Customs Unions (Section 13.3). The recent trend towards Regional Trading Blocs is examined in Section 13.4.

13.2 The Free Trade Area

13.2.1 Outline of the issues

A Free Trade Area (FTA) is a group of countries that permit free trade between them. Tariffs, and other barriers to trade, may be retained on trade between a country in the group and others outside it.

What differentiates the FTA from the customs union (which we shall examine in Section 13.2.2) is that decisions about tariffs against imports from non-member countries *are left to the governments of the individual countries* within the FTA. By contrast, a customs union sets a common external tariff. If A and B are members of a customs union, their tariffs against a third country's exports will be uniform, and fixed in unison. If A and B are from an FTA, A's tariff rate on exports from an excluded country C can be quite different from B's. Another difference is that a country can be a member of two or more FTAs, while membership of a customs union precludes participation in any other trading bloc.

The structure of this section is as follows. We shall start by considering a small country that cannot affect any price in any foreign country by its own actions. We shall ask what happens when it enters an FTA, abolishing its pre-existing barriers to trade with a partner country B, but retaining existing barriers trade with an outside country C. We shall be interested in the positive effect on the magnitude and pattern of A's trade, and on consumption and production in A. Then we shall ask whether potential social welfare in A has risen or fallen. Perfect competition will be assumed.

The next question we shall ask is whether country A is better off joining the

FTA and retaining its original tariffs against non-partner countries, or adopting either of two other policies. One of these is to abolish all its tariffs against all countries unilaterally. The other is to enter the FTA, and simultaneously abolish its tariffs against non-FTA member countries. In an FTA, this is an option; in the customs union, it is not.

We shall then re-examine our answers to all these questions after postulating a framework where country A is large enough to influence prices in other countries by its own actions. Finally, we shall take a brief look at what difference imperfect competition can make.

13.2.2 Analysis of the FTA when A is too small to affect prices elsewhere

We start, then, with a small country A that enters an FTA with B. There is a third country (or set of countries), C, which lies outside the FTA.

Consider a good which A imports. Before it enters the FTA, let us assume it imposes a non-discriminatory tariff, at the rate t_0, on imports of the product from either B or C. Because A is so small, we can assume that the supply curves of exports of the product, from both B and C, are horizontal. Which country will A import this commodity from?

The answer is whichever offers it at a lower price. This could be either B or C. If B offers the product more cheaply, removing the tariff against B (and retaining it against imports from C) will not affect the source of imports. They will continue to come in from B, but their price facing domestic consumers falls; so demand expands. If the product is also made (in modest amounts) inside A, with an upward-sloping supply curve, domestic production will drop. It could, indeed, cease altogether.

What can be said about the welfare effects of this? Setting aside repercussions on other markets, and imposing a partial equilibrium framework, it appears that the change is all to the good. There is a big rise in domestic consumers' surplus. The surplus of home producers of the product falls. So does government revenue (the tariff has been abolished). But these two sources of loss are, in sum, smaller than the gain to consumers' surplus. If national social welfare is defined simply as the sum of consumers' and producers' surplus, plus net government revenue, we can be sure that social welfare has risen for country A. Figure 13.1 illustrates this.

The reason for this optimistic result is essentially that the remaining tariff against imports from C is redundant. It does no damage because A would always want to purchase only from B, which is a lower-cost source. Let us now assume the opposite. Suppose that the supply price from B is much bigger than from C by a margin that exceeds the tariff rate that will continue to be imposed on imports from C. Then entry into the FTA will have no effect at all, at least as far as this product is concerned. The product will still be imported from C, because B's supply price is simply too high. Since the tariff rate on imports from C is unchanged, there will be no change in the price facing domestic consumers (or home

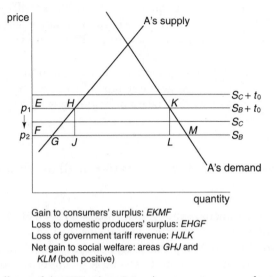

Gain to consumers' surplus: *EKMF*
Loss to domestic producers' surplus: *EHGF*
Loss of government tariff revenue: *HJLK*
Net gain to social welfare: areas *GHJ* and
    KLM (both positive)

Fig. 13.1. The effects of the FTA when B is a lower-cost source of supply

producers). So there is no change in consumers' or producers' surplus here, and no loss of government tariff revenue.

The third possibility is that B's supply price exceeds C's, but by a smaller margin than the surviving tariff rate on imports from C. This case is complex and interesting. Under a non-discriminatory tariff (the original position) A buys the good from C, the lower-cost source. Removal of the tariff against B's exports *only* has to bring the domestic price down, with consequent benefits to consumers' surplus, and damage, but necessarily lower damage, to home producers' surplus. So far, all well and good. The new domestic price equals B's supply price, with no tariff add-on.

The problem is that A now buys the good from B rather than C. This is inefficient. C supplies the good more cheaply. Import-sourcing has become wasteful. This is a source of welfare loss, reflected by the fact that what used to be government tariff revenue on imports from C has gone. It is split into two rectangles in Figure 13.2, R_1 and R_2. R_1 is a transfer to consumers' surplus; our assumption about social welfare makes this a matter of indifference. It is the rectangle R_2 that causes trouble. It simply vanishes into thin air. No one gains from it. It represents the pure waste of switching the source of imports from C to B, where the product is more expensive.

Area R_2 in Figure 13.2 is generally identified as the welfare loss due to *trade diversion*. Taken by itself, it suggests that entry into the FTA has been a mistake.

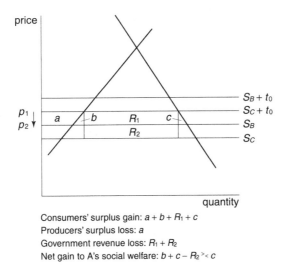

price

p_1
p_2

a b R_1 c

R_2

$S_B + t_0$
$S_C + t_0$
S_B
S_C

quantity

Consumers' surplus gain: $a + b + R_1 + c$
Producers' surplus loss: a
Government revenue loss: $R_1 + R_2$
Net gain to A's social welfare: $b + c - R_2 \overset{>}{<} c$

Fig. 13.2. The effects of the FTA when C is a lower-cost source of supply

But the FTA could still represent an improvement in domestic social welfare in A.
This is because of the gain in consumers' surplus. This equals the area $a + b + R_1 + c$.
Area R_1, as we saw, is a transfer from government revenue, and therefore nets out
as far as social welfare is concerned. Area a is also a transfer to consumers' surplus, this time from domestic producers' surplus (which has fallen, in line with
the reduction in the home price of the product, and the contraction in supply this
induces). Our assumption that competition is perfect ensures that the supply
curve reflects domestic marginal cost. The area under marginal cost represents
total cost; receipts for producers above this area are surplus, and the surplus area
is cut back by area a.

Given our definition of social welfare for country A, we have two areas of net
gain—the (approximately) triangular areas of b and c—and, to set against them,
a loss due to trade diversion of area R_2. There can be no general presumption
about whether R_2 exceeds, or is less than, $b + c$. The areas b and c are evidence of
trade creation: if you look beneath b to the horizontal axis you will see the extent
to which imports (from B, now) expand at the expense of shrunken domestic production, while the base of area c reflects the rise in imports due to enlarged
domestic demand.

What determines whether R_2 exceeds $b + c$, or not? Essentially, three factors.
One is the relative magnitudes of t_0 and the vertical gap between B's and C's supply curves. The bigger t_0 is, the greater the drop in the domestic price (one determinant of the areas b and c). The bigger the gap between P_B and P_C, the larger is

area R_2. The other two factors that are relevant here are the elasticities of the domestic supply and demand curves. If S_A and D_A are highly inelastic, b and c will be very small; if highly elastic, very much larger.

Let us review our findings so far. The small FTA participant, incapable of influencing any foreign prices by its own actions, stands to gain if its partner is a lower-cost source of imports than excluded countries; is unaffected if it continues to import from outsiders; and may lose its gain when entry into the FTA leads it to switch from a cheaper outsider to dearer imports from its partner.

Our next question is trickier. We wish to contrast entry into the FTA, not with an initial position distorted by non-discriminatory tariffs against imports from all sources, but with unilateral free trade, and entry into the FTA, accompanied by removal of tariffs against outsiders. We will also be interested in comparing these two policies.

Since it was trade diversion that posed the only threat of damage to domestic welfare, the first seems to be a superior policy to entry into an FTA accompanied by retaining tariffs against imports from outsiders. If tariffs are removed on all imports A will never switch sources of supply from C to B. If C's supply price is lower than B's, and imports from both C and B can enter free of tariffs, all purchases will come from C. At least as far as imports are concerned, the picture is clear.

The snag, however, is that the two policies we are contrasting have different implications for exports. The free-trade area with B means that B removes its tariffs against exports from A. Unilateral free trade on A's part means that A takes off all its tariffs, but B (and C for that matter) may well continue to levy tariffs on imports from A (and each other). How is A affected by B's removal of its tariffs on A's exports?

Assuming that B (and also C) is a very large country in comparison with A implies that A faces an infinitely elastic demand curve for its exports to B. The incidence of any tariff B imposes on A's exports will then fall squarely on A's exporters. It cuts the price of the good in A, because A's exporting firms will only be in equilibrium if they receive the same price in A as in B (and the price in B that they get there is, of course, squeezed by the tariff). This is good news for A's consumers who buy this product, but the consumers' surplus gain is more than outweighed by the loss in producers' surplus. This has to be so, since the good is an exportable: production exceeds demand in A. It follows that the removal of B's tariff against A's exports can only be beneficial for A. There is just one qualification here: if A's exporters can get a better price in C, they will not export to B, and if the price in C still exceeds that in B even after B's tariff has come off, A will experience no benefits on this score.

We conclude from this that entry into the FTA, with a positive tariff retained by A on imports from non-partner countries, could still be better from A's standpoint than a policy of unilateral free trade on A's part. This is so because the FTA does away with partner tariffs on A's exports, which could have no effect, but can only bring benefits if it has any effect at all. What A may gain on this score could exceed the loss from trade diversion on the import side. But it may not; so it is in general an open question whether unilateral free trade is better for A than entry into an FTA with tariffs retained on imports from outsiders. Our analysis has, however, indicated precisely what the potential sources of gains and losses are in the two cases.

Now let us compare the FTA with tariffs retained on imports from outsiders with the second policy, the FTA with tariffs on outsiders removed. Under our stated assumptions, this policy delivers the best of both worlds. Efficient import sourcing cannot be violated for country A, because there cannot be trade diversion once A has removed all its tariffs. At the same time, A can only gain when B takes off its tariffs against imports from A. The domestic price of these A-exportables inside A can only rise if it changes at all, and this spells a rise in producer surplus that necessarily exceeds the squeeze in consumers' surplus there. This result is clear-cut.

There is another unambiguous result as well. Unilateral free trade must dominate the original position where A levied non-discriminatory tariffs against every country. This follows, essentially, because of our assumption that A is a price-taker. There is no optimum tariff argument for A to have tariffs. And we can refer back to our standard result on tariffs, that even when second-best arguments (public revenue, unemployment, externalities, or other distortions) mean that a tariff could be welfare-increasing, provided that the country is small, there must in principle exist a superior solution to the problem that avoids the additional distortions brought about by tariffs.

Let us formalize this. Contrast the two policies discussed with

3. an initial position of positive tariffs levied by A on all imports, on a non-discriminatory basis, and
4. entry into an FTA where A retains positive, unchanged tariff levels against outsiders.

Our results are: (1) must dominate (3); (2) must dominate (4); but we cannot in general rank (3) against (2) or (4). These propositions relate only, of course, to country A. Whether (3) is superior to (2) or to (4) can only be answered by examining the particular facts of the case.

13.2.3 Analysis of the FTA when A is large enough to influence world prices

When A is large, it will no longer face horizontal supply curves of its imports or horizontal demand curves for its exports.

The analysis of this case is exceedingly complex. We shall confine ourselves to a more limited discussion of the issues involved. Since A faces upward-sloping supply curves for its imports now, both from B and, let us assume, C as well, it enjoys some monopsony power. Buying fewer imports means bringing down their price. Let us assume that A has no power to discriminate between different units of supply, or supplying firms, in either B or C.

A now faces an upward-sloping 'average cost' of imports from B, and also from C: the no-discrimination assumption ensures that all its imports from B, for example, are secured at a common price. The import supply curve from B gives the average cost of imports from B, and similarly from C. Since average cost slopes up, marginal cost lies above it.

Optimum import sourcing, in this case, entails equating the marginal cost of imports from each country of supply. (The second-order condition, which we shall assume to hold, is that these marginal costs are non-decreasing.) The optimum tariff is set, from A's standpoint, where the marginal cost of imports equals the domestic price of the good in A. It follows that country A does best to set common tariff rates on imports from B and from C when these two countries' supply curves of exports to A are of equal elasticity.

If the supply curves of imports from B and C differ in elasticity, A does best to set higher tariffs on goods coming in from the country whose supply is less elastic. In the special case where B's supply curve is horizontal and C's slopes up, A optimizes by letting B's exports in free of tariff and levying a tariff against C that equates the marginal cost of imports from C with B's given supply price. It can only be in this very special case that the FTA with B is ideal from A's standpoint.

It follows from this that removing the tariff on imports from B, and retaining it on C's exports, may well be welfare-reducing. This is certain when the initial tariff rates A levied against both were optimal. Unilateral free trade, and entering the FTA together with abolishing all A's tariffs, are likely to be still less attractive for A—at least from the standpoint of its imports. The only possible exception to this arises when the initial tariffs were set well above their optimal levels.

On the export side, analogous arguments apply. If A is large, the demand for its exports that it will face in both B and C will surely be downward-sloping. Barring price discrimination, that means marginal revenue in both markets lies below demand. An optimum trade policy from Country A's standpoint will involve (a) equating marginal revenue from exports across all destinations, and (b) equating this equalized marginal revenue with domestic price. The second-order condition here qualifies this by the stipulation that marginal revenues be non-increasing.

Policies (a) and (b) will call for export taxes, at uniform rates when B's and C's demand elasticities are the same, but otherwise at different rates. In the limiting case where B's demand curve is horizontal and C's slopes down, it is best to levy no tax on exports to B, but tax exports to C up to the point where marginal revenue from that market equates with the price earned in B. The FTA (which will presumably prohibit intra-area export taxes) would then be first-best from A's point of view. In other circumstances it cannot be best; when the initial export taxes that A levies happen to be optimal, entry into the FTA will involve inevitable departure from the optimal export policy.

All that we have said so far about the large-country case is, however, open to an important qualification. If B was also large, it would also enjoy monopsony and monopoly power. From a purely national standpoint, it would also be tempted to levy import tariffs and export taxes against other countries, including A. B's taxes on trade with A can only have damaged A. The FTA not only calls upon A to remove its trade barriers against its partner, B; it also requires B to do the same for A. If A and B happen to be similar in size and in flexibility in both production and consumption, the damage that one's trade taxes inflict on the other will be similar in magnitude.

The FTA can, therefore, be beneficial for both A and B after all. What A gains from B's liberalization can certainly compensate for A's losses from having to depart from its own optimal taxes on trade with B. If A and B were the only countries in the world, and symmetry applied, the Nash equilibrium with each taxing trade with the other would unquestionably deliver lower potential welfare for both countries than the 'cooperative' solution of free trade.

We cannot ignore country C, however. The FTA specifically excludes C. What difference does this make? One point is incontrovertible. The optimum free-trade area is the world as a whole. Qualifications aside—barring, for example, the intriguing Newbery-Stiglitz (1984) case of Pareto-inferior trade, due to market incompleteness[1]—we know that global free trade must be best, at least under ideal conditions. It is only then that consumers' marginal rates of substitution between product pairs can be equalized across international boundaries, which is a necessary condition for efficiency in exchange. It is only then that marginal rates of transformation between product pairs can be equalized for all producers in all countries, a necessary condition for productive efficiency.

When C is excluded, however, the only threat to welfare inside the FTA is posed, essentially, by trade diversion. This threat is at its greatest when FTA partners levy large trade taxes against C. Yet we know that if A and B, separately, levy optimal trade taxes against C, these should be set at lower rates than if A and B set their trade taxes against C in unison. This is because A and B have only oligopsony power in trade with C. When they act in concert, they enjoy monopsony power. If A and B were to set optimal monopsony-exploiting trade taxes against C, they would already be achieving an optimum balance between the distortions of those trade taxes—which include the wasteful incentive to expand.

13.3 The Customs Union

The Customs Union (CU) differs from the Free Trade Area (FTA) in one key respect. In a CU, external tariffs levied on non-members' exports are common. They are no longer, as in the FTA, left to the discretion of the individual member states. So external tariffs are uniform in the CU. More importantly, one sees them as being set by negotiation between the member states.

From the standpoint of the CU itself, the harmonized fixing of common external tariff walls carries one advantage and one disadvantage. The disadvantage is that individual member states' beliefs about their own optimal tariffs (if any)

---

[1] This is discussed in detail in Chapter 7.

against excluded countries could well diverge. Member A may have a large domestic industry producing substitutes for good x which it also imports from an outsider, C. If member B may rely on imports for its entire supply of x, B will have much more to lose from a tariff on C's exports of x than A will. If the owners of the factors of production employed intensively in, or specific to, A's x industry receive a large weight in A's social welfare function, it may be keen to urge a high tariff. B will want a much lower one, and perhaps a zero one. In the FTA, A can have its high tariff and B its low tariff. In a CU, they must compromise, and presumably fix a tariff rate that is less than ideal for both.

The advantage that the CU has over the FTA arises when the union partners, acting in concert, can exert appreciable influence over world prices. They can set an optimal tariff on imports and thereby beat down the world price of a good they import from the rest of the world, necessarily gaining more from improved terms of trade than what is lost in reduced trade volume. Had A and B set their optimal tariffs independently, assuming that both of them are importers of the range of goods in question from the rest of the world, these tariffs would be lower. A and B on their own have less oligopsony power than they do when they act together. This advantage for the CU is absent, of course, when the CU is too small to influence world prices, because its optimal common external tariffs are then zero.

How is this conflict between the plus and the minus of the CU in comparison to the FTA resolved? Clearly we need to examine the question case by case to see which consideration dominates; but there are some general points to be made. One concerns symmetry. If the customs union partners are similar in their structures of consumption and production, factor endowments and technologies, and social welfare functions, they will not disagree about what an optimal tariff will be. Then the potential disadvantage will not apply; nothing is lost by confining external tariff rates to uniformity.

Another relevant factor is the size of the CU, and the number of countries within it. Suppose all of them buy x from the rest of the world. A two-member CU will roughly double the oligopsony power each country could exert on its own. For a five-member CU, the increase in oligopsony power is correspondingly increased. So the more numerous its members—so long as we are dealing with a good they all import—the greater the gain from coordinated external tariff-setting that the CU implies. Against this, if the CU is a small player in world terms the magnitude of this oligopsony power, no matter how magnified by coordination, will remain trivial.

How is the rest of the world affected? Would excluded, non-European countries, let us say, prefer to see a Europe that sets common external tariffs as the EU currently does, or a Europe closer to the model of the EFTA, or the North American Free Trade Area where external tariff decisions were, or are, left to individual member countries?

Those countries in the rest of the world that are net importers of the goods on which Europe levies import tariffs would prefer to see an EU-style Europe. They can free-ride on the reduction in import prices that the EU common tariffs will bring, a larger reduction, assuming that these tariffs are set optimally, than would have been set by individual European states acting independently. But the rest of the world as a whole must be an exporter of such goods. For those countries in the rest of the world that export them, a European FTA would be a much friendlier animal than a European CU.

13.4 The emergence of regional trading blocs

In 1988 Canada and the United States signed a comprehensive free trade agreement, and created a North Atlantic Free Trade Area (NAFTA). In 1993 agreements were reached with Mexico that secured its participation. Chile and Columbia are among other Latin American countries that have recently been considering whether they should also join NAFTA.

The European Free Trade Association, EFTA, was created in 1959. It embraced Denmark, Norway, and Sweden, together with Austria and Switzerland, and Portugal, Ireland, and the UK. Iceland and Finland joined later. The European Economic Community was formed in 1957, with Belgium, Luxembourg, the Netherlands, Italy, France, and West Germany as original members. As in EFTA, internal tariffs were progressively reduced and eventually eliminated, but external tariffs were fixed in common, making the EEC a CU, not an FTA. Denmark, Ireland, and the UK joined the EEC (now renamed the EC) in 1973, followed by Greece in 1981, Portugal and Spain in 1986, and, in 1995, Austria, Finland, and Sweden. Earlier agreements between the EC and other European states had meanwhile led to free trade in almost all manufactures.

Regional trade blocs have emerged in many other areas in the world. Some early ones foundered: economic unions in East Africa (Kenya, Uganda, and Tanzania) and Central Africa (Malawi, Zambia, and Zimbabwe, under their previous, pre-independence names) were to collapse in the 1960s. The Council for Mutual Economic Assistance (CMEA), while neither a FTA nor a CU in the normal sense, presided over rapidly expanding (if strongly regulated) trade between the former USSR and East Germany, together with Bulgaria, Czechoslovakia, Hungary, Poland, and Romania, and broke up only with the collapse of communism in 1990–1. Others, such as the South African customs union linking Botswana, Lesotho, Namibia, and Swaziland to South Africa, were to thrive and survive major political changes. Argentina, Brazil, Paraguay, and Uruguay have formed a free trade area known as Mercosur. There are numerous regional trading blocs in Asia and the Pacific Rim.

These developments have created both excitement and alarm among economists and policymakers alike. Would the trend towards ever-larger regional trading blocs create more trade than it diverted? What would happen to rates of protection between the blocs, and to welfare?

A pessimistic view was proffered in highly influential work by Krugman (1991). Krugman explored a model where each country was endowed with a given supply of a unique good that could be found nowhere else. Consumers in all countries had similar tastes, displaying preferences that were symmetrical between all these products, which were less than perfect substitutes for each other in consumption. Governments were modelled as setting tariffs optimally, to get the maximum net benefit for their terms of trade. Krugman then considered what would happen if countries joined to form trade blocs that set their tariffs in unison, like CUs, on external trade, while removing tariffs against each other within the bloc.

Krugman's results were startling. A symmetric process of bloc enlargement would lead inexorably to higher and higher tariffs. For this reason—and because intra-bloc trade creation was never powerful enough to swamp the damage due to growing diversion and external tariff changes—welfare would fall. Welfare would reach a minimum, Krugman concluded, when the world was composed of three regional blocs. Trends at the time were increasingly suggesting that the world would indeed be forming itself into three blocs—a North American bloc with a Central and South American 'hinterland'; a West European bloc, with Eastern Europe and Africa as appendages; and an Asia-Pacific bloc centred round Japan.

Krugman's gloomy conclusions, it was found, would not necessarily follow under modified assumptions. Were the trade blocs to act as FTAs rather than CUs, Sinclair and Vines (1995) showed, a process of trade bloc enlargement would lead to progressively lower tariffs and higher welfare. The key issue, then, was whether the European Union with its common external tariff was the typical trade bloc, or whether the NAFTA model, where tariff-setting lay with individual countries' governments, would be the model. Krugman's results had stemmed from the enhanced oligopsony power that the trade bloc would exploit, with growing ferocity, as it expanded. Because of the model's symmetry, what each bloc gained from its own tariffs was cancelled, and indeed outweighed, by the damage it experienced from the increasing tariffs imposed by other trade blocs as they grew in parallel. In the FTA model of Sinclair and Vines the constraint of a zero-tariff against all bloc partners implied a falling optimal tariff, at the individual country level, against outsiders as the size of the bloc grew. In a second paper, Krugman (1993) showed that the earlier results could be reversed for a different reason. Because of international transport costs, countries would trade more with neighbours than with more distant countries, so provided that blocs had the regional—what he called 'natural'—feature of proximity or contiguity, trade creation gains would dominate trade diversion losses, and bloc enlargement would be beneficial.

13.5 Summary

- Members of a Free Trade Area (FTA) tax trade with non-members as they wish, and trade freely with each other. In a Customs Union (CU), tariffs on trade with non-members are set in unison.

- A country that enters a FTA or CU, preserving tariffs on imports from non-members, can gain or lose. The primary source of loss is import diversion from cheaper non-partner to dearer partner sources of supply. A CU constrains a member's external trade policy, perhaps damagingly, but may offer scope for exploiting enhanced monopoly power in trade.
- The trend to fewer, larger trade blocs may raise protection and lower welfare if the blocs are CUs, but should raise welfare if they are FTAs.

TRADE, COMPETITIVENESS, EMPLOYMENT, AND WAGES

14.1 Introduction

As countries have become more open, international trade has increasingly become the focus of political rhetoric regarding economic performance in Western industrialized countries, including the countries of the EU. It is not uncommon to hear politicians bemoaning lack of international competitiveness, attributing the high and persistent unemployment experienced since 1980 to increased imports from low-wage developing countries, and blaming these imports for increasing the difference in wages between skilled and unskilled workers. Many people perceive that domestic economic problems would disappear if only their country or countries were as 'competitive' as Japan, Taiwan, or Korea.

But what is competitiveness? Does it have any meaning for a country? To what extent is the economic well-being of a particular country determined by its performance relative to other countries? Can we, like President Clinton, treat a country like 'a big corporation competing in the global marketplace'? Does economic theory and the available empirical evidence support the assertion that more openness to international trade and, in particular, greater imports from low-wage countries have contributed to increased unemployment and larger wage differentials? These are the issues that we will consider in this chapter. We should start by remembering that in most countries, and certainly for the EU as a whole, although its importance has been increasing, international trade plays a relatively minor role in the economy. In 1994 imports from outside comprised less than 12 per cent of EU GDP. For the vast majority of sectors of the economy over 80 per cent of demand in the EU is satisfied by EU suppliers. The United States exhibits a similar degree of openness to international trade. Thus from the very outset one should expect that domestic issues are likely to lie at the heart of the economic problems that have afflicted industrialized countries since the 1980s. This is not to rule out at the start any role for international factors, but rather, to put their potential impact into some perspective.

In this chapter we will show that international competitiveness is not a well-defined concept, and discussions of how to improve a country's ability to compete with other countries are prone to give incorrect and hence dangerous policy prescriptions. We also show that there is no compelling evidence that international trade is at the root of overall changes in unemployment. For particular industrial sectors, however, increasing import competition may have a significant impact upon employment in that sector. Unskilled labour-saving technical progress is clearly at the heart of changes in employment opportunities and the relative wages of unskilled labour. There is some theoretical support for the notion that trade with low-wage economies has increased the dispersion of wages of different types of labour. However, trade cannot be the single, or the most important, reason for this phenomenon. The contribution of trade to these changes is an empirical issue which has yet to be properly addressed.

14.2 Trade and competitiveness

In 1993 the European Commission published a White Paper (policy proposal document) entitled Growth, Competitiveness and Employment (CEC 1993). Here the rhetoric of competitiveness is writ large. For example, the document talks of the 'responsibility on the part of national and Community authorities as regards competitiveness'. The Commission has also instituted an annual competitiveness review. But what is competitiveness? Nowhere is it defined in the White Paper.

A popular misconception is that the size of the trade balance reflects a country's competitiveness. 'A country with a large trade deficit must suffer from a competitiveness problem!' In the 1980s highly indebted developing countries in Africa and Latin America, with access barred to additional lending, had to run a trade surplus to pay for the interest on this debt. This is hardly a sign of the competitive strength of these countries. A trade deficit may simply reflect the intertemporal preferences of the citizens of a country, a desire for greater consumption now, to be paid for in the future.

Competitiveness has also been at the forefront of economic policy discussion in the United States. In an influential book, Tyson (1992) defines competitiveness in terms of a country's ability to 'produce goods and services that meet the test of international markets while our citizens enjoy a standard of living that is both rising and sustainable'. But again, what is the test that international markets provide? An answer is not provided.

A further issue is the linking of competition in international markets and rising living standards. To what extent do developments in international trade affect living standards? Throughout this book we have highlighted ways in which participation in international trade benefits a country in terms of a higher level of welfare. There are both static resource-allocation gains highlighted by traditional trade theory and the dynamic benefits that may accrue from the influence of trade upon the level of technology and the rate of growth. Remember that here we are

discussing the overall level of welfare of the country, and that we are not considering the distributional impact of trade within a country. As we have discussed in
Chapter 5, and will return to below, the Stolper-Samuelson theory shows that
greater openness to trade will increase the returns to the relatively abundant factor and reduce the returns to the relatively scarce resource; but overall, welfare
rises. Tyson and others seem to suggest that trade may reduce overall living standards in a country. How can this happen?

Krugman (1994) uses a very simple experiment to highlight the issue. Imagine
a country which undertakes no trade. In this case the extent to which standards
of living rise will be determined solely by domestic factors, the most important
being the rate of growth of productivity. If we now introduce international trade,
the only way that the benefits of rising productivity can be undermined is if the
terms of trade continually deteriorate. In other words, the price that the country
has to pay for its imports relative to the price it receives for the goods it exports
may rise such that overall purchasing power and standards of living fall.

This is an empirical issue which can be investigated using what is known as
command GDP, a measure of the volume of goods and services that a country can
purchase. This compares with real GDP, which is a measure of the volume of output of the country. Command GDP is given by the volume of goods and services
produced for domestic consumption plus the volume of imports that can be purchased with the proceeds of exports, the latter being given by dividing the value
of exports by the price of imports. So, only if command GDP is substantially
lower than real GDP can we say that external factors have influenced the growth
of living standards and hence 'competitiveness'.

Table 14.1 shows the growth rates of real GDP, command GDP, and productivity for each of the EU, Japan, and the USA for the period since 1961. The data
show that for the thirty-year period covering the 1960s, 1970s, and 1980s the rate
of growth of command GDP was very close to that of real GDP. The difference
between the two, the terms-of-trade effect, was very small for all three countries
or regions. For example, for the EU, command GDP grew on average each year by
2.31 per cent. The contribution of the terms of trade effect was 0.05 per cent per
annum, whilst real GDP grew at 2.26 per cent per annum. The same feature per-

Table 14.1. Growth in real GDP, command GDP and productivity

	Growth of	1961–1993	1961–1973	1973–1983	1983–1993
EU	Real GDP	2.26	4.59	2.23	2.23
	Command GDP	2.31	4.90	1.89	2.69
	Productivity	2.82	4.27	2.19	1.83
Japan	Real GDP	5.75	9.14	3.75	3.61
	Command GDP	5.98	9.81	3.15	4.05
	Productivity	4.68	7.81	2.90	2.46
USA	Real GDP	2.28	3.88	2.05	2.62
	Command GDP	2.19	3.98	1.92	2.59
	Productivity	1.07	1.97	0.38	0.81

Source: Gros and Jones (1995)

tains to the US and Japan. Thus, over these three decades the effect of external developments, via the terms of trade, on the growth in living standards (competitiveness) was negligible. This leads Krugman to conclude that 'competitiveness is a meaningless word when applied to economies. And the obsession with competitiveness is both wrong and dangerous.' Thus, it is domestic factors, and in particular productivity growth, which are the primary determinants of rising living standards.

Gros and Jones (1995) show that for shorter periods the terms-of-trade effect can be important. Between 1973 and 1983, and 1983 and 1993, productivity growth in the EU fell, whilst the rate of growth of real GDP remained constant. The annual rate of growth of command GDP, however, increased from 1.89 per cent to 2.69 per cent due entirely to a favourable movement in the terms of trade. Nevertheless, domestic factors remained the dominant force in pushing forward living standards in the EU.

The difficulty with the term 'competitiveness' is that whilst it has a clear meaning at the level of the firm, ambiguities arise if it is applied at the industry level and particularly at the national level. For a firm, if a rival becomes more efficient, or competitive, it may find it more difficult to maintain sales. The idea of international competitiveness only arises if the rival is located abroad. At the industry level, competitiveness is an issue only if all firms in the industry become less efficient relative to foreign rivals.

So, over the longer term, changes in the terms of trade have contributed little to the growth of living standards in industrial countries. Diverting attention to international issues as a source of poor economic performance serves only to delay decisions necessary to improve domestic economic factors.

Although terms-of-trade effects have proved to be insignificant for industrial countries, this is not the case for some developing countries. Countries whose exports are dominated by a few, non-oil, resource-based products, and who primarily import manufactures, have suffered from a long-run tendency for the price of primary products to deteriorate relative to those of manufactures. Thus, international factors have had a significant effect upon the growth of living standards in many countries in Africa. In these cases international 'competitiveness' is an important issue. Attempts to address this problem by intervention using, for example, commodity stabilization schemes have, in general, not been successful. Thus, many countries have sought to diversify away from dependence upon a narrow range of primary products and into manufactures. The experience of the NICS suggests that this is best achieved in an export-orientated environment. This is confirmed by the poor performance of countries which sought to industrialize behind protective import barriers.

In conclusion, in a diverse, dynamic economy in which new firms and new products are continually being introduced, the notion of national competitiveness cannot be clearly defined. The primary determinant of rising living standards will be domestic factors such as growth of productivity. It is not productivity relative to other countries that is important. This is highlighted in Table 14.1, which shows that Japanese productivity grew at a rate almost double that of the EU in the 1960s, whilst in the 1970s Japanese productivity growth exceeded that of the EU by only 30 per cent. With EU GDP in the 1960s growing, on average, at twice the rate of the 1970s it is hard to conclude that performance improved in the 1970s.

14.3 Trade and jobs

Although the international economy may be of little significance for standards of living in the economy as a whole, greater openness to international trade may have significant effects upon particular groups within a country. An issue which has come to dominate discussions in the 1980s and 1990s is the role of international trade in the reduction of the size of the manufacturing sector in western countries and the historically high and persistent levels of unemployment. Figure 14.1 shows the change in manufacturing employment in the EU, the United States, and Japan since 1980.

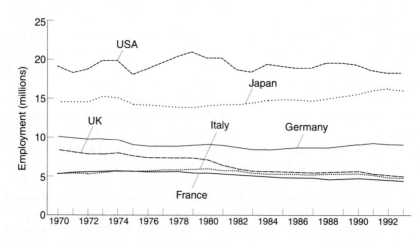

Fig. 14.1. Employment in manufacturing

Can unemployment be attributed to international trade, and in particular, to trade with low-income countries? In the previous chapters we have shown how more openness to trade increases specialization. In standard neo-classical trade theory, described in Chapter 5, the industry which uses intensively the factor which is in relatively short supply will contract, whilst the industry which uses the abundant factor intensively will expand. Most economists would argue that if markets work fairly efficiently then this adjustment, although it may take a little while, will be achieved without creating large numbers of unemployed workers.

Indeed, the massive increase in trade between European countries in the 1960s was achieved without generating large numbers of unemployed workers. Much of this trade was between similar countries, in terms of factor endowments, and was of an intra-industry nature. Adjustment costs were mitigated by the need for resources to shift primarily within industries, rather than between industries, as in the traditional trade models.

During the late 1980s and 1990s there has been considerable concern in Europe that trade with the newly industrializing countries of Asia and the transformation, and consequent increase in openness, in Eastern Europe will lead to a flood of imports which will undermine employment in industries which use unskilled labour intensively. Similarly, in the US there has been much discussion of the potential effects of the NAFTA and free trade with Mexico on manufacturing employment in the US. Thus, here the attention is focused upon trade with countries which are different from EU countries, and in particular imports from whom embody the intensive use of unskilled labour.

In general, empirical studies have suggested that, for the economy as a whole, the net effect of increasing exports and imports on employment has not been important in industrial countries (Baldwin 1994). A detailed study of OECD countries (OECD 1992) found that during the 1970s and 1980s trade had a positive effect on employment in Canada, Denmark, France, Germany, Japan, and the Netherlands. In the UK and the US imports tended to displace more jobs than were created by exports. However, in all countries the effect on employment of changes in the demand for domestically produced goods far exceeded the effect of changes in the demand for imports. Rising labour productivity was also identified as a more significant cause of job losses than was greater imports.

This analysis uses input–output tables to decompose changes in output and employment according to whether the source was changes in domestic demand for domestically produced goods, changes in demand for exports, changes in demand for imports, technical change, or labour productivity. Interestingly, technical change, measured as the change in the input–output coefficients, appears to have played an insignificant role in net employment creation. This approach is very mechanical, and the lack of a theoretical base makes interpretation of the results difficult. The breakdown of the employment effects assumes that the various components are independent of each other. It has been argued that actual or potential imports will encourage domestic producers to invest in labour-saving technologies. The decline in the use of labour will be attributed to rising productivity, rather than as being due to competition from imports.

An alternative approach to estimating the effect of trade on employment has been to use the factor content of trade. The amounts of different factors embodied in a country's exports are computed, and, when multiplied by the increase in exports, they give the positive effect of trade on the demand for the different factors. The factor content of imports is then used to derive the quantities of the factors that would be employed if goods which are now imported were produced domestically. This is the negative effect of trade upon the demand for factors of production. In general, studies using this approach have not attributed large changes in the demand for factors, and in particular unskilled labour, to increased trade.

Underlying this approach is the application of the same factor-input coefficients (those of the importing country) in the computation of the factor content of both exports and imports. This implies the assumption that the goods produced by an industry are the same whether produced in the North or the South. Wood (1994) criticizes this assumption, and argues that many of the manufactured goods imported by the North do not have a domestic substitute, and so are non-competing. These goods are not produced in the North because the highly intensive use of unskilled labour makes them unprofitable.

Wood suggests that a more relevant approach is to compute the amounts of factors required in the North to produce non-competing imports from the South using the factor input coefficients of the South. For example, when computing the amounts of factors that would be required in the EU to produce the quantity of footwear currently imported from Asia, the amounts of unskilled and skilled labour and capital required to produce a unit of footwear in Asia should be used. However, these magnitudes then have to be adjusted to take account of the fact that unskilled labour is relatively more expensive in the North. That is, producers in the North would not use unskilled labour in the same proportion as in the South because of the relatively high price of unskilled labour in the North. Finally, since costs and prices are higher in the North, the increase in the output of labour-intensive manufactures would be less than the level of imports.

Using this method suggests that trade liberalization has had a major impact upon labour markets in Western economies. Wood estimates that increased trade between developed and developing countries has reduced the demand for labour in the manufacturing sector of the advanced countries by an amount equivalent to 12 per cent of employment in manufacturing. These calculations are around ten times greater than those based upon the factor-input coefficients of the North. This figure, it is claimed, will be an under-estimate, since it fails to take into account that increased trade with the South will encourage labour-saving technical innovation in the North.

The estimates of Wood therefore suggest that trade between the North and South has had a significant effect upon employment in manufacturing in the North. However, there are a number of reasons to be very suspicious of these estimates. First, there is the assumption that all manufactured products imported from the South, except processed primary products such as food, have no substitute produced domestically in the North. Baldwin (1994) notes that the constructors of input–output tables have to decide whether a particular import is a substitute for a domestically produced good. Only 14 per cent of US imports were classified as non-competing for the 1977 and 1982 input–output tables. Therefore, the assumption that imports of all manufactures, excepting processed primary products, are non-competing looks extreme.

A further issue relates to technology. If products from the South do not compete with those produced in the North, why should producers in the North adopt new labour-saving technologies? It may rather be that producers in the North have access to better technology which raises the productivity of all factors of production relative to productivity in the South. If this is the case then the calculations of Wood will overstate the amount of labour that would be required if imports from the South were replaced by domestic production.

Perhaps of greatest importance, finally, is the fact that the demand for unskilled workers relative to those with skills has declined across a whole range of industries in the industrial countries, not just those where there is a high degree of import penetration by developing countries. In the standard neo-classical model the decline in the relative price of unskilled labour will lead to the substitution of unskilled for skilled labour in all sectors including the skill-intensive export sector. In other words, if more open trade has led to a significant shift towards the skill-intensive sector it should also have contributed to a shift within sectors to the more intensive use of unskilled relative to skilled labour.

Furthermore, there is no apparent reason why greater openness to international trade should lead to a decrease in the demand for unskilled workers in non-traded sectors. Again, if the relative wages of unskilled workers have fallen relative to the returns to other factors, then these industries would be expected to increase their demand for unskilled labour, and the ratio of skilled to unskilled labour should fall. International trade cannot be held responsible for the loss of jobs of unskilled workers in sectors subject to low import-penetration from countries with relatively low labour costs.

Thus, the argument that international trade is responsible for the wholesale destruction of the jobs of unskilled workers in the manufacturing sector of industrial countries is far from convincing. Many economists view the loss of unskilled jobs in manufacturing as primarily the result of technological change. Standard trade theory shows that the impact of technological change depends upon whether the innovation occurs in the skill-intensive or unskilled-intensive sector. Further, it is important whether the innovation is biased towards saving unskilled labour. It is this latter type of innovation which is seen to be responsible for the employment trends in industrial countries.

Unskilled labour-saving technical progress which occurs to the same extent in both sectors will lead to within-industry shifts away from the use of unskilled relative to skilled labour. In the simple two-factor (unskilled and skilled labour), two-commodity (skill-intensive and unskilled, labour-intensive goods) model the maintenance of full employment requires that the output of the unskilled, labour-intensive sector rises relative to the output of the skill-intensive sector. If the country is large these changes will influence the international prices of the two goods. The relative price of the unskilled, labour-intensive good will fall relative to the price of the skill-intensive good. This change in product prices will tend to reduce the relative wage of unskilled labour which will encourage the substitution (if input coefficients are not fixed) of unskilled for skilled labour, partly offsetting the effect of the technological change.

Unskilled labour-saving technical progress does appear to have occurred to a substantial extent in industrial countries over the last two decades. There has been a considerable substitution of skilled for unskilled labour across industries, despite a fall in the relative wage of unskilled workers. However, this is not to preclude a role for international trade in the shift away from unskilled labour; both technological change and international trade can affect the use of unskilled relative to skilled labour. The need is to go beyond interpreting general trends, and carefully to disentangle the influences of these two determinants. As yet there are no studies which provide a clear answer to this issue. Leamer (1994) argues that the breakdown between production and non-production workers used in many studies is inappropriate for distinguishing between skilled and unskilled labour.

14.4   Trade and wages

A further issue which has received a great deal of attention in the 1990s is the view that the increase in competition from more open trade is responsible for lowering the wages of unskilled workers in the industrial countries relative to other workers. In general, wage inequality declined or remained constant in OECD countries in the 1970s, but increased throughout the 1980s. The increase in inequality was most pronounced in the US and the UK. In contrast, there is some evidence that during the 1980s wage inequality in the more advanced developing countries in Asia and South America was reduced. The increase in wage inequality in Western Europe and North America is associated with a trend towards higher relative returns to skilled or educated workers. This is compatible with the neo-classical explanation of trade.

Above we concluded that greater openness to trade cannot provide a strong explanation of the decline in demand for unskilled workers relative to skilled labour. A number of authors have then concluded that trade cannot explain increasing wage inequality. For example, studies using the 'factor content of trade' approach, having found little influence of trade on relative labour demand and supply, conclude that trade can have had only a small influence upon relative wages. The study by Wood, on the other hand, suggests that trade has had a pronounced effect upon earnings and inequality. International trade theory shows that it is wrong to conclude that if trade has not influenced relative factor demands it cannot have had an effect upon relative factor rewards. Similarly, even if trade has led to changes in relative factor demands there need not be any effect upon relative factor rewards. In other words, there is no specific relationship between the factor content of trade and relative factor prices.

In the Heckscher-Ohlin model, with constant and identical technology in all countries, relative factor prices can only change as relative product prices vary. In a small country facing constant terms of trade, changes in trade flows will have no effect upon relative factor prices. In a large economy, movements in domestic economic variables may offset a change in the international environment so that relative product prices (and hence relative factor prices) remain unchanged. So, trade theory highlights the link between product prices and factor prices.

The correct framework for analysing the influence of more open trade upon relative factor returns is the Stolper-Samuelson theory. This states that a decline in the relative price of products intensive in the use of unskilled labour will reduce the real return to unskilled labour. The return to factors which are used less intensively will rise. The fall in the return to unskilled labour can happen even if the level of output is unaltered. So, in this framework we should not be surprised that the real wages of unskilled workers in industrial countries have declined, if increased trade with developing countries has reduced the relative price of unskilled labour intensive products.

However, the Stolper-Samuelson result is predicated on the assumptions which underlie the Heckscher-Ohlin model of trade. If the reason for trade lies in the presence of imperfect competition, economies of scale, and product differentiation then the Stolper-Samuelson effect can be offset or even overturned. Thus, an increase in intra-industry trade should have less of an impact upon income distribution within a country than an increase in inter-industry trade.

Initial experience suggests that trade liberalization between the EU and the countries of Eastern Europe has led to a substantial increase in intra-industry trade.[1] The fears of some that competition from producers in these countries would undermine employment and the wages of unskilled workers in the EU have not materialized. A similar feature is apparent for more open trade between the US and Mexico. Oliveira-Martins (1994) finds statistical evidence that in OECD countries import penetration has tended to reduce wages (there is no distinction between skilled and unskilled labour) in industries characterized by low product differentiation. Examples of these industries are textiles, wood products, and non-metallic mineral manufactures.

The Stolper-Samuelson theorem that changes in relative prices are the only channel through which relative returns can vary requires that technology is constant. Again, the effect of introducing technical change depends upon the nature of innovation (whether it is unskilled or skilled labour-saving) and whether it is concentrated in one sector. Assuming that technical progress is unskilled-labour saving, if innovation occurs in the skill-intensive sector, then with fixed product prices the relative wage of skilled labour will rise. Innovation in the unskilled, labour-intensive sector will raise the relative wage of unskilled labour.

As we saw above, the relative wage of unskilled labour will fall if unskilled-labour saving technical progress occurs in both sectors. This will encourage the substitution of unskilled for skilled labour, but this may not offset the initial decline in the use of unskilled labour due to the technological change. In industrial countries in the past twenty years there has been a substantial increase in the supply of skilled labour relative to unskilled workers. This increase in the endowment of skilled workers should have led to a fall in the price of the skill-intensive good, and a fall in the return to skilled relative to unskilled labour. Baldwin (1994) suggests that if unskilled-labour saving technological progress has been

---

[1] Between 1989 and 1993 the level of intra-industry trade in total trade with the EU rose from 36% to 48% for Bulgaria, from 29% to 58% for the former Czechoslovakia, for Hungary from 46% to 58%, from 39% to 45% for Poland, and from 21% to 31% for Romania (from Brenton 1995).

concentrated in the skill-intensive sector this could explain why the relative wage of skilled workers has risen despite a fall in the relative price of skill-intensive products. However, the terms of trade improvement (implying a rise in the relative price of skill-intensive goods) experienced by the US and the EU during periods of the 1980s does not fit with this explanation. Baldwin concludes that international competition must be introduced as an explanation for this relative price change. So, the fall in the relative wage of unskilled labour is due partly to technical progress being biased towards the skill-intensive sector, and partly to the fall in the relative price of the unskilled labour-intensive good due to increased international trade.

Again, the relative contributions of trade and technology need to be identified by empirical analysis. The fact that the ratio of skilled to unskilled labour has increased in most industries shows that increased openness to trade cannot be the sole or the major explanation for the increase in wage inequality between skilled and unskilled labour. However, the lack of empirical evidence means that it is not possible to conclude that trade has played an insignificant role in the relative decline in the wages of unskilled labour. There are reasons to believe that the effect of trade has not been negligible.

14.5　Implications for policy in the EU

The problems of declining employment opportunities for unskilled workers and rising wage inequality have not led to the response of widespread trade protection. The analysis above confirms that there is no strong evidence by which to conclude that trade has been the fundamental factor causing these trends. Even if it were, trade protection would not be appropriate. The fact that declining employment for unskilled labour has led to the persistent unemployment of a proportion of such workers suggests problems with the efficient working of labour markets.

Most economists advocate the removal of restrictions which constrain the ability of the labour market to work and suggest that there is a role for governments in increasing the supply of skilled labour. This can be achieved through investment in education and in training and retraining programmes. Some economists argue for greater redistribution of income from skilled to unskilled workers to offset, in part, the increase in wage inequality. Finally, there may be a case for intervention to stimulate technological innovation. Because of problems relating to securing a reasonable return on investments in R&D, firms may provide less than the socially optimal amount of funds for such activities. Further, in fragmented market structures there may be socially wasteful duplication of research effort.

Many of these arguments have been accepted by the Commission as reflected in the White Paper, 'Growth, Competitiveness and Employment'. This rejects protectionism as a suitable policy, but stresses the need for the liberalization of labour markets, investment in education and training, and policy towards technology. The Commission has adopted horizontal policies which are designed to affect the inputs used across industries and has rejected vertical policies which target the outputs of particular sectors. The latter policies have failed in the past to provide solutions to the problems of falling employment and declining relative wages for the unskilled.

However, the principal determinant of welfare within EU members will be domestic conditions in each state. Policies which facilitate strong growth of productivity are likely to have the greatest effect upon the rate of growth of living standards. Intervention to reduce the level of international trade, whilst having a distributional impact, will shrink the size of the cake that can be divided.

14.6 Summary

- Command GDP and real GDP have grown at similar rates in the EU, suggesting that 'competitiveness' is not an important issue at the national level.
- Trade could influence domestic labour markets in the EU countries, but the evidence suggests that it does not play a major role. Domestic technological developments could lower the demand for unskilled labour if progress is concentrated in skill intensive sectors or has a bias against unskilled labour.
- Policies of protection against imports from newly industrializing countries are not an appropriate response to the labour market problems of the European Union.

15

THE POLITICAL ECONOMY
OF PROTECTION

15.1 Introduction

Protectionist policies levied by a small country in an otherwise ideal world are inevitably a cause of economic inefficiency. The level of potential social welfare in this economy can only drop as a result. It is for this reason that they must be evidence of some kind of political failure, too. An ideal political system would follow rules that made the national pie as large as possible. Protection typically wastes some of that pie.

We can go further. There are plenty of circumstances that can give rise to a distortion. Markets could be incomplete. Insurance against all eventualities may be unavailable. Externalities may be present. Competition may be imperfect, due to increasing returns and sunk costs, let us say. The government may have obligations to provide public goods because the citizens are selfish and provide too few themselves; and this will create a need for distortionary taxes if lump-sum taxes are infeasible or ruled out on equity grounds. There could be unemployment, for any of a number of reasons. In all these cases, a tariff on imports *could* be better than nothing (although it might well make things worse, depending on the exact nature of the distortion). But it will always be true that removing the distortion at source must in principle achieve whatever gain a tariff could bring at lower cost. So we reach the same conclusion: trade barriers set up by government are wasteful, and testify to domestic political failure—a failure, for whatever reason, to apply the best response to the distortion.

This need not be true in a large economy, however. A large country can influence the prices at which it conducts trade. By restricting its imports, it can secure more favourable terms. Holding exports down can have the same effect: export prices are levered upwards, in terms of import prices. The damage from reduced trade volume can be more than outweighed by the benefit of improved terms of trade. Optimum tariffs on imports, or taxes on exports, maximize the net benefit from improved terms of trade, over and above the cost of lowered trade volume.

Yet improved terms of trade for one country are worsened terms of trade for its partners. At the world level, at least under otherwise ideal conditions, the inefficiencies that spring from reductions in the volume of trade can only make world income less than it would have been, and could have been, in their absence. So the presence of artificial barriers to trade created by national governments must testify to an international political failure.

Inside a small country, then, cooperation between interested parties to ensure maximum efficiency would be the hallmark of an efficient political system. A cooperative equilibrium to the game would necessarily entail free trade. This would also be true for large countries, when the game, and the definition of cooperative equilibrium, was extended to cover players in other countries too.

So why do we observe policy-induced trade barriers in the real world? Why do they take the form they do? This is the subject matter of the present chapter, which is devoted to the political economy of protection.

15.2 Autocrats and rent-seeking

This section starts by examining how an autocrat would tax trade. It then explores some lessons from history, and investigates the concept of rent-seeking.

15.2.1 Trade taxes levied by autocrats

Let us begin with an autocracy. Suppose that the ruler is motivated solely by greed. He faces some risk, let us say, of being removed by coup or revolution, if his exactions levied on the populace are perceived as too harsh; and the ruler has some unavoidable spending requirements on public goods (which could have the added advantage, for him, of making his removal less likely). But these are the only things that temper his actions, which are designed to maximize his expected stream of income. These assumptions might characterize the regimes of Ferdinand Marcos in the Philippines, or Colonel Mobutu of Zaire, or Papadoc Duvalier of Haiti. In the European arena, we might place the pre-1989 Communist régime in Romania in this category.

Avaricious tyrants will wish to maximize their receipts, then, subject to a constraint, perhaps, that the representative citizen's utility should not be driven below some threshold (at which he would revolt). If the tyrant's taxes take the form of imposts on consumption, and the economy is closed, the general solution to this problem is the same as Ramsey's optimum taxation principle, established in Ramsey (1927): the set of taxes should lower the compensated demand for every good by the same proportion. Ignoring cross-effects, this amounts to saying that the rate of tax on each good should be inversely proportional to the elasticity of compensated demand for it if all supply curves are horizontal. If they are not, it is the sum of the reciprocal of the demand elasticity and the reciprocal of the supply elasticity to which each tax should be proportional.

The problem with taxes levied on consumption and production for the tyrant, however, is that they are rather conspicuous. They also presuppose a very extensive (and expensive) army of tax-collectors. In a poor agricultural society, taxing income or consumption is hard, because farmers can eat their own product (and swap it with neighbours) unobservably. When the economy is open, this is where trade taxes have a big advantage. Levied at ports or border posts, they are much easier to collect. The citizenry, particularly if denied the right to travel or to information about the outside world, may hardly realize it is being taxed at all.

What the tyrant may do is to confer monopoly rights to import certain goods to members of his family or to state agencies or companies in which he has a controlling interest. Assuming that world prices are given, and that there is no domestic production of the good, the tyrant will mark up domestic prices by the reciprocal of the elasticity of domestic demand. If there is some production of the good at home, it will be the sum of the reciprocals of the demand and domestic supply elasticities by which prices are marked up above world levels. The similarity with the Ramsey formulae given earlier is no accident.

An equivalent device for the tyrant is to conduct an auction of the continuing monopoly right to sell the good at home. This way the ruler receives a capital sum, equal to the discounted present value of the revenue stream, up to an infinite horizon if the monopoly right is treated as irrevocable. The Bourbon kings of France behaved like this. The biggest incentive to bid for the import monopoly arises for the domestic producer for the good. If he is the sole domestic producer, he eliminates the problem of duopolistic competition between imports and home output. Price is pitched at world price times one plus the reciprocal of the home demand elasticity; home output is set where domestic marginal cost, if rising, matches the world price; if home production is too costly, it will be set at nil.

Either way, the ruler receives more income from the quantitative import restriction than from a tariff that lowers import volume to the same degree, if the good is produced at home by a single firm. The tariff makes that home firm a price-taker: it has no influence on the domestic price of the product, which is simply the world price plus the tariff. But a quota, whether it is the home producer that controls it or not, confers market power upon him. If he does not control the quota himself, the home firm may act as a Cournot duopolist, noticing that a production cutback leads to a rise in the price. So price exceeds marginal revenue (with the tariff, set at anything below prohibitive rates, these are equal). If he and the quota-holder collude, or if he controls the quota himself, the monopoly result follows, much to the detriment of consumers, but greatly to the gain of the tyrant.

It bears emphasis, however, that trade taxes involve deadweight loss. Had the ruler been anxious to extract surplus from his state in the least costly manner, he would have chosen lump-sum taxes. These would not have violated any conditions for efficient allocation of economic resources. But lump-sum taxes are costly in political terms: they were tried, in the form of poll taxes, in England in 1377, and with disastrous results. They led to the Peasants' Revolt, and came close to bringing down the government. What commends trade taxes is that they are less visible and cheaper to collect than alternative revenue sources, and that they can often, though not always, be tilted to fall most heavily on the rich.

Even an autocrat cannot take all decisions, however. He will often find it efficient to delegate certain authority. Subordinates are likely to do a better job if they share in rewards. The ruler has to rely on others for information. Information is power. Officials, military and police chiefs, judges, regional magnates, and party or religious leaders are all likely to participate in political decisions, including those on trade taxes. At this point, a brief excursion into economic history will help to explain why some governments, autocratic or less autocratic, are protectionist and others not, and the character of such trade taxes as are imposed.

15.2.2 Some evidence from history

In much of medieval Europe, retail trade was largely confined to fairs. These were often subject to regulation and fees levied by the Church. The Church also derived income from land it held directly and from harvest tithes on other land; its outgoings included some rudimentary provision of schooling, and hospital and social services. A few privileged communities, boroughs, won the right to regulate and tax their own trade fairs, with commerce controlled by guilds of specialized merchants. International trade was regulated and taxed by central government. The sketchily documented history of trade taxes stretches back 2,000 years to 'portoria', export–import duties levied on inter-provincial trade by the imperial fiscal authorities of ancient Rome. Portoria were a key component of their revenue, needed for many purposes—amongst them good pay for soldiers and bread and entertainment for the urban poor in Rome, without which an emperor's survival prospects would be grim.

Among the goods subject to heavy taxation in medieval and early modern Europe were condiments and spices, and particularly salt. Since their primary function was to preserve meat, or improve its flavour, these were progressive taxes: the diet of the poor rarely extended beyond grains and seasonal vegetables. Another merit, from the taxman's standpoint, was that they were typically imported. That meant few collection points, and little evasion (meat itself would have been untaxable). The new luxuries of tea, coffee, and tobacco came into this category in the seventeenth and eighteenth centuries. Many countries, particularly in Northern Europe where Protestantism and inappropriate local growing-conditions made them prime candidates for stiff import duties, also levied taxes on wines and spirits.

The states of early modern Europe seem to have differed markedly in their trade policies. Many of the richest families and institutions in pre-revolutionary France had acquired fiscal immunity; this, coupled with the perceived need for large military expenditures, made it strongly protectionist. The same was true of many other large, autocratically governed states. Trade taxes were understandably much lighter in city-states like Venice, where government was in the hands of merchant oligarchies, and fiscal arrangements were not unlike those in today's international entrepôt centres like Singapore and Hong Kong. For similar reasons the great Dutch Republic, easily Europe's most prosperous community in the seventeenth century, espoused free trade.

In England, fiscal decisions had long passed to ministers selected from, and answerable to, a Parliament where the landed interest was paramount. Little wonder, then, that it had legislated a set of regulations limiting international trade in wheat, a leading import after 1750. The 'Corn Laws' kept wheat and grain prices higher in England than outside it. The effect was to raise the income of landowners. This was a classic example of the Samuelson-Stolper tariff. Land was the factor used intensively in wheat and grain production. Franchise extension in the 1832 Reform Act shifted parliamentary representation in favour of manufacturing towns, which had previously sent hardly any members to Parliament, and the owners of capital and labour to whose interests the Corn Laws were clearly damaging.

Fourteen years later the Corn Laws were repealed, and Britain embarked on a policy of unfettered free trade. The policy was to last with no breaches until 1915, and in essentials until the inter-war slump, or even later: Britain reimposed her first taxes on imported food only after accession to the European Community in 1973 (and with considerable reluctance). Landowners suffered with the repeal of the Corn Laws, especially after world grain prices collapsed by two-thirds in the two decades after 1873. The real income of capital and labour rose sharply. France and Germany, on the other hand, reacted to the food price slump in international markets by levying tariffs on imported grain. Part of the reason for this, doubtless, was the greater political strength that farming and landowning interests could muster there than in nineteenth-century Britain. The Franco-German protection for grain farmers survives to this day in the form of the Common Agricultural Policy of the European Union.

The inferences that we may draw from this brief review of European historical experience are as follows. One is that taxes on trade are likelier in agricultural societies, where income and spending are harder to measure and to tax. Industrialization brings specialization and the spread of account-keeping practices in larger units of production, providing the basis for broad systems of direct and indirect taxation. It is chiefly for this reason that trade taxes are much more prevalent and exacting in contemporary Africa than in contemporary Europe. If the need for revenue is the key motive for taxing imports, and home production of import-substitutes is appreciable, why not simply tax consumption of these goods?

A second conclusion is that smaller polities tend to be warier of trade taxes than large ones. Consumption needs are likelier to depend on overseas supply. The proportion of the citizens who derive income from exports and trading will be higher. The government will be more sensitive to the need to avoid retaliatory tariffs levied by its trading partners.

A third, more tentative inference that one might draw is that democracy tends to favour freer trade. The fascist and communist régimes in twentieth-century Europe all adopted highly protectionist policies. Restrictions on foreign trade are the external, economic face of social and political *dirigisme*. Individuals' incomes are typically derived from the ownership of factors in specialized uses, while consumers' incomes are spent on a very wide range of goods. If democracy enthrones consumer interests it will display a constitutional aversion to taxing imports; if other forms of government give pride of place to a narrow range of producer interests, the extra producer surplus generated by tariffs on imports will receive greater political weight. As we shall see below, however, there are reasons for thinking that democracies can also sometimes succumb to protectionist pressures. Before examining that issue, however, we shall turn to an important additional argument against protection that has emerged from recent analyses of political economy: this concerns the notion of 'rent-seeking'.

15.2.3 Rent-seeking

Rent-seeking describes any non-productive activity designed to secure economic rewards. Lobbying for transfers from the State is one example. Lobbying for a monopoly right is a second; lobbying for protection, a third.

Lobbying uses up real resources. Computers, pen, ink, paper, telephones, copiers, printers, office space, and time—time of secretaries and assistants, time of officials and politicians, and time of the lobbyists themselves. Suppose two firms are contending for a certain privilege, which will be awarded to just one of them on a comparison of the quality of their submissions, and carries a prize valued at £1 million. How much will the two firms spend on the submissions they make? In equilibrium, if they are neutral to risk and do not collude, the answer will presumably be, up to £1 million.

What this implies is that much, possibly all, of the direct private producer benefits conferred by the granting of an economic privilege may be wasted on campaigning for it. We have argued that a tariff, let us say, levied by a small country generates valuable revenue to firms who produce that good at home. The extra surplus is the increase in their receipts, net of the rise in costs of production. True, there is also extra revenue to the authorities in the form of tariff receipts; but this, and the extra producers' surplus, has to be set against—and will necessarily fail to match—the resulting loss of consumers' surplus. The significance of the notion of rent-seeking is that the net social damage from protection may be seriously underestimated. What is spent on the dark arts of political persuasion has to be subtracted from (and might cancel) the addition to producers' surplus.

The standard partial equilibrium measure of the deadweight loss from protection (in a small, price-taking economy) is the sum of the two little triangles familiar from Chapter 9. Rent-seeking suggests this is too small. We need to add some, possibly all, of the quadrilateral of gain to domestic producers' surplus. On the most pessimistic assumption, that all the extra producers' surplus was wasted in this way, we would need to multiply the standard measure of deadweight loss by one plus the ratio of pre-tariff home output to half the tariff-induced fall in imports, and then adding in the little triangle directly above the production distortion, to arrive at a true figure of net loss. (This formula assumes that the domestic demand and supply curves are linear.)

If a certain tariff cuts imports by £2 million, therefore (half of this from reduced demand), and pre-tariff home production of the importable goods was £8 million, inclusion of its rent-seeking effects would increase our measure of the deadweight loss eightfold (plus an additional 50 per cent for the little triangle of extra producers' surplus above the production distortion). What would have been a deadweight loss of £1 million, let us say, before allowing for rent-seeking effects, becomes a loss of £8.5 million when they are included. Figure 15.1 illustrates this. Without taking rent-seeking into account, the deadweight loss is $b + d$. When it is, it increases to $a + b + d$.

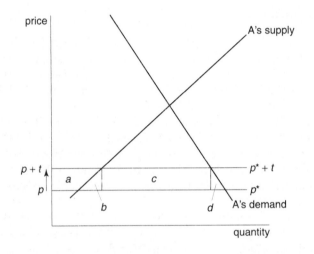

Fig. 15.1. The partial equilibrium effects of a tariff: rent-seeking may increase deadweight loss by area a

Turning from partial to general equilibrium, one way we may capture the effects of rent-seeking is to remove the resources devoted to it from the nation's endowment of factors of production. What that means is that the country's production possibility frontier is brought inwards. It simply shrinks. If lobbying uses a mix of resources, the way it moves inwards depends on a comparison of that mix with the mixes of inputs in the countries' 'other' industries.

Suppose there are two sectors, two factors of production, capital and labour, and that lobbying uses labour only. That would lead to a Rybczynski effect: at unchanged commodity prices, there would be a (modest) rise in the output of the capital-intensive product, and a (much bigger) fall in the output of the labour-intensive one. If the capital–labour ratio in lobbying lay between those in the economy's two productive industries, output would go down in both. These are interesting results, for they imply that a tariff of this kind, even one levied by a small country as is the case here, can lead to a fall, not a rise, in the domestic output of the importable once the rent-seeking effects are taken into account. Added to these output effects from shrinkage of the production possibility frontier would come the standard effects of moving along it in response to the alteration in relative prices.

One point to stress is this. Rent-seeking for tariffs can make tariffs far more damaging to potential social welfare than the case studied in Section 15.2.1 above, where the tariff revenues were siphoned off by the tyrant. This is paradoxical: a ruler's extortion strikes one as morally repugnant, much more so than 'honest' competition for rents. The reasoning is that a transfer to the ruler does not lead to a pure waste of resources, while rent-seeking does. And if social welfare is defined simply as the sum of all agents' utilities, with the marginal utility of income common and constant for all (including the ruler), redistribution between ruler and ruled leaves social welfare unaffected. Only when social welfare registers a sharp decline following transfers to the ruler shall we able to say that tariffs of that kind are more deleterious, in the main, than ones accompanied by rent-seeking.

However regrettable the waste of resources to which rent-seeking leads, an important distinction has to be drawn between exogenous and endogenous protection. Exogenous protection keeps the tariff rate fixed: the government announces, let us say, that it will put a 10 per cent tariff on imports of widgets, provided it is presented with a strong enough case for it. We then imagine that the owners of a factor of production used intensively in the widget sector, or of any factor specific to that sector, then hire smart young economists and other resources to produce some unanswerable arguments about the pervasive and dramatic social gains that this widget tariff will bring. The smart young economists are bid away from other uses, where their talents would have proved genuinely useful, instead of being prostituted to the PR business. The government, let us say, concedes that the tariff is worth having, and enacts it.

That is a case of exogenous protection, exogenous because the rate of tariff, if granted, is given. Endogenous protection is different. More and still smarter young economists can dream up even more effective arguments to bamboozle the authorities, with the result that the tariff rate that is granted increases above 10 per cent. With endogenous protection, the height of the tariff depends upon the quality of the case argued, and therefore with the cost of resources needed to develop it.

Endogenous (or exogenous) tariffs may be given not only in response to eloquent research papers. Agricultural protection in Europe may be defended (or enhanced) by other means. When farmers drive their tractors at walking speed, in line abreast, down the highways of France, they are using up their time and gasoline to remind the powers that be of their importance. This is standard rent-seeking activity. But on top of this comes the massive externality of delays enforced on countless others. The externality dimension to this kind of lobbying-by-blackmail also needs to be brought into the picture.

Suppose that those who gain from the tariff can behave as a cohesive group (a somewhat doubtful assumption, as we shall see). How much should they spend on presenting their case? They will be in equilibrium if (a) they select the least-cost combination of inputs for lobbying and (b) lobby up to the point where the expected marginal gain, in terms of the enhanced tariff rate conferred, just balances the marginal cost.

To these conditions we must add a second-order condition: here, this is that marginal cost cut marginal revenue from below. There is also a side-condition to rule out a corner solution of no lobbying. What is gained from lobbying must not fall short of the total cost. Panels (1) and (2) of Figure 15.2 depict cases where all these conditions are met. In case (1), the costs of lobbying are less than the gains. In case (2) they are equal. In panel (3) the optimal interior solution, where the gains from lobbying are parallel, at point E, to the costs, is none the less ruled out, because such a point is unprofitable. It is better for the interest group in panel (3) to avoid lobbying and live with free trade.

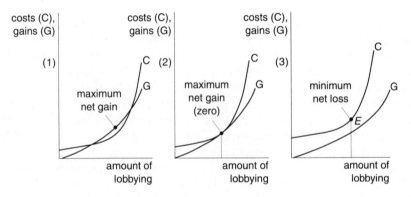

Fig. 15.2. Private gains and costs from lobbying

The welfare ranking of these three cases is straightforward, because each involves the same rate of tariff, or none. With the simplest social-welfare function, that makes the distribution of income between domestic residents a matter of indifference, case (3) will be best because there is no tariff and no shrinkage of resources due to lobbying costs. Next comes (1), with its disadvantageous tariff; but (1) has the advantage over (2) of shrinking resources less. In more complex cases, welfare comparisons are more intricate. But it will always be true, all else equal, that smaller endogenous tariffs are less damaging than bigger ones (assuming they bring no indirect benefit), for two reasons: less waste of resources on lobbying, and smaller distortions in the patterns of consumption and production.

Furthermore, we do gain one crumb of comfort from Figure 15.2. This is the fact that lobbyists in equilibrium can never spend more on lobbying than the private gain that lobbying confers. Panel (3) testifies to that. But it is perfectly possible for lobbyists to be in equilibrium by spending less than what they gain. This is the case in panel (1). If panel (1) is typical, the production possibility frontier shrinkage will still apply, but it will be quantitatively much less alarming than the case depicted in panel (2). Panel (1) would imply, in partial equilibrium terms, that a healthy chunk of area a in Figure 15.1 would remain as net gain to producers' surplus in our earlier diagram, and hence not be added to $b + d$ as social loss. Rent seeking may not be quite so bad after all.

Another argument that qualifies the view that rent-seeking leads to a massive increase in our estimates of the economic damage done by tariffs is this. We really have to doubt whether the parties that gain from it are sufficiently cohesive to lobby in the manner described above. Let us assume perfect competition. When all factors are perfectly mobile within the economy, the gainers are the owners of the scarce factor (wherever it works) that is used intensively in the importable sector on which tariff privileges are conferred. In the presence of domestic factor immobility, it is the owners of factors specific to the industry in question. It is not the 'firm or firms producing the importable'—that is a facile view, the weaknesses of which become apparent as soon as we start to think in general equilibrium terms.

It is clear, therefore, that the gainers could be a numerous group of individuals, possibly even almost everyone in the economy in the mobile-factor case (though many of them could lose out from the fall in rewards to other factors). Getting all these people to coordinate their decisions, and their subscriptions to the lobby, will be no small matter. There will be a strong incentive for them to free ride. 'The lobby may produce gain for me if it succeeds,' people will think, 'but whether it succeeds or not will hardly depend on my subscribing towards its costs, which will only make me poorer.' It will be very difficult, and probably impossible, for the lobby to ensure that gains are confined to lobby-subscribers. In the case of England's Corn Laws there was no difficulty, because many of the big landowners played a major part in framing laws themselves as members of Parliament. (This made their grain tariffs resemble peculation by the tyrant himself.) But this was probably a very special case.

So far we have presented tariffs as mechanisms of extortion by political leaders, or as prizes to lobbies which are granted when they employ enough resources to dress up their political case for them in sufficiently persuasive terms (the rent-seeking case). This does not exhaust the list of possibilities. We have so far taken a somewhat naïve and unflattering view of the political process and those participating in it. We have also emphasized what are probably the most negative features of the activities that give rise to tariffs (bare-faced peculation on the one side, and the waste of resources posed by rent-seeking on the other). In the following sections, we shall describe two other types of approach to the political economy of protection.

15.3 Protection and the political process

We begin by investigating the role of lobbies, politicians and elections in protection, and then examine what happens when tariff rates set by governments are endogenous.

15.3.1 Lobbies, politicians, and elections

Political propaganda is like advertising. It has an informative role, which may be helpful. Voters get to learn more of rival candidates' political platforms, and may therefore make better and more informed decisions on their ballot papers. There is also a persuasive effect, and that may be meretricious. Voters may have a tendency to vote for the party whose messages they have heard longest, most often, or last.

In the United States, there are no limits on what politicians may spend fighting elections. Some European countries do restrict direct expenditure by individual candidates, and apply rules to broadcasting time that individual parties are allotted. But there are typically no ceilings on what parties can spend on newspaper and hoarding advertisements. In elections to national legislatures in Europe, it is not uncommon for all the parties together to spend at least two Deutsche Mark, or about eight French francs or £1, per elector on political campaigning. In the United States, the total annual average figure, including presidential, congressional, gubernatorial, and state legislature elections, both final and primary, is much higher than this.

Where do these political campaigning costs come from? One source is individual party membership subscriptions. But this produces little more than small change. The main contributions come from firms and, to a lesser extent, trade unions. Some firms' contributions are channelled via pressure or interest group bodies.

Political parties and politicians will frame their political programmes with the overriding objective of winning elections. This means tailoring proposals so that they command wide appeal. But appeal will not be forthcoming unless the message gets across, which means finance. The political programme must be devised to appeal to contributors. It also reflects awareness, in equilibrium, of what the rival party or parties are proposing.

Suppose there is a political duopoly. One party's probability of electoral victory, its maximand, will be a function of its programme, its rival's programme, and the two parties' propaganda messages (in volume, as well as content). The messages and the programme are linked to a budget constraint. The constraint depends on contributions, which are themselves influenced by programmes offered by the party and its rival. Parties optimize by trading off direct-voter appeal against contributor-appeal (which indirectly affects voters too, via the messages that contributions buy); and one party's programme choice is also sensitive to its rivals'.

Voters dislike tariffs, in the main, because they will see that they raise the prices of the goods they buy, although particular groups of voters may be attracted by the prospects of higher or securer income. But parties may propose tariffs because that attracts contributions. Firms and lobbies choose what to contribute to whom as a simple portfolio decision, based on expected returns from the policies on offer. Tariff or import quota proposals are, of course, only one aspect of the economic elements in a party's programme: other aspects will include proposals on income, indirect and corporation tax rates, policies towards the regulation of monopolies, state procurement, and employment.

In very simple cases, where there is just one dimension on which voters' attitudes differ, the two parties may in equilibrium propose identical programmes, in an attempt to secure the approval of the median voter. But competition for contributions, and limits on the information available to voters that make these contributions, and, so importantly, the messages they buy, will generally prevent this outcome. When voters are worried by two or more issues, and have heterogeneous attitudes towards them, the median voter can no longer typically be identified.

What results from a story like this is a set of endogenous tariffs the character and height of which depends on a number of variables. One critical one is the quality of voter information. The better this is, the less powerful messages will be; and the smaller the contributions that parties will seek, and the lower the tariffs or other special-interest concessions that they will be forced to concede. This reinforces the point made at the start of this chapter, that what ultimately explains phenomena like tariffs is some kind of political failure.

Another is the size of the group that benefits from such concessions. The free-riding argument discussed in Section 15.2.3 above suggests that small groups may be more powerful than large ones when it comes to the clout provided by political contributions (although the opposite is true, clearly, in the ballot box). It is a generic feature of tariffs that the losers are very numerous, with each bearing only a small loss, while the gains are highly concentrated. The more concentrated these gains, the more each beneficiary stands to benefit, and the weaker the free-riding obstacle to getting them.

The model just described is a sketch of a number of theories propounded by some American economists. The massive scale of political campaign expenses, and the political duopoly, are clearly features of the US political system that do not carry over to the same extent to polities in Western Europe. There is another difference. The US has great latitude in setting its own commercial policies. It is bound to respect its international agreements under GATT (and its successor from 1995, the World Trade Organization). It is also obliged to adhere to free trade in a large class of products with Canada, and, from 1994, with Mexico. But these commitments still leave room, under its own legislation, for a wide range of countervailing duties, and non-tariff barriers, that can be levied on particular products from other countries.

Western European countries that are members of the European Union (and this only excludes Norway and Switzerland after January 1995) do not set tariffs or restrictions on non-EU imports themselves. This is a matter for the European Commission. In the West European context, therefore, the leverage that political parties enjoy in the various nation states is very limited. All they can do is lobby for changes in common external trade barriers, with little prospect of success unless they can secure a wide measure of support for governing parties in several other EU member states. External trade policy has therefore come to disappear from the agenda in national elections. For Norway and Switzerland, however, and for the emerging democracies of Central and Eastern Europe, this is not so.

This section has concentrated on elections. Elections are only one aspect of the political process, however. It is also worth remembering that promises delivered at the hustings may not be honoured after victory in the polls. Parties that do this lose credibility, and endanger future contributions; but the next election may be many years away, and politicians may be deflected by more immediate concerns. We shall turn now to a rather different explanation of endogenous tariffs, which places focus on the party in government rather than on the party facing the electorate.

15.3.2 Endogenous tariffs: the Grossman-Helpman model

No government likes to be hated. Let us assume that it seeks to maximize the goodwill towards it on the part of the governed. Goodwill may be sought for its own sake, or because it makes the task of governing less unpleasant, or because it is associated with improved prospects of eventual re-election.

Goodwill is likely to have two key elements. First, there is 'social welfare' to consider. Social welfare will presumably be some increasing function of the utilities of all residents. It could be their sum or their product, for example. The social welfare function is called Utilitarian in the first case, or Benthamite; in the second, it is often named after Champernowne, who first proposed that functional form.

The second element in goodwill will consist of expressions of support by lobbies. Such support might take the form of political contributions, of the kind considered in either Section 15.2.1 or Section 15.3.1 above. Or it may mean something closer to acquiescence or consent, the absence of complaint, troublesome publicity, or noisy demonstrations. In general, we may think of goodwill as an increasing function of social welfare (however defined) on the one side, and lobby support on the other. It could be their weighted sum.

When it comes to protection, groups that have perhaps the strongest incentive to organize as lobbies are the owners of specific factors attached to the various industries in the economy. A tariff on an imported good will raise the incomes of those who own a factor specific to the domestic industry producing that good, if there is one. A subsidy on exports will do the same for owners of a factor specific to the exportable industry in question.

If there were perfect mobility of all factors of production in the economy, and all factors were employed in several industries, no factors would be specific. But it takes time for factors to migrate between industries, often far longer than the life of a Parliament. Labour is often trained to do a specialized task, with skills that are not easily transferred from one industry to another; much of the economy's stock of capital is in this category, too, particularly machinery. Let us simplify matters by assuming that every sector employs one mobile factor and one specific one.

If our country is small it is a price-taker in world markets. There is no terms-of-trade benefit to be had from taxing trade. Let us assume that this is so. Let us also dispense with all of the problematical wrinkles that can cause a country to gain from imposing trade restrictions as a second-best device (such as unemployment, factor market distortions, externalities, and the like). Let us further assume that the social-welfare function is indifferent to distribution (or, if not, that there exist other ways of securing an optimal distribution of income costlessly). This being so, we can be sure that our government will never protect any of its industries if its goodwill consists solely of social welfare.

When political support from organized, potentially noisy lobbies is a constituent of goodwill towards the government, however, this result will not follow. The lobbies consist, we have supposed, of at least some of the sets of specific factor owners. Let some groups of specific factor owners be represented by organized lobbies, and others not. What will the government do?

The answer is that it will confer some positive protection on the 'lobby industries'. When the industry produces an importable, it will be given a tariff to shelter behind. The tariff will induce a rise in that industry's output, and an increased reward, for sure, to the factor specific to it. If a lobby industry produces an exportable, it will be given an export subsidy, with similar effects on the specific factor's rent. Non-lobby industries, on the other hand, will be given negative protection. Imports of those goods will be subsidized, and exports taxed.

The size of these tariffs and subsidies, positive or negative, will be sensitive to demand and supply conditions. If domestic demand and supply are highly inelastic, resulting deadweight losses will be very small. The opposite is true when these curves are very elastic. Steep tariffs or subsidies on such products, of either sign, will be very distortionary.

Another relevant consideration will be the range of industries covered by lobbies. If this is small, we can expect quite large positive import tariffs or export subsidies, as the case may be, on the industries included by lobbying. The other sectors will be given relatively light negative protection. The opposite will be true when most industries are represented by organized lobbies.

The size of the industry's output will matter, too: the bigger this is, the greater the political muscle its specific factor owners can exert when they are organized as a lobby, so the higher protection it will get. A large industry not covered by a lobby can expect larger 'disprotection' because there are more political gains to be had from transferring income from its specific factor owners to others.

The final determinant of the height of protection will be the way that goodwill is weighted between social welfare as against lobby support. The larger the relative weight on the former, the more modest all the rates of protection will be.

A precise formula for all tariff and subsidy rates, which reflects the various considerations we have discussed in an exact algebraic form, can be found in

Grossman and Helpman (1994). They devised the model we have been discussing in this section.

15.4 Summary

- In a small country, protection represents a political failure to secure ideal, maximum efficiency; in a large one, a political failure to secure international cooperation.
- Taxes on trade tend to be higher in developing than industrial societies, and in larger and/or more authoritarian countries.
- Lobbying for protection wastes real resources, with Rybczynski effects on production patterns. Such costs are amplified if protection rates are endogenous. Endogenous protection may result from electoral processes, or government sensitivity to particular interest groups.

16

TRADE AND THE ENVIRONMENT

16.1 Introduction

The heightened concern over degradation of the environment has coincided with increasing international economic integration. This has led environmentalists to question the presumption that trade liberalization is beneficial. International trade increases the volume of production of goods, and influences the pattern of production and consumption in different countries. If the production or consumption of some of these goods has detrimental effects upon the environment which are not fully reflected in the costs of production, then more trade may impinge upon the quality of the environment, leading some environmentalists to advocate the use of restrictive trade policies for environmental reasons. Alternatively, by raising income levels and the demand for environmental quality, more open trade could lead to an improvement in the environment. In short, trade policies have environmental consequences.

In addition, environmental policies will affect trade. A fear has been expressed that countries will intentionally reduce their environmental protection below the socially optimal level so as to give domestic firms a competitive advantage in home and foreign markets. This ecological dumping will lead to a deterioration in the environment, as governments compete with each other in a downward spiral of standards.

The criterion adopted by economists for defining optimal environmental policies is that the cost of preventing an additional unit of pollution (the marginal abatement cost) should be just equal to the cost of an additional unit of pollution (the marginal damage cost). This implies that the optimal level of pollution is not zero. It also means that the extent of environmental protection will differ from country to country, depending upon the endowment of environmental resources and the preferences of citizens towards the environment. Here we equate abundance of environmental resources with a relatively large capacity to absorb pollution, the physical ability of land, air, and water to engross waste and pollution.

In this chapter we look at the relationship between trade and the environment. We will evaluate the arguments that trade liberalization should be foregone to prevent further damage to the environment, that trade will lead to ecological dumping, and that trade policies should be used to encourage countries to participate in international environmental agreements and then to enforce such agreements. A feature of recent research on the incentives for distortion of environmental policies, which is discussed in the chapter, is the importance of allowing for imperfectly competitive markets so as to take account of possible strategic behaviour by both governments and firms.

16.2 Trade liberalization and the environment

In previous chapters we have seen that standard trade theory predicts that more open trade will be beneficial to both importing and exporting countries. Some 'environmentalists' have recently argued against trade liberalization, suggesting that any gains from increased trade will be outweighed by the costs of greater damage to the environment. In this Section we assess whether the recommendation for free trade can be supported when the good or goods which are traded generate pollution. The pollution could be caused in either the act of production, the act of consumption, or in both. The analysis merely acts to reinforce the conclusions of Chapter 9, which showed that in the presence of negative externalities more open trade may reduce welfare, but that the best policy is to directly target the source of the externality. Trade policies are at the utmost second-best and, in practice, are likely to be third-best policies.

The standard analysis (see, for example, Anderson 1992) assumes that the country under consideration is small, so that changes in trade have no effect upon the world prices of the goods concerned. Further, there are no other distortions affecting other markets. The environmental implications of trade liberalization depend upon whether the country being studied will be an importer or an exporter of the good at the world price. We consider each possibility separately.

Consider, first, a single good which generates pollution in production, for example, clothing, where effluent from the colour dyeing of garments pollutes local rivers. In the absence of any other policies, trade liberalization will improve the environment and unambiguously raise the welfare of the country if the good is imported. Welfare is the sum of the surplus of producers and the surplus of consumers less the costs of any damage to the environment. The gains from trade are reinforced by a fall in pollution as domestic production of the good declines.

If the country exports the good after trade liberalization, then the gains from trade may be offset by a decline in environmental quality, the volume of production of the good will rise, and welfare may fall. However, as we shall see, if optimal environmental policies are in place then gains from trade liberalization will be guaranteed.

Figure 16.1 shows, firstly, the case of an importing country. Pollution is generated in production. This negative externality will lead to a divergence between marginal private costs (MPC) of producing the good and the marginal social costs (MSC), the difference being equal to the marginal costs of pollution. Now trade liberalization, the removal of the tariff on imports of t, will reduce the price

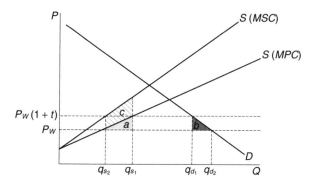

Fig. 16.1. The effects of trade liberalization for a small country importing a good which generates pollution in production

paid by consumers to the world price, P_w. This will stimulate an increase in the demand for the good from q_{d1} to q_{d2}. Producers, basing their decisions on the private costs of production, will contract supply in the face of a lower selling price, from q_{s1} to q_{s2}. Trade liberalization, then, brings the traditional welfare gains of the triangles a and b. There is an additional benefit as the decline in domestic production leads to a fall in the level of pollution. This is shown by the area c.

The welfare gains from trade liberalization for such an importing country will be reduced if it has already in place optimal policies to deal with the pollution. Starting from the tariff-ridden situation, the optimal environmental policy would be a tax on producers of t_{e1}, set at the point where the marginal social benefit (as reflected by the price of the good) equals the marginal social cost. Another way of expressing this is that the optimal policy is the one which equates the marginal abatement cost with the marginal damage cost. Figure 16.2 shows that the welfare gain from the improvement in the environment following this policy is given by

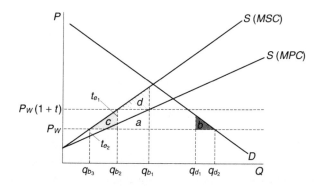

Fig. 16.2. The effects of trade liberalization for a small country importing a good which generates pollution in production: optimal environment policy in place

the area *d*. Trade liberalization will now generate gains of the areas *e* and *b*. Following trade liberalization, the optimal environmental policy would be a tax of t_{e2}. The welfare gain of *e* is smaller than the area *a*, so that the gain from trade liberalization is smaller once the optimal environmental policy is in place.

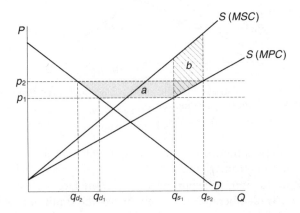

Fig. 16.3. The effects of trade liberalization for a small country exporting a good which generates pollution in production

We now consider, in Figures 16.3 and 16.4, the case of a small country which exports a good which generates pollution in production. Here trade liberalization, such as the removal of an export tax, leads to an increase in the price faced by producers and consumers from p_1 to p_2, the latter being the world price. This leads to a contraction of demand and a rise in exports and an increase in welfare shown, in Figure 16.3, by the area *a*, the vertically shaded area. However, the increase in output raises the emissions of pollutants which has a negative effect upon welfare shown by the (horizontally shaded) area, *b*. It is perfectly feasible that the loss from greater degradation of the environment could exceed the benefits from trade liberalization.

If optimal environmental policies are used to counter pollution then trade liberalization will raise welfare. In Figure 16.4 before trade liberalization, when the price in the market is p_1, the optimal environmental policy is a tax of t_{e1}. This fully internalizes the externality by ensuring that marginal social costs equal marginal private costs. The benefit from lower levels of pollution is shown by the area *d*. The tax leads to a contraction of output from q_{s1} to q_{s2} and for each unit of output that is lost the social cost, shown by $S(MSC)$, exceeded the social benefit (represented by p_1).

Trade liberalization, and the consequent increase in exports, brings a welfare gain shown by the area *c*. This increase in output from q_{s2} to q_{s3} increases the amount of pollution. However, it does not have a negative effect upon welfare, because the presence of the environmental policy ensures that for each extra unit

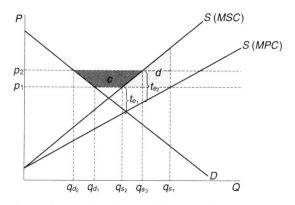

Fig. 16.4. The effects of trade liberalization for a small country exporting a good which generates pollution in production: optimal environmental policy in place

of output the social benefit equals the social cost. As output rises the size of the environmental tax rises, with the optimal tax in the liberal trade equilibrium being t_{e2}. Hence trade liberalization unambiguously raises welfare if optimal environmental policies are in place.

The above analysis has considered a good which generates pollution in production. If pollution occurs in the act of consumption, for example, the creation of litter from eating confectionery, then trade liberalization will unambiguously benefit an exporting country, whilst welfare may fall if the country imports the good. Again, if optimal environmental policies are in place then welfare gains from trade liberalization will be ensured.

Finally, we will show that trade policies can always be used to achieve environmental objectives, but that they will be less efficient than other policies which can be more directly targeted at the source of the pollution. Figure 16.5 returns to the case of the small exporting country which produces a good which generates pollution in production. At the world market price of p_1 the optimal environmental policy is a tax of t_e, which reduces output from q_{s1} to q_{s2}, generating a welfare gain of a. This improvement in the environment could be achieved by an export tax which has the effect of reducing the price to p_2 and hence output to q_{s2}. The export tax, however, gives rise to an additional distortion, in consumption, which leads to a loss of welfare denoted by the triangle b. Thus, the welfare gain to the country of achieving a given level of environmental improvement is lower when an export tax rather than an environmental tax is used. In fact, the area b could exceed the size of area a so that overall welfare could fall, if trade policy is used to achieve environmental objectives.

In reality producers are not identical, as assumed above, so that some generate more pollution than others. In this case a tax on output which is uniform across all producers would not be efficient, since the output of the most highly polluting firms would decline at the same rate as the less environmentally damaging producers. Trade policies would be an even more inefficient means of addressing the

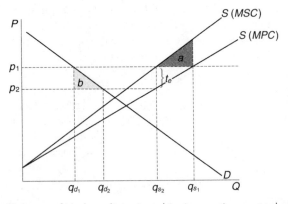

Fig. 16.5. The inefficiency of trade policies in achieving environmental objectives

negative externality. The optimal policy in this case would be a tax levied per unit of pollution.

What if the optimal environmental policies are not available to the country? In a second-best world the clear ranking of policies is no longer feasible, and it is possible that trade policies may increase welfare. Although such cases can be found in principle, it is difficult to generalize to provide practical guidelines. This, together with a range of empirical evidence, leads to the presumption that even in a second-best situation trade policies should not be used to tackle environmental problems. A number of studies have found that trade policies have little impact upon the source of pollution, so that large-scale resource misallocation is likely to result from intervention into international trade. In fact, intervention to correct for environmental effects using trade policies may worsen the environment.

Deforestation of tropical rainforests is a well-known environmental problem.[1] The source of the externality leading to the over-exploitation of timber reserves is, however, often internal rather than a result of international trade. Problems of identifying and enforcing property rights, the presence of monopolistic practices, uncertainty, government subsidies, and the design of logging contracts are the key factors underlying deforestation. The majority of timber felled in developing countries is for domestic consumption. Studies of the effectiveness of trade policies as a means of controlling deforestation in Indonesia and Brazil have demonstrated their inefficiency. Restrictions on exports depress the price of timber in the domestic economy and lead to an increase in the quantity of timber used in domestic production, and the ban on exports of logs from Indonesia may have increased domestic consumption by as much as 10 per cent. It should be remembered that policies in the EU and other Western economies which constrain the amount of timber imported from developing countries would have a similar effect.

---

[1] This example is derived from the summary in Beghin *et al.* (1994).

So far we have limited our analysis to considering a small open economy. We know that if the country can influence the terms at which it trades then policies which constrain the amount of trade may raise domestic welfare. Again assuming that pollution is generated in production, then if the optimal environmental policies are available, the first-best strategy would require the use of two instruments: a tariff on imports (or export tax if the country exports the good) to improve the terms of trade, and an environmental tax to offset the pollution. If the environmental policy cannot be implemented and only trade policies are available then the effect of constraining trade on the level of pollution must be considered. The tariff (export tax) which maximizes the benefit from the improvement in the terms of trade may not be the optimal tariff or tax. If the country is an importer (or exporter) of the good the tariff (or export tax) which maximizes welfare in the country will be lower (or higher) than that which extracts the most rent from foreigners. The importer of the good must take into account the increase in pollution that accompanies a rise in the output of domestic firms following the imposition of the tariff. Similarly, if the country exports the good the benefit to the environment from constraining exports with a tax must be added to the gain from a rise in the relative price of exports.

A perhaps more realistic case, given that tariffs and export taxes do not appear to be imposed for terms of trade reasons and the GATT has constrained their application, is where only environmental policies are available. Here the optimal pollution tax will be higher (or lower) for an exporting (or importing) country than that which would fully reflect the divergence between private and social costs, because of the additional effects upon the terms of trade. For the exporter there are benefits from pushing up the price of the good and, in the absence of an export tax, environmental policies can be used to achieve this aim. Thus, in addition to improving the environment, such policies bring terms-of-trade gains. For the importer, on the other hand, there are gains to be had from allowing domestic production to rise, by relaxing environmental policy, and so reducing import demand and pushing down import prices.

This shows that countries may distort their environmental policies to take account of trade effects. However, it does not support the case of those who argue that the interaction between trade and environmental policies will lead to 'ecological dumping', where countries deliberately lower their environmental standards to prevent activity migrating to countries with lower standards. A standard approach has been to extend trade theory to take account of environmental issues by treating the environment as an additional resource. Countries differ in their environmental resources and the preferences of their residents for the state of the environment. Countries well-endowed with environmental resources will tend to specialize in the production of pollution-intensive goods. The analysis above shows that such countries will want to set environmental policies which are stricter than those which fully internalize the externality. This casts doubt on the view that countries well-endowed with environmental resources, usually thought to be the poorer, developing countries, where low incomes constrain concern for the environment, will wish to become havens for polluting industries. We shall return to the issue of the links between trade and environmental policies below, when we consider if the analysis is modified with imperfect competition. We note, finally, that if pollution is generated in consumption, then the above arguments hold in reverse: importers will set environmental standards which are stricter than the first-best rule for dealing with the pollution.

16.3 Transboundary pollution

The analysis above has considered the case for trade policy in the presence of an externality which causes pollution within the confines of the domestic country. A more intractable problem arises if pollution spills over national boundaries and has regional effects, such as acid rain, or impacts upon the global environment, as in the case of the emission of greenhouse gases. The principal implication of transboundary pollution is that policies which may be optimal for a country taking account of only its own interests may not be the best from the regional or global perspective. However, again the most effective policy to improve the environment will be that most directly targeted at the source of the pollution. Trade policies are likely to be inappropriate.

The most efficient way to implement policies to tackle transboundary pollution is through international cooperation. International cooperation permits the design of policies with the world or region concerned being treated, in effect, as a single country. Economists have strongly argued that international solutions are required to address the problem of global warming. The Montreal agreement on reducing CFCs (the cause of ozone depletion) highlights the fact that coordinated policies can be agreed and implemented at an international level. The Montreal Agreement is, however, primarily an agreement between rich industrial countries. An international agreement on greenhouse gases would have to include developing countries.

The problem with international agreements is that, whilst their implementation may be optimal from a global point of view, they often neglect the effect upon welfare of individual countries. Thus some countries may experience a lower level of welfare under the optimal global policy than under some other form of intervention, such as trade policy. In other words, not all countries will have the same incentives to participate in international agreements, and for some there may be a disincentive. This has led to the suggestion that the threat of trade sanctions be used to discourage the free-rider problem which is inherent in international agreements, and to encourage cooperation. The Montreal agreement referred to above provides for trade measures against countries which act against the terms of the agreement.

Of course, an alternative mechanism to encourage countries to participate in international action against pollution is to provide them with compensation. Subramanian (1992) shows that the choice between the compensation or sanction mechanism to encourage compliance has an important effect upon the distribution of welfare between countries in the post agreement situation. We assume here that the rich industrial countries are seeking to encourage the poorer developing countries to participate in agreements to reduce transboundary pollution. If the developing countries were persuaded to join with compensation then they would achieve a higher level of welfare than if the threat of trade sanctions had been used. This is because the threat of trade sanctions implies that the outcome for the developing countries will be worse in the absence of an international agreement. This then reduces the bargaining position of these countries in the negotiations. Thus, the principal issue in allowing the rich countries the potential to use trade sanctions unilaterally to promote international environmental agreements is the distributional impact upon the developing countries. The threat of sanctions leads to a larger share of world welfare going to the rich countries.

Within a country the 'polluter pays principle' (PPP) is a sensible approach to the implementation of environmental policies. If a factory discharges waste into a river then the appropriate response is to introduce a tax on the output of the factory, such that the marginal costs of abatement are equal to the marginal costs of pollution. This provides an incentive for the search for methods of production which generate less pollution. The alternative is the 'victim pays principle' (VPP) whereby the polluting firm receives subsidies to reimburse the costs incurred in cutting pollution. The use of PPP in effect means that the environment is the property of the citizens of the country. Under VPP, property rights are assigned to the polluter.

At the international level the assignment of property rights to environmental resources becomes much more difficult. Permitting rich countries to threaten the use of trade sanctions to encourage developing countries to participate in international environmental agreements implies that the latter countries are the source of the pollution. China, for example, is a major contributor to current global emissions of greenhouse gases. However, environmental problems such as global warming arise from the stock of pollution. Accordingly, it is the rich countries which have contributed most to the problem, and compensation should flow to the developing countries. In other words, compensation could be consistent with the PPP.

There are two instances when the threat of trade sanctions may be useful. Firstly, to combat genuine free-riders, that is, individual countries which deliberately refrain from participating in an international agreement so as to benefit from the improvement in the global environment without having to contribute to the costs of achieving a cut in levels of pollution. The second instance is where trade sanctions provide a means of punishment to ensure compliance once agreements have been achieved. In both cases it is important to recognise that sanctions would be imposed on a multilateral basis. The unilateral use of trade policies would not be relevant. Trade sanctions are, however, unlikely to be the most efficient policies to achieve these aims, although they may be the easiest to implement.

16.4 Ecological dumping

Policies designed to reduce the level of pollution of domestic firms may affect the costs of production of these firms. This has led to a number of opposing arguments concerning the effects of environmental policies on the competitiveness of domestic firms in pollution intensive industries. Industrialists, on the one hand, argue that tough environmental policies, relative to those of other nations, undermine their ability to compete. Environmentalists, on the other hand, fear that this concern with the competitiveness of domestic firms in highly polluting sectors will lead to a relaxation of environmental protection. In the absence of trade policies it is argued that governments may distort their environmental policies to protect domestic firms. It has been proposed that there should be international harmonization of environmental regulations, but, failing that, imports from countries with relatively weak environmental standards should be subject to countervailing tariffs. The latter policies find support from the industrialists.

An alternative view, espoused by Porter (1991), is that a country which now imposes environmental policies which are tougher than those of other countries will help domestic firms to have a competitive advantage in the longer term. The reasoning is that tough environmental policies will encourage the development of new, less polluting technologies of production before firms in other countries, and that this will improve the long-run profitability of the domestic firms; thus there is no conflict between strict environmental regulations and long-run economic performance.

The analysis earlier in this chapter provides no support for the notion that countries will engage in ecological dumping. If markets are competitive then there is no incentive for governments to reduce their environmental standards below the optimal level, the level at which the marginal cost of abatement is just equal to the marginal damage caused by pollution. We also saw that if the government has market power, in the sense that it can influence the terms of trade, but cannot use trade policies, then countries which export commodities whose production is pollution-intensive will be encouraged to set environmental policies which are too strict.

Countries will differ in their environmental policies because of differences in environmental endowments and in preferences towards the environment. It is not unreasonable that, because of their low incomes, the citizens of poor countries place less value on the environment than the citizens of wealthy countries. The fact that poorer countries tend to export the more pollution-intensive goods can be interpreted as these countries exploiting a comparative advantage in these goods. Policies in the rich countries which distort trade by placing countervailing import taxes on pollution-intensive goods from the poor countries will produce an inefficient outcome and constrain the incomes of the poorest countries.

There is some evidence that for certain pollutants there is an inverted-U-shaped relationship between emissions and income per head (see Grossman and Krueger 1992). In other words, as income rises from a low level there is an increase in pollution; then, at some average level of development, emissions reach a maximum. Subsequent growth leads to decreasing levels of pollution. As growth occurs the scale of economic activity increases, and so pollution rises. With unfettered trade there will also be a tendency towards specialization. At low levels of income this will shift resources towards more pollution-intensive industries. However, open trade will also tend to highlight and make available more efficient production techniques, which will typically be less polluting. As income rises there will be greater demand for more stringent environmental standards. In the longer run environmental standards in different countries may be expected to converge. The decline in emissions at higher levels of income is not typical of all pollutants. For example, the contributions of rich countries to global warming, in terms of emissions of greenhouse gases, do not appear to have declined as they have become richer.

If, however, markets are not competitive, then it has been shown (see, for example, Barrett 1994) that there will be an incentive for governments to lower their environmental standards. This follows from an application of the models of strategic trade policy discussed in Chapter 10. Consider again the Brander and Spencer duopoly model, with a single domestic firm competing in third markets with a single foreign rival. Assume that production of the good generates pollution which does not spill over national borders. The governments of the two firms have available to them only environmental policies. The governments move first and set their pollution tax. Given the environmental policy, the firms then make their decisions so as to maximize profits. As in the case of strategic trade policy, if the firms compete in terms of quantities (Cournot competition) and the government can stimulate the domestic firm to raise output, then national welfare will rise. The government can do this by reducing the environmental tax below the level which equates marginal abatement and marginal pollution costs. Setting weak environmental policies will shift profits from the foreign rival.

As with strategic trade policy, this policy implication is not robust. As the number of firms increases then the incentive for the government changes from setting too weak environmental policy to setting standards which are too strong, that is, the marginal abatement cost will exceed the cost of an extra unit of pollution. If the firms compete in terms of prices then the government will wish to impose environmental standards which are too strong whatever the number of firms. Again, the argument is very similar to that presented under strategic trade policy. An increase in environmental taxes will lead the domestic producer to increase its price. The foreign rival will respond by raising its price by an even greater extent. In the resulting equilibrium the domestic firm will enjoy a larger share of the market and higher profits.

If the government also has industrial policies available to it then a production subsidy could, alternatively, be used to encourage the firm to act as the Stackelberg leader. In this case profits would again be shifted, but without any environmental damage to the domestic economy. Thus, the distortion of environmental policies will always be inferior to industrial policies. This all suggests that governments will face enormous difficulties in deciding whether to adopt environmental standards which are either too weak or too strong depending upon the structure of the industry concerned. So, the incentive to distort environmental policies may not be that important.

These simple models examine the case where only governments have the ability to take strategic decisions that affect the final outcome. Ulph and Ulph (1994) argue that to assess properly the possibilities for ecological dumping, and the claim of Porter that governments have an incentive to adopt more stringent standards than are implemented elsewhere, it is necessary to also allow for producers to take decisions which have a strategic impact. This is incorporated by allowing firms to make decisions regarding the level of R&D that they undertake. It is important to distinguish between process R&D, which generates innovations which reduce the costs of production, and environmental R&D, which provides for innovations which reduce pollution from the production process. It is assumed that international trade agreements prohibit the use of subsidies to R&D, so that the issue to be analysed is how strategic competition between firms, in terms of the choice of R&D, influences the government's decision on the level of environmental policy.

The structure of these models is such that in an initial stage of the game governments decide upon the level of environmental policy. Taking this as given, firms then choose the total level of R&D to maximize profits, assuming the level of R&D of the rival firm remains unchanged. The distribution of resources between process and environmental R&D is such that production costs, inclusive of the emissions tax, are minimized. In the final stage of the game each firm decides upon its level of output (Cournot) or price (Bertrand). It is assumed that costs are decreasing and convex in total R&D, and rise with the tax rate.

Consider first the case where producers can only invest in process R&D. Relaxing environmental policy, and setting pollution taxes below the level which equates marginal abatement costs and marginal damage costs, now has an effect additional to the direct impact of reducing the producer's costs of production. There is an indirect effect via an increase in the return to R&D. The lower tax will lead to an increase in R&D. The direct effect implies that since the producer is acting strategically there is less of an incentive for the government to act strategically and relax environmental standards. However, the fact that there is an additional, indirect effect of strategic action by the government encourages such action. Thus the overall incentive for more or less ecological dumping than when only governments act strategically is ambiguous, depending upon whether the direct effect dominates the indirect effect. Nevertheless, an incentive for lower environmental standards remains.

If firms can only undertake environmental R&D it becomes unclear whether governments will want to set environmental policy that is too weak or too strong. A reduction in the pollution tax with constant R&D will reduce the costs of the firm. This is the direct effect. But there will also be an impact upon the level of R&D. The lower tax increases the profit incentive for investing in R&D and increases the effect of a unit decline in costs on profits. However, the fall in the tax reduces the effectiveness of a given amount of R&D in reducing the firm's costs, and so discourages investment in R&D. The total effect is ambiguous.

This conclusion also applies to the more general case, where both process and environmental R&D can be undertaken. It is unclear whether governments will have incentives to adopt too-weak or too-strong environmental policies; so the hypothesis that governments will seek tougher environmental policies receives only limited support. The effect of environmental policy on R&D is ambiguous: even if tougher standards raise R&D this may be offset by the direct effect upon costs. So when both governments and producers act strategically there is an incentive for the distortion of environmental policies for strategic reasons, although there can be no presumption in which direction policy will be distorted.

So far we have considered taxes as the only available environmental policies. Ulph (1993) shows that use of an alternative policy, the setting of emission standards, will tend to reduce the extent of ecological dumping. The reason for this is that, with a constant tax on pollution, as the domestic firm raises output in response to a loosening of environmental policy it faces a fixed tax on additional emissions. With an emissions standard, as output rises the marginal cost of abatement increases; hence strategic use of environmental taxes is more effective than use of emission standards in raising the output and market share of the domestic firm. This then leads to a prisoners' dilemma in the choice of instruments when all governments use environmental policies. Whichever environmental policy the government of the foreign country chooses, the domestic government will choose taxes, since these are more effective in raising the market share of the domestic firm. Thus, all governments will choose taxes which imply higher output and greater deterioration of the environment than if emission standards were adopted in all countries.

Finally, empirical evidence provides little to sustain the fears that environmental policies have a large impact upon the costs of firms. A number of studies have found that the impact of pollution abatement policies in industrial countries is low, between 1 and 3 per cent of a firm's total costs (Dean 1992). This is unlikely to have a significant effect upon the ability of firms in countries with such policies to compete with firms in countries which do not impose them. Similarly, such policies will have minor, if any, impact on the locational decisions of firms. The worry that environmental policies in rich countries will push firms to shift their production facilities to poorer countries with lax environmental policies would appear to be unfounded on the basis of these figures.

16.5 Environmental policy in the EU

We have argued above that the appropriate response to pollution which is confined within the boundaries of a particular state is national policy by that country. This is consistent with the subsidiarity principle enshrined in the Single European Act of 1987, which states that policy intervention should always occur at the lowest level consistent with dealing with the problem. It has also been argued that the use of trade policies to tackle environmental problems cannot be supported. It should be remembered that these arguments do not preclude the use of trade policies to support domestic environmental policies. Indeed, the GATT/WTO (General Agreement on Tariffs and Trade/World Trade Organization) is designed to outlaw the use of policies which discriminate between domestically produced goods and imports. In a now-famous statement, the GATT has decreed that 'generally speaking, a country can do anything to imports or exports that it does to its own products, and it can do anything it considers necessary to its own production processes'. Legislation in the US which taxed imports containing certain chemical substances, to provide funds for improving waste disposal sites, was deemed to be GATT-consistent when challenged by the EU, because similar taxes were imposed on the domestic use of such chemicals.

Within the EU, environmental policies, the legal basis for which is defined in the Single European Act, are based upon three principles: the Prevention Principle, the Polluter Pays Principle, and the Subsidiarity Principle. Consistent with the analysis of this chapter, Subsidiarity states that the responsibility for dealing with an environmental policy lies with the lowest possible level of the political hierarchy; so intervention at the level of the EU should only occur for transnational pollution issues. The completion of the Single Market allows for the free movement of goods and factors throughout the EU. All measures which have the potential to restrict the free movement of goods are prohibited. However, Article 36 of the Single European Act provides for the suspension of free movement of goods to permit environmental regulations that protect the life and safety of people and protect fauna and flora. To be legally consistent with the Act such measures must not discriminate against foreign suppliers, or no better (less discriminatory) policy should be available.

Italy has been able to restrict the amount of phosphates in imported detergents, since the restriction applies equally to detergents produced in Italy. The European Court of Justice allowed a Danish regulation requiring, for environmental reasons, all imported drinks to be sold in returnable containers. In contrast, an Irish scheme to prohibit beer being sold in aluminium cans because of the environmental problems caused by such containers was not permitted, because other drinks in aluminium cans were not covered. Trade policy objectives rather than environmental policy appeared to be at the heart of the scheme.

Finally, subsidiarity permits each country to set its own policies with regard to national environmental problems. If governments implement policies which equate marginal abatement costs to marginal damage costs there may well be different levels of protection in different countries. This will lead to pollution-intensive activities being concentrated in countries with lower environmental taxes or emission standards. Similar arguments pertain to the environmental policies adopted in countries outside of the EU. These differences in standards should be viewed as being related to the comparative advantage of a country. A greater endowment of environmental resources and/or a lower valuation on environmental goods are not a source of unfair trade, but a genuine reason for international specialization. In the longer run there will be a tendency towards the harmonization of environmental standards.

As we see above, there may be incentives for governments to distort their environmental policies for strategic reasons. This suggests that subsidiarity may not be relevant for environmental policies and that the Commission should carefully monitor national policies. However, there is no certainty as to whether governments will wish to relax or tighten the policy relative to that which fully internalizes the environmental externality. One proposal is for the EU to agree upon a range for environmental standards, movement outside of this range being possible if supported by suitable evidence that marginal damage costs warrant such action.

16.6 Conclusions

In general trade cannot be held responsible for environmental degradation. Pollution arises from some form of market failure, and the relevant policy is that which is most directly targeted at the distortion. Since the market failure which gives rise to environmental problems is not in the process of international trade, the use of trade policies is not relevant. Welfare is maximized with appropriate environmental policies and free trade.

If appropriate environmental policies are not available, then using trade policies to achieve environmental objectives may raise welfare. However, other policies, such as production taxes, will typically be superior to trade policies. It is possible that trade restrictions will worsen the environment in the domestic economy.

The use, or threat, of trade restrictions to ensure that developing countries participate in international environmental agreements is also inappropriate. Their use implies that these countries are the source of an environmental problem that may have developed over many decades and that redistributes resources away from such countries to the wealthy industrial nations. The threat of the use of trade policies may be useful to dissuade countries from genuine free-riding and to ensure that countries abide by international agreements. There will, however, be superior policies to achieve these aims.

Finally, the fear of ecological dumping finds little support in traditional trade models. In fact, countries which export pollution-intensive commodities will either have no incentive to distort their environment policies or will be encouraged to set policies stricter than the optimal level. With imperfect competition, strategic behaviour by governments and firms provides an incentive for the manipulation of environmental policies. However, it is not clear whether the incentive will be towards tighter or weaker environmental standards. The nature of the market, and the way investment in R&D responds to changes in environmental policies, are crucial in determining the relevant outcome, and will vary from industry to industry. Since these are very difficult to ascertain, it is clear that there is no firm basis for governments to devise a policy to distort environmental standards.

Throughout this chapter we have assumed that, when they are available, governments will use appropriate environmental policies. If close-to-optimal environmental policies are in place the standard benefits from a more open trading regime will follow. Determining what are the appropriate levels of such policies is a complicated issue. Nevertheless, it is hard to conclude that close-to-optimal policies are being applied in most countries. The reason why optimal policies are not used, even when they are available, is an important issue and requires analysis of the role of different interest groups in influencing policy choices. We do not cover this issue further here, but conclude by arguing that, if relevant environmental policies are not being imposed, it is better to seek to improve these policies rather than looking for alternatives, such as trade policies, which usurp them.

16.7 Summary

- Per se, trade does not degrade the environment. Pollution externalities should ideally be internalized by bargaining, taxation or regulation, and trade left free.
- In the absence of appropriate environmental policies, trade policies might enhance welfare, but other measures will typically dominate them.
- Trade models provide little support for the idea of ecological dumping.

17

EUROPEAN UNION TRADE POLICY AND DEVELOPING COUNTRIES

17.1 Introduction

This chapter discusses economic policy of the European Union as it relates to developing countries. After summarizing the motivation of policy, it proceeds with a brief description of the policy and trading environment. The chapter next discusses policy concerning certain so-called sensitive products, and then comments upon the Union's diverse system of preferential arrangements towards various groupings of developing countries. There is then a discussion of the Union's aid policy, and of the relationship between aid and trade. This is followed by a consideration of the harmonization of standards. The chapter is concluded with a brief discussion of how policies are being reformed as a result of the conclusion of the Uruguay Round and the establishment of the World Trade Organization, and the implications that these reforms have for the developing countries.

'Developing countries' is a rather vague category that can be defined in various ways. We shall describe developing countries by elimination as being all countries except the industrial market economies, the formerly centrally planned economies of Eastern Europe, and the former USSR. Trade policies affecting these are discussed in Chapter 18. This leaves a very heterogeneous group consisting of a large number of small countries, many with populations of less than a million; two very large countries, China and India, each with a substantial proportion of the world's population; several other large countries with populations exceeding or approaching 100 million; and a considerable range of intermediate-size countries. Similarly 'developing countries' are heterogeneous with respect to income and level of development. The description ranges from the newly industrializing countries that are rapidly approaching or are overtaking the income levels of Western Europe, and the 'least developed countries', where incomes are very low and often stagnant. It also includes oil-exporting countries, some of which have high income but are underdeveloped by other criteria, such as literacy. It must also be realized that the classification has a policy dimension because, as discussed below, 'developing countries' receive preferential treatment with respect to access to the markets of developed countries, and with respect to the time permitted to adjust to some of the requirements of the World Trade Organization agreed in the Uruguay Round settlement. Thus, quite reasonably, some of the newly industrializing countries have lost or are losing their 'developing country' status and their rights to preferential treatment. They are graduating into developed-country status. Some of the high-income oil-exporting countries are also excluded from developing-country status with respect to preferential treatment. Far less reasonably, and very importantly, the European Union and the United States are unwilling to accord China with 'developing country' status because of fear of the export potential of that giant economy, even though China is clearly a developing country on objective criteria such as per capita income.

17.2 Motivation of European policy towards developing countries

Trade and aid policy as it affects developing countries is motivated by various considerations. These, not necessarily in order of importance, are: to facilitate the completion of the single European Market; to protect the Union's domestic industries—in particular, agriculture, sensitive labour-intensive manufacturing industries, and some high-technology industries—from import competition; to promote Union exports; to facilitate economic development in developing countries generally; and, more specifically, to maintain the political and economic influence of the Union in countries and regions where such influence has traditionally been strong, or to enhance its influence in countries or regions that are perceived to be of growing importance to the Union. These considerations determine the general structure of trade and industrial policy of the Union. They also determine the willingness of the Union to provide aid and non-reciprocal preferences on imports from developing countries. They determine the countries which receive preferences, the range of products on which preferences are conferred, and the instruments by which preferences are implemented or by which imports are restricted.

   These objectives are often inconsistent. Furthermore, the governments of the European Union have priorities that differ from each other and from those of the European Commission, so that the resultant policies often reflect political expediency rather than a coherent matching of policies and objectives.

17.3 The trading environment

The policies of the European Union with respect to trade have evolved in the context of the participation of its member countries, initially individually and latterly collectively, in GATT since the Second World War, culminating in the completion of the Uruguay Round of trade negotiations in 1994. They have been conditioned by the internal arrangements of the Union for the implementation of the Single European Market, and for the production of certain types of products—in particular, the Common Agricultural Policy—and by the desire to protect sensitive labour-intensive industries from import competition. They also reflect historical trading relationships between members of the Union and former colonies and overseas dependencies.

In the various GATT rounds of multilateral trade negotiations prior to the Uruguay Round, considerable progress was made in reducing protection on a wide range of manufactured goods. Spokesmen for the developing countries, particularly within the forum of UNCTAD, have, however, argued with some justification that the trade liberalization in these GATT rounds was mainly confined to products of interest to the developed industrial economies, and systematically omitted products of particular interest to the developing countries. Evidence for this has been the omission of agriculture from the GATT rounds prior to the Uruguay Round, the rapid expansion of trade, particularly intra-industry trade among the developed countries, and the proliferation of non-tariff barriers on the exports of some labour-intensive products from developing countries. Reasons for the rapid expansion of trade among the industrial countries relative to trade between developed and developing countries might be explained in three ways: bias in the trade liberalization negotiations, the ease of liberalizing intra-industry trade relative to factor endowment trade, and the high-income elasticity of demand for the intra-industry trade type products. Trade policy of the European Union as well as that of other industrial countries may well have favoured the expansion of trade between these rich countries. Nevertheless, it must also be recognized that some developing countries have followed extreme import substitution policies that have systematically and seriously reduced their participation in international trade. The empirical evidence on European Union trade with developing countries is mixed. The share of developing countries in extra-European Union trade (defining the Union as the twelve members as of 1994) has fallen steadily—apart from a rise in the 1970s associated with increases in the price of oil—from 45 per cent in 1958 to about 32 per cent by 1993. This is a considerable decline, and is consistent with the view that the developing countries have not been able to participate effectively in the expansion of world trade. There is, however, considerable variation among the developing countries, with considerable decline in the share of OPEC countries in spite of the sharp rise in the 1970s, and an almost continuous decline in the share of the African, Caribbean, and Pacific (ACP) countries in spite of preferential trading arrangements, discussed below. The ASEAN countries, on the other hand, have increased their share in European trade—particularly since the mid-1970s—albeit from a low initial level, in spite of Union policies that have generally been hostile to their exports.

There has been a considerable change in the structure of EC imports. In the early 1960s the twelve countries that constituted the Union from 1986 until the enlargement in 1995 were in aggregate essentially exporters of manufactured

Table 17.1. Share of selected country groups in Extra-EU trade (*percentage of exports plus imports with partner countries*)

	1958	1975	1993
Western Industrialized (non-EU)	48.45	46.84	55.11
EFTA	16.80	46.84	55.11
USA	15.21	18.77	22.30
Japan	1.02	3.16	7.25
Developing Countries	44.65	42.33	32.11
ACP	10.48	7.45	3.20
OPEC	14.55	22.45	8.25
Latin America	9.61	6.10	4.70
ASEAN	2.86	1.97	5.02
Central & East European Countries	4.15	8.08	8.32

Source: Eurostat.

goods and importers of primary products. By the 1990s the composition of imports had fundamentally changed, with the share of manufactured goods having risen from 30 per cent to 70 per cent. It is this decline in the importance of primary products in Community imports, caused partly by the policies of the Union and partly by the tendency for the income elasticity of demand for such products to be low, that mainly explains the diminishing role of developing countries in European trade. Those countries—mainly in East and South-East Asia—that have developed the capacity to produce manufactured goods have been able to capture an expanding share of the Union's imports, in spite of Union policies that are generally inhospitable to the import of labour-intensive manufactured

Table 17.2. Extra-EU imports by commodity groups (*percentage of imports*)

	1961	1975	1993
Food, beverages and tobacco (SITC sections 0 + 1)	24.27	13.42	7.57
Other primary products (excl. fuel) (SITC sections 2 + 4)	29.42	14.20	6.52
Fuel products (SITC section 3)	15.15	32.32	12.69
Manufactured goods (SITC sections 5 + 6 + 7 + 8)	29.91	37.31	69.72

Source: Eurostat.

goods.

In contrast to imports, the structure of the European Union exports has been very stable. The Union has remainded predominantly an exporter of manufactured goods, as is shown in Table 17.3.

Table 17.3. Extra-EU exports by commodity groups (*percentage of exports*)

	1961	1975	1993
Food, Beverages and Tobacco (SITC sections 0 + 1)	8.61	7.10	7.54
Other Primary Products (excl. Fuel) (SITC sections 2 + 4)	3.80	2.18	2.16
Fuel Products (SITC section 3)	3.86	4.51	3.22
Manufactured Goods (SITC sections 5 + 6 + 7 + 8)	80.79	84.67	85.18

Source: Eurostat.

17.4 Policies concerning products

We now briefly discuss European Union policy in three sectors: agriculture, steel, and clothing and textiles. These are chosen because of their importance to developing countries, and because they illustrate the types of protectionist measures employed, and the effects of these measures on developing countries.

17.4.1 Common Agricultural Policy

The most important of the internal policies of the European Union that affects developing countries is certainly the Common Agricultural Policy. The CAP, as is discussed more fully in Chapter 18, maintains the internal price of a wide range of agricultural products at well above the world price, and to a considerable extent isolates the internal market from developments in the international economy. This is achieved by a variety of controls on imports, and by export subsidies and other measures to dispose of agricultural surpluses outside of the Community. The net effect of the policy is to lower the world price of many products, in particular temperate-climate products such as grains and livestock, but also tropical products that compete with Community production, such as sugar and oil-seed. It also makes the world market more volatile, since most of the instability that originates in the conditions of demand and supply in the Community is exported to the residual world market. Thus the general effect of the CAP is to lower and destabilize prices in the rest of the world. Clearly this is damaging for land-abundant countries, particularly those of South America, and for the tropical producers of such crops as sugar. What is less obvious is the effect on food-importing developing countries. The naïve presumption is that such countries gain from the lower price of their imports, and that this gain is particularly beneficial for the poor in these countries who tend to spend high proportions of their income on food. The reason why this argument may not be correct is that many developing countries have been implementing trade and development strategies that severely discriminate against agricultural production. Such countries may well have potential comparative advantage in agricultural production; and some of them are now attempting to implement structural adjustment and liberalization programmes that would encourage them to produce food both for export and for their domestic markets. It is now widely believed that shifting resources towards agricultural production in developing countries is not only correcting the existing misallocation of resources, but is also encouraging labour-intensive production and improved income distribution. The Common Agricultural Policy is inhibiting such desirable reform.

17.4.2 Steel, and textiles and clothing

Tariffs applied by the European Union to most industrial products are now quite low, on average about 5.7 per cent, and are due to fall to an average of 3.6 per cent after the Uruguay Round agreement on tariffs is fully implemented by the end of the century (see Table 18.2 in Chapter 18). Although tariffs on sensitive products have tended to be somewhat higher than the average levels stated above (for example, the pre-Uruguay Round tariffs for clothing and textiles are 12.6 per cent and 9 per cent respectively) they have been insufficient to protect the domestic industries from degrees of import penetration that are considered to be excessive by Union policy makers, and so have been supplemented by other measures.

Two important examples of European Union protection of manufactured products of interest to developing countries are provided by steel and by textiles and clothing. In both of these industrial groups protection is maintained by non-tariff barriers and by aid and subsidies to the Community producers.

17.4.3 Steel

The steel industry in Europe and worldwide faced increasing difficulty in the second half of the 1970s when expanding productive capacity coincided with economic recession. European Union producers found themselves under increasing pressure from imports from Eastern Europe and from some of the more industrially advanced developing countries, in particular South Korea, Brazil, Mexico, and Venezuela.

For most of the 1970s, the Union maintained a set of bilateral VERs for regulating steel imports; but in 1978 these were supplemented by a system of basic import prices. Under this system the invoiced prices of imports of iron and steel products into the Union have to be compatible with the levels of basic prices published by the Commission. This is enforced by means of anti-dumping measures. This system has been a particular problem for low cost suppliers; but they have been encouraged to accept alternative bilateral arrangements under which they are allowed to undercut Union producers' delivery prices by 4 to 6 per cent, but only in return for restrictions on quantity. These bilateral quantitative arrangements are intended to allow the signatory countries to maintain their traditional trade patterns with the Union in the context of the development of the EU market. Readers will appreciate the irony of a trade policy that prohibits or at best severely restricts the foreign suppliers from offering gains from trade to Community consumers in the form of lower prices. The negative implications that this policy has for the competitiveness of Community producers in other sectors that utilize steel should also be noted.

17.4.4 The Multi-Fibre Arrangement (MFA)

The most important and the most damaging restriction on the export of manufactured goods from developing countries is undoubtedly the Multi-Fibre Arrangement that controls, on a country-by-country and product-by-product basis, the export of clothing and textiles from developing to developed countries.

The MFA evolved in 1974 from earlier bilateral arrangements that protected the industry in the United States and Europe from competition, particularly from Japan. A striking feature of the MFA, which since 1974 has been extended with respect to country and product coverage, is that it particularly discriminates against developing countries.

Clothing and textiles is an industry that has been particularly important in the progress towards development of countries such as Japan in the 1960s, of Korea, Taiwan, Singapore, and Hong Kong, and more recently of the rapidly industrializing countries of South East Asia as well as Latin America and Eastern Europe. The production of clothing is also of great importance to countries with much lower levels of income and development—in particular the countries of the Indian sub-continent and China. In contrast to steel, discussed above, clothing can be produced efficiently at small scale and without much capital equipment. It is an industry that is therefore appropriate for countries that are small or that have low levels of industrial capacity, or both. Thus the MFA is widely regarded as having delayed the transfer of comparative advantage in these industries to low-income countries, and thereby as having reduced the prospects for development of millions of the world's poor. Fortunately agreement under the Uruguay Round provides for the dismantling of the MFA system, albeit slowly.

The ways in which the quota system of the MFA creates production and consumption inefficiencies are analysed by Faini *et al.* (1995) on which this discussion has drawn.

Individual European Union countries have bilateral quota arrangements with individual developing countries for particular categories of textile and clothing products. There has been considerable variation between the members in the size and distribution of the quotas. Thus, Germany with about 25 per cent of the Union's GNP had 53.6 per cent of the total Union quota for women's and girls' woven coats, but only 20.7 per cent of the quota for woven cotton fabrics. The UK in contrast, with 17 per cent of Union GNP had 34.4 per cent of the quota for woven cotton fabrics, but only 3.3 per cent of the quota for cotton yarn. France, with about 21 per cent of Union GNP had 20.2 per cent of the quota for T-shirts, but only 7.3 per cent of the quota for men's and boys' shirts.[1] Faini *et al.* use this and other evidence relating to price and quota utilization as indications that the national MFA restraints have been effective in segmenting the Union market. This has been a source of consumption inefficiency because Union consumers have been faced with diverse prices, and production inefficiency because Union producers have been receiving diverse levels of protection. Implementation of the SEM has included the repealing of Article 115 of the Treaty of Rome which permitted the suspension of the free movement of products within the Union and so allowed the segmenting of the Union market. With a unified market, it is the total Union quotas rather than the national quotas that determine prices, and so these particular sources of inefficiency should be eliminated.

The expansion of the share of developing countries in the imports of textiles and clothing into the EC seems to have been halted in recent years, with the share of clothing having been fairly stable since the mid 1970s, with that of yarns and fabrics falling since the mid 1980s, and with that of fibres falling since 1970. It is not clear, however, to what extent this can be attributed to the MFA, since there is some indication that comparative advantage in textiles, in contrast to that of clothing, may have been shifting back towards developed countries in recent years, as technical progress is transforming textile production into a capital intensive industry (Spinanger 1995).

Faini *et al.* provide some interesting evidence concerning trade diversion within the OECD arising from the discriminatory focus of the MFA. Italy, which is presumed to have a comparative advantage within the OECD in the production of clothing and textiles, has been able in recent years to stop a substantial decline in its share of the developed-countries market; and the textile and clothing industry in Italy has had an expanding share of national investment, in contrast to declining shares in investment experienced by the industry in most European countries. This, Faini *et al.* suggest, is an indication of an inefficient production shift from constrained developing-country producers to an unconstrained developed-country producer.

Finally, it should be recognized that the allocation of quotas is a source of inefficiency: between exporting countries, and between firms within the exporting countries. Quotas are usually allocated on the basis of past performance. This inefficiently discriminates against newcomers—whether countries or firms within a country—that may be emerging low-cost producers.

The MFA quotas will be fully liberalized by the year 2005 as part of the implementation of the Uruguay Round, bringing substantial benefits to developing-country exporters as well as to European consumers. This is discussed further later in this chapter and in Chapter 18.

---

[1] The data is for 1987, and is from Table 2 of Faini *et al.* (1995).

17.5 The hierarchy of developing countries

We have been discussing the trade policy of the European Union with respect to particularly sensitive industries. We now turn to consider the differential trade policies of the EU with respect to countries. The treatment of countries is not independent of the treatment of industries, since the choice of countries upon which the Union is willing to confer preferences, as well as the extent of those preferences, depends partly upon the extent to which the country is perceived to be a potential threat to the Union in the sensitive industries. There are, however, other considerations. As mentioned at the beginning of this section, the Union has been concerned to maintain and to promote trade relations with those developing countries with which its members have had close cultural, economic, and political links; or with countries with which it wishes to establish such links. This is reflected in the concept of 'associationism' whereby the Union extends to the associates various privileges, particularly with respect to access to Union markets, but also including technical and industrial cooperation. The differing treatments accorded to various countries create what is often described as a hierarchy of privilege. As we shall describe, this hierarchy is somewhat fluid at the present time.

17.5.1 The Lomé convention

The 'most-favoured' countries are the sixty-eight African, Caribbean, and Pacific (ACP) countries whose economic relations with the Union are governed by the Lomé convention. This was originally agreed in 1975 subsequent to the UK joining the Union, and it evolved from the earlier Yaoundé conventions that covered relations between the original six members of the Union and their various associated states and territories.[2] The Lomé convention, which was most recently revised in 1990, provides preferential access to the markets of the EU. Tropical products and many manufactured products can be imported into the Union duty-free; and restrictions on the imports of more sensitive products tend to be more relaxed. Some of these preferences are formulated in special protocols such as those for sugar and for bananas. In addition to the trade preferences, Lomé provides a wide range of arrangements for industrial, financial, technical, commercial, and cultural cooperation, and for the provision of aid. There are some features of Lomé that are particularly worthy of note, as follows.

Membership　　The Asian countries, some of which, as former colonies of the UK and other Community members, might have been considered as candidates, are not included. Partly as a result of this, most of the Lomé countries (with the exception of Nigeria) tend to be small. They also tend to be at low levels of industrial development, and so do not pose much threat to Union manufacturing industries.

---

[2] The relationship between the EU and its associates, and the evolution of the Yaoundé and Lomé conventions, are described in Grilli (1993).

Non-reciprocity   The Lomé convention, in contrast to the Yaoundé conventions that preceded it, is non-reciprocal in the sense that the Union does not receive preferential access to the markets of the developing country members. The issue of reciprocity had been a serious source of conflict between the EU and the United States, which perceived the preferential access that the EU received as being a breach of the fundamental non-discrimination principle of GATT.

The elimination of reciprocity also met one of the demands for the 'New International Economic Order'.[3]

STABEX   An innovation of Lomé was the introduction of a 'System for the Stabilization of Export Earnings' (STABEX). This is financed by the EU, and provides grants or loans, under quite generous terms, to the developing-country participants whose export revenue earnings on any commodity fall below some norm. This commodity-earnings stabilization scheme also meets one of the central demands formulated by the developing countries as part of their search for a new international economic order.

Sugar and bananas   There are two protocols that are of particular interest, concerning sugar and bananas. The sugar protocol is of interest, partly because it is an important product, but also because it is a rare example where the EU has been prepared to give duty-free access to an agricultural product that competes with domestic production.

The sugar protocol is essentially an extension of the UK's Commonwealth Sugar Agreement. It allows and commits the Lomé associates and India to export agreed amounts of sugar to the Union at prices determined by the Common Agricultural Policy. Thus the exporters receive the same price guarantees as the domestic Union producers. This is valuable because the Community sugar price has usually been well above the world price (in recent years roughly double). Only in two years, 1975 and 1980, has the world price exceeded the Community price so that the ACP exporters experienced welfare losses. The welfare effects of the CAP system are analysed more generally in Chapter 18. Here we note some of the findings of Herrmann and Weiss (1995) with respect to the Sugar protocol. They estimate that over the period from 1975 to 1991 the total sugar export earnings of the countries receiving EU quotas was raised by 32 per cent, and the instability in earnings was reduced by an average of 34 per cent. They point out that the quota sugar is transported into the Community, and then, because the EU is self-sufficient, it is re-exported as surplus to requirements. Therefore there is a waste of transportation resources, lowering world welfare. They also emphasize—as can be deduced from the general principles discussed in Chapter 9—that, from the

---

[3] The New International Economic Order is the term used to describe the body of reforms to the international financial and trading systems that were advocated—particularly during the 1960s and 1970s—to redress distortions in the existing systems that were perceived as being detrimental to the interests of developing countries.

donors' point of view, the sugar quota system is an inferior method of redistributing income towards the ACP producers.

The Community banana policy is interesting for three reasons. Firstly, it is an example of a cost being imposed upon Union consumers to protect mainly non-Union producers. Secondly, it is an example of the muddle that can arise from attempting to achieve conflicting or inconsistent objectives with too few policy instruments. And thirdly, it illustrates how such attempts are likely to damage relations with other countries.

The policy that the EU is implementing attempts to satisfy three conflicting objectives while complying with the GATT rules. The objectives are the desire of the German government to ensure that their consumers have access to low-price, high-quality bananas; the policy of the UK and French governments in particular to fulfil the commitment under the Lomé convention to maintain protection for their traditional ACP suppliers; and the implementation of the Single European Market.

In addition to some production in Crete (Greece), bananas are supplied to the EU from three sources: former ACP colonies under the Lomé convention; overseas territories—Departements d'Outre-Mer (DOM) of EU states including the Canary Islands (Spain); and third-country, mainly Latin American producers, known as 'Dollar Area' suppliers. Prior to the implementation of the Single European Market, ACP suppliers had preferential access to the EU under the banana protocol of the Lomé convention, while the dollar area imports were subject to a 20 per cent tariff. However, individual EU states were able to make their own national arrangements. Notably: Germany was permitted to import Dollar-Area bananas duty-free; France imported only from its DOM producers and Franc-zone, ACP states; UK had a global quota, but issued licences to Dollar-Area producers only when ACP imports failed to fill the quota; Italy reserved some imports from Somalia, but also imported Dollar-Area bananas; and Spain accepted supplies only from the Canary Islands.

These disparate arrangements enabled the individual countries to meet their various objectives; but they gave rise to diverse prices throughout the EU that could only be maintained by segmenting the market and restricting the internal movement of bananas. This was inconsistent with the SEM.

The regime which came into force on 1 July 1993 as part of the implementation of the SEM is complicated. The EU was prohibited by the rules of GATT from raising the average tariff on bananas; so, since German imports were previously duty-free, a common external tariff including Germany would have needed to be reduced from 20 per cent to about 14 per cent, but this was not deemed to be high enough to provide effective protection to the favoured producers. Furthermore, GATT was trying to abolish non-tariff barriers, so a proposed scheme involving quotas and deficiency payments was ruled out. The present regime is a 'tariff quota' system, in that the tariff levels to which imports from the various sources are subject are determined by volume quotas. The EU producers, including the DOMs, have individual specific annual quotas which are eligible for deficiency payments under the Common Agricultural Policy. The ACP countries have specific quotas for 'traditional' imports, based on pre-1991 levels of imports, which enter duty-free. In addition there is a global quota for non-traditional imports from the Dollar-Area suppliers and the ACP. Up to the limit of this global quota, ACP bananas enter duty free, while Dollar-Area bananas are subject to a tariff of 100 ecus per tonne (equivalent to an *ad valorem* tariff of 20.8 per cent in 1991). Imports above the quota are subject to very high levies of 750 ecus per tonne for ACP supplies, and 850 ecus per tonne for the Dollar-Area supplies. In addition, the régime includes provision of aid to the ACP countries to improve productivity, quality, and diversification. The quotas sum to an amount quite close to that which was imported under the previous régime, so it is not clear whether the new régime is more or less restrictive than the old one. It is almost certainly illegitimate under the rules of the WTO. This complicated system of protection has created a diversity of production distortions and is clearly very inefficient. It imposes a high cost upon the European consumers, and it has become a source of acrimony between Germany and France. It is also a source of conflict between the EU and some of its trading partners, particularly the Latin American producers, and also the USA since US-based multi-national firms are involved in Latin American production and distribution (see Read 1994).

We conclude this discussion of the Lomé convention by noting that although the ACP associates have consistently received the most favoured treatment provided by the EU to non-members, their share of EU trade has steadily declined. This is because many of the ACP countries have experienced poor economic growth over the past few decades and remain at low levels of industrial development. They have not been able to participate effectively in the expanding world and European trade in manufactured goods, nor have they been able to expand their primary product supply capacities.

17.5.2 Mediterranean and European Associates

The second tier of countries in the EU hierarchy of preferences are the Associates in the Mediterranean basin, and more recently in Eastern Europe. These are outside the Lomé convention, but nevertheless are subject to non-reciprocal, preferential trade and cooperation agreements.

The Union has always been concerned to maintain or to establish close links with the countries of the Mediterranean, although the priority given to this objective has varied. It was given particular priority during the 1970s, when the securing of access to supplies of oil seemed imperative. Nevertheless, trade relations with these countries have developed more slowly than with the ACP countries, mainly because of the difficulties concerning the access of products that are competitive with those of the southern members of the EU: in particular citric fruit, wine, and olive oil. That these difficulties have to a considerable extent been surmounted reflects the political expediency of securing good relations with these countries.

The collapse of the Soviet hegemony over Eastern Europe, and the decline of the power of OPEC, may in recent years have reduced the importance of the Southern Mediterranean to the EU. Nevertheless, the EU has recently given approval to a proposal by the Commission to create by the year 2010 a European-Mediterranean economic area in which the countries of the Maghreb (Morocco, Tunisia, Algeria, and Libya) and the Mashreq (Egypt, Jordan, Lebanon, and Syria) participate along the same lines as European associates.

The relationship between the European Union on the one hand, and the ACP countries and the Mediterranean Associates on the other, is now quite asymmetric. This is discussed by Haggard (1995: 100). 'For both groups of countries the special relationship with the EU constitutes the most important international institutional structure for their foreign economic policy,' and 'Lomé and associate relationships remain essentially preferential ones in which little is demanded of the partners who are developing countries.'

The main focus of Union attention has now shifted to establishing economic relations with Eastern Europe. These relations are discussed in more detail in Chapter 18. Here it will suffice to note that for some of these countries there is the prospect of eventual membership of the European Union, and it seems likely that the existing Union will be prepared to make considerable economic sacrifices in order to integrate them securely into the Western European democratic system. The Community policy is to incorporate the Southern Mediterranean and all of Europe into a free-trade area for manufactured goods.

A third tier in the hierarchy is formed by some of the least developed countries that are not members of the Lomé convention but which receive some preferential treatment in excess of that afforded to more advanced developing countries.

Another level in the hierarchy of privileges is provided by a diversity of cooperative arrangements that various countries and country groupings have with the European Union. At the present time the Union is attempting to strengthen economic relations with Latin America—a region that had previously been neglected—by initiating or extending cooperative arrangements and negotiating free trade arrangements with that region.

Finally, most developing countries receive some tariff preferences relative to the developed countries under the EU's Generalized System of Preferences that was introduced in 1971.[4] This permits duty-free access for manufactured and semi-manufactured products subject to quotas or tariff ceilings for sensitive and semi-sensitive products. Since tariffs on most manufactured products are now quite low after successive rounds of trade liberalization, and since the ceilings on the sensitive products are strictly enforced, the usefulness of these preferences for most countries has been minimal, and only a few of the relatively advanced developing countries have been able to make effective use of them. Much of the problem has been the late and arbitrary allocation of quotas on a yearly basis, and the tendency of the EU to punish success of particular exporters by reducing their quotas and restricting the range of products eligible for preferences. Peers (1995) describes the resulting uncertainty as having been 'poisonous'. The complex

[4] Taiwan and initially China were excluded.

and arbitrary regulations concerning rules of origin have been a further barrier preventing developing countries from making effective use of the preferences. A new European Union GSP for industrial goods came into effect at the beginning of 1995. Peers assesses this to be a modest improvement; but he notes that it has failed to increase the value of the benefits to compensate for the loss of preferences resulting from the lowering of tariffs and from the extension of free trade arrangements within Europe: 'developing States (outside the Lomé States and the Mediterranean) have moved from near the top of the EU's hierarchy of preferences to near the bottom'.

Preferential access to the developed countries' markets was one of the main planks of the New International Economic Order, and an enormous amount of political and administrative effort was expended in attempting to achieve it. But most political economists would now agree that the effort would have been better spent in attempting to achieve liberalization of relevant products rather than general preferential treatment.[5] It is interesting to note that one of the most successful countries in achieving an expansion of manufactured products to developed countries has been Taiwan, which did not receive preferences.

17.6 Aid

It might be imagined that aid should be considered as a separate issue from that of trade since, in principle, the former is determined by governments upon humanitarian and developmental grounds, whereas the latter is determined by private agents on commercial grounds. In practice, the two are closely interrelated because the motivation of aid policy is broadly the same as that of trade policy, as has been described above. Aid policy is, to a considerable extent, an instrument of trade policy, in that aid is used to promote trade. But the opposite is also true, in that the fostering of economic and social development through the promotion of trade is an explicit objective of the EU's trade policy with its associates.

Official aid is provided centrally from the Union budget through the European Development Fund, and nationally from the governments of the member countries. In addition, there is an aid component in some of the conventions governing economic relations between the Union and developing countries—in particular in the Lomé convention, described above. Some European aid is channelled through international organizations, and considerable aid is provided by individual residents of the Union through various international charities. This discussion concentrates on aid provided by the European Commission and the member governments.

The interaction of aid and trade policy is most manifest in the tying of aid to expenditure on exports from the donor country. A particularly restrictive form of

---

[5] See Little (1982) for an early and forceful exposition of that view.

tying is the 'mixed credit' system, under which firms of a particular country receive subsidies from their government to finance exports to selected developing countries. This last practice is aid in the sense that the subsidies are financed out of the donor country's aid budget, and that the availability of the exports at prices below those that would obtain in the absence of the subsidies may confer a benefit upon the importing country. A much looser, informal type of tying aid is to direct it at developing countries which have sufficiently close commercial links with the donor country that a high proportion of the aid will voluntarily be spent upon the exports of that country.

The rationale of tying aid from the perspective of the donor is that it stretches the aid budget and increases its political acceptability to domestic taxpayers. Tied aid is also seen as having a smaller balance-of-payments cost than untied aid. A further consideration concerning mixed credits is that they can be focused on goods that are produced under conditions of increasing returns to scale and imperfect competition. They are in fact export subsidies, so the issues of strategic trade policy discussed in Chapter 10 above are relevant.

Tied aid is of less value to the recipients than untied aid. There are two considerations. First, more resources might have been obtained if the recipient had been free to acquire those resources from the cheapest source of supply; and secondly, the tying of aid might constrain or encourage the recipient to import different products or to develop different projects than if the aid had not been tied. This last point may be of considerable importance. Morrissey (1993), upon which this discussion is partly based, provides reasons for believing that tied aid will tend to promote capital-intensive exports from the donor countries. Since many of the developing countries have trade and industrial policies that promote excessive capital-intensity in their industrial sectors, it seems likely that further subsidies on the import of capital-intensive equipment worsen the existing distortions and so may be immiserizing.[6] On the other hand, untied aid may be used to support an over-valued exchange rate, and so may have the same sort of effect.

It is difficult to measure the extent to which aid is tied, because much tying is informal or implicit, but Morrissey cites data of the Development Assistance Committee (DAC) of the OECD that suggest that between a third and a half of official development assistance provided by the larger members of the EU is formally tied. This seems to be of about the same proportion as that of the United States, and somewhat higher than that of Japan. The DAC is trying to limit the extent of tied aid, especially mixed credits. The 'Helsinki Package' agreed by the DAC in November 1991 recommended that tied aid should be restricted to projects which could not attract commercial finance; but Morrissey expresses doubt whether this can be implemented or enforced.

The implementation of the SEM may be expected to ameliorate the restrictiveness of tied aid, since there should be no restrictions within the SEM upon the procurement of goods financed by expenditure of member countries. Thus

---

[6] The possibility that an increase in the availability of a factor of production may make a country worse off (i.e. be immiserizing) has been discussed in Ch. 9 above.

individual governments are not permitted to restrict expenditure of aid to their own exports. Furthermore the 'level playing-field' concept for exporters should prohibit individual governments from providing export subsidies in the form of mixed credits to their own firms.

Less encouraging is the impact that European integration is likely to have upon the quantity of aid. To the extent that integration and expansion involve transfers of income from richer to poorer members within the European Union, the willingness to provide aid to developing countries may be crowded out. There is also likely to be a diversion of aid towards the Eastern European countries.

Only about a third of Union aid is directed towards the poorest or least developed countries, and there is little relationship between the quantity of aid received and the extent of poverty in the recipient country. Mixed credits, in particular, tend to be available to finance exports to the middle-income and rapidly developing countries.

Some aid is provided directly from the budget of the European Union; in particular, some of the surpluses of the Common Agricultural Policy are disposed of as food aid. There is no doubt that some of this has provided much-needed relief in circumstances of famine. Nevertheless, food aid has to be assessed with caution. In particular, the provision of food that disrupts or prevents the development of domestic sources of production and distribution may be damaging to long-term development in the recipient country. For example, food aid made available to the urban populations of a developing country may exacerbate rural poverty by reducing incomes and employment opportunities in the agricultural sector. There may also be problems of the appropriateness of the food aid being provided. For example, the provision of surplus EU powdered milk to schools that do not have an adequate supply of clean water can be detrimental to the health of the children attending those schools.

A tension in the relationship between donors, including the European Development Fund, and the recipient governments is the extent to which the former are entitled to impose their own developmental and libertarian values upon the latter. The EDF, for example, has in recent years been focusing aid upon rural projects that are intended to enhance food production for domestic consumption, but this has not always been in accordance with the development strategies of the recipient governments, which tend to be biased towards urban and industrial development. A more specific example has been the linking of EDF aid to Kenya to economic reform such as the dismantling of parastatal organizations. Since the parastatals are important vehicles of political patronage, this conditionality has been resisted and is viewed as unwarranted interference in Kenyan internal affairs. The European Union, in common with other donors, has also been making aid to Kenya conditional upon political reform: in particular, the abolition of one-party government.

Grilli discusses how by 1985 (Lomé III) the emphasis of Community lending had shifted from projects reflecting the priorities of the borrowers to structural adjustment loans. He argues that the ability of the Union to impose conditionality upon the Lomé and Mediterranean associates is an indication of a substantial change in the bargaining power of the Union relative to these associates. It might reflect, however, an increasing awareness among these associates of the necessity for adjustment.

We conclude this discussion of European Union aid policies with the apposite observation of Hughes Hallett (1994): that for every ECU spent on aid, roughly two are spent on restrictions to keep the exports of developing countries out.

17.7   Harmonization of standards

An issue which will be of increasing importance in the post-Uruguay-Round era concerns the upward harmonization of labour and environmental standards between countries. This issue is already of significance within trading blocks: in particular between Mexico and the United States within the North American Free Trade Area; and to a lesser extent within the European Union between countries that have committed themselves to the Social Chapter of the Maastricht Treaty and those that have not.

Environmental standards have already been discussed in Chapter 16, so here we shall mainly focus on the issue as it relates to labour standards between developed and developing countries.

The basic issue is simple: a country that does not adhere to some 'acceptable' minimum standard of labour conditions is contravening fundamental human rights, and may be gaining an 'unfair' cost advantage. This generates two quite different arguments for trade controls. The first is to signal moral abhorrence at the unacceptable conditions, thereby encouraging the offending authorities to modify those conditions. This argument is quite separate from any consideration of economic efficiency. An example would be the sanctions imposed by various countries and groups of countries upon economic relations with South Africa during the apartheid regime. The second argument for trade controls is to protect import-competing industries that are damaged by competition from foreign firms whose low costs are attributable to the non-enforcement of the standards. GATT has anti-dumping and counter-subsidy provisions, but the conditions under which these may be used have been tightened and clarified in the WTO accord, as is described in Chapter 18. In particular, it has to be demonstrated that subsidies against which countervailing action may be taken distort trade. This would seem to rule out most cases, since lax standards are likely to apply in all sectors and so cannot be considered as subsidies specific to the export industries.

Let us illustrate this discussion in the context of the important and sensitive issue of child labour. Here we have a continuum of circumstances ranging from the employment of very young children under conditions that are clearly injurious to their health, safety, and general welfare, to the employment of teenagers for longer hours than would, in a developed country, be considered as compatible with full-time education. Both of these cases might affect trade by increasing the supply and lowering the cost of labour, but it is difficult to see how they distort trade unless the use of the child labour is only permitted in specific export industries. The argument for restricting trade in goods produced by young children has nothing to do with damage to import competing industries. It is an ethical one, involving the desire to discourage the use of such labour, tempered by the concern that the trade restrictions will actually improve the conditions of the children. The problem is, of course, where to draw the line between conditions that are unacceptable and those that reflect the social preferences and the economic realities of relatively poor countries. It would surely be unreasonable, for example, to restrict the import of beef from Botswana on the grounds that the cattle were being raised by herdsmen of an age at which in Europe school attendance would be compulsory.

There are three issues in considering whether trade should be restricted on the grounds of inadequate labour, environmental and safety standards, in the exporting countries. The first is to note that low labour cost is the basis of comparative advantage of poor, labour-abundant countries. A strict harmonization of standards erodes this basis of comparative advantage and reduces the ability to export labour-intensive products. On Stolper-Samuelson arguments, this will worsen the condition of labour in the exporting country.

The second consideration is the need to prevent import-competing groups from hijacking the decision-making progress. Rodrik (1994), in an interesting discussion of these and related issues, emphasizes the desirability of involving consumer and exporting-interest groups in assessing whether imports should be restricted in the public interest. The Uruguay Round goes some way to meeting this requirement, but Rodrik would like it to be strengthened by requiring the testimony of these interests.

The third consideration concerns the payment of compensation to developing countries whose trade has been restricted on the basis of standards imposed by the richer countries. Rodrik uses the criterion of whether the exporting country is broadly democratic for the payment of compensation on the grounds that in a democratic regime the standards can be presumed to reflect the social preferences of that country. This seems too limited. If, for example, the wildlife of East Africa is considered a world resource, then the richer countries should contribute to the preservation of that resource whether or not the East African régimes are democratic.

Finally we would like to reiterate that although these issues have been discussed in the context of trade relations between developed and less developed countries, they may be important within the European Union. This is illustrated by the example of the export of British beef into Germany. There is a perceived risk associated with British beef due to the BSE disease which has affected some British herds. So are the Germans justified in restricting its import if the perceived risk is higher in Germany than in the UK, or if the Germans are more risk-averse than the British? The implementation of the Single European Market implies that standards have to be uniform even though social preferences are diverse.

17.8 Prospects

We conclude this discussion of European Union policies towards developing countries with some brief comments on the prospect in the light of the completion of the Single European Market, the completion of the Uruguay Round, and the establishment of the World Trade Organization. Policies towards developed and Eastern European countries are discussed more fully in Chapter 18.

17.8.1 Single European Market (SEM)

We have already noted in the discussion of aid that the implementation of the SEM should improve the position of the recipients of aid by reducing some of the negative effects of that aid being tied to the products of specific countries. There is however, danger of some aid being diverted to facilitate structural adjustment within the Union.

Hughes Hallett (1994) discusses the implications of the SEM for trade and investment. He suggests that any trade diversion or creation effects from implementation of the SEM are likely to be small. But he argues that there is danger of investment being diverted from developing countries towards the EU, with negative effect upon economic growth in the developing countries. What is critical, although unpredictable, is whether the EU will be inward-looking and protectionist, or outward-looking and liberal.

17.8.2 Uruguay Round and the World Trade Organization

The developing countries were seeking to obtain from the developed countries, including the European Union, liberalization of agriculture and textiles and tighter controls on the use of safeguard procedures against the import of sensitive products. The Union, on the other hand, in common with other developed countries, was pressing the developing countries for liberalization of services, for protection of intellectual property rights, and for reform on practices concerning foreign investment.

Some progress has been made in all of these areas, although most of the gains are potential rather than immediate. Thus, a major achievement of the Uruguay round has been to integrate agriculture into the GATT procedures for the first time, although the extent of the liberalization achieved has been modest. Similarly, a framework for the management of international trade in services has been established, the General Agreement in Trade in Services (GATS), but only a limited range of services have so far been included. Another achievement of importance to developing countries is the agreement to abolish the use of quotas to control trade in clothing and textiles. This is in effect a dismantling of the Multi-fibre arrangement; but the time permitted for it is long—ten years—with much of the reform being postponed until near the end of that period. The developed countries gained agreement on the protection of intellectual property, but here again there is a long phase-in period.

The major institutional reform arising from the Uruguay Round has been the establishment of the World Trade Organization to replace GATT. This includes strengthened procedures to settle disputes, and to monitor and control the use of safeguards against import penetration in sensitive industries. Noteworthy in this last respect is a prohibition on the use of voluntary export restraints.

An interesting feature of the WTO, and one that has been a cause of concern for some developing countries, is the provision whereby signatories have to accept the whole package, and cannot—as was possible under GATT—select a menu of its provisions. A country cannot, for example, accept the trade policy agreements for goods but reject those for services.

Attempts to quantify the gains from the Uruguay Round tend to yield rather modest results, typically not more than one percent of world GNP (see Cline 1995, Hamilton and Whalley 1995). These tend to be the static gains in producer and consumer welfare arising from improved allocation of resources and the reduction in consumption distortions. It is interesting to note that often the gains from liberalization accrue to the citizens of the countries that have been resisting that liberalization. Thus the major beneficiaries of reform of the Common Agricultural Policy would surely be the consumers and taxpayers of the European Union. Hamilton and Whalley (1995) point out that most of the estimated gains from the liberalization of clothing and textiles accrue to the consumers in the developed countries through lower prices.

In considering the distribution of the gains among the developing countries it seems that it is the relatively advanced countries of Asia that have the most to gain or the least to lose from liberalization (Page and Davenport 1994). The least developed countries tend to lack the flexibility to be able to exploit new opportunities in a changing world. Some of these countries—in particular the ACP countries—may lose from the erosion of preferences that they receive under the Lomé convention.

Finally we should emphasize that the estimates of gains from the Uruguay Round that we have been discussing do not take into account the prospects for improved economic growth. It is feasible that a less arbitrary trading environment provided by an effective World Trading Organization will encourage investment and innovation throughout the world. A potentially important feature of the WTO is that it commits its members not to increase trade protection. Thus membership provides a useful mechanism by which governments that are embarking upon reform, such as India and many in Latin America, can enhance confidence that the reforms will not be reversed. More generally, the WTO, by restricting the use of protectionist measures, strengthens the capacity of its member governments to resist the pressures of special interest groups, and so potentially enhances the quality of governance in developing and developed countries alike.

The citizens of the European Union can hope to gain from liberalization in

Europe and the rest of the world through lower prices and a growing world economy.

17.9 Summary

- The European Union's protectionist policies in labour intensive manufactured goods—particularly clothing and textiles—are inhibiting the growth of developing countries. The effects of agricultural protection are, however, less clear since poor consumers may benefit from the import of cheap EU food, whereas poor agricultural producers are harmed.
- The EU has a shifting hierarchy of preferences towards developing and East European countries. Generally, it has been middle income developing countries that have been able to benefit from trading opportunities with the EU.
- Aid from the EU and its member countries is motivated mainly by considerations of trade and political expediency. The direction of EU aid bears little relationship to need. The tying of aid reduces its value to recipients, and is often inconsistent with the requirements of the Single European Market.
- The completion of the Uruguay Round and the establishment of the World Trade Organization provide the prospect of modest gains for developing countries. It is, however, European consumers who have the most to gain from European trade liberalization.

THE EUROPEAN UNION'S TRADE POLICY, AND THE CAP

18.1 Introduction

This chapter is devoted to examining the international trade policies of the European Union. In Section 18.2, the main focus is on policy towards trade in manufactures and services. The operation of the EU's Common Agricultural Policy is analysed in Section 18.3.

18.2 EU trade policy

The external trade policy of the EU is often characterized as having a pyramid of preferences. At the top are countries with whom the EU has negotiated free trade agreements. At the end of the 1980s the EU had reciprocal free trade arrangements with the EFTA countries and had unilaterally removed tariffs and quantitative restrictions (QRs) on imports from the ACP countries. Below these countries in the pyramid of preferences came the Mediterranean countries, who were exempt from customs duties and QRs, excepting certain textile products. Limited tariff exemptions were granted to all other developing countries within the framework of the Generalized System of Preferences (GSP).

Next in the hierarchy came the industrial countries, imports from whom were subject to MFN duties and the general rules of the GATT. However, contrary to the spirit of the GATT and counter to a common commercial policy, there existed a number of nationally imposed QRs, most notably against specific products, such as road vehicles from Japan, and footwear from Taiwan and Korea. Finally, at the base of the pyramid came the countries of Eastern Europe, the Soviet Union, China, and other 'state trading economies'. These were all granted MFN treatment. However, all the 'state trading countries' were subject to significant non-tariff barriers despite Czechoslovakia, Hungary, Poland, Romania, and Yugoslavia being members of the GATT. Romania and Yugoslavia were granted treatment under the GSP, although subject to many restrictions. A number of studies (see e.g. Messerlin 1989) have highlighted a strong bias against 'state trading countries' in EU anti-dumping investigations in both the tendency to find dumping and in the size of the estimated dumping margin.

So, prior to transformation, the countries of Eastern Europe were at the base of the EU's pyramid of preferences. Developing countries were somewhat higher in the structure, having been granted GSP treatment. The GSP involves preferential tariff treatment within specified limits. It has been heavily criticized for the selective inclusion of products and beneficiary countries by the country granting the preferences, the importing country. The use of quantitative limits on preferred imports, rules of origin, and safeguard clauses tend to ensure that the imports which have a close domestic substitute receive, at best, only a modest increase in access to developed country markets. Empirical studies have tended to support the view that the GSP has not had a significant impact on imports from developing countries into markets such as the EU.

Following transformation, the countries of Eastern Europe have moved up the pyramid of preferences. Trade and cooperation agreements incorporating tariff preferences were quickly signed. Poland and Hungary were incorporated into the GSP from the beginning of 1990, with Czechoslovakia and Bulgaria following in January 1991. Then, in December 1991, association agreements, the Europe Agreements (EAs), were signed with Czechoslovakia, Hungary, and Poland. In spring 1993 similar agreements with Bulgaria and Romania were initialled. Since the whole of the Agreement involved complex political discussions and required ratification by each member of the EU and the Eastern European country, interim arrangements implementing the trade parts of the Agreements were introduced almost immediately, taking effect from March 1992 for Czechoslovakia, Hungary, and Poland, from March 1993 for Romania, and from December 1993 for Bulgaria. However, following much criticism of the rather tentative steps towards more open-market access in certain products, the Council of Ministers, at the Copenhagen Summit of June 1993, decided to quicken the pace of trade liberalization. In Section 18.2.1 we describe these agreements in some detail.

18.2.1 The Europe agreements[1]

The trade aspects of each of these agreements are very similar, and provide for a free trade area in industrial products within a maximum of ten years. The agreements are not symmetrical in that liberalization of trade policy in the Eastern European countries will proceed at a slower pace than in the EU. Here we concentrate on the liberalization of EU trade policy and how this will affect imports from Eastern Europe.

The agreements are summarized in Table 18.1. The liberalization of trade provided for in these agreements is not uniform across products. For the majority of industrial products, defined in the General Provisions of the Agreements, tariffs

---

[1] This section draws heavily upon Schumacher and Mobius (1994) and CEC (1994).

Table 18.1. Summary of trade liberalization for industrial products in the interim Europe agreements

		Mar. 1992	Jan. 1993	May 1993	July 1993	Dec. 1993	Jan. 1994	Jan. 1995	Jan. 1996	Jan. 1997	Jan. 1998
General provisions											
Bulgaria	Tariffs	GSP	GSP	GSP	GSP	0					
	QRs	Yes	Yes	Yes	Yes	Abolished					
Czech Slovak	Tariffs	0									
	QRs	Abolished									
Hungary	Tariffs	0									
	QRs	Abolished									
Poland	Tariffs	0									
	QRs	Abolished									
Romania	Tariffs	MFN	MFN	0							
	QRs	Yes	Yes	Abolished							
Basic products tariffs											
Bulgaria	Ann IIa	GSP	GSP	GSP	GSP	50	0				
	Ann IIb	GSP	GSP	GSP	GSP	80	60	0 (40)	0 (20)		
Czech Slovak	Ann IIa	50	0								
	Ann IIb	80	60	60	60	60	0 (40)	0 (20)			
Hungary	Ann IIa	50	0								
	Ann IIb	80	60	60	60	60	0 (40)	0 (20)			
Poland	Ann IIa	50	0								
	Ann IIb	80	60	60	60	60	0 (40)	0 (20)			
Romania	Ann IIa	MFN	MFN	60	0						
	Ann IIb	MFN	MFN	60	60	60	60	0 (40)	0 (20)		
Sensitive products within tariff quota											
Bulgaria	Tariffs	GSP	GSP	GSP	GSP	Suspended					
	QRs	100	100	100	100	120	150 (140)	180 (160)	Abolished (180)	(Abolished) (200)	
Czech Slovak	Tariffs	Suspended									
	QRs	120	140	140	150 (140)	150 (140)	180 (160)	Abolished (180)	(200)	(Abolished)	
Hungary	Tariffs	Suspended									
	QRs	115	130	130	130 (140)	130 (140)	165 (145)	Abolished (160)	(175)	(Abolished)	
Poland	Tariffs	Suspended									
	QRs	120	140	140	150 (140)	150 (140)	180 (160)	Abolished (180)	(200)	(Abolished)	
Romania	Tariffs	MFN	MFN	Suspended							
	QRs	100	100	120	120	120	150 (140)	180 (160)	Abolished (180)	(Abolished) (200)	
Sensitive products outside tariff quota											
Bulgaria	Tariffs	GSP	GSP	GSP	GSP	85	70	55	0 (40)	0 (25)	
	QRs	85				Abolished					
Czech Slovak	Tariffs	Abolished									
	QRs	90	70	70	70	70	55	0 (60)	0 (50)		
Hungary	Tariffs	90	80	80	80	80	70	0 (60)	0 (50)		

Product / Country		Regime								
Poland	Tariffs	MFN	85	70	70	70	55	0 (60)	0 (50)	0 (25)	0 (1/7)
	QRs		Abolished								
Romania	Tariffs	MFN	70	85	85	70	55	0 (40)	1/7		0 (1/7)
	QRs		Abolished								

Textiles and clothing

Country									
Bulgaria	Tariffs	GSP	5/7	5/7	5/7	4/7	2/7	1/7	0 (1/7)
	QRs	Unspecified rate of reduction to 0 after 5 (6) years from Jan. 1994							
Czech Slovak	Tariffs		5/7	5/7	5/7	2/7	1/7	0 (1/7)	
	QRs	Unspecified rate of reduction to 0 after 5 (6) years from Jan. 1994							
Hungary	Tariffs		5/7	5/7	5/7	2/7	1/7	0 (1/7)	
	QRs	Unspecified rate of reduction to 0 after 5 (6) years from Jan. 1994							
Poland	Tariffs		5/7	5/7	5/7	2/7	1/7	0 (1/7)	
	QRs	Unspecified rate of reduction to 0 after 5 (6) years from Jan. 1994							
Romania	Tariffs	MFN	5/7	5/7	5/7	4/7	2/7	1/7	0 (1/7)
	QRs	Unspecified rate of reduction to 0 after 5 (6) years from Jan. 1994							

Steel

Country								
Bulgaria	Tariffs	GSP	80	80	60	40	0 (20)	0 (10)
	QRs		Abolished					
Czech Slovak	Tariffs		60	60	60	40	20	0 (10)
	QRs		Abolished					
Hungary	Tariffs		60	60	60	40	20	0 (10)
	QRs		Abolished					
Poland	Tariffs		60	60	60	40	20	0 (10)
	QRs		Abolished					
Romania	Tariffs	MFN	80	80	60	40	20	0 (10)
	QRs		Abolished					

Coal

Country							
Bulgaria	Tariffs	GSP	100	100	50	50	0
	QRs	MFN	Abolished (with exceptions)				
Czech Slovak	Tariffs		100	100	50	50	0
	QRs		Abolished (with exceptions)				
Hungary	Tariffs		100	100	50	50	0
	QRs		Abolished (with exceptions)				
Poland	Tariffs		100	100	50	50	0
	QRs		Abolished (with exceptions)				
Romania	Tariffs	MFN	100	100	50	50	0
	QRs		Abolished (with exceptions)				

Source: CEC (1994).

These figures represent the agreement at the Copenhagen Council of 1993. This agreement provided for faster liberalization than in the initial interim Europe Agreements. The figures reflect tariffs and quotas as a percentage of those applied before the agreement.
The initial liberalization timetable is shown by the figures in parentheses.

and QRs were removed immediately upon implementation of the Interim Agreement. These products comprise about 50 per cent of Eastern European exports to the EU. Only for Romania do exports of such products to the EU fall substantially below 50 per cent. The importance of textiles and clothing to Romania means that immediate tariff and QR removal affected only 25 per cent of Romanian exports.

Products exempted from immediate tariff and non-tariff barrier liberalization in the EU are classified as basic industrial products, sensitive products, textiles and clothing, and coal and steel products. Basic industrial products are listed in Annex II of each agreement and differ between each associated country. These special products include base metals, such as aluminium and zinc, together with other primary products such as leather and salt. The Annex further subdivides items according to tariff treatment. For products in Annex IIa, tariffs were halved upon implementation of the agreement and removed one year later. Thus, from January 1994 these products entered the EU duty free from all Eastern European countries. Tariffs are reduced more slowly for products in Annex IIb, 20 per cent annually for the first two years of the agreement followed by abolition. This reflects an increase in the rate of liberalization following the Copenhagen Summit. The original agreements provided for two further consecutive reductions in duties of 20 per cent.

The classification of products to Annex IIa or IIb differs according to country. For example, Aluminium imports from Hungary are included in Annex IIb, whilst Aluminium imported from Bulgaria is classified in Annex IIa. However, these products are not of great significance to the eastern European countries, accounting for less than 1 per cent of exports to the EU.

Products deemed to be 'sensitive' in the EU are listed in Annex III of each agreement. Again, there are some differences between the individual agreements as to the products involved. In general, the products in this list correspond to those treated as sensitive under the GSP. Included are footwear, glassware, furniture, passenger cars, cement, certain chemicals, and leather goods. For all 'sensitive' products QRs were abolished upon implementation of the agreement; March 1992 for the Czech and Slovak Republics, Hungary and Poland, May 1993 for Romania, and December 1993 for Bulgaria.

The agreements suspend tariffs on sensitive products provided the quantity of imports remains below a predetermined level each year. Above these levels imports are subject to tariffs that are progressively reduced and finally abolished in January 1996. In certain cases the quantitative limit is treated as a ceiling after which the Commission has the discretion to reintroduce duties. The Copenhagen Summit brought the date of abolition forward from January 1998, as envisaged in the original agreements, the annual rate of reduction of the duties on above quota imports being 15 per cent (10 per cent for Hungary) of the level immediately prior to the initiation of the agreement. In addition, the levels at which duties are imposed are progressively liberalized, increasing by at least 20 per cent (15 per cent for Hungary) in each year following implementation of the agreement. The limits are to be abolished in the fourth year after the agreement came into effect.

Again, the Copenhagen Summit promoted faster liberalization. The increase in quotas mentioned above is faster than in the original agreements, and they are abolished two years earlier. The Commission has argued (CEC 1994) that the arrangements with regard to 'sensitive' products are more liberal than they appear, since many of the tariff quotas do not bind.

Liberalization of trade in textiles and clothing is slower than that for 'sensitive' products. Tariffs are reduced to zero after a period of five years, by two-sevenths in the first two years and in the fourth year, and by one-seventh at the beginning of each of the third, fifth, and sixth years after implementation of the agreements. Following Copenhagen, tariff elimination will be achieved one year earlier than laid down in the original agreements. Quantitative restrictions will be abolished at the beginning of 1998 for the Czech and Slovak Republics, Hungary, and Poland, and in January 1999 for Bulgaria and Romania. Again, this is one year earlier than planned in the original agreements. The way in which these constraints will be removed is not specified in the agreements.

Steel and coal products are another exception. For steel products quantitative restrictions were removed by the EU when the agreements came into effect. Tariffs are reduced annually by 20 per cent, with complete abolition being achieved by the beginning of 1996 for Bulgaria, Poland, Hungary, and the Czech and Slovak Republics. For Romania, zero tariffs will not be achieved until one year later. For coal products all duties will be removed by 1996. Quantitative restrictions were abolished after one year of the agreement, although national restrictions remain in Germany and Spain which must be eliminated within four years of the agreement coming into effect.

Thus, the Europe agreements provide immediate liberalization from tariffs and QRs of approximately 50 per cent of products exported by Eastern Europe to the EU. However, liberalization is considerably slower for some of the principal industrial exports of the Eastern Europeans, most notably textiles and clothing, footwear, and road vehicles. The approach of the EU to the liberalization of trade in the 'sensitive' sectors and in textiles and clothing and iron and steel has been subject to much criticism, primarily on the grounds that transition in the East would be further enhanced by the more immediate removal of trade barriers against these products. These are products in which these countries currently appear to have a comparative advantage. The agreements have also been criticized for leaving imports from these countries open to the vagaries of the EU's anti-dumping policies.

The reason why liberalization is slower for these sectors, so that within the EU enterprises are given time to adjust to greater competition, appears misconceived. Rollo and Smith (1993) show that although the 'sensitive' sectors are economically important at both the regional and national level within the EU, the share of imports from Eastern Europe in the output of EU members is so small, typically less than 1 per cent, that a large increase in imports should not cause major disruption to EU producers.

In addition, calculating the share of 'sensitive' products in exports to the EU shows that they are no more important for Eastern European countries than for the southern EU members. In 1993 the share of such products ranged from 54 per cent (Portugal) to 60 per cent (Greece), whereas for Czechoslovakia the share of 'sensitive' products was only 46 per cent, and for Hungary and Poland it was 51 and 55 per cent respectively.

18.2.2 The single market and the Uruguay Round

Access for foreign exporters to the EU markets will be influenced by two major policy changes in the 1990s: the Single European Market (SEM), and the 1994 GATT accord. The removal of barriers within the EU will stimulate intra-EU trade. For external suppliers there appear to be two key issues: firstly, whether the removal of barriers to trade within the EU will lead to trade diversion, and secondly, whether more intense competition within the EU will lead to greater demands for external protection, which, if granted, would create a 'fortress Europe'.

Trade diversion is not necessarily the consequence of trade-barrier removal within Europe. In markets where goods are differentiated and economies of scale are important, there may be an increase in demand for the products of external suppliers. The integration-induced increase in demand for a product produced within the EU may stimulate the demand for complementary goods, some of which may be supplied by non-member countries. Furthermore, some of the barriers which will be dismantled have impinged upon imports from outside the EU, so that their removal will stimulate external trade. For example, the removal of border controls will permit a EU-wide approach to distribution. The harmonization of technical standards should make it easier for non-EU suppliers who serve several of the national markets within the EU. The replacement of national quotas with EU-wide restrictions will benefit the exporting countries, as a given amount of sales can be more efficiently allocated between countries. In other words, the supplier will be able to shift sales from low-price, previously unrestricted, EU markets to higher-price EU markets, those where imports were previously constrained.

Empirical studies of the effects of the SEM have concentrated upon the implications for EU members. The dominant approach has been based upon numerical simulation models which try and capture the effects of imperfect competition and returns to scale. This research has highlighted the potential for large welfare gains from completing the single market, as much as 5 per cent of EU GDP. However, this prediction is controversial. Standard statistical measures of the accuracy of these models are not available. Furthermore, over half the gain emanates from economies of scale and imperfect competition. There is little evidence by which to judge the importance of unexploited scale economies in the EU, or the extent to which the available economies would have been reaped even in the absence of the SEM; and, as we have already argued, we have little information by which to ascertain the way in which firms compete in imperfectly competitive markets. The nature of this competition is important in determining the results produced by the model. Very crudely, we do not know whether the Cournot assumption is empirically more relevant than the Bertrand assumption, but we do know that Cournot gives bigger gains than Bertrand!

In these simulation models the non-EC sector is poorly specified, if at all. Brenton and Winters (1992), using a traditional econometric approach with limited product differentiation (only by country), suggest that if the SEM entails just simple trade-barrier removal this will lead to an increase in demand in the EU for imports from all sources. Since the removal of some barriers will benefit imports from outside of the EU there will be no trade diversion. If, however, the creation of the SEM leads to an increase in the efficiency of output for domestic sales, then non-EU suppliers may suffer from trade diversion. This could occur if the stimulation of exports provides for increased exploitation of scale economies which reduces the unit cost of all output.

In this case the implications of the SEM for non-EU countries would depend upon the extent to which their exports to the EU are concentrated in sectors where scale economies are important. Scale economies are generally not viewed as being important for traditional industries such as clothing, footwear, and furniture. Exports of machinery, telecommunications equipment, and vehicles are typically held to offer scope for exploiting scale economies.

Sapir (1995) has highlighted that, over the period 1986 to 1992, which should include adjustments to the creation of the SEM on 1 January 1993, a wide range of sectors in the EU experienced both internal and external trade creation. The share of both intra- and extra-EU imports in apparent consumption has increased. Trade creation (both internal and external) has been much greater in sectors classified as having medium trade barriers than in those thought to be the most heavily protected. External trade creation is found to dominate the medium-trade barrier sectors, whilst internal trade creation is more important in the sectors with high barriers. Sectors with medium-trade barriers are typically those where national trade barriers against non-EU suppliers were important. Sectors with high internal trade barriers are typically high-technology sectors where bias in public procurement has been prevalent.

The second issue relates to the concern that, deprived of protection from competition within the EU, there will be increased pressure from European firms for stricter external trade barriers. The study by Sapir (1995) shows that for the period prior to 1992 this fear has been unfounded. The share of imports from outside the EU in total EU consumption has been continually growing. Furthermore, the commitments to more open access to the EU market made as part of the Uruguay Round settlement, to be discussed below, will help to ensure that external liberalization occurs at the same time as internal liberalization, so minimizing the potential for trade diversion. The strengthening of the rules of the world trade régime as part of the GATT deal will provide greater confidence for non-EU countries that a 'fortress Europe is no longer a possibility'.

18.2.3 The Uruguay Round

On 15 April 1994 an agreement was signed in Marrakech, Morocco, which ended seven years of trade negotiations under the 'Uruguay Round'. This was the eighth round of multilateral trade negotiations. The previous rounds were marked by their success in reducing tariffs on trade in industrial products between the advanced countries. The current agreement is most notable for bringing under GATT rules sectors previously immune from the trade policy disciplines applied to industrial products, namely agriculture and textiles and clothing. There was also success in including new issues: trade in services, intellectual property, and investment-distorting trade policies. With regard to trade in industrial goods, the main features of the Uruguay Round are tariff concessions and the strengthening of the rules of the world trading system. We now briefly consider each of these issues separately.

The agreement on agriculture was crucial to the overall success of the Uruguay Round. Failure to reach a consensus on liberalizing trade in agricultural products would have put into jeopardy other aspects of the negotiations. The major achievement is that agriculture is now subject to the discipline of the GATT. Previously this sector was subject to 'special treatment' which allowed for the use of import quotas, export subsidies, and instruments which were not covered by the GATT, such as variable import levies and domestic subsidies.

The agreement on agriculture entails specific commitments (see e.g. Ingersent *et al.* 1995). Total domestic subsidies to agriculture, defined by the Aggregate Measure of Support (AMS), must be reduced by 20 per cent over six years. Certain types of subsidy involving direct payments to farmers are excluded from the AMS, such as the deficiency payments system applied in the US, and the compensation payments to EU farmers implemented following the CAP reform of 1992. All non-tariff barriers must be converted into equivalent tariffs. Tariffs must then be reduced by an average of 36 per cent, with a minimum 15 per cent reduction for each product, over the six-year period from the completion of the Uruguay Round. Tariffs will then be bound at this final rate. Export subsidies remain legal, an exception to basic GATT principles, but are capped in terms of both the level of expenditure and the volume of subsidized exports prevailing in the base period, the average over the years 1986 to 1990. Thus, the possibility of subsidy wars in agriculture has been removed. There is also a commitment to reduce expenditure on export subsidies by 36 per cent, and to contract the volume of subsidized exports by 21 per cent over the six-year period.

The agreement allows for a considerable degree of flexibility in its implementation. The reduction of 20 per cent in domestic subsidies relates to all expenditures. Subsidies to certain commodities may be cut by less than 20 per cent, and perhaps may not be cut at all. The agreement is rather vague on the procedure by which non-tariff barriers are to be converted into tariffs; for example, adjustments may be made for quality and variety, and the base period for tariffication (1986 to 1988) was a period of historically high prices for food products on the world market. Thus, initial tariffs are in many cases very high and exceed the current protective effect of the barriers they replace. For example, the tariff equivalents of the EU's variable import levies are 314 per cent for butter, 267 per cent for skimmed-milk powder, 267 per cent for white sugar, 181 per cent for beef carcases, and 171 per cent for barley (reported in Ingersent *et al.* 1995). Small reductions to, and then the binding of, such high tariffs will have little impact in practice.

Thus, the commitments in agriculture will not have a significant impact upon world food markets or the CAP. However, the agreement for the first time makes agricultural protection more open and transparent, which will provide for a more certain environment for agricultural producers. The agreement will be reviewed in 1999. In the mean time, domestic pressure for the reform of agricultural support is likely to mount, and the EU is already committed to further reform of the CAP. By early in the next century it may be possible for the initial liberalization of trade in agricultural products agreed as part of the Uruguay Round to be reinforced by genuine commitments which offer greater market access to imported products.

The Uruguay Round seeks to bring textiles and clothing back into the GATT so that trade in such products will again be governed by the accepted rules which apply to trade in other industrial goods. Trade restrictions were originally imposed under the euphemistically titled Short-Term Agreement to provide a 'breathing spell' to permit adjustment in industrial countries to 'new market conditions' (see Spinanger 1995). But thirty years later, under the Multi-Fibre Arrangement (MFA), a complex set of bilateral trade constraints remained.

The Uruguay Round contains an agreement that the bilateral quotas of the MFA will be phased out over a ten-year period from the creation of the WTO. There is a commitment that from the date of implementation of the agreement, each member will integrate into the WTO at least 16 per cent of the volume of their imports in 1990 of textile and clothing products covered by the MFA, but not necessarily restricted by it. At the start of the fourth year of the agreement, 1998, a further 17 per cent will be brought under the normal rules of the GATT. In the eighth year 18 per cent will be integrated, with the final 49 per cent being brought into the GATT at the end of the phase out in 2005.

The agreements also entail that the restrictions which remain must be progressively relaxed. In stage one, the first three years, the yearly growth rate of quota carried forward from the MFA will be increased by 16 per cent. A quota which increased by 3 per cent per annum under the MFA must now rise by 3.48 per cent each year. During the next four years, stage two, the rate of increase in quota levels must be 25 per cent higher than those established in stage one. For the last three years, stage three, the rate of increase must be 27 per cent above that of stage two. Thus a quota rising by 3 per cent per annum prior to the agreement will increase by 5.52 per cent in the final stage of the phase-out. For countries subject to restrictions which accounted for less than 1.2 per cent of the total volume of a country's restricted imports at the end of 1991, the rates of increase in quotas are advanced by one stage, that is, 25 per cent in stage one and 27 per cent in stage two.

Importing countries are permitted a great deal of discretion in choosing which products should be liberalized in the various stages and thus in the structure of their quota liberalization. All that is required is that some products are included from each of tops and yarns, fabrics, made-up textile products, and clothing. The amount of each category that should be liberalized at each stage is not specified. This flexibility means that the most sensitive items will be excluded from the initial stages and will not be liberalized until the MFA phase out is completed at the end of 2004; thus 49 per cent of trade covered by MFA quotas, including the most sensitive and most highly constrained products, will not be freed from quota restrictions until the end of 2004.

This has led to much scepticism as to whether this final stage of the agreement will be implemented, or whether, in the face of strong pressure from domestic import-competing interests, the importing countries will seek to extend the transitional period or will revert to using safeguard measures. Thus, there is considerable uncertainty concerning whether textiles and clothing trade will be brought fully under the umbrella of the GATT by 2005.

The liberalization in the transition period may also be offset by the use of safeguard measures and anti-dumping restrictions. The Uruguay Round agreement seeks to prevent the introduction of new restrictions on trade in textiles and footwear, but provides for the use of selective safeguards measures on products where quotas have been fully removed, and for anti-dumping actions on products whether quotas have been removed or not. This has led to concern in some exporting countries that protection will be shifted from quotas to safeguards and anti-dumping measures (Schott 1994).

The Uruguay Round agreement also included understandings on three areas not previously covered by the GATT: trade in services, trade related intellectual property rights (TRIPs), and trade-related investment measures (TRIMs). The importance of trade in services has grown markedly over the past two decades. In 1993 it is estimated that the value of world exports of services was approximately one quarter of the value of world trade in goods. The General Agreement on Trade in Services (GATS) provides an initial framework for the liberalization of trade in services. There are three elements to the agreement: a set of general obligations that apply to all services, the key obligation being Most Favoured Nation treatment; sectoral annexes showing how the rules apply to specific sectors; and market access commitments on a sector and country basis. Progress in obtaining specific commitments towards liberalization was rather mixed. Significant moves towards greater market access were achieved for advertising, construction and engineering, insurance, accounting and consulting, and land transport. Little or no headway was made for audiovisual services, banking and securities, telecommunications, and maritime services. Nevertheless the GATS provides a platform for further, more extensive, liberalization in the future.

The TRIPs agreement provides for copyright protection in a number of areas, such as computer programs, pharmaceuticals, and agricultural chemicals. As we discussed in Chapter 6, the key issues with regard to international copyright protection have a North–South, Rich–Poor dimension. The negative effects of the agreement on the South are to some extent mitigated by the long transitional periods that are permitted: for example, ten years in the case of pharmaceuticals.

The agreement on investment measures outlaws practices which are inconsistent with national treatment, such as local content requirements and trade balancing and foreign-exchange-balancing conditions. Issues such as the right of establishment were not covered and investment incentives were included in the discussion of domestic subsidies. Again, the TRIMs agreement represents a tentative first step towards the establishment of multilateral discipline and liberalization of trade measures in the field of international investment. There is, however, a commitment to review the accord within five years and to consider whether it should be 'complemented with provisions on investment policy and competition policy'. This is an important issue. There are indications that investment by EU car producers in Eastern European countries has been accompanied by demands from those producers that trade barriers be raised in the Eastern markets.

The negotiations on tariffs took place on two fronts: tariff bindings and tariff liberalization. The issue of tariff bindings, the commitment not to raise the tariff on a product above a certain level, by industrial countries was not an important issue in the Uruguay Round, since previous rounds had already generated a high level of bound rates. Prior to the Uruguay Round, 94 per cent of imports into industrial countries were subject to bound tariff rates. The Uruguay Round increased this percentage to 99 per cent. The main developments regarding bindings were in developing countries (the proportion of imports being covered by bound rates rising from 13 per cent prior to the Round to 61 per cent) and transition economies (74 per cent to 96 per cent; data from Abrea 1995).

Tariff liberalization was also an important element of the Uruguay Round, as in previous rounds. The extent of tariff liberalization translates into improved market access for suppliers of imports when tariff rates have been bound. Thus, for industrial countries such as the EU, where most tariffs are bound, the proportionate decline in tariff rates is a useful indicator of the increase in openness. Improvements in market access are more difficult to determine when tariff rates are not bound.

The commitments on tariff reductions will be phased in over five years from the date of approval of the WTO, that is, from 1995. The average duty across all products applied by the EU will decline from 5.7 per cent to 3.6 per cent. However, this hides important differences in the extent of tariff reductions between sectors. The first two columns of Table 18.2 show the trade-weighted average tariffs applied by the EU on broad industrial groups of products both before and after the Uruguay Round. These data are indicative of tariff cuts being proportionately greater for products which were subject to below-average tariffs prior to the Uruguay Round. Most notable is the case of textiles and clothing. The average tariff on textiles and clothing products was 1.9 times higher than the average tariff for all products prior to the Round. After the Uruguay Round, tariffs on clothing products, on average, are more than 2.5 times higher than the average for all products.

An important issue that the Uruguay Round was to address was that of tariff

Table 18.2. Average tariffs and the distribution (per cent) of EU imports according to different tariff rates: pre- and post-Uruguay Round

| | Average Duty | | Distribution of imports | | | | | | | | | |
| | | | 0 | | 0.1–5.1 | | 5.1–10.1 | | 10.1–15.0 | | 15.1–35.0 | |
	pre	post	pre	post	pre	post	pre	post	pre	post	pre	post
Fish and fish products	12.3	10.2	6.2	6.9	15.2	14.5	20.7	29.6	19.9	31.2	38.0	17.8
Wood products	3.0	0.7	60.3	88.5	3.3	3.0	34.8	8.5	1.6	0.0	0.0	0.0
Textiles and cloth	11.0	9.1	0.6	1.3	5.3	19.1	29.7	25.5	64.3	54.1	0.1	0.0
Leather, rubber, and footwear	6.5	5.1	23.3	24.5	12.1	40.7	52.8	23.0	0.0	0.0	11.8	11.8
Metals	2.3	1.1	60.8	73.7	18.7	19.6	19.4	6.7	0.0	0.0	1.1	0.0
Chemicals	7.3	4.5	2.7	27.2	11.2	4.0	70.3	68.8	15.6	0.0	0.2	0.2
Transport equipment	7.2	6.5	22.0	23.4	6.9	15.7	65.5	59.9	4.4	0.8	1.2	0.2
Non-electric machines	4.4	1.4	6.0	33.9	84.1	63.1	8.8	3.0	1.1	0.0	0.0	0.0
Electric machines	8.6	5.2	2.2	3.9	25.9	69.9	37.0	8.3	34.9	17.9	0.0	0.0
Minerals	0.9	0.6	68.2	85.2	24.3	10.4	6.1	3.3	1.4	1.1	0.0	0.0
Other manufactures	6.4	3.5	8.4	24.2	13.0	58.9	70.7	12.0	7.3	4.3	0.6	0.6
Total	5.7	3.6	23.6	37.7	26.3	34.2	35.5	19.0	13.2	8.2	1.4	0.9

peaks in industrial countries, that is, tariffs of 15 per cent or more. Table 18.2 shows that this was not a particularly important matter in the EU tariff schedule: for only fish and fish products and leather, rubber, and footwear were a significant proportion of imports subject to tariffs over 15 per cent. The latter product is one of the major exports of Eastern European countries to the EU. However, as the table shows, there was no progress in reducing the proportion of imports subject to such high tariffs in this sector. Table 18.2 shows more generally the structure of EU tariffs both before and after the Uruguay Round. The most striking feature of the Table is the relatively large proportion of imports of textiles and clothing which are subject to tariffs of between 10 and 15 per cent.

A further important achievement of the Uruguay Round is the strengthening of the rules of the trade system. The GATT provides for any member country to impose trade restrictions under certain conditions: emergency measures to protect industries seriously injured by imports (Article XIX); measures to counter dumping by foreign firms (Article VI); countervailing duties to offset subsidies to foreign firms (Article VI); and restrictions by developing countries for balance of payments reasons (Article XVIII). The reason for these provisions is to provide an outlet for protectionist interests and so facilitate general trade-liberalizing agreements that would otherwise have been blocked by such interests. Finger (1995) rather bluntly describes the situation as 'all dogs have fleas, therefore all dogs have legs with which to scratch. Likewise, any government that maintains a liberal trade policy must have ways to deal with the constituent pressures for exceptions—pressures for "exceptional protection" of particular domestic sectors'. The problem for the GATT is how to place appropriate constraints through the establishment of agreed rules upon their use whilst still allowing trade restrictions.

Article XIX of the GATT provides for importing countries to use measures to give temporary respite from a surge in imports that is causing or has the potential to cause serious injury to a domestic industry. A notable feature of the Uruguay Round is the prohibition of voluntary export restraints and orderly marketing agreements. However, as we have seen in Chapter 9, the EU will continue to maintain an agreement with Japan on imports of cars until 1999. The conditions under which safeguard measures can be applied have been clarified, and the attraction of using GATT legal responses, rather than VERs, to dislocation caused by imports has been increased. Thus, during an initial three-year period, exporting countries may not retaliate even if compensation is not offered by the importing country. Cline (1995) suggests that this addresses a reason why GATT illegal safeguard measures were used in the past.

The agreement states that an investigation must find actual damage or threat of injury, and that safeguards measures can only be imposed to the extent necessary to prevent injury. Measures can only be applied for up to four years, although a further four-year extension is possible to prevent or remedy serious injury if it can be shown that the industry is adjusting. Application of safeguards during the initial four-year period is not predicated on any adjustment policy being implemented in the importing country. Finally, the agreement allows for some selectivity in safeguard measures. Thus, particular supplying countries can be targeted if imports from those countries have increased disproportionately relative to total imports. It has been argued (Schott 1994) that this will allow industrial countries to target protection against fast growing Asian and Eastern European countries, and, in particular, is a mechanism that will be used to deal with rapidly rising imports from China.

The safeguards agreement has led to differing interpretations of its likely impact. Schott (1994) suggests that because of the Uruguay Round, safeguards will 'continue to play a minor role in international trade relations'. Cline (1995), on the other hand, suggests that the removal of the exporting country's right to retaliate and the allowance of discriminatory restrictions 'could make safeguards a more actively used vehicle'. Time will tell.

The agreement on anti-dumping is one of the least satisfactory aspects of the Uruguay Round. The GATT provides for countries to unilaterally impose duties upon imported products which are dumped, that is, sold at less than their 'normal' value, if such imports cause or threaten injury to domestic producers. Traditionally the 'normal' value or price is taken to be the price at which the product is sold in the exporter's home market.

The use of anti-dumping measures increased substantially during the 1970s and 1980s. In the early 1960s there were less than twelve cases per year initiated by GATT members. In the decade prior to 1994 there were on average 164 antidumping cases per year. This compares with an average of 3 cases per year of safeguard actions notified to the GATT under Article XIX. Antidumping cases have become the most desired method for industries seeking protection in industrial countries. The United States, the EU, Canada, and Australia are the principal users of anti-dumping measures. Over 80 per cent of all anti-dumping cases between 1985 and 1992 were initiated by these four countries or country groups (Schott 1994).

This increase in the demand for, and use of, anti-dumping measures also led to concern about the misuse of this instrument. There are two main issues. Firstly, the broad definition of dumping in national regulations permits anti-dumping actions in a wide range of cases. There is considerable evidence that regulations are such that there is a bias towards finding dumping and to exaggerating the margin of dumping, and hence to inflating the size of the anti-dumping duties. Secondly, the mere initiation of an anti-dumping investigation curtails imports. This is because exporters face the possibility of large legal and administrative costs, whilst importing agents may have to pay backdated anti-dumping duties.

The Uruguay Round improves the current system by increasing the amount of information that the country initiating the anti-dumping action has to make public, and by increasing the transparency of the procedures. The data used in the investigation must be made public, and an explanation has to be provided of how a decision was reached. Interested parties must be provided with the opportunity to defend themselves.

The negotiations were also concerned with methodological aspects of the procedures followed in anti-dumping investigations. The most important changes are the introduction of a sunset clause requiring that all duties or undertakings (foreign firms can avoid anti-dumping duties by giving a commitment that they will raise their prices) will cease after a maximum of five years. However, cases can be reviewed prior to the sunset date and measures continued if it is deemed that dumping and injury will persist.

The new agreement also legitimizes much of the approach to anti-dumping in the United States and the EU. The relatively high propensity of these countries to use anti-dumping measures in the past suggests that the Uruguay Round may increase the use of such 'process protection'. Standard definitions of dumping emphasize the selling of products abroad at prices lower than the good is sold in the home market. US practice concentrates upon whether the product is sold in the importing country at a price below the average cost of production, whether or not the good is sold for the same price in the home market. This induces arbitrariness in the identification of dumping, and allows scope for excessive calculations of dumping margins. The agreement does seek to exert some discipline by defining how the 'cost' calculation should be undertaken. In summary, the agreement on anti-dumping provides for greater clarity, but does little to reduce the potential misuse of such measures. The reduction in protection in other sectors, such as textiles and clothing, is likely to push protectionist demand towards anti-dumping and safeguard measures. One commentator has summarized the agreement as providing 'a bandage to a festering sore of trade policy; more extensive treatment will be required in future negotiations' (Schott 1994).

The GATT has anti-subsidy provisions. Prior to the Uruguay Round there existed a prohibition on export subsidies, except for agriculture. However, there was a lack of clarity concerning domestic subsidies which impinge upon international trade. The new agreement, which is confined to non-agricultural products, clearly defines a subsidy and states which practices are covered by the new commitments. Thus, a subsidy covers all financial contributions by any government body or organization acting on behalf of the government. Another key aspect of the agreement is that actions by state bodies which may indirectly confer a competitive advantage in international trade but which involve no transfer of funds or of goods or services are excluded. This clearly implies that relatively weak environmental standards are not covered by the agreement, so that rich countries with high standards cannot take action against imports from poorer countries with relatively less stringent environmental policies.

There is a distinction between subsidies which are generally available to all firms and those which are specific, that is, targeted, or restricted, to certain enterprises. The agreement then defines three categories of subsidy: those that are prohibited, those that are actionable, and non-actionable subsidies. Prohibited subsidies include those which are related to export performance. Non-actionable subsidies cover those associated with research and development, regional subsidies, and subsidies linked to pollution control and compliance with environmental regulations.

Actionable subsidies are those which, although not prohibited, are subject to countermeasures by other GATT members (countervailing duties) if it is shown that they distort trade. The agreement provides clear guidelines for evaluating whether such trade distortion occurs in terms of causing injury to the domestic industry, causing serious 'prejudice' to another GATT member, or undermining GATT benefits. Finally, the agreement clarifies the rules concerning the implementation of countervailing measures and includes a sunset clause similar to that in the anti-dumping agreement. There has, in general, been a positive response to the agreement on subsidies which it is felt has strengthened the GATT in this area.

Finally, the Uruguay Round implemented institutional changes including the establishment of a permanent institution, the World Trade Organisation (WTO), to govern international trade relations between members; the improvement of the dispute settlement procedure; and the introduction of the Trade Policy Review Mechanism. The WTO brings together all the various agreements negotiated in the forum of the GATT since its inception in 1947, including the GATS and the agreements on TRIMs and TRIPs. Countries which do not wish to sign the agreement on the GATS, for example, cannot join the WTO. Of most significance is the 'single undertaking', whereby members of the WTO will have to conform, with a few exceptions, to all previous agreements. In the Tokyo Round, for example, new codes on non-tariff barriers were negotiated, but were only signed by a subset of GATT members. These obligations will now apply to all members.

The Dispute Settlement Understanding has been well received as an agreement that will improve decision-making and should stimulate countries to conform with decisions made by the WTO. The Trade Policy Review Mechanism provides for the WTO to undertake periodic surveys of the trade policies of member countries. Such reviews, which have been conducted since an interim agreement in 1988, increase the transparency of trade policies and will encourage compliance with the agreed rules that govern international trade. Furthermore, by highlighting the economic costs of trade restrictions such reviews could help governments in resisting protectionist pressures.

To sum up, the Uruguay Round has succeeded in extending international trade rules to two sectors previously immune to multilateral discipline: agriculture, and textiles and clothing. Whilst this is to be welcomed for the greater certainty it gives to exporters, the extent to which trade is actually liberalized will depend upon the spirit with which the agreements are liberalized. Initial indications for agriculture suggest that there will be little impact upon degree of openness in the highly protected markets. Similarly for textiles and clothing, concessions are likely to be greatest for products which are already relatively unconstrained. Much depends upon whether the major step toward liberalized trade is actually taken at the end of the agreement in 2005.

The reinvigoration of the rules of the GATT should provide exporters with a measure of greater certainty regarding access to foreign markets. In this context it should help to allay fears that the internal market and the Europe Agreements will lead to an increase in protectionism against other suppliers. However, serious doubts remain over the use of anti-dumping duties. This, together with the initial tentative agreements in services, intellectual property, and investment measures suggest that a renewed effort towards negotiated trade liberalization will be required shortly into the new century. In addition, the WTO faces the demanding task of successfully integrating China, Russia, and other countries of the CIS into the world trading system.

18.3 The Common Agricultural Policy

The European Union's Common Agricultural Policy (CAP) has two fundamental roles. One is to *stabilize* consumer and producer prices for most locally grown foodstuffs within the Union, in the face of both internal and external disturbances, which would otherwise have made prices volatile. The other is, on average, to *raise* these prices above levels prevailing in the rest of the world. Very occasionally EU prices, for key commodities such as wheat, are close to or even below world levels: this was observed briefly in 1973–4, and again in 1995 for some products. But much more often EU internal prices are far above world levels.

It is helpful to explore these two roles of the CAP separately. Let us consider the price-stabilization role first, and begin with the case of external disturbances. The European Union has a given excess demand for a particular foodstuff, let us say wheat, which is shown by the curve *E* in Figure 18.1. EU imports are measured rightwards along the horizontal axis, from the origin at *O*; EU exports, leftwards from *O*. There is a family of rest of world excess supply curves. The middle one, $\bar{R}$, depicts, let us say, an average level of rest of world excess supply. $\bar{R}$ intersects *E* at point *c*. Let us assume that the EU fixes European prices at *c*. So when the rest

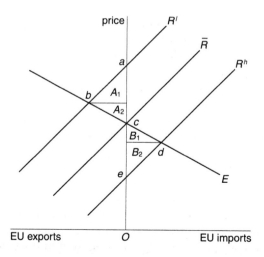

Fig. 18.1. CAP price-stabilization when the rest of the world's excess supply is volatile

of the world's excess supply is average, the EU neither exports nor imports wheat.

The rest of the world's excess supply is, however, volatile. Grain harvests in North America and Russia are susceptible to big swings. Suppose that harvests in the rest of the world are poor. The rest of the world's excess supply curve is now given by R^ℓ. In a completely free world market, untrammelled by intervention in the EU or elsewhere, the equilibrium would lie at b. The EU would export grain to the rest of the world. But with the EU price fixed at c, this does not happen. The equilibrium price in the rest of the world is at a. There are no grain exports from the EU. The partial equilibrium welfare effects of EU policy in this case lead to a deadweight loss of A_1 in the rest of the world, and A_2 in the European Union, when compared with the no-intervention, ideal equilibrium at b. Behind these adverse aggregate effects lie gains for certain people: the EU's price-fixing policy benefits European consumers. It also raises producer surplus in the rest of the world. But within the EU producer surplus falls by more than consumer surplus rises. The net difference between the two is A_2. In the rest of the world, consumer surplus falls by more than producer surplus rises (with A_1 measuring the difference).

Now take the case where rest of world harvests are high. The rest of the world's excess supply moves rightwards to R^h. But for the CAP, a new equilibrium would be established at d, where the EU is a net wheat importer. But for the CAP, the EU would benefit from a net welfare gain of B_1, which measures the excess of consumer surplus gain above producer surplus loss within the EU. The rest of the world would benefit by area B_2, which is the amount by which their producer surplus gain exceeds their consumer surplus loss. But the CAP freezes EU prices at c. The EU's grain imports do not happen. The rest of the world price falls to e. The net welfare gains from the trade that would otherwise have materialized, B_1 within the EU, and B_2 for the rest of the world, are sacrificed. So the deadweight cost of the CAP in this case is B_1 for the EU and B_2 for the rest of the world.

The message of Figure 18.1 is that EU price-fixing in the face of volatile world excess supply is damaging. Both the EU and the rest of the world suffer. Efficient trades are blocked. Prices are stabilized in the EU, but destabilized elsewhere. The size of the damage done is (approximately) proportional to the square of the variance in rest-of-world excess supply, and exactly so when, as in Figure 18.1, the EU and rest of world's excess demand and supply curves are linear. The distribution of the deadweight losses between the EU and the rest of the world will be equal when the gradients of these two curves are the same in absolute value. If the rest of the world's excess supply curve is flatter (steeper) than the EU's excess demand curve, it is the EU (the rest of the world) that shoulders the larger part of these costs.

A fuller treatment would complicate these statements somewhat, but would not really overturn them. If the EU's consumers are averse to risk, they benefit from steadier food prices. Similarly for the EU's producers, if, as seems reasonable, they too are risk-averse. But the destabilization of prices in the rest of the world hurts consumers and producers there, to the extent that they are also averse to risk. Furthermore, producer risk-aversion implies that the EU will tend to produce more food on average, and the rest of the world less, than they would have done without the CAP. There are also the agricultural policies in the rest of the world that could be brought into the story, as well as the general equilibrium effects of production and consumption shifts into and out of other goods, and also the separate welfare effects on individual groups in the two parts of the world which are important if social welfare is not defined as the simple sum of consumers' and producers' surpluses. Within the EU, the producer-risk-aversion argument for price stabilization is also open to the objection that it could be much more efficient for farmers to enter into forward contracts, which would eliminate the uncertainties associated with price-volatility.

This is what happens when the source of market disturbances lies in the rest of the world. Now let us see how the picture changes when it is harvest volatility within Europe that leads to swings. Figure 18.2 refers to this. There is now a single rest-of-the-world excess supply curve, R. But there are three excess demand

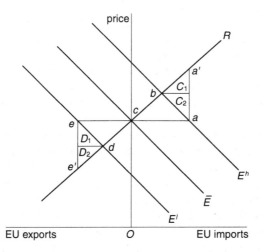

Fig. 18.2. CAP price-stabilization when excess demand is volatile in the European Union

curves for the European Union: $\bar{E}$, representing an average value, and E^h and E^ℓ, which depict high and low EU excess demand respectively.

Without the CAP, the world price would be at b when the EU's excess demand is given by E^h, and at d when by E^ℓ. In the first case, the EU is a grain importer; in the second, it exports. When the EU excess demand is given by $\bar{E}$ there is no trade, and the equilibrium world price is at c.

When CAP locks the EU internal price at c, the EU imports the horizontal distance from a to c when its excess demand is E^h. With excess demand low, at E^ℓ, its exports the distance ec. In the outside world, the price jumps to a' in the first case, and falls to e' in the second. The price-fixing by the CAP therefore introduces a pro-trade bias when the source of market disturbance is internal, in marked contrast to the external disturbances in Figure 18.1, which exerted an anti-trade bias. But in both Figures 18.1 and 18.2, the effect of price-fixing inside the EU is to exaggerate price swings in the rest of the world.

The enhanced trade volumes under the CAP in Figure 18.2 are not efficient. When comparing the equilibrium with CAP fixing with the one without, areas $C_1 + C_2$ amount to the net deadweight loss that distinguishes the former from the latter. This is the welfare cost of the excessive trade in the high excess demand case; $D_1 + D_2$ capture the equivalent cost when the EU's excess demand is E^ℓ. The CAP arrangements call for export subsidies with E low, and import subsidies when E is high.

In the E^h case, $C_1 + C_2$ measures the amount by which the EU's financial loss on import-subsidization exceeds the increase in the EU and rest-of-world surpluses over and above what would have been gained without CAP fixing, under the equilibrium at b. Similarly, when E is at E^ℓ, $D_1 + D_2$ measures the excess of the EU's export subsidies over and above the net surplus gains (relative to the no-CAP equilibrium at d).

Our conclusions about the price-stabilizing aspect of the European Union's Common Agricultural Policy is that it buys intra-European food-price stability at the cost of increased price destabilization in other countries, no matter whether the source of disturbance is internal or external. When disturbances are external, it serves to squeeze agricultural trade between the EU and the rest of the world. If disturbances are internal, it artificially boosts this trade, but at a large financial cost (because exports when EU harvests are high have to be subsidized, and imports likewise when EU harvests are poor). Under both types of disturbance, internal and external, there is a net welfare cost to be borne, which is unambiguous under simple assumptions and not at all likely to disappear when more complex effects are introduced. The size of this deadweight loss is trivial if a disturbance is small, but goes up, roughly, with the square of its size. Both the EU and the rest of the world are liable to suffer when disturbances are external; internal disturbances tend to benefit the rest of the world but damage EU welfare by more.

We now turn to the issue of average price *levels*. We saw that the CAP typically raises EU prices for foodstuffs above rest-of-world levels. In the case of grain, butter, and beef, EU prices have averaged nearly double rest-of-world prices for the past twenty years. The European Union consists of fifteen rich countries, well-endowed with capital and skilled labour. It is one of the most densely populated regions on earth. In certain areas (the Po valley in northern Italy, the Île-de-France region, Denmark, Holland, Prussia, and East Anglia, particularly) it is blessed with some well-watered and highly productive land; but large parts of this small and crowded continent are mountainous, arid or both. In arable and pasture acreage per head, the EU is impoverished, and especially so in comparison with the US Midwest, the prairies of Canada, Argentina, New Zealand, the western Cape of South Africa, the Australian east coast, and the Ukraine.

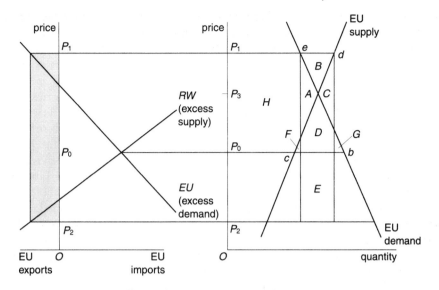

Fig. 18.3. The general effects of the CAP, without volatility

The European Union is, then, a natural food importer as a whole, although there are particular regions where Heckscher-Ohlin arguments would lead us to predict agricultural exports. Despite this, the European Union has tended to export temperate-zone foodstuffs on balance for many years. The credit—or blame—for this rests largely with the CAP.

Figure 18.3 shows why this is so. In the right-hand panel, we see the EU's demand and supply curves, labelled D and S, for a representative product, such as wheat, butter, or beef. The two curves cut at point a. This would depict equilibrium under autarky; the price here would be P_3.

Rest of world prices are typically lower than P_3, and sometimes far below. In the absence of the CAP, world equilibrium would give rise to a price of P_0. This is where the EU's excess-demand curve, labelled EU (which is found by subtracting S from D in the right-hand panel) crosses the rest of the world's excess supply curve, RW. If P_0 ruled as an internal price within the EU, consumption would occur at b and production at c, giving rise to EU imports of the horizontal distance cb.

The CAP has led, for numerous products and on numerous occasions, to internal 'excess supply' within the EU. This will happen if prices are pitched inside the EU at a level above P_3, such as P_1. The size of excess supply is indicated by the horizontal distance between d and e if the CAP price that rules within the EU is set at P_1. This is not to say that the EU imports no agricultural products from the rest of the world. It does. But the Union is generally a net exporter of temperate-zone agricultural products as a whole.

What happens to the excess supply? It is sold 'into intervention' and (at least temporarily) stored. It is the addition to the 'mountain' of beef or butter, or the 'lake' of wine. Some of it is destroyed, or fed to animals (which induces more excess supply later, in another market). But much of it is dumped on world markets. It may be sold at especially low prices to Russia, for example; or exported anywhere for what it will fetch.

In Figure 18.3 we assume that the EU's excess supply is all sold to the rest of the world. Its effect is to depress the price in the rest of the world, from P_0 (where it would be if CAP were abolished) to P_2. The financial cost of this is absorbed by the European Agricultural Guarantee and Guidance Fund (EAGGF, with a French acronym FEOGA). It is ultimately paid for by taxes levied on European Union residents, through national taxation, and then transferred to the European Commission. The total financial cost is shown in the right-hand panel of Figure 18.3 by the rectangle $edfg$. In the left-hand panel, it appears as the shaded rectangle to the left of the vertical axis. In the right-hand panel, the rectangle is subdivided into areas A, B, C, D, and E, which will be useful later.

The CAP acts as a consumption tax on food, and as a subsidy on its production. The good news is a large increase in producer surplus. The gain to producer surplus is the area $P_1 dc P_0$ in the right-hand panel of Figure 18.3, when the CAP price of P_1 is compared with the equilibrium price, P_0, which would have ruled in its absence. This filters through to farmers in higher income, and agricultural workers in higher wage rates. But in the long run, the mobility of labour between agriculture and other sectors suggests that these benefits are only temporary. The real long-term beneficiaries of the CAP are the owners of the land. The CAP raises implicit rents for owner-managed farms, and explicit rents that tenant farmers pay to their landowner.

There is another piece of good news from the CAP, too. The rest of the world, in aggregate, imports food from the EU which would have been more expensive otherwise (P_2 as against P_0). So rest-of-world consumer surplus goes up. Buenos Aires industrial workers enjoy more beef, Auckland office-workers cheaper lamb, Torontonians and New Yorkers cheaper bread as a direct result of CAP.

That is the end of the good news. In the rest of the world, producer surplus in the food industries is cut. In Europe, there is a large loss of consumers' surplus (which falls by the area $P_1 eb P_0$). And finally there is the EAGGF loss, of $edfg$, to be made up by taxes on European Union nationals (typically in the form of contributions levied through VAT—often on food as well as other goods!).

Let us now examine the separate welfare effects in more detail. There are eight areas in the right-hand panel to consider, labelled A, B, C, D, E, F, G and H. Table 18.3 presents these in tabular form. The EU's taxpayers have to meet the EAGGF loss of areas $A + B + C + D + E$. Of this, B is a straight transfer to EU producers' surplus. Producers' surplus also increases by areas $A + H$, which form part of the loss in consumers' surplus. Total consumers' surplus loss equals areas $A + D + F + G + H$. The block at the bottom of the EAGGF loss rectangle, E, is a transfer to the rest of the world (where consumers' surplus rises, and producers' surplus drops).

From the EU's standpoint, if EU social welfare is simply the sum of gains to tax-

Table 18.3. Separate components of overall welfare effects of high EU food prices under the Common Agricultural Policy

Food prices	European Union			
Area	Taxpayers	Producers' surplus	Consumers' surplus	Total
A	loss	gain	loss	loss
B	loss	gain		
C	loss			loss
D	loss		loss	loss × 2
E	loss			loss
F			loss	loss
G			loss	loss
H		gain	loss	
Total net gain	$-A - B - C - D - E$	$+A + B + H$	$-A - D - F - G - H$	$-A - C - 2D - E - F - G$

payers and to consumers' and producers' surplus, the total loss is $A + C + 2D + E + F + G$. Areas B and H do not count here, because they are transfers within the EU (from taxpayers to producers' surplus). Area D counts twice: it is lost by consumers' surplus and also by taxpayers, with no gain by anyone to offset either of these effects.

It is possible (but would only occur by chance) that areas $D + F + G$ equal area B. This might happen if point a, the autarky price P_3, were moved down within the box *edfg*, which could cause the S and D curves to intersect the P_0 line inside the box so that areas F and G vanished. If $D + F + G = B$ in area, the EU welfare loss from this aspect of the CAP would exactly equal the financial loss borne by taxpayers, *edfg*. When point a is sufficiently high up, as in Figure 18.3, $D + F + G > B$ in area, so that the welfare loss *exceeds* the financial loss. This appears likely, and, if so, the true cost of the CAP to the EU is still larger than the massive EAGGF financial cost.

The simple partial-equilibrium analysis of Figure 18.3 conceals a number of possible further effects that deserve mention. One of these is the knock-on effects on other markets, both within the EU and outside it. For example, the balance of payments effects of the CAP, which replace imports by exports of temperate-zone foodstuffs, could cause European currencies to appreciate in real terms against other world currencies, with at least transitory damaging repercussions for unemployment. The additional VAT rates needed to finance the EAGGF losses will aggravate existing distortions on, for example, the work–leisure frontier, suggesting that the real resource cost of financing area *edfg* is even larger than appears in the diagram.

Then there is the important point that foodstuffs are necessities. They occupy a larger share in the budget of the poor than the rich. The income-elasticity of demand for foodstuffs as an aggregate appears to be about 0.4. This means that CAP is a regressive tax, that increases income inequalities. If this effect is to be offset by more progressive income tax, and higher transfers to the poor, there are further distortions that enter the picture in the form of higher marginal rates of taxation levied on wages and incomes and/or employers' payrolls. If it is not offset, we have to add in the welfare effect of adverse income redistributional consequences implicit in the CAP.

In the EU's poorer member states, such as Greece, Ireland, Portugal, and Spain, we need to remember that CAP involves transfers from relatively rich non-agricultural communities to some considerably poorer farmers and farm-workers. This presumably counts as a gain if the European Union as a whole is deemed to be averse to income inequalities, at individual or national levels. The CAP is not, therefore, regressive in all its effects.

There are two counter-arguments to raise against this last observation. One is that the long-run effects of the CAP are, as we have seen, to raise rents earned by owners of land. The boost CAP provides to farm-workers' relative wage-rates, in comparison with pay available in other sectors, should only be transitory. Those who own land, either directly or through, for example, their pension funds, are hardly likely to be poorer than average.

The second point is that all EU member states adopt progressive tax-and-transfer policies within their boundaries. What is so special about a poor farmer, that elevates his claims for financial support above that of a poor shopworker or a poor poet? Even if the poor farmer is especially meritorious, hard as this is to believe, why not let individual EU countries tinker with their tax/transfer arrangements to give him or her favourable treatment (as, for example, Ireland does)? Why should the EU involve itself with this problem?

Another issue concerns externalities. Suppose agricultural production within the EU confers important external benefits that are not rewarded through the market-place. We should then accept that EU agricultural output should be higher than under a *laissez-faire* equilibrium. To the extent that the CAP achieves this, all well and good. But one now needs to ask whether the CAP is the right method. The answer is no. CAP involves taxing food consumption and subsidizing food production within the EU. Even if the latter is appropriate on some externality ground, the former is not.

If there is a sound externality argument for subsidizing European agriculture, a superior method of achieving this—in the absence of other distortions—must be through a production subsidy on its own. Between the late 1930s and 1973, British governments did just this, through a system of 'deficiency payments'. Farmers were promised a particular minimum price for a particular product, reviewed annually, and when world prices fell below this, the Exchequer would make up the difference. Deficiency payments involved no tax on consumption.

The idea that agriculture production generates positive external benefits it itself, of course, open to challenge. Woods and forests may be preferred to intensive agriculture from aesthetic, environmental, and tourism standpoints. And the military security argument for achieving high European agricultural output is qualified by the observation that land yields more when it has recently been fallow. It may be that the externality argument for agricultural support is a baseless ex-post rationalization, used by farming lobbyists to gain adherents for their cause.

There may be deeper and subtler points here, however, such as the idea that urbanization brings social congestion: costs imperfectly registered in relative prices confronting individuals. A more even geographical spread of population and economic activity may lead, on this view, to greater social harmony and long-run economic efficiency. Such arguments are often advanced in France, Greece, Ireland, Italy, and Spain, in defence of the CAP, since it is clearly one way of attempting to secure this. Yet the question this provokes is whether the CAP is the most efficient instrument for redressing spatial misallocations. Again one has to be sceptical here. There are ample fiscal mechanisms, such as regionally differentiated tax allowances for investment and transfers between central and local government, that could achieve these effects at lower cost. It can also be argued that urban areas generate positive as well as negative externalities, and that sooner or later the spread of information, and relative price adjustments, should ensure that location decisions are reasonably efficient.

The fact that the rest of the world's excess supply curve of foodstuffs slopes upward does imply that the EU's *optimum* tariff on food imports is positive rather than zero. This is not, however, an argument that applies at the world level, where free trade must be presumed best. Furthermore, the optimum-tariff argument cannot possibly justify a level of protection that literally goes 'over the top' by switching the direction of trade from net imports to net exports.

The rest of the world is not, of course, homogeneous. Consumers' surplus goes up there, but producers' surplus falls, and quite possibly by a larger amount. There are some countries that are conspicuously harmed by it. Prime examples include cane-sugar producers like Guyana, whose terms of trade suffer from the EU's protection for beet-sugar production. CAP-induced income distribution effects in the rest of the world, both between countries and within them, are complex and varied.

In defence of the CAP, it may be argued that the EU's supply and demand curves for foodstuffs are relatively inelastic, so that the deadweight losses from excessive prices are smaller than they would be for some other goods. This is not to justify the CAP, but to qualify the magnitude of the adverse welfare effects it brings. A more potent point is the fact that the EU is certainly not alone in protecting agriculture. Among the world's twenty-four richer countries (the OECD area), New Zealand is unique in not doing so.

Agricultural support policies in Japan and the United States work differently from the CAP (and from each other). But in total financial costs, and in their estimated real resource costs, they are far from dissimilar (Winters 1987 provides an admirable survey on this).

Japan's agricultural policies impose stiff tariffs on imports of foodstuffs. In the case of rice, they lead to a domestic Japanese price of rice some four times higher than that prevailing in, for example, the Philippines. The object is to protect the livelihoods of Japanese rice-farmers. The end-result, given long-run labour mobility, is to push up the price of, and rents on, agricultural land in Japan.

Japan's agricultural policies do not involve financial outlays from central government: they actually generate positive revenue for the State, from the tariff proceeds.

By contrast, the US allows consumer prices of foodstuffs to be low, not far from world levels, but provides a gamut of producer subsidies and payments that effectively allow farmers a higher price, on average, than they would have earned otherwise. In this, American policies bear some resemblance to Britain's old system of deficiency payments. The US protects consumers' surplus, and generates some additional producers' surplus at the taxpayer's expense. There are also periodic attempts, in the United States, to persuade farmers to reduce production of some products when world prices are low; these take the form of compensation payments for taking land out of production for certain specified products.

The CAP embodies features of both the Japanese and US systems. The high consumer and producer prices, shielded from import competition by variable levies or tariffs, are common to the CAP and to Japan. The EU has increasingly relied also on US-style compensation for production cuts in recent years. Set-aside provisions to farmers have been established to reduce excess supply when and where this has been particularly serious. Milk production has been subject to quotas, so that farmers face the high price, P_2, only on pre-specified output volumes. Any excess production surplus to quota earns farmers little or nothing.

The EU also took steps in 1992 to shift some of the forms of producer support from a price subsidy (which is proportional to production, and gives most to big farmers) to an income subsidy (which switches support to smaller, poorer farmers). Detaching farmer support from production concentrates transfers on poorer, presumably needier farmers; it helps to limit wasteful and costly overproduction; it enables consumer prices to be lowered and brought closer to international levels; and, suitably administered, it may permit substantial reductions in EAGGF costs. These 'MacSharry Reforms' have been widely welcomed.

The GATT Uruguay round of international negotiations tariff reductions, initiated in 1986 and finally concluded in 1994, widened the agenda to include trade in agricultural products. Previous GATT rounds had been limited to trade in manufactured goods. Under pressure from Canada, the United States, and Southern Hemisphere agricultural exporters, the GATT proposed a phased programme of tariff cuts designed to reduce the gap between internal support prices and world prices by 60 per cent over a ten-year period. The proposal was welcomed by Britain, but viewed with less favour by other EU members, particularly France. Protracted and often bitter debate within the EU, and between the EU, the United States, and the GATT, was finally resolved in 1994.

The 1994 GATT agreement, reinforced by the prospects of future steps towards liberalizing international trade in agricultural products under the World Trade Organization, and of EU enlargements to the East, make it probable that the average gap between internal EU and world prices will decline sharply in coming decades. The CAP in its current form is doomed. If one adopts the hypothesis of linearity in EU demand and supply curves, the deadweight costs of the CAP are proportional to the square of that gap. The 1994 GATT agreement will cut the gap by 60 per cent. That implies a welfare gain equivalent to 84 per cent of the pre-1994 costs. This may amount (on an average of various estimates, suitably updated) to some 41 billion ECUs at 1994 values, or an increase in EU GDP of nearly 0.7 per cent.

There will be losers as a result of these changes. Farm-workers' wages and employment prospects will suffer temporarily, perhaps for several years, until the labour released is absorbed by other sectors. Landowners will anticipate a fall in rents, and hence in the capital value of their assets. Certain regions within the EU will experience a drop in aggregate income.

Against this, total real income in the EU will rise as a result of these reforms, and also in many countries in the rest of the world. Within the EU, lower food prices should lead to reduced economic inequalities, since food occupies a higher budget share for the poor than the rich. There will be opportunities for reductions in burdensome and distortionary taxes currently levied to finance EAGGF losses. Finally, and most importantly, the European Union will be moving closer to the principles of Comparative Advantage and Efficient Trade to which much of this volume has been devoted.

18.4 Summary

- Two key developments in the 1990s have influenced the conditions under which the EU trades: the Single European Market, and the Uruguay Round of multilateral trade negotiations.
- EU trade with formerly Communist countries in Central and Eastern Europe has been liberalized, but imports of steel, textiles, clothing and motor vehicles remain subject to tight restrictions.
- The Common Agricultural Policy imposes severe welfare costs, both by raising internal prices relative to average world levels, and by stabilizing internal prices.

REFERENCES

Abrea, M. de P. (1995), 'Trade in Manufactures: The Outcome of the Uruguay Round and Developing Country Interests', paper presented at the World Bank Conference, *The Uruguay Round and Developing Countries*, January 1995.

Aghion, P., and Howitt, P. (1992), 'A Model of Growth through Creative Destruction', *Econometrica*, 60: 323–51.

Aitken, N. (1973), 'The Effect of the EEC and EFTA on European Trade: A Temporal Cross-Section Analysis', *American Economic Review*, 63: 881–92.

Anderson, K. (1992), 'The Standard Welfare Economics of Policies Affecting Trade and the Environment', in K. Anderson and R. Blackhurst (eds), *The Greening of World Trade Issues* (London: Harvester Wheatsheaf).

Ark, B. van (1990), 'Comparative Levels of Manufacturing Productivity in Postwar Europe: Measurement and Comparisons', *Oxford Bulletin of Economics and Statistics*, 52 (November): 343–74.

—— and Pilat, Dirak (1993), 'Productivity Levels in Germany, Japan, and the United States: Differences and Causes', *Brookings Papers on Economic Activity: Microeconomics*, 2: 1–48.

d'Aspremont, C., Gabsziewicz, J. G., and Thisse, J. F. (1979), 'On Hotelling's Stability in Competition', *Econometrica*, 47: 1145–51.

Audretch, D. B. (1995), 'Industrial and Trade Policies for the Emerging Market Economies', in Winters, L. A. (ed.), *Foundations of an Open Economy: Trade Laws and Institutions for Eastern Europe* (London: CEPR), 155–77.

Balance, Robert H. (1988), 'Trade Performance as an Indicator of Comparative Advantage', in David Greenaway (ed.), *Economic Development and International Trade* (London: Macmillan), 6–24.

Balassa, B. (1963), 'An Empirical Demonstration of Classical Comparative Cost Theory', *Review of Economics and Statistics*, 4 (August): 231–8.

—— (1989), *Comparative Advantage, Trade Policy and Economic Development* (London: Harvester Wheatsheaf).

—— and Bauwens, L. (1988), 'The Determinants of Intra-European Trade in Manufactured Goods', *European Economic Review*, 32: 1421–37.

Baldwin, R. (1971), 'Determinants of the Commodity Structure of US Trade', *American Economic Review*, 61: 126–46.

—— (1989), 'The Growth Effects of "1992" ', *Economic Policy*, 9: 247–82.

—— (1994), 'The Effects of Trade and Foreign Direct Investment on Employment and Relative Wages', *OECD Economic Studies*, 23: 7–54.

Barrett, S. (1994), 'Strategic Environmental Policy and International Trade', *Journal of Public Economics*, 54: 325–38.

Barro, R. J. (1991), 'Economic Growth in a Cross Section of Countries', *Quarterly Journal of Economics*, 106: 407–44.

368   *References*

Barro, R. J. and Sala-i-Martin, X. (1992), 'Convergence', *Journal of Political Economy*, 100: 223–51.

Becker, G. S., Murphy, K. M., and Tamura, R. (1990), 'Human Capital, Fertility and Economic Growth', *Journal of Political Economy*, 98: S12–37.

Beghin, J., Roland-Holst, D., and van der Mensbrugghe, D. (1994), 'A Survey of the Trade and Environmental Nexus: Global Dimensions', *OECD Economic Studies*, 23: 167–92.

Bhagwati, J. (1964), 'The Pure Theory of International Trade: A Survey', *Economic Journal*, 74: 1–84.

—— (1968), 'Distortions and Immiserizing Growth: A Generalisation', *Review of Economic Studies*, 35: 481–5.

—— (1971), 'The Generalised Theory of Distortions and Welfare', in Bhagwati *et al.* (1971), 69–90.

—— (1988), *Protectionism* (Cambridge, Mass.: MIT Press).

—— *et al.* (1971), *Trade, Balance of Payments and Growth* (Amsterdam: North Holland).

—— and Ramaswami, V. K. (1963), 'Domestic Distortions, Tariffs and the Theory of Optimum Subsidy', *Journal of Political Economy*, 72: 44–50.

—— and Srinivasan, T. N. (1969), 'Optimal Intervention to Achieve Non-Economic Objectives', *Review of Economic Studies*, 36: 27–38.

Blackhurst, R., Enders, A., and Francois, J. (1995), 'The Uruguay Round and Market Access: Opportunities and Challenges for Developing Countries', paper presented at the World Bank Conference, *The Uruguay Round and Developing Countries*, January 1995.

Bliss, C. (1994), *Economic Theory and Policy for Trading Blocks* (Manchester: Manchester University Press).

—— (1996), 'Long-Run Wealth Distributions with Random Shocks' (mimeo, Nuffield College, Oxford).

Bowen, H., Leamer, E., and Sveikauskaus, L. (1987), 'Multicountry, Multifactor Tests of the Factor Abundance Theory', *American Economic Review*, 77: 791–809.

Brander, J. (1995), 'Strategic Trade Policy', Working Paper No. 5020 (Cambridge, Mass.: NBER).

—— and Krugman, P. R. (1983), 'A Reciprocal Dumping Model of International Trade', *Journal of International Economics*, 15: 313–21.

—— and Spencer, B. (1985), 'Export Subsidies and Market Share Rivalry', *Journal of International Economics*, 18: 83–100.

Brenton, P.A. (1995), 'External Liberalisation and Russian Trade' (mimeo, Centre for European Policy Studies, Brussels).

—— and Gros, D. (1995), 'Trade between the European Union and the Countries of Central and Eastern Europe: An Economic and Policy Approach', Working Document (Centre for European Policy Studies, Brussels).

—— and Winters, L. A. (1992), 'Bilateral Trade Elasticities for Exploring the Effects of "1992"', in Winters, L. A. (ed.), *Trade Flows and Trade Policy after 1992* (Cambridge: Cambridge University Press), 266–85.

Brilli, Enzo R. (1993), *The European Community and Developing Countries* (Cambridge: Cambridge University Press).

Bulow, J. I., Geanakopolous, J. D., and Klemperer, P. D. (1985), 'Multimarket Oligopoly: Strategic Substitutes and Complements', *Journal of Political Economy*, 93: 488–511.

CEC (1993), 'Growth, Competitiveness and Employment', *Bulletin of the European Communities*, supplement 6/93.

—— (1994), 'Trade Liberalisation with Central and Eastern Europe', *European Economy*, Supplement A, No. 7 (Brussels).

Cecchini, P. (1988), *The European Challenge: 1992* (London: Wildwood House).

Chin, J. C., and Grossman, G. M. (1990), 'Intellectual Property Rights and North-South Trade', in R. W. Jones and A. O. Krueger (eds), *The Political Economy of International Trade: Essays in Honour of Robert E. Baldwin* (Cambridge, Mass.: Basil Blackwell), 90–107.

Cline, William R. (1995), 'Evaluating the Uruguay Round', *The World Economy*, 18(1): 1–23.

Corden, W. M. (1971), 'The Effects of Trade on the Rate of Growth', in J. N. Bhagwati, R. W. Jones, R. A. Mundell, and J. Vanek (eds), *Trade, Balance of Payments and Growth: Essays in Honor of Charles B. Kindleberger* (Amsterdam: North Holland).

—— (1974), *Trade Policy and Economic Welfare* (Oxford: Oxford University Press).

—— (1983), 'The Normative Theory of International Trade', in R. W. Jones and P. B. Kenen (eds), *Handbook of International Economics*, i (Amsterdam: North-Holland), 63–130.

—— and R. Findlay (1975), 'Urban Unemployment, Intersectoral Capital Mobility, and Development Policy', *Economica*, 42: 59–72.

Currie, D., Levine, P., Pearlman, J., and Chui, D. (1996), 'Phases of Imitation and Innovation in a North-South Endogenous Growth Model' (mimeo, London Business School).

Dean, J. M. (1992), 'Trade and the Environment: A Survey of the Literature', in P. Low (ed.), *International Trade and the Environment* (World Bank, Washington), 15–28.

Deardorff, A. (1984), 'Testing Trade Theories and Predicting Trade Flows', in R. Jones and P. Kenen (eds), *Handbook of International Economics*, i (Amsterdam: North-Holland), 467–517.

—— (1990), 'Should Patent Protection be Extended to all Developing Countries?' *The World Economy*, 13: 497–507.

Dick, A. (1994), 'Does Import Protection Act as Export Promotion? Evidence from the United States', *Oxford Economic Papers*, 46: 83–101.

Diwan, I., and Rodrik, D. (1991), 'Patents, Appropriate Technology, and North-South Trade', *Journal of International Economics*, 30: 27–47.

Dixit, A., and Grossman, G. (1986), 'Targeted Export Promotion with Several Oligopolistic Industries', *Journal of International Economics*, 21: 233–50.

Dixit, A., and Stiglitz, J. E. (1977), 'Monopolistic Competition and Optimum Product Diversity', *American Economic Review*, 67: 297–308.

Dollar, D. (1986), 'Technological Innovation, Capital Mobility, and the Product Cycle in North-South Trade', *American Economic Review*, 76: 177–90.

Dornbusch, Rudiger, Fischer, S., and Samuelson, P. A. (1977), 'Comparative Advantage, Trade and Payments In a Ricardian Model with a Continuum of Goods', *American Economic Review*, 67: 823–39.

Eaton, J., and Grossman, G. (1986), 'Optimal Trade and Industrial Policy under Oligopoly', *Quarterly Journal of Economics*, 101: 383–406.

Emmanuel, A. (1972), *Unequal Exchange* (London: New Left Books).

Englander, A. Steven, and Gurney, Andrew (1994a), 'Medium-Term Determinants of OECD Productivity Growth', *OECD Economic Studies*, 22 (Spring), 49–109.

—— (1994b), 'OECD Productivity Growth: Medium-Term Trends', ibid., 111–29.

Faini, Riccardo, de Melo, Jaime, and Takacs, Wendy (1995), 'A Primer on the MFA Maze', *The World Economy*, 18(1) (January), 113–35.

Ferrantino, M. J. (1993), 'The Effect of Intellectual Property Rights on International Trade and Investment', *Weltwirtschaftliches Archiv*, 129: 300–31.

Francois, J. F., McDonald, B., and Nordstrom, H. (1995), 'Assessing the Uruguay Round', paper presented at the World Bank Conference, *The Uruguay Round and Developing Countries*, January 1995.

Graham, F. D. (1923), 'Some Aspects of Protection Further Considered', *Quarterly Journal of Economics*, 37: 199–227.

Gros, D., and Jones, E. (1995), 'European Competitiveness: Is the Record that Bad?', mimeo (Centre for European Policy Studies, Brussels).

Grossman, G. M., and Helpman, E. (1993), *Innovation and Growth in the Global Economy* (Cambridge, Mass.: MIT Press).

—— (1994), 'Protection for Sale', *American Economic Review*, 84: 833–50.

Grossman, G. M., and Krueger, A. B. (1992), 'Environmental Impacts of a North American Free Trade Agreement', Working Paper 3914 (Cambridge, Mass.: NBER).

Haberler, Gottfried (1929), 'The Theory of Comparative Costs Once More', *Quarterly Journal of Economics*, 43: 376–81.

Haggard, Stephen (1995), *Developing Nations and the Politics of Global Integration* (Washington DC: Brookings Institution).

Hamilton, Colleen, and Whalley, John (1995), 'Evaluating the Impact of the Uruguay Round Results on Developing Countries', *The World Economy*, 18(1) (January), 31–48.

Harris, R. (1985), 'Why Voluntary Export Restraints are Voluntary', *Canadian Journal of Economics*, 18: 799–809.

Heffernan, S. A., and Sinclair, P. J. N. (1990), *Modern International Economics* (Oxford: Blackwell).

Helpman, E. (1987), 'Imperfect Competition and International Trade: Evidence from Fourteen Industrialised Countries', *Journal of the Japanese and International Economies*, 1: 62–81.

—— and Krugman, P. (1989), *Trade Policy and Market Structure* (Cambridge, Mass.: MIT Press).

Herrmann, Roland, and Weiss, Dietmar (1995), 'A Welfare Analysis of the EC-ACP Sugar Protocol', *Journal of Development Studies*, 31(6): 918–41.

Hirsch, S. (1967), *Location of Industry and International Competitiveness* (Oxford: Oxford University Press).

Holmes, P., and Smith, A. (1995), 'Trade, Competition and Industrial Policy: Conflicts of Aims and Instruments in the Car Sector', mimeo (University of Sussex).

Horstmann, I., and Markusen, J. (1986), 'Up the Average Cost Curve: Inefficient Entry and the New Protectionism', *Journal of International Economics*, 20: 225–47.

Hotelling, H. (1929), 'Stability in Competition', *Economic Journal*, 39: 41–57.

Hufbauer, G. (1970), 'The Impact of National Characteristics and Technology on the Commodity Composition of Trade in Manufactured Goods', in R. Vernon (ed.), *The Technology Factor in International Trade* (New York: NBER), 145–231.

Hughes Hallett, A. J. (1994), 'The Impact of EC-92 on Trade in Developing Countries', *The World Bank Research Observer*, 9(1): 121–46.

Hummels, D., and Levinsohn, J. (1993), 'Monopolistic Competition and International Trade: Reconsidering the Evidence', Working Paper 4389 (Cambridge, Mass.: NBER).

Hunter, L., and Markusen, J. (1988), 'Per Capita Income as a Determinant of Trade', in Feenstra, R. (ed.), *Empirical Methods for International Trade* (Cambridge, Mass.: MIT Press).

Ingersent, K. A., Rayner, A. J., and Hine, R. C. (1995), 'Ex-post Evaluation of the Uruguay Round Agricultural Agreement', *The World Economy*, 18: 707–28.

Jacquemin, A., and Sapir, A. (1992), 'Competition and Imports in the European Market', in L. A. Winters and A. Venables (eds), *European Integration: Trade and Industry* (Cambridge: Cambridge University Press), 82–95.

Johnson, H. G. (1965), 'Optimal Trade Intervention in the Presence of Domestic Distortions', in R. E. Baldwin *et al.*, *Trade, Growth and the Balance of Payments* (Amsterdam: North-Holland Publishing Company), 3–34.

Jones, R. W. (1965), 'The Structure of Simple General Equilibrium Models', *Journal of Political Economy*, 73 (December), 557–72.

—— (1971), 'A Three-Factor Model in Theory, Trade and History', in Bhagwati, J. *et al.* (eds), *Trade, Balance of Payments and Growth* (Amsterdam: North-Holland), 3–21.

Krishna, K. (1989), 'Trade Restrictions as Facilitating Practices', *Journal of International Economics*, 26: 251–70.

Krugman, P. (1979a), 'Increasing Returns, Monopolistic Competition, and International Trade', *Journal of International Economics*, 9: 469–79.

—— (1979b), 'A Model of Innovation, Technology Transfer, and the World Distribution of Income', *Journal of Political Economy*, 87: 253–66.

—— (1984), 'Import Protection as Export Promotion; International Competition in the Presence of Oligopoly and Economies of Scale', in H. Kierzkowski (ed.), *Monopolistic Competition and International Trade* (Oxford: Clarendon Press), 180–93.

—— (1986), 'A "technology gap" model of international trade', in K. Jungenfelt and D. Hague (eds), *Structural Adjustment in Advanced Economies*.

—— (1987), 'Is Free Trade Passé?', *Journal of Economic Perspectives*, 1: 131–44.

—— (1991), 'Is Bilateralism Bad?' in E. Helpman and A. Razin (eds), *International Trade and Trade Policy* (Cambridge, Mass.: MIT Press).

—— (1993), 'Regionalism versus Multilateralism: Analytical Notes', in J. de Melo and A. Panagariya (eds), *New Dimensions in Regional Integration* (Cambridge: Cambridge University Press).

—— (1994), 'Competitiveness: A Dangerous Obsession', *Foreign Affairs* (March/April), 28–44.

Lancaster, K., and Lipsey, R. G. (1956), 'The General Theory of Second Best', *Review of Economic Studies*, 24: 18–20.

Leamer, E. (1980), 'The Leontief Paradox Reconsidered', *Journal of Political Economy*, 88: 495–503.

—— (1984), *Sources of Comparative Advantage, Theory and Evidence* (Cambridge, Mass.: MIT Press).

—— (1994), 'Trade, Wages and Revolving Door Ideas', Working Paper 4716 (Cambridge, Mass.: NBER).

—— and Bowen, H. (1981), 'Cross-Section Tests of the Heckscher-Ohlin Theorem: Comment', *American Economic Review*, 71: 1040–3.

Leamer, E. E. (1994), 'Testing Trade Theory', in D. Greenaway and L. A.Winters (eds), *Surveys in International Trade* (Oxford: Blackwell), 66–106.

—— and Levinsohn, J. (1994), 'International Trade Theory: The Evidence', Working Paper 4940 (Cambridge, Mass.: NBER).

Leontief, W. W. (1933), 'The Use of Indifference Curves in the Analysis of Foreign Trade', *Quarterly Journey of Economics*, 47: 493–503.

—— (1953), 'Domestic Production and Foreign Trade: The American Capital Position Re-Examined', *Proceedings of the American Philosophical Society*, 97: 332–49.

Levine, L., and Renelt, R. (1992), 'A Sensitivity Analysis of Cross Country Growth Regressions', *American Economic Review*, 82: 942–63.

Levinsohn, J. (1993), 'Testing the Imports-as-Market-Discipline Hypothesis', *Journal of International Economics*, 35: 1–22.

—— (1994), 'Comment on Smith', in Krugman, P., and Smith, A. (eds), *Empirical Studies of Strategic Trade Policy* (Chicago: University of Chicago Press), 81–3.

Linnemann, H. (1966), *An Econometric Study of International Trade Flows* (Amsterdam: North-Holland).

Little, Ian M. D. (1982), *Economic Development: Theory, Policy, and International Relations* (New York: Basic Books Inc.).

Lucas, R. E. (1988), 'On the Mechanics of Development', *Journal of Monetary Economics*, 22: 3–42.

McCallum, J. (1995), 'National Borders Matter: Canada-US Regional Trade Patterns', *American Economic Review*, 85: 615–23.

MacDougall, G. D. A. (1951), 'British and American Exports: A Study Suggested by the Theory of Comparative Costs, Part 1', *Economic Journal*, 61: 697–724.

Messerlin, P. (1989), 'The EC Antidumping Regulations: A First Economic Appraisal', *Weltwirtschaftliches Archiv*, 125: 563–87.

Mill, John Stuart (1848), *Principles of Political Economy* (London: Parker & Co.).

Minhas, B. S. (1962), 'The Homohypallagic Production Function, Factor Intensity Reversals, and the Heckscher-Ohlin Theorem', *Journal of Political Economy*, 60: 138–56.

Morrissey, W. Oliver (1993), 'The Mixing of Aid and Trade Policies', *The World Economy*, 16(1) (January), 69–84.

Mussa, Michael (1979), 'The Two-Sector Model in Terms of its Dual', *Journal of International Economics*, 9(4): 513–26.

Neary, J. P. (1978), 'Short-Run Capital Specificity and the Pure Theory of International Trade', *Economic Journal*, 88: 477–510.

Newbery, D., and Stiglitz, J. E. (1984), 'Pareto Inferior Trade', *Review of Economic Studies*, 51: 1–12.

O'Mahony, Mary (1992), 'Productivity Levels in British and German Manufacturing Industries', *National Institute Economic Review*, 139 (February): 46–63.

OECD (1992), *Structural Change and Industrial Performance: A Seven Country Growth Decomposition Study* (Paris: OECD).

Oliveira-Martins, J. (1994), 'Market Structure, Trade and Industry Wages', *OECD Economic Studies*, 22: 1–23.

Page, Sheila, with Davenport, Michael (1994), *World Trade Reform: Do Developing Countries Gain or Lose?* (London: Overseas Development Institute).

Peers, Steve (1995), 'Reform of the European Community's Generalized System of Preferences: A Missed Opportunity', *Journal of World Trade*, 29: 79–96.

Pohl, Gerhard, and Sorsa, Piritta (1994), 'Is European Integration Bad News for Developing Countries? A Comment on Hughes Hallett', *The World Bank Research Observer*, 9(1), 147–55.

Porter, M. (1991), 'America's Green Strategy', *Scientific American*, 16.

Posner, M. V. (1961), 'International Trade and Technical Change', *Oxford Economic Papers*, 13: 323–41.

Quah, D. (1996a), 'Twin Peaks: Growth and Convergence in Models of Distribution Dynamics', *Economic Journal*, 106: 1045–55.

—— (1996b), 'Empirics for Economic Growth and Distribution', *European Economic Review*, 40: 1353–76.

Ramsey, F. P. (1927), 'A Contribution to the Theory of Taxation', *Economic Journal*, 37, 47–61.

Rawls, J. (1972), *A Theory of Justice* (Oxford: Oxford University Press).

Read, Robert (1994), 'The EC Internal Banana Market: The Issues and the Dilemma', *The World Economy*, 17(2) (March): 219–36.

Rebelo, S. (1992), 'Growth in Open Economies', *Carnegie Rochester Conference Series in Public Policy*, 36: 5–46.

Ricardo, David (1817), *On the Principles of Political Economy and Taxation* (Harmondsworth: Penguin, 1971 edn).

Richardson, J. D. (1989), 'Empirical Research on Trade Liberalisation with Imperfect Competition: A Survey', *OECD Economic Studies*, 12: 7–50.

Robson, P. (1987), *The Economics of International Integration* (3rd edn, London: George Allen and Unwin).

Rodrik, Dani (1994), 'Developing Countries after the Uruguay Round', Centre for Economic Policy Research Discussion Paper No. 1084.

Rollo, J., and Smith, A. (1993), 'The Political Economy of Eastern European Trade: Why So Sensitive?' *Economic Policy*, 16: 140–81.

Romer, P. M. (1986), 'Increasing Returns and Long-Run Growth', *Journal of Political Economy*, 94: 1002–37.

—— (1990), 'Endogenous Technological Change', *Journal of Political Economy*, 98: S71–102.

—— and Rivera-Batiz, L. A. (1991), 'Economic Integration and Endogenous Growth', *Quarterly Journal of Economics*, 106: 531–55.

Rybczynski, T. M. (1955), 'Factor Endowments and Relative Factor Prices', *Economica*, 22: 336–41.

Salop, S. (1979), 'Monopolistic Competition with Outside Goods', *Bell Journal of Economics*, 10: 141–56.

Samuelson, P. A. (1949), 'International Factor–Price Equalisation Once Again', *Economic Journal*, 59: 181–97.

—— (1962), 'The Gains from International Trade Once Again', *Economic Journal*, 72: 820–9.

Sapir, A. (1995), 'Europe's Single Market: The Long March to 1992', Discussion Paper 1245 (London: CEPR).

Schott, J. J. (1994), *The Uruguay Round: An Assessment* (Institute for International Economics, Washington DC).

Schumacher, D., and Mobius, U. (1994), 'Analysis of Community Trade Barriers Facing Central and East European Countries and Impact of the Europe Agreements', *European Economy*, 6 (Brussels), 94: 17–76.

Sinclair, P. J. N. (1993), 'World Trade, Protectionist Follies and Europe's Policy Options for the Future', *Oxford Review of Economic Policy*, 9(3): 114–25.

—— (1995), 'Monopolies, Localized Ownership and Pauperizing Trade', University of Birmingham Department of Economics Discussion Paper 95–31.

—— and Vines, D. (1995), 'Bigger Trading Blocs Need Not Entail More Protection', University of Birmingham Department of Economics Discussion Paper 95–32.

Smith, A. (1994), 'Strategic Trade Policy in the European Car Market', in P. Krugman and A. Smith (eds), *Empirical Studies of Strategic Trade Policy* (Chicago: University of Chicago Press), 67–81.

—— and Venables, A. (1988), 'Completing the Internal Market in the European Community: Some Industry Simulations', *European Economic Review*, 32: 1501–25.

—— —— (1991), 'Counting the Cost of Voluntary Export Restraints in the European Car Market', in E. Helpman, and A. Razin (eds), *International Trade and Trade Policy* (Cambridge, Mass.: MIT Press), 187–220.

Solow, R. M. (1956), 'A Contribution to the Theory of Economic Growth', *Quarterly Journal of Economics*, 70: 65–94.

Stern, Robert M. (1962), 'British and American Productivity and Comparative Costs in International Trade', *Oxford Economic Papers*, 14: 275–304.

—— (1975), 'Testing Trade Theories', in P. B. Kenen (ed.), *International Trade and Finance: Frontiers for Research* (New York: Cambridge University Press), 3–49.

Stolper, W. F., and Samuelson, P. A. (1941), 'Protection and Real Wages', *Review of Economic Studies*, 9: 58–73.

Subramanian, A. (1992), 'Trade Measures for the Environment: A Nearly Empty Box?' *The World Economy*, 15: 135–52.

Trefler, D. (1993), 'International Factor Price Differences: Leontief was Right!' *Journal of Political Economy*, 101: 961–87.

Tyson, L. (1992), *Who's Bashing Whom: Trade Conflict in High-Technology Industries* (Institute for International Economics, Washington DC).

Ulph, A. (1993), 'Environmental Policy and International Trade when Governments and Producers Act Strategically' (Discussion Paper 9318, University of Southampton).

—— and Ulph, D. (1994), 'Trade, Strategic Innovation and Strategic Environmental Policy: A General Analysis' (Discussion Paper 9416, University of Southampton).

UNESCO (1993), *Statistical Yearbook* (Paris: UNESCO).

Vanek, J. (1968), 'The Factor Proportions Theory: The N-Factor Case', *Kyklos*, 21(4): 749–56.

Venables, A. (1985), 'Trade and Trade Policy with Imperfect Competition: The Case of Identical Products and Free Entry', *Journal of International Economics*, 19: 1–19.

—— (1994), 'Trade Policy under Imperfect Competition: A Numerical Assessment', in P. Krugman and A. Smith (eds), *Empirical Studies of Strategic Trade Policy* (Chicago: University of Chicago Press), 41–63.

Vernon, R. (1966), 'International Investment and International Trade in the Product Cycle', *Quarterly Journal of Economics*, 80: 190–207.

Winters, L. A. (1987), 'The Economic Consequences of Agricultural Support: A Survey', *OECD Economic Studies*, 9 (Autumn), 7–54.

Wood, A. (1994), *North-South Trade, Employment and Inequality* (Oxford: Clarendon Press).

INDEX